NEW ZEALAND'S FRANCE

A different view of 1835–1935

Alistair Watts

Published by Aykay Publishing

Author contact: https://www.facebook.com/alistairwattsauthor/

A catalogue record for this book is available from the National Library of New Zealand.

For Karen, who waited patiently

But history consists entirely of contemporary references that have gone out of date...

— Clive James, *North Face of Soho: More Unreliable Memoirs*

CONTENTS

Introduction

This is the story of how the French became the 'others' to the New Zealanders. Historians use the term 'othering' to describe how one nation, tribe, social or culturally based group identifies themselves by seeing the 'others' as different. The concept owes much to the ideas and writing of Edward Said. In his book *Orientalism: Western Conceptions of the Orient*, Said drew attention to the way one group can develop generalised ideas about the 'others'. He had experienced being one of the 'others' himself, because he was a naturalised American of Christian-Palestinian descent. His boyhood in the Middle East meant he had first-hand knowledge of a land that had been repeatedly conquered, colonised and traded, as if it were a possession of other nations.

Over time, generalisations about the 'others' come to be seen as their defining characteristics. Edward Said's example was the exoticism of the East as it was seen by those who lived in the Western world. Notice that when we talk of the Eastern or the Western World or the western hemisphere or the Middle East and so on we use geographical divisions based on the assumption that London and Europe are at the centre of the world. Yes, Greenwich is in the United Kingdom but that is itself an arbitrary location for the meridian line that divides the eastern lines of longitude from those in the west. Edward Said argued that the Eastern world was characterised by the West as a place of intrigue, cruelty, eroticism, and any one of many other features that supposedly typified Eastern cultures. He pointed out that cultural points of view are taken from the perspective of the writer or person observing and describing them. In this case it was the Western historians, anthropologists and the like who were the observers. There was not necessarily deliberate malice or ill-will in their studies and observations, but they typically saw their own culture as normal and used that to reference the 'others' who were therefore different or even incorrect. This is the process of ‘othering’; the development and definition of generalised ideas about the ‘others’ who are different from us.

Taking this a step further, imagine you are comfortably at home in a Western-style household. A stranger arrives and knocks on the door, asking if they can have a look at your home. You know they are a stranger because their clothing, language, behaviour and perhaps skin colour tell you so. You politely let them in and stand bemused as they examine your dwelling. They leave, only to return with some experts who start to forensically examine not only you and your family but your culture, your religion and your daily habits. They measure, they sketch, they record and they film. You have ceased to be another human; you are now an unwitting participant in their study. You are an object, a data point, one of the ‘others’ to be studied. Worse still, more of the visitors arrive and by peaceful or aggressive means they occupy your home and overwhelm your culture, perhaps by destroying your religion and substituting theirs. You are being subjected to the colonisation process. The colonisers may believe that you will be better off as a result of their intervention, but that is their view, not yours.

What happens under a more complex scenario when there is more than one group of colonisers? This happened in New Zealand when both the French and the British attempted to possess and colonise the same land, regardless of the views of the existing inhabitants. Clearly the British came out on top in the colonial contest. Only the archaeological traces of the French remain at Akaroa and in the Bay of Islands … or is there more? I will argue that the real story is more complex and deserves telling because it shows how ‘othering’ can occur and persist in our everyday lives without us being aware of it. Of course the past cannot be changed so we must deal with the situation as we now find it. But, if we do not re-examine the past, how can we learn more about ourselves and how we respond to challenging circumstances and unpredicted events and different groups of people?

I will also argue that New Zealand has had three views of France and the French. When the Treaty of Waitangi was signed in 1840, France was seen as the place of the Revolution and Napoleon Bonaparte. For the early European settlers this France was the mortal enemy of the British, a potential invader determined to expunge the British way in favour of a chaotic republicanism. In the aftermath of the New Zealand Wars of the 1860s came the colonial years, when the image of France as a direct enemy faded only to be replaced by France as a colonial competitor in the Pacific. France, the immediate enemy, could, however, swiftly re-emerge when European or Pacific matters forced Britain to confront her former enemy elsewhere in the world. The pre-World War I *entente cordiale* between the British and the French then recast France as an ally and later a fellow peace process affiliate at Versailles. This France also briefly became for New Zealand a potential commercial trading partner. That option of a closer relationship was soon cast aside in favour of resurrecting the earlier pre-war colonial competitor in the Pacific, albeit one that played rugby tolerably well and cared for New Zealand graveyards on its home soil.

It proved impossible for the New Zealanders to reconcile these conflicting versions of France. New Zealand therefore tried to minimise or ignore both the France of Revolution and Napoleon as well as France the World War I ally. This deflection is exposed in the histories covering this period, for when writing of 1918 to 1935 New Zealand historians have usually portrayed the New Zealand–France relationship as a series of occasional, exceptional, sometimes competitive but usually implicitly unimportant, post-colonial incidents. This was, after all, a period when there was reinforcement of a British-centric New Zealand identity that implicitly rejected non-Empire influences. This rejection combined the residues of British colonialism with pro-Empire sentiments that were then amplified through local political cheerleading and domestic cultural attitudes in favour of perpetuating the myth of the British heritage that including a rejection of the French.

Despite this rejection, France had (and still has) an important role in shaping British and New Zealand cultural norms and political events. By adopting Britain's tumultuous historical relationship with France along with Britain's ambivalent attitudes towards the French in contemporary affairs, New Zealand has minimised the French link. To do otherwise would recall the inconvenient truth of the strong anti-French bias that has left its often-ignored markers on the national landscape. In the spirit of developing independence and a distinct national identity, the New Zealanders have tried to leave these matters behind and taken instead to writing self-contained national histories that perpetuate the theme of a distinctly New Zealand identity gradually emerging after World War I. For today's New Zealanders, any reminder that the French were an ongoing presence disrupts the uneasy historical equilibrium evident in these post-colonial narratives because this challenges the idea that New Zealand's emergence as a nation was simply a reluctant separation of Britain and New Zealand, from which there emerged a new bicultural entity that has now (re-) discovered Te Tiriti o Waitangi as its founding event. This is the story of how this happened.

PART I

Shaky Beginnings

> The question of the sovereignty of these islands has not yet been decided. The *status quo* has been established by agreement between Captain Lavaud and the English Commandant, until the two Governments shall have come to an understanding on the subject.
>
> *Paris Constitutionnel* requoted in the *New Zealand Gazette and Wellington Spectator*, 26 January 1842.[1]

The French made two attempts at establishing a permanent presence in early colonial New Zealand but in the event neither succeeded. The Banks Peninsula settlement at Akaroa did not result in the establishment of an identifiably French population in the South Island – such as occurred at Quebec in Canada – while the French religious mission begun by Bishop Pompallier in the Bay of Islands did not result in New Zealand becoming a predominantly French-led Catholic nation. Both ventures are therefore usually treated as insignificant historical curiosities with little direct impact on New Zealand as it is today. Such is the nature of history, for it is usually written as if the outcome as we now know it was inevitable. This presumed inevitability gives the present situation legitimacy, for if the outcome is assumed to have been unavoidable, what more could or should have been done?

Consider the case of that early French presence in New Zealand. This did not apparently result in the French having a significant role in today's New Zealand. Is that because we now know that a significant historical French presence did not result in any obvious French presence today or is it because the French presence was insignificant? I believe there is a case for the former claim. There was a significant French presence and influence in New Zealand's past but because it did not result in any immediately obvious presence today it has been largely ignored in the mainstream versions of New Zealand's history.

There are two reasons for this understatement of the French role. Firstly, the earliest, popular version of the New Zealand story described the British colonisers winning over the indigenous Māori population and acquiring their land through a combination of discovery, annexation, treaty settlement, purchasing and war. The mainly British Protestant missionaries concurrently gained religious ascendancy as part of this process while Catholic evangelising from France faltered. Secondly, generations of Pākehā historians perpetuated this version of New Zealand's history. They were mainly associated with the British colonial winners, having either been trained in Britain or taught by British-educated academics. The formal histories they learned were those of the English nation. Their histories had a strongly pro-British undertone along with a significant bias against the French. Events such as William the Conqueror's invasion of England, the excesses of Louis XIV, the chaos of the French Revolution and Napoleon's wars were common topics when these historians were educated. Even when taught as factual histories, these subjects were coloured by an inherited Francophobia that had been renewed during the Napoleonic Wars, and then nurtured and sustained well into the nineteenth century.

These themes were adopted and perpetuated in New Zealand, with local variations. Re-examining the New Zealand public record (as it was preserved in the newspapers of the time) and the official archives shows that the contemporary reporters and writers could either exaggerate or understate the French influence, depending on the viewpoint of the author and their intent in interpreting the events they described. The French were usually the 'others' from the British point of view, and so were a useful contrast or foil against which British actions could be assessed, be it favourably or otherwise. What the French really intended to do in New Zealand did not matter because the British colonists and their successors created a perception of French intent or actions, whether real or imagined, which was then used to shape the history of New Zealand's colonisation as they wanted the world to know it. In fact, the reality of day to day interactions with the French in New Zealand as described in the press of the day, be it through their naval, religious or colonial presence, appears to have been at the very least civil and in many cases complementary. Surprisingly, an element of admiration appears in many of the comments on French actions.

Discrepancies from this generalisation fall into three categories. The first and broadest of these is the use by the early colonists (particularly those associated with the New Zealand Company) of the French presence or the threat of French action to further their own ends in their dealings with the Colonial Government. Secondly, reports about events in other French colonies were used as a reference point to show how much worse New Zealand would be if it were to have come under French rule. Finally, the Colonial Government excused its own shortcomings by attributing unfavourable events to the French, when it suited them.

Chapter One

Fortune-seeking in mid-nineteenth-century New Zealand

The enthusiasm for colonisation during the nineteenth century showed that no nation could realistically hope to exist as a completely independent territory, isolated from world events. Sooner or later an explorer, an opportunistic fortune-seeker, an imperial power with a desire for new territory or another tribe or population would arrive and disturb the status quo. Whether these uninvited immigrants intended to exploit a new (for them) environment to improve their own fortunes, or whether they saw themselves as benevolent do-gooders (as the missionaries did) was largely irrelevant because whatever their motives, the fact of their arrival and ongoing presence disturbed the local equilibrium.

The earliest European visitors to New Zealand observed and then judged their new surroundings based on their own values and experience. These past experiences tinted the new arrivals' views of the local situation through their European bias. When a newly discovered population is described as (say) peaceful or perhaps uncivilised, the yardstick used is the writer's own experience and social background. Even with the best intentions, the early European arrivals in New Zealand could not describe events as if they were viewing a scene with unfiltered impartiality. Moreover, just as these mindsets coloured their observations – perhaps an ordinary British seaman viewed the behaviour of local women as immoral and sexually permissive or maybe a French priest saw the people as sinners and heathens waiting to be saved – their biases shaped the historical record we have today. The local population probably reciprocated and viewed some of the visitors' customs as uncivilised or immoral. When given the choice, the locals no doubt showed the visitors a selection of their cultural customs, material goods or local environment that they thought to be appropriate, just as we do for visitors today. They probably assumed that the newcomers would interpret what they were shown from the local viewpoint, not by judgement using a foreign moral code. Even the natural philosophers of their time (such as Joseph Banks) could not therefore have observed and described so-called pre-contact customs and behaviours while staying quarantined from the influence their very presence induced. Nor could they impartially observe without introducing their own past experiences, even if that was not their intent. Consider the viewpoint of Te Rauparaha, expressed after the Wairau engagement when he contemplated the fate of his prisoners. He was in one view an inhumane brute and in another a man of learning and wisdom simply applying the rule of law as it was on his land:

> A little while ago I wished to talk with you in a friendly manner, and you would not; now you say save me, I will not save you. It is not our custom in war to save the chiefs of our enemies. We do not consider our victory complete unless we kill the chiefs of our opponents.
>
> Te Rauparaha's response to Magistrate Thompson's plea for his life.[1]

Contrast this with Saladin's (Ṣalāḥ al-Dīn Yūsuf ibn Ayyūb, the great Muslim Sultan) statement made to King Guy during the Crusades. Saladin had beaten Guy's army, Guy's ally (Raynald) had been beheaded, and Guy presumed he faced the same fate, but Saladin told Guy that: 'A king does not kill a king.'[2]

Historians often focus on muskets, muslin-cloth and malted liquors, but it was the ideas and intellectual baggage of these strange European visitors and invaders – not just their material goods – that added much of the uncertainty and led to such unpredictable results in New Zealand. Three of the themes that came from the mid-nineteenth-century world with the new arrivals are directly relevant to the early interactions between the British, the French and Māori in Aotearoa New Zealand. The first was the historical love-hate relationship between France and England. Such constructs were not left behind in their original Western European cultural setting. They were brought to New Zealand by the British and used by the colonists to evaluate and judge the French as circumstances demanded. Thus, when considering the British and French interactions in distant New Zealand, the idea of a new beginning was still built on the historical constructs brought by both the European nations to guide their respective judgements.

Second was the imperialism of the great powers. The idea of acquiring territory and 'civilising' the natives (claimed as being in their interests) was an accepted part of maintaining a global footprint while sharing out the world's resources. This was common ground between the British and the French, although the means to do so, especially in the case of religion, were diametrically opposite.

Third was the debate over the abolition of slavery. References by Māori to the threat of enslavement were probably a reflection of the controversy that the issue was still generating in the Western world (a controversy that culminated in the American Civil War of 1861–1865), while the British continued to transport convicts to Australia until the late 1860s. It was also an implicit warning of what backing the wrong side might mean. The concept of slavery with its associated loss of individual identity and mana was already known to Māori, so any perceived threat of enslavement carried extra gravitas in the New Zealand context.

Before the Treaty of Waitangi was signed in 1840, French and British activity in New Zealand consisted of exploration, exploitation of natural resources, trade and religious missions, executed with varying degrees of support from their respective governments and from Māori. The most significant of these, as far as the eventual resolution of the sovereignty question went, was the early exploration and associated claims of possession, followed by the evangelising of various Christian denominations. European attempts at colonisation through private land purchases added a further level of complexity.

Prior to the French colonisation attempt at Akaroa in 1840, at least nine officially recognised French expeditions had visited, starting with de Surville's visit in 1769.[3] These visits appear to have been either opportunistic or, when planned, explorative but without specific intent. Clashes often resulted as two societies unaware of the protocols, culture and religion of the other interacted. Anne Salmond's account of Marion du Fresne's visit in 1772 provides a typical example of the points for potential friction. Not only was there the impact of some 200 additional people helping themselves to the local resources, including fish, fresh water and trees for timber and fuel (activity that Europeans would have called raiding or theft if it had occurred in Europe), there was the indirect impact on local politics. Du Fresne's popularity with the locals apparently disturbed the Māori hierarchy and that, coupled with a broken tapu and interaction between the local women and the sailors, helped precipitate the conflict that followed. Du Fresne was killed, along with a boat crew. Reprisal raids by the French resulted in Māori deaths and destruction of property.[4]

Visits by French ships had consequences beyond their direct impact on Māori, for they aroused British fears that the French might establish a penal colony in the Pacific as a forerunner to occupying the land. Dumont D'Urville sailed to the Pacific in 1826 with 'secret political orders' instructing him to search the upper North Island of New Zealand for a location suitable for a penal colony.[5] Penal colonies were used by both the French and the British to provide manpower for developing the infrastructure of new colonies and to serve as an offshore prison-in-exile for criminals. They were also, at least in theory, intended to reform the inmates. 'The basic idea behind the early proposal (for penal colony establishment) was that crime was the product of a hostile and evil environment, and that perfect people could be produced in a well-ordered agricultural society where man could live "naturally" away from temptations.'[6]

France had used the American territory of Louisiana as a penal colony during the first revolutionary period in the late eighteenth century. Once Louisiana was sold, France had no territory suitable for deportations, despite such punishment being included in the Napoleonic Penal Code of 1810. After the 1848 revolution, use of deportation for political prisoners was revived with Algeria the initial destination. French interest in establishing a penal colony in New Zealand fortunately fell between these two significant events in French history, a period when deportation was perhaps less in demand.[7] Hence the venture was not pursued.

Probably the French had in mind the British penal settlement model used in Australia. These were meant to be prisons as well as bases for whaling and transit ports for accessing New Zealand timber and flax needed for naval supplies. Hobart and Sydney became a means of 'pre-empting other European powers' by occupation in the South Pacific and Tasman Seas while giving the British a strategic advantage over their main Pacific competitors – the French and the United States.[8] Penal colonies were, however, not only a bad look, they were also unproductive, expensive to run and clearly they did not act as a deterrent. They did provide tangible evidence that a newly claimed territory was occupied, although they arguably hindered free colonisation since the prisoners – being more or less slaves in all but name – could provide cheap labour.

Despite the suspicions aroused by various early French visitors, there is little evidence of a planned French presence in New Zealand prior to 1838, but given the history of hostility between Britain and France it is hardly surprising that each country saw the other as a potential competitor in any situation where their activities overlapped.

Defining events particularly Trafalgar (1805) and Waterloo (1815) were still within living memory. Despite this, the scaremongering from New Zealand's British residents probably had as much to do with drumming up support at Home for their ambition of creating a British-dominated, Protestant country as it did with any genuine threat of French domination.

Although the 1831 visit by Cyrille Pierre Théodore Laplace was principally for his crew to recuperate, it was nonetheless used by the British residents to arouse fears of French annexation. Laplace had in fact received 'a very generous reception' in Sydney from 'both Government and Society' before sailing on to New Zealand.[9] Although he considered New Zealand to be a hostile place, the missionary wife Maryanne (sic) Williams wrote that his visit in 1831 was really to '…spy out the land'. Such fears led to a coalition of Māori chiefs petitioning William IV for protection from the 'tribe of Marion'. The petition was probably instigated by the Protestant missionaries who had their own reasons for discouraging the French. Nevertheless, this was the start of an ongoing pattern of pleas and requests for help in response to fears whether real or not, as to what the French might do if British support was not forthcoming. The petition was not withdrawn, even when it became apparent to the missionaries that Laplace did not intend to claim sovereignty, for he departed without doing so.[10]

In 1835, as the eccentric Anglo-French Baron de Thierry attempted to establish himself as the ruler-sovereign of New Zealand by way of a declaration issued from his base in the French territory of Tahiti., some New Zealand chiefs responded with their own Declaration of Independence while James Busby, the British Resident, wrote to the Governor in Sydney to acquaint him with his fears of a French settlement. The de Thierry threat again failed to goad the British colonial authorities into action, for after de Thierry's arrival any local interest in this hopeless romantic and fantasist faded as he lapsed into 'harmless obscurity'. The French Government's attitude towards New Zealand similarly 'lapsed into indifference' once D'Urville confirmed the illegitimacy of de Thierry's land purchases. Up to this point it seems safe to conclude that notwithstanding the de Thierry initiatives, British concerns over French intentions were largely based on paranoia, exacerbated by self-serving local rumours that were in turn generated by the missionaries and early colonists.[11]

The hollow fears of a French presence were nonetheless an important influence in persuading the Māori leadership, presumably with European guidance, to adopt the political language and implied sovereign identity of what would have seemed to European eyes to be a unified nation-state. The Chief's 1835 declaration of independence began:

> We, the absolute leaders of the tribes (iwi) of New Zealand (Nu Tireni) to the north of Hauraki (Thames) having assembled in the Bay of Islands (Tokerau) on 28th October 1835. [We] declare the authority and leadership of our country and say and declare them to be prosperous economy and chiefly country (Wenua Rangatira) under the title of 'Te Wakaminenga o ngā Hapū o Nu Tireni' (The sacred Confederation of Tribes of New Zealand).[12]

The use of terminology associated with unified governance over the northern portion of country – as if the geographic whole was one political entity – was to have profound consequences when it was later abutted with European concepts of treason, rebellion and collective punishment in the 1860s. Using the construct of a Western political state may have made sense for petitioning a British king, but it mischaracterised the traditional tribally based governance structures used in New Zealand wherein each tribe held sovereign status within its own portion of the land. Moreover, petitioning King William IV implied that the British King had authority over the British subjects resident in New Zealand. This was an unintended step closer to accepting British power to act in respect of New Zealand affairs even when these primarily concerned Māori possessions and territory. Had the Declaration of Independence that Busby promoted been more widely supported by Māori and British alike it may well have achieved the same outcome as the Treaty of Waitangi.[13] Instead, as a result of a lessened threat owing to French inaction and indifference the matter rested until earlier, vague threats of French occupation finally seemed vindicated through the arrival of Bishop Pompallier on 10 January 1838. Here was hard evidence for the British colonists that justified their earlier '...well founded suspicions that the French had their eye upon New Zealand'.[14]

The first mission station had been established in New Zealand in 1814, just before Napoleon's 100-day reign was ended at Waterloo in 1815. France had effectively been under naval blockade since the Battle of Trafalgar ten years earlier, so the British missionaries had a clear advantage in time and sea transport. To make up for the lapse, the French initiated a policy of aggressive support for French mission activity. French naval commanders were authorised to issue warnings and threats in support of French missions when needed. The British gave less direct support, especially to colonies deemed to be of low economic worth. They acquiesced when the French annexed Tahiti, despite the fact that the London Missionary Society had largely won over the local population.[15] Nonetheless, the British appeared to be well ahead in the contest for Pacific territory of economic significance, and to outward appearances had a clear plan for further acquisitions of territory deemed to be consistent with British interests.

Given the British missionaries' significant head start over their Catholic rivals it is unsurprising that an 1862 survey of mission activity noted that 'everything' was working against the Catholic missionaries who had arrived twenty-five years after the Protestants' mission had begun. This was, however, another judgement made with hindsight, for initially even Protestant progress was slow. The conversion tactics were originally based on the idea that the 'cannibal savages' had to be civilised before they would become Christian. Samuel Marsden tried to recruit 'artisans' to live amongst Māori and teach them a civilised way of life. This strategy didn't work as planned, a failure attributed to the character of Māori and a lack of artisans so the order was reversed, and it was decided that '…the Gospel is the pioneer of civil life'. It seems more likely that education presented a mutually beneficial intersection between Māori and missionary interests. On the one hand, Māori gained knowledge of Pākehā ways while paying lip service to religion and on the other the missionaries could add to their tally of souls saved and hence petition for more funding. From the late 1820s onwards there was '…a new eagerness among some Maoris for the skills of reading and writing' so that education became, '…one of the most effective tools of the imperial machine'.[16] This point was not lost on the French missioners who established New Zealand's first printing establishment at Kororāreka/Russell in 1842.

The joint interests of the French Church and State led to the formation of a Catholic Western Oceania Vicariate under Bishop Pompallier's leadership in the 1830s. This development heightened British fears of a possible backdoor annexation of New Zealand territory by religious conversion. The subsequent arrival of French Catholic missionaries in New Zealand therefore began a fierce inter-religious competition at a grassroots level between the Protestant and Catholic faiths.[17] The French Chief Minister (Soult), who was also the Foreign Minister, was quite open with the head of the Marists, Father Colin, in linking religion with colonisation; 'If they (i.e. the natives) become Catholic, they will become French' he wrote to Father Colin in 1839.[18] Whether intentionally or not, the presence of French warships protecting the missionaries meant the latter were overtly linked to French imperial ambitions. The visit of the French ship *Heroine* in 1838 elevated the status of the Catholic mission in Māori eyes and contributed to subsequent conversions. It seems on balance that the local links between the French Church and State in the Pacific were to outward appearances at least as close as they were in France itself, and directly supportive of colonial sovereignty aspirations.[19]

The integrated and aggressive interaction and mutual support between the French missionaries and the French Navy therefore made territorial gains appear to be more than a coincidental outcome, even when only one or the other was apparently involved. Soult's offer to pay the missionaries' fares and provide direct naval support for their expedition to New Zealand was welcomed by Father Colin (the Mission leader) but Colin was very aware of the dangers for the Church of being seen as an agent of the French state. Nevertheless, Soult's support along with the morale-boosting news of a French settlement planned for Akaroa raised French hopes of successful colonisation in New Zealand. Unfortunately, the Treaty of Waitangi had already been signed by the time Bishop Pompallier received Father Colin's letter sharing the good news of state support.[20]

The arrival of the French missionaries brought more than theological differences, for this other Pākehā tribe were clearly the traditional enemies of the British. Māori could see a different culture, language, political structure and religion.[21] Collectively these differences help explain the depth of feeling between the French and the British that eventually became a local fissure far greater than any theological debate. It was hostile and acrimonious to a degree that led William Colenso, who was himself no 'yes-man' for the Church Missionary Society (CMS), describing the Catholics as 'bitter enemies'.[22] CMS missionaries claimed that conversions to Catholicism were invalid because they did not require Māori to renounce old customs, while Catholicism itself was theologically incorrect and leading Māori astray.[23] As James Buller, the missionary and explorer, put it, 'It was their (the Catholic missionaries) one great object to assail and denounce the (Protestant) missionaries who had preceded them'.[24] No doubt the French would have made the reverse claim.

While French interests were directed through an association between religion and the nation as shown by Bishop Pompallier's presence, official British interests were pursued through a political pathway that led via James Busby's appointment as British Resident to the selection of William Hobson as New Zealand's first Lieutenant-Governor. The British Government's interest in New Zealand was ostensibly non-denominational, but James Stephen, then Permanent Under-Secretary at the Colonial Office in London, was strongly Protestant and most concerned that the New Zealand Association, a private colonial business enterprise, was led by Catholics. Stephen appears to have believed that preventing New Zealand from becoming Catholic by blocking any chance of the Association becoming the real power in New Zealand was grounds enough for British Government action. If this was so, it seems odd that Governor Hobson agreed with Pompallier's suggestion during the Treaty of Waitangi negotiations that freedom of religious choice be included in the agreement.[25] Hobson may have been unaware of the anti-Catholicism within the Colonial Office and the Association's supposed bias or, as seems more probable, he was aware but did not refer to it in his despatches to avoid reproach for allowing this amendment.[26]

But what had led to a treaty being contemplated, let alone signed? Official French interest in New Zealand in pre-Treaty times (until about 1838) was explorative, opportunistic and circumstantial, rather than a coordinated strategy. The result was the haphazard exploration already described, alongside an uncoordinated mix of religious missions, whaling and a few settlers. On a global level, France was preoccupied with colonies and events elsewhere, while being at a severe disadvantage in naval power compared to the British when it came to defending distant islands in the South Pacific. Annexation was in any case arguably unnecessary from a commercial point of view as long as trade continued, and so it proved. Even after the British took possession of New Zealand, French whaling in the Southern Ocean using New Zealand's British-controlled ports for provisioning and rest periods continued uninterrupted.

Ignoring a colonial opportunity on the other hand risked ceding territory to an imperial competitor by default, assuming that the competitor wanted to take possession. Moreover, British colonisation was taking place in New Zealand without official sanction. In such circumstances annexation was 'usually' the easiest course, rather than trying to stop or reverse actions taken by the people on the spot.[27] If so, British annexation of New Zealand was inevitable based on the scale of British activity. Suggestions that the British Government viewed colonisation by the enemies of the British Empire – such as France – as detrimental to Māori were probably less of a concern in London than the immediate need to get some control before a private colonial enterprise took over the entire country.[28] The door was open for the British because the European presence in New Zealand was already predominantly British and the Māori population had shown hostility towards the earlier French visitors.

Thus, when Bishop Pompallier and the Marists began converting Māori to Catholicism it was seen by the British colonists and Protestant missionaries as an attempt to direct Māori sympathies and loyalty towards France. The despatch of the ships the *Aube* and the *Comte de Paris* to Banks Peninsula then made overt what was previously construed by the British colonists as a covert strategy. The French plan was apparently to occupy the Middle (South) Island by establishing a French colonial settlement at Akaroa under the guise of the commercial operations of the Nanto-Bordelaise Company, and then to proclaim sovereignty as a complement to the religious conquest begun in the north.[29]

As far as anyone in Europe knew, at the time Captain Lavaud's expedition departed for New Zealand the British had not pursued any legal claim to territory in southern New Zealand since the time of Cook's possession (by raising the flag at Queen Charlotte Sound on 31 January 1770). Nor had any claim been affirmed through a display of civil government action, or by occupation as required under international convention.[30] Hence when the French left Europe, they would have assumed they had as much right to claim territory in New Zealand as the British, given that Lavaud could not have known that the Treaty of Waitangi had already been signed. This uncertainty explains why the New Zealand Company had written with some alarm to Foreign Secretary Palmerston in November 1839, alerting him to the danger of

French attention being drawn to New Zealand's uncertain sovereign status. If Cook's claim by discovery was not to be pursued there was nothing to stop the French acquiring sovereignty by exactly the same means that Hobson had been instructed to use, i.e. gaining Māori assent.[31] When Lord Russell at the Colonial Office became aware of the Lavaud expedition he informed the Foreign Secretary (on 27 May 1840) that '...we cannot object to the proceedings of the French Government in relation to New Zealand'. (He would have been unaware that the Treaty had been signed and validated by Hobson's proclamations of 21 May 1840.)[32]

Once the Treaty of Waitangi was signed, there was concerted British activity in New Zealand aimed at adding Māori signatures and extending the geographical boundaries of the territory that could henceforth be deemed to be under British sovereignty. Governor Hobson knew there were French ships in New Zealand waters and that the arrival of a French colonial expedition was imminent, but given the international commercial interests already in the Pacific, especially in the whaling industry, French ships in New Zealand waters can hardly have been a new development. While on one signature-collecting expedition, Major Bunbury's vessel (the *Herald*) had sighted and exchanged salutes with the two French vessels of D'Urville's Antarctic expedition.[33] This encounter does not appear to have been exceptional.

Captain Lavaud finally arrived at the Bay of Islands, Hobson's seat of Government, on 11 July 1840. The original plan had called for the *Aube* to stop at Hobart in Tasmania to disembark some missionary passengers who were bound for the Bay of Islands. They could then take onward passage to their final destination while Captain Lavaud was supposed to sail directly to Banks Peninsula to meet up with the settlers who were travelling in the *Comte de Paris*. Rather than landing the missionaries at Hobart as instructed and then going directly to Banks Peninsula, Lavaud took the prejudicial approach of first calling at the Bay of Islands. Why the missionaries were not simply taken to Banks Peninsula and then told to make their way up to the Bay of Islands has not been explained. Whatever the reason, Captain Lavaud's decision avoided the possibility of any misunderstanding that may have led the British authorities to assume he was making a surreptitious landing.[34]

Historians have suggested various reasons for Lavaud's decision. These include the vague catch-all explanation that it was the wisest choice, personal discord between the missionaries making their disembarkation a priority (perhaps they did not want to transit Hobart and face a stopover together followed by another voyage), a wish to consult Pompallier, and/or to simply check on the state of the sovereignty claims. Any or all of these are possible since they are not mutually exclusive, but without knowledge of the onboard mood and Lavaud's own assessment of sea and weather conditions (the weather in the southern Tasman Sea is unpredictable during the southern hemisphere autumn and winter with prevailing westerly winds) it seems possible that all were factors in his decision. Whatever the reason, since the French claim was to have been based on occupation of land at Banks Peninsula, calling at the British capital in the north would seem to have been as predictably counterproductive as it proved to be.

Lavaud's arrival obviously alerted the New Zealand authorities, thus setting the scene for much of what followed in the New Zealand–French relationship. Lavaud accepted the fait accompli of the Treaty and he did not attempt to annex the Middle Island when he finally arrived at Banks Peninsula. Despite urging from Pompallier he never seems to have seriously considered this course. Lavaud does quote Pompallier as saying to him during his stay in the Bay of Islands '...how grateful he was to the French Government for the protection it granted him...'.[35] English and French authority was to exist side by side on Banks Peninsula until Hobson died in September 1842. Willoughby Shortland then became acting Governor/Administrator and he wasted no time in reasserting British possession by raising the British flag.[36] Meanwhile, the Catholic missionaries had their own problems with a conflict between Pompallier and the Marists slowing the pace of conversions.[37] With no further settlers arriving from France and the missionary work stalling, the attempt at colonisation and establishing French sovereignty was apparently finished.

These events have been re-examined by many well-known writers and distinguished historians with surprisingly different conclusions. All are tidied-up explanations that suited the sensitivities prevalent when they were written, just as acceptance of the Treaty as the nation's founding document reflects the current (2020) consensus. Michael King's reflections raise an additional dilemma that historians' face, namely should they consider what might have been? As King wrote in 2012: 'Had Hobson not acted three months earlier, this (French) settlement might have resulted in part or the whole of the South Island being annexed by France.'[38]

We will not of course know what might have happened if some other event had not occurred, but it can be helpful to at least consider the options faced by the participants at the time, even though we cannot replicate the exact circumstances under which they faced them. There were at least four grounds under which British sovereignty over New Zealand could have been claimed. As well as the Treaty, there were claims by right of Cook's discovery, by occupation of vacant (so-called 'waste') land and by the assertion of sovereignty. Annexation by conquest is the only means excluded in most historical writing, a matter of some irony given the dispossession of Māori as a result of the land wars of the 1860s.

Much of the contemporary debate in New Zealand accepts that the Treaty of Waitangi was and still is the defining document for sovereignty claims. The Treaty, however, relied on two different concepts of nationhood, sovereignty and representation. The European concept of a single binding treaty depended for its legitimacy on a recognised nation-state contained within clearly defined geographic boundaries, represented by authorised representatives (ambassadors) who could claim to speak on behalf of their respective rulers. Such representatives still require some form of validation from their own sovereign state in order to claim the authority to enter into agreements on behalf of the state.

Under Māori rule, sovereignty over Aotearoa was not contained within a single nation-state with a unified political structure, although the earlier Declaration by the northern chiefs suggested it was.[39] Trying to arrive at a mutual agreement using the Western European political constructs without initially establishing and agreeing to shared ground rules therefore led to continual misunderstandings and ultimately conflict. This was the foundation problem that the apparently unified new nation of New Zealand had to grapple with: the ground rules for political interaction between two peoples who were supposedly unitary entities joined in partnership were dissimilar. Conversely, disputes between the French and the British led to fewer problems because the two European nation-states shared a common understanding of the rules (as they applied under European conventions) for international treaty making and territorial acquisitions. It was easier for the two foreign powers – Britain and France – to come to an arrangement over New Zealand than it was for either European nation to negotiate a workable agreement with Māori.

Chapter Two

The facts? Formal records and official perspectives

When the French expedition left France for Banks Peninsula there was clearly some uncertainty as to the sovereign status of New Zealand, for on 7 July 1840, the British House of Commons debated a petition requesting the appointment of a select committee to investigate various issues concerning colonisation and the associated sovereign claims.[1] The petitioners were 'merchants, bankers, and ship-owners, of the city of London' who, judging from their occupations and the tone of the petition, had a commercial interest in the subject. Not only had Colonial Office actions raised serious doubts, it had in its instructions to Hobson also questioned the validity of earlier land purchases. Presumably concerned about their investments in the colonisation project, those with commercial risks needed to muster what arguments they could in favour of British sovereignty. British sovereignty would entrench the British legal system under which the purchasers believed they could validate their claims of ownership to the land already acquired.

Chartism was at its peak in England in 1839, partly because only property owners could actively participate in the political process. The disruptive Chartists and their supporters might, however, be persuaded to emigrate to a new country, if it had a British-based legal system under which they could become property owners and therefore eligible to vote. During the parliamentary debate the purpose of colonisation was defined with more finesse as being to help the 'working classes' who due to: '...the increasing state of the population, and the great improvements that were daily being made in machinery, (were unable) to obtain sufficient employment for the support of themselves and their families'.

In short, the result of industrialisation and unchecked population growth was unemployment and poverty. The solution was to send these problems elsewhere. The issue was whether Britain had suitable, uncontested territory available and whether the relocation could be profitably and legitimately achieved through private enterprise, unhindered by official intervention.

Lord Edward Eliot (1798–1877) presenting the petitioners' case was concerned that despite Cook's visit and subsequent arm's-length government involvement from Australia, New Zealand's sovereign status had still not been fully resolved. Even despatching Hobson raised questions as to the validity of prior British claims, since the need to assign Hobson to this new position provided evidence that Britain had not previously undertaken any act of civil authority in New Zealand. A directive to the land commissioners to concentrate on Australia could further weaken the British case and attract the interest of 'foreign states to this derelict colony'. Even more alarmingly, French settlers were heading to the 'southern' (sic) island, which Lord Eliot said Hobson had already declared (after his tour in HMS *Rattlesnake*) could not won by treaty since it was: '…inhabited by persons in a savage state, and incapable, from ignorance, of entering into any treaty; and he (Hobson) recommended the assertion, on the ground of discovery, of Her Majesty's sovereign rights over the island…'

Hobson's own observations were being used as evidence that a sovereignty claim over the South Island based solely on Treaty signatures was impossible. Furthermore, some disturbing if unofficial news had already been received from New Zealand. Whether this was a communication from Hobson or some other source and whether it was directed to Lord Eliot or one of his conferees is not clear. Although there was no mention of a Treaty, the Commons was told that: 'By private letters it appeared that Captain Hobson had upon landing issued a proclamation stating, that her Majesty had directed a commission to be appointed to inquire into the validity of the titles of the colonists to the lands which they held.'

Lord John Russell (1792–1878), who at the time was Secretary of State for the Colonies, raised the point that a claim based solely on discovery without subsequent action – such as colonisation – would be open to question, since such claims would be numerous and conflicting. He quoted two Acts of Parliament that specifically stated New Zealand was not under British rule. He went on to argue that the Government was not going to act just to help out a 'number of gentlemen', i.e. the New Zealand Company. Doing so would set a precedent for anyone to request retrospective legislation to validate private purchases of native land for later resale.

> What he [Lord Russell] objected to was, that a company in London should send persons into a country, and do those things which it belonged to the Crown to do, which had at all times been considered as the undoubted prerogative of the Crown, and which ought to remain a Crown prerogative.

Sir Henry Ward claimed that it wasn't until the French had shown some interest that the Government had acted. Vernon Smith (Under-Secretary of State for the Colonies from 1839 to 1841) pointed out that the only reason the Colonial Office had been forced to show that New Zealand was not under British sovereignty was because the New Zealand Company had wrongly claimed that it was, and that the New Zealand Company through publicising part of Hobson's instructions, had provoked the French to act.

Under further questioning, Lord Russell added that:

> ...the duties of Captain Hobson were, in the first place, to endeavour to acquire the sovereignty of those lands in which any of her Majesty's subjects were located. If he should find, in the course of his negotiations

> with the chiefs, that they were desirous of placing the whole sovereignty of their country in the hands of the Crown of England, he would be authorised to accept such a proposition. It was, however, a subject very much left to the discretion of Captain Hobson...[2]

(It is noticeable that Lord Russell spoke of the chiefs as if they were the joint, collective rulers of New Zealand, capable of placing the 'whole' land under Crown rule rather like a Cabinet in control of a sovereign, legal entity.) In short, the Government devolved responsibility to Hobson and was now metaphorically stepping back from the sovereignty conundrum. The supporters of the petition to the British Parliament were arguing that a benevolent New Zealand Company was helping the unemployed and poor of England to emigrate while (coincidentally) saving New Zealand from being colonised by the French.[3]

Under the accepted Western rules for discovery and possession of international territory, a British sovereignty claim based solely on the grounds of discovery without occupation would fail. In such circumstances it was entirely possible that at least part of New Zealand could be turned into a French (penal) colony, if France established a settlement first. The threat from France, whether realised or not, gave cause for the New Zealand Company and its supporters to push for political action. The other viewpoint is of land profiteering by a private company, which was exploiting the indigenous Māori population. When this enterprise was threatened through government intervention the Company mustered every argument it could including a possible French threat, to force the British Government to protect the Company's interests. Then, as now, there was no one definitive view as to which was 'correct' nor were there well-defined grounds for intervention. The many versions depended on the participants' objectives and the interpretations placed on them through the legal and cultural mindsets of the history writers. It hardly needs stating that the one voice of unquestioned validity – the Māori owners who were the sole legitimate authority in their own country – were largely absent from this debate.

The timing of information flow was a significant factor in 1840. While dates on letters and other documents have never been a guarantee of the date of signing, despatch, receipt or reading whether officially or otherwise, slow transmission meant news lagged events to the extent that documents were often redundant or superseded before they could be read. Therefore, when considering reconstructed versions of historical events it is impossible to know whether the chronology used in the reconstruction is the same as the sequence of events at the time. When the *Aube* sailed from France for New Zealand on 19 February the House of Commons debate of 7 July 1840 was still four months away, but an article that covered some of the same ground was published in *The New Zealand Journal* (a London-based bulletin) on 22 February 1840, just three days after the *Aube* sailed.[4] This *Journal* article included a translated column ('The French in New Zealand') that had originally appeared in the *Journal du Havre.* Based on the timing and tense it must have been published in France to coincide with the departure of the *Aube*. Presumably the French expedition leaders were aware of the content because the *Journal du Havre* item makes the point that 'a mere attempt at colonization' is not the sole objective of the French expedition. It would also investigate establishing a penal colony at Banks Peninsula. Possession of the land was to be claimed by proprietary right (i.e. purchase) with subsequent validation obtained by French occupation.

The (presumably British) author of 'The French in New Zealand' article carefully avoids objecting to the French Company business model of a private enterprise funded, free-settler colony, presumably because this was similar to the New Zealand Company's venture. The writer does, however, attempt to legitimate pre-Treaty claims of British sovereignty, probably to calm British nerves, bearing in mind that news of the signing of the Treaty of Waitangi just sixteen days earlier could not have yet reached Europe. The article states that the British sovereignty claim is based on Cook taking formal possession of New Zealand, validated 'quarter of a century ago' by the exercise of sovereignty through the appointment of magistrates. This implies that British magistrates were appointed in New Zealand in 1815. It probably refers to the appointment of the lay missionary, Thomas Kendall, as a Justice of the Peace in 1813.[5] It was a shaky case but probably sufficient to settle any investor nervousness in London resulting from the *Journal du Havre* item.

Although we now know that the first ship carrying New Zealand Company settlers – after the *Tory*'s explorative voyage of the previous year – arrived in Wellington in January 1840, the article writer cannot have been certain that a British settlement had been successfully established.[6] Therefore, rather than actively opposing the anticipated French arrivals *The New Zealand Journal* suggested a backup plan. The 'foreign' settlers would be adopted by naturalisation as British subjects and then employed to introduce new skills to the colony.[7] On the penal colony issue, the writer takes comfort from the view that this is just a preliminary investigation or 'feeler', and that in any case any French prisoners sent to New Zealand would be immediately set free. The author clearly wanted to validate the actions of the New Zealand Company as confirmation of British possession, as well as to rehearse the arguments for denying the legitimacy of either a French settlement in the Middle Island or the proposed penal colony. There were nonetheless obvious doubts about the sovereign status since the New Zealand Company colony was in the North Island not the South (or Middle Island as it was known). With doubt came an increased risk to the fortunes of investors in the New Zealand Company and their settlers. Had Captain Lavaud been delayed and then seen this article he would have been reassured by the tenuous basis for claiming sovereignty over the South Island and the British uncertainty as to how to proceed. He may then have been more determined in his efforts to proceed directly to Banks Peninsula, take possession of the South Island by occupation and contest the British claims from there.

The reprinting of the 'French in New Zealand' newspaper article in *The New Zealand Gazette and Wellington Spectator* on 11 July 1840 coincided with the arrival of the *Aube* in the Bay of Islands. It therefore predated the 9 August 1840 arrival of the *Comte de Paris* at Pigeon Bay in Banks Peninsula with the French settlers and their equipment on board. The *Comte* had not departed from Ile d'Aix until 20 March 1840 owing to various mishaps.[8] Presumably the settlers and crew would have seen the *Journal du Havre* article and probably the leaders were aware that it had been reprinted in London but they had no way of letting their already departed consort vessel know of this development.

The arrival of the *Aube* in the Bay of Islands was not reported (in the *Gazette and Wellington Spectator*) until 22 August 1840.[9] An article noted that HM brig *Britomart* was sailing south to warn the French settlers of British sovereignty claims. This issue included the news from Banks Peninsula (received on the previous Monday, i.e. 17 August 1840) that none of the French expedition had arrived as yet. In the next issue (29 August 1840) the *New Zealand Gazette and Wellington Spectator* reported in one sentence that three hundred emigrants in a '...French frigate and two ships...' had arrived at Banks Peninsula.[10] This was an exaggeration for on 5 September the *Gazette* reported that the French frigate (*L'Aube*) had arrived at Banks Peninsula three days after *Britomart* followed by the *Comte de Paris*, two days later. The expedition was now said to consist of just fifty settlers. The British flag had been hoisted and the account says that matters had been 'conducted in a most amicable manner'.[11] These reports are undramatic and, given their brevity, do not appear to have signified any great concern about French colonisation, particularly given that a social visit to Port Nicholson by Captain Lavaud and his ship was proposed. A separate account of the unrelated visit of a French whaling vessel to provision and re-equip was printed just above this article. Again, the tone is amicable and written in a friendly style without rancour. The New Zealand Company and the Wellington establishment clearly did not want to give undue weight in public to the French arrivals.

Hobson nevertheless appears to have had earlier doubts about the efficacy of the Treaty as grounds for claiming British sovereignty over the South Island, notwithstanding the signatures added since the original signing.[12] His fears were justified. Even Major Bunbury, who was sent to collect the signatures, was doubtful whether the South Island chiefs who signed the Treaty were the legitimate owners of the land and therefore authorised to do so.[13] On 19 June 1840 the *New Zealand Advertiser and Bay of Islands Gazette* published two proclamations under the signature of Lieutenant Governor Hobson claiming British sovereignty over New Zealand by way of treaty (North Island) and by right of discovery (the Middle and Stewart Islands). Hobson was specifically authorised by Lord Normanby in his instructions to make such a claim.[14] The differing treatment of the two islands was forced by Hobson's own 'misconception' (as previously noted) that the islands differed in their degree of 'civilisation', and therefore the ability of local Māori to enter into a legal agreement affecting their sovereign status.[15]

Hobson clearly believed he needed to act to thwart the New Zealand Company at Port Nicholson, to block Australian-based land speculators in the South Island and to deal with the probable arrival of the French. Extending British sovereignty by proclamation over the South Island superseded whatever legitimacy the Treaty could provide, even when bolstered by Bunbury's additional signatories. Hobson rationalised his actions by claiming he had in any case gathered sufficient legitimate signatures to justify his proclamations.[16] Despite this, there was still obvious uncertainty when the *Aube* arrived at the Bay of Islands on 11 July 1840. Hobson therefore wrote to Lavaud on 18 July 1840 while Lavaud was still at Russell. In his letter Hobson makes it clear that he will not address the validity of the French land claim in the South (Middle) Island until Lavaud recognises Hobson as Lieutenant-Governor. This leaves Lavaud in an impossible situation. By first calling at the Bay of Islands, Lavaud had already implied that Russell was the seat of government in New Zealand. Recognising Hobson as

Lieutenant-Governor would be a further validation of British sovereignty. On the other hand, failure to do so risked any chance of recognition by the local ruling authority of the French claims at Banks Peninsula.

Two days after his letter to Lavaud, Lieutenant-Governor Hobson wrote to Captain Stanley on HMS *Britomart.* Stanley was instructed to proceed southward to validate and reassert the British claims. This letter expresses Hobson's considerable disquiet if not outright alarm. It is quoted here in full as it clarifies both Hobson's views on the sovereignty issue and his state of mind after he became aware of Lavaud's intention.[17] (Indecipherable and unclear words are shown as '?').

Government House
Russell New Zealand
20th July 1840

Sir

It being of the utmost importance that the authority of Her Majesty should be unequivocally exercised throughout the remote parts of this Colony and particularly in the Middle and Northern Islands where I understand Foreign influences and even interference is to be apprehended I have the honour to request you to proceed immediately in HM Sloop under your command to those islands.

On the subject of this communication I have to request the most inviolable secrecy from all but except your immediate superior Officers to whom it may be your duty to report your proceedings.

The ostensible purpose of your (?) may appear to be the conveyance of two Magistrates to Port Nicholson, to whom I will (?) more particularly after. The real object to which I wish particularly to direct your attention is to defeat the movements of any Foreign Ship of War that may be engaged in establishing a settlement on any part of the coast of New Zealand.

I have on various ominous (?) current that Captain L'Avaud of the French Corvette L'Aube now at anchor in this Port is employed in the furtherance of designs such as I have before mentioned.

From some observations that fell from him I discovered that his intention was to proceed to the Southern Islands being under an impression that the land about Akaroa and Banks' Peninsula in the Middle Island is the property of a French subject.

These circumstances combined with the tone in which Captain L'Avaud alluded to Akaroa and Banks' Peninsula excite in my mind a strong presumption that he is charged with some mission in that quarter incompatible with the Sovereign rights of Her Britannic Majesty and which as I have before observed it will be your duty be every means to frustrate.

If my suspicions prove correct the L'Aube will no doubt proceed direct to Akaroa and Banks' Peninsula for which place I have earnestly to request that you will depart with the utmost expedition as it would be a point of the utmost consideration that on his arrival at the port, he may find you in occupation, so that it would be out of his power to dislodge you without committing some direct act of hostility.

Captain L'Avaud may however anticipate you at Akaroa (or should ? be defeated and his movements) may endeavour to establish himself at some other point; In the event of either contingency occurring I have to request (suggest?) that you remonstrate and protest in the most decided manner against such proceeding and impress upon that such interferences must be considered as an act of decided hostile invasion.

You will (?) by the enclosed copy of Major Bunbury's declaration that independent of the assumption of the Sovereignty of the Middle and Southern Islands as announced by my Proclamation of the 21st May ultimo, a copy of which is also enclosed, the principal Chiefs have ceded their rights to Her Majesty through that Officer who was fully empowered and authorised to treat with them for that purpose it will not therefore be necessary for you to adopt any further proceedings. It will be however desirable that some Act of Civil authority should be exercised on the Islands and for that purpose the Magistrates who accompany you will be

> instructed to hold a Court on their arrival at each Port and a record of their proceedings (?) and transmitted to me.
> You will by every opportunity which may offer forward intelligence of the French Squadrons movements to me and should you deem it necessary to the Secretary of State for the Colonies through the Admiralty and to His Excellency Sir George Gipps Governor of New South Wales.
> Mr Murphy and Mr Robinson the Magistrates who accompany you will receive a Memorandum of Instructions for their future guidance which you will be pleased to hand to them when you arrive at your destination.
> As your presence in these Islands will be of the utmost importance to keep in check any aggression on the part of Foreign Powers, I have earnestly to request that should you require any further supply of Provisions, that the same may be procured if possible at port Nicholson or at any other Ports on the Coast without your returning to Sydney.
> I have the honour to be …
> To Captain Stanley
> HMS Britomart.

There was doubt and there was an obvious need for Stanley to get to Banks Peninsula first. Hobson insisted on 'inviolable secrecy' and a rapid departure ('depart with the utmost expedition') to either occupy the region to the extent that Lavaud could not 'dislodge you without committing some direct act of hostility' or, if *Britomart* was beaten to Banks Peninsula, to treat any French landing as a 'hostile invasion'. This was an extremely aggressive approach, suggesting that Hobson believed there was a genuine threat to the British claim that should be met with force if necessary.

When Hobson first arrived in New Zealand on 29 January 1840, he had proclaimed that all titles to land not acquired from the Crown were invalid, but nevertheless he felt it necessary to reinforce his position. Once Stanley had his instructions, Hobson therefore pushed his advantage by writing again to Lavaud, on 23 July 1840. This letter stated that he (Hobson) would delay any recognition of French claims until he received instructions from Britain, ‘except where they are contested by Englishmen’. In other words, if there is an English claim Hobson reserved the right to decide its legitimacy, even if instructions had not arrived from Britain. In his next paragraph Hobson advised Lavaud that the ‘whole parcel including Banks’ Peninsula and Akaroa and the coasts adjacent of it for many leagues to the North and South is claimed by English born subjects’.[18] Lavaud could recognise Hobson as Lieutenant-Governor but even if he did, given that there were British subjects contesting the French land claims, he had no certainty that Hobson would confirm the French purchases. Awaiting word from England might bring a favourable result for Lavaud if the French claim went uncontested, but Hobson had made clear that it was disputed. Hobson had taken a very firm stance with little opportunity for counter-argument.[19]

Instructing Stanley by letter not to pursue sovereignty by obtaining further signatures or making additional declarations suggests that any claim over the South Island was now to be based on discovery and occupation, rather than by a proclamation/declaration of sovereignty by cession. An ‘Act of Civil Authority’ by the magistrates would provide the evidence that a civil administration was in place and the land was occupied. Hobson was clearly concerned that the alternative of further claims based on signatures and a proclamation would fail if a foreign power occupied the land. Historian Guy Scholefield states unequivocally that: ‘The probable explanation is that he (Hobson) doubted the validity of the title to the South Island either on the grounds of cession or of ‘effective occupation’, as required by international law.’[20]

Land claims in the South Island have been debated ever since, so it is useful to review the respective British and French positions on the sovereignty issue to determine how strong these claims were. In his third despatch to the Colonial Secretary Hobson had written that: ‘Actuated by similar motives and a perfect knowledge of the uncivilised state of the natives, and supported by the advice of Sir George Gipps previously given I also proclaimed the authority of Her Majesty over the Southern Islands on the grounds of discovery.'[21]

The Waitangi Tribunal considered the sovereign status of what we now commonly refer to as the Chatham Islands and the South Island as part of the Waitangi settlement claims of Moriori and Ngāti Mutunga.[22] The Tribunal Report makes the same point that Lord John Russell did in 1840. Under Western/European customary law, discovery alone is not enough to establish possession, as Hobson initially tried to do. Some form of colonisation or civil activity is also required independent from any assessment of the state of civilisation of the 'natives'. (If claims were allowed based solely on discovery presumably every land mass in the known world would have been subject to similar multiple claims.) Applying that reasoning and aware that the only alternative was sovereignty by accession persuaded Hobson to send Major Bunbury on 27 April 1840 to gather Treaty signatures from the South Island chiefs. Hobson could then proclaim that he had obtained sovereignty by way of voluntary cession. This was his only option since the land was only sparsely occupied by British subjects and there was no official civil presence in the South Island.[23] While Major Bunbury was away, Hobson issued two proclamations on 21 May 1840. The first asserted sovereignty by cession through Treaty over the North Island. The second covered the Southern Islands. The version of this proclamation in Lindsay Buick's account is ambiguous.

> Whereas I have it in command from Her Majesty Queen Victoria, through her principal Secretary of State for the Colonies, to assert the Sovereign rights of Her Majesty over the Southern Islands of New Zealand, commonly called 'The Middle Island' and 'Stewart's Island,' [sic] and, also the Island commonly called 'The Northern Island,' the same having been ceded in Sovereignty to Her Majesty.[24]

The wording appears to assert sovereignty over the Southern Islands without giving the grounds for doing so. It could be read from the words 'and, also' that the same grounds were used for the Southern Islands as for the North. This was clearly not the case since Major Bunbury was still trying to gather enough signatures to allow a claim by cession to be made.[25] This wording may have been used in anticipation of a successful outcome from Bunbury's signature-gathering expedition. Whatever the rationale, the version published in the *New Zealand Advertiser and Bay of Islands Gazette* of 19 June 1840 includes the critical words 'on the grounds of discovery' inserted between 'to assert' and 'the Sovereign rights'.[26] This removed any ambiguity, although it does raise the issue as to whether the other versions were copied in error or had the critical words omitted through design or oversight. Bunbury's biographer has Bunbury proclaiming sovereignty over Stewart Island on 5 June 1840 by right of Cook's discovery and then over the South Island on 17 June 1840 by cession of sovereignty through the additional Treaty signatures. This presumably superseded Hobson's proclamation of 21 May.[27]

Who did own the land the French wanted to colonise and on what authority did the French assert a right of possession? Documents and discussion relevant to the French land titles at Banks Peninsula are filed with the Inward despatches from the Secretary of State but much of the supplementary material and enclosures are missing. Despite being dated as 9 December 1840 to 16 February 1841, the file includes a copy of a letter dated 26 February 1841, written by J. Backhouse, an official on Foreign Secretary Viscount Palmerston's staff, to James Stephen Esq., his opposite number on Colonial Secretary Lord Russell's staff.[28] (This was the same James Stephen who wanted a Protestant New Zealand.) News of the previously described events following the arrival of the French expedition in New Zealand had reached London and Paris. Viscount Palmerston's official informed his opposite at the Colonial Office that the French Chargé d'Affaires in London had sent a note pointing out the 'alarm' amongst the French settlers in New Zealand owing to the claim of possession by the British and the invalidation of earlier land titles. The note from the Chargé seeks an assurance that the intent cannot have been to invalidate 'arrangements' made prior to British authority being established. This request was in itself de facto recognition of British sovereignty since the French were asking the British to confirm the legality of their earlier land purchases. Despite this supplication, the British Government rejected the French request. Lord Russell's official asked his opposite to tell Viscount Palmerston that given the 'extravagant' and 'frivolous' nature of some claims, the French claim will have to be scrutinised.[29] He did offer an assurance that any decision would be 'such as to prevent any complaint on the part of the French Settlers, whom it will be the duty of the British Govt. to protect in their lawful possessions & useful occupations'. Again, the offer of protection assumes the existence of legitimate British control and authority.

The issue was still being contested in 1844. The despatches for that year include a letter written by G.W. Hope, Under-Secretary of State 1841–45, on Lord Stanley's behalf to the then Governor, Robert FitzRoy.[30] It explains that Lord Stanley, Secretary of State for the Colonies (1841–45) has seen the claim of the Nanto-Bordelaise Company. If the Colonial Land and Registration Committee dealt with the French claim in the same way as the New Zealand Company's claims, the Nanto-Bordelaise Company would be granted 3000 acres, based on their original expenditure. There is, however, no report from the Committee on the claim and no Deed of Sale, although the latter will 'shortly' be in England. In a convoluted procedure, designed to take care of delays and crossovers in communication, Stanley offers to send the Deed once it is received direct to the Governor (bypassing the local Committee) accompanied by an order that it was to be considered by the Land Commissioners forthwith. There was no guarantee of a favourable outcome. Communication delays, bureaucracy, contested claims and procrastination had effectively completed Hobson's original intent. Without certainty of title the possibility of further private colonisation from France, or indeed anywhere else, had ground to a halt, and with it went any hope of eventually establishing French sovereignty via a backdoor presence on Banks Peninsula.

So, was there an Anglo-French contest? The language of Hobson's letter suggests there was, but if so Lavaud was effectively delayed at the Bay of Islands and so the race started before both contestants were ready. Why then did Lavaud originally go to the Bay of Islands? Apart from Tremewan's explanation there is another scenario that fits the facts. France would not have wanted another competition or even conflict with the British, especially one requiring naval resources in a location where the British already had an adjacent base (Australia). Even a local disagreement could escalate into a confrontation between two empires out of all proportion to the significance of the original affront, as will be shown when the Fashoda incident is considered. Given the relative strengths of their respective navies and geographic locations in the Pacific, caution was needed on the part of France.[31] However, a great deal of political, religious, financial and indeed what we would now call human resource effort and support had been expended during the lengthy gestation of the French scheme. To accept failure without attempting to establish a French presence may well have been beyond the limits of what was acceptable politically and financially as well as in damaged national pride.

In June 1861, an unattributed letter written in a scholarly style was published in the *Nelson Examiner*.[32] This stated that the French frigate 'St Aube' (sic) arrived at Akaroa to claim sovereignty on 15 August, five days after the English vessel. On 6 April 1869, some thirty years after the French had arrived, another unattributed article was published in the *New Zealand Herald*. It included an account of the 'race of eight hundred miles between two ships-of-war, a race between France and England for the sovereignty of the Middle Island of New Zealand'.[33] This version of events gives the impression that the Union Jack was hoisted in the nick of time to save the Middle Island from the French only because of 'the indomitable energy of Captain Hobson'. The true intent of this article then becomes clear. Despite this heroic start, events thereafter had left the British subjects living in New Zealand in a 'more than disastrous' position. The writer had a point to prove because he or she then speculated that if the French had won sovereignty, they would 'never have been satisfied with the worthless shadow of the land'. As the French had shown in New Caledonia, 'without needless bloodshed, savages can be brought to order'. The past was being twisted using the French as an example to suit the writer's views.

Noted Historian Lindsay Buick took a very different view in 1914, referring to 'much beating of the air' about the 'so-called race'. Notably, Buick's version was published just as New Zealand was joining the World War I alliance alongside the British in support of France. The period of the *entente cordiale* was not the time to suggest that New Zealand's foundations rested in part on a claim disputed by the French. According to Buick, Lavaud requested a meeting with Hobson after arriving at the Bay of Islands. Lavaud satisfied himself as to the legitimacy of the British claims. He then decided to wait for French Government instructions before formally recognising British sovereignty. Hobson is reported as conciliatory and 'much impressed' with Lavaud's sincerity. Buick's assessment is that despite this reassuring stance, Hobson was 'not entirely satisfied' and he 'saw that some executive act was advisable'.[34] Buick appears determined to kill the race-to-Akaroa version of events beyond all doubt, yet even Buick cannot account for Lavaud first calling at the Bay of Islands contrary to his instructions, nor for Hobson's urgency in sending Stanley south while delaying Lavaud with negotiations and letter writing.

Peter Tremewan's work (published in 2010) concluded that Governor Hobson and Captain Lavaud, the commander of the French frigate, had come to a compromise on the sovereignty issue when they met in the Bay of Islands, prior to Lavaud sailing for Akaroa. Hobson nevertheless sent Captain Stanley in the *Britomart* to Banks Peninsula, just to be sure. In any case, the *Herald* had already delivered Hobson's sovereignty proclamation two months earlier so the so-called race for the Middle Island was rather a precautionary measure.[35] Peter Tremewan's interpretation is very close to the *Gazette* report, although the *Gazette* doesn't mention an agreement or deal reached in the Bay of

Islands. If there was an agreement one can only speculate as to what the public reaction would have been if it had become public property.

Lavaud was an experienced forty-two-year-old naval officer in 1840, but even before he sailed he was pessimistic as to his chances of leading a successful expedition. Perhaps he already suspected that he was unlikely to succeed, based on his private instructions and intelligence gathering. He may have been told, either implicitly or explicitly but not in any written record that has survived or been discovered, to proceed to New Zealand as planned, but then to ascertain the sovereign status of the country before landing and not to contest it if the Middle Island had already been annexed by the British. This would explain his first call in Australasia being at the Bay of Islands, despite official orders to the contrary. Lavaud's promotion and career thereafter do not suggest any retribution or recriminations arose from his actions. He went on to the rank of Rear Admiral, and later served as Governor of Tahiti.[36]

The tiny French presence at Akaroa continued (as noted) as a more or less independent state within a state for the remainder of Hobson's governorship. In January 1842 *The New Zealand Gazette and Wellington Spectator* published an article sourced from the *Paris Constitutionnel*.[37] The 'conciliatory spirit' between Captain Lavaud and the English magistrate (the French article reported) meant that the French colony at Banks Peninsula remained independent and 'it is the opinion of all parties' that this should continue. The prosperity and rapid growth at Port Nicholson was, however, contrasted with the slower progress at Banks Peninsula, where only one successful vegetable grower was cited as evidence of success. M. de Beligny, the Mayor of the French colony, had visited Port Nicholson and exchanged declarations of mutual respect and harmonious relations between France and England. Resolution of the sovereignty issue was still pending but a fair solution would be to declare both islands and their ports as 'free'. A second French expedition was in the offing. This report provoked a heated response from one correspondent who from the cover of a nom de plume criticised Governor Hobson for not actively enforcing his proclamation of sovereignty at Akaroa, presumably by occupation.[38] The issue was again linked to the constant complaints of the Port Nicholson settlers regarding the seat of government in the north of the country. The same theme reappeared in September of 1842 when Hobson was again taken to task for not keeping an eye on the French owing to the location of his government.[39] Exactly what these correspondents wanted done with respect to the French was not clear. Most probably the French were used as cover to demand the Government's relocation to Port Nicholson, thereby increasing the commercial growth and wealth of the presumptive capital.

The pre-Treaty British residents of New Zealand had clearly read more intent into the occasional visits by French vessels to explore and resupply than was meant. Admittedly some French visits were to investigate colonising opportunities, but most were not. Despite this, they were still used as a convenient pretext to demand British action. The Māori chiefs' petition requesting King William IV's protection was a front behind which the British religious and settlers concealed their own interest in blocking the French. The French Catholic mission arrived far later than the British Protestants but was still met with fierce theological opposition. The apparently half-hearted French enthusiasm for securing a site for a penal colony, the tardy despatch of French colonists and Captain Lavaud's apparent lack of resolve alongside the problem-plagued Catholic mission thwarted the French plan of achieving sovereignty by occupation. It would seem that poor coordination and a lack of determination, rather than an absence of intent or agreement over the tactics to be used by the various French participants, was the main shortcoming. Despite the indifference in London it was, however, at least in the timing a close-run thing and could well have resulted in a small part of the South Island being occupied by the French and sovereignty proclaimed, given a little more fortitude and luck on their part and a less determined reaction from

Hobson who proved to be fiercely defensive when his newly founded domain was threatened.

Seen in this light, the story of the race for the South Island takes on a different tone, closer to the romanticised close-run race narrative, rather than the understated version that appeared in the newspapers at the time. Lavaud may have believed that a negotiated settlement was possible or that sovereignty was already decided and therefore there was no urgent need to follow Stanley south from the Bay of Islands. Perhaps Lavaud was misled into believing that Stanley was going on some unrelated errand. While not a race in the classic sense of two or more contestants departing simultaneously from the same point to achieve a common goal, the net effect was much the same, notwithstanding Hobson's success in delaying the only other competitor – who happened to be French – at the starting line. Through all these events Captain Lavaud kept a cool head and acted with restraint.

These events raise the intriguing question as to Hobson's overall disposition towards the French. He had after all served as a career Royal Navy officer when the British naval prowess shown at Trafalgar was still largely incontestable. Was he therefore a Francophobic, ardently nationalistic, post-Napoleonic War chest-beater or was he just a newly promoted governor who wanted to excel in, and defend, his first assigned territory? Perhaps two of the more prescient comments Hobson made shortly after his arrival in New Zealand give some indication of his views. In his very first despatch, written on board HMS *Herald* in the Bay of Islands on 16 February 1840, Hobson noted that '…the passion for land jobbing now pervades every class….'. Hobson wrote in the same despatch with considerable foresight: 'I greatly fear that the conflicting claims for lands that will be brought under the consideration of the Commissioners who are to be appointed to investigate them will create a violent foment through every class of Society, both Native and European.'[40]

Hobson's report shows he was aware of the land purchases and 'extensive settlement' at Port Nicholson by the New Zealand Company. By the time he wrote his third despatch, Hobson was referring to the formation of a Council and land purchasing at Port Nicholson as 'high treason' because the Company was usurping the function of the Crown.[41] Seen in this context it is difficult to imagine Hobson acting in any other way. Another private colonisation expedition had arrived in New Zealand with a contested land claim. Being under the escort and command of the French Navy, the newcomers would probably have been reluctant to recognise British sovereignty. From Hobson's viewpoint, it would have been quite conceivable that they would contest his right to govern all of New Zealand in the name of the British Crown. Hobson was not in this context being Francophobic, provocative or unnecessarily vexatious. He was being consistent. It was the challenge to the British right to rule rather than the fact that the challenge was French that was of concern.

Chapter Three

Misinformation and misrepresentations

Following their colonisation failure, the French presence faded, becoming a vague background identity whose status, whether positive or hostile, varied according to circumstances. There was a divergence between accounts of cordial first-hand interactions with the French in New Zealand and the opaque but adversarial arm's-length version of France the nation. Some British colonists, who might otherwise have shown animosity, unashamedly used the French in a broader context to promote their own agenda. Others disparaged the French nation. This contradiction was never openly debated nor was it resolved. It was left in abeyance as an uncomfortable inconsistency but one to be readily used as needed to cultivate a French presence within the New Zealand story.

While on station in New Zealand waters Captain Lavaud proved to be both a canny political operator and an excellent ambassador for France. When the crew of the *L'Aube* inadvertently consumed poisonous berries the English Dr William Davis who treated them was recommended by the French for a Gold Medal award. Dr Davis was quoted as saying that his feeling about providing free treatment in such circumstances would be the same, whether the ship was English or French.[1] The crew of *L'Aube* assisted the firefighting effort during a blaze at the Surveyor-General's office in Auckland. 'Too much praise cannot be bestowed upon the officers and seamen from the French frigate L'Aube, who were unremitting in their exertions.'[2] In another incident a British lady was reported as being cared for by the French navy at Akaroa after she was badly burned in a domestic kitchen fire. 'Commodore Lavaud most kindly gave up his own bed…'.[3]

In May 1843 the officers of *L'Rhin* were given a full civic reception in the Wellington town hall complete with a municipal dinner, speeches and mutually congratulatory toasts from the representatives of the two nations. In his speech the Wellington Mayor said:

> Enough cannot be said to express our sentiments of profound regard, and the happiness which we feel, in welcoming and addressing the representative of one of the most highly chivalrous, brave, and second to none, of the nations of the earth. For ever be silenced and buried that horrible heresy, that the French and English have separate interests.[4]

The absence of any Colonial Government representatives at this gathering was noted. Many other favourable examples were used to critically contrast Colonial Government inaction with French accomplishments. Compliments directed to the French often came from the Wellington and Nelson press where discontent with Hobson and the colonial regime still lingered as a hangover from the earlier treatment of the New Zealand Company, and the presumed slight inherent in the decision to locate the capital at Auckland. One newspaper correspondent resident in the Chatham Islands was incensed that the Government had taken no action when his property was stolen and destroyed by local Māori. He referred to the French sending a man-of-war to take revenge against the Chatham Islanders when the French had lost a whaler there. In retribution the French crew had 'burned down all their pahs', thus implying that the British authorities should do likewise.[5]

The Wairau Incident (as it is now commonly referred to) of 17 June 1843 was another opportunity to use the (uninvolved) French as a contrasting viewpoint.[6]

> France has never suffered injuries to be inflicted on her distant children such as our Government tamely submit to. She asks for no surrender of a minor chief, but inculcates, by the vigour of her arms, respect for her name, and insures protection for her offspring. She is paralyzed by no instructions from a Government House … the tricolour gleams over the waves, and France vindicates and protects her own.[7]

The presence of HMS *North Star* proved more of a provocation than a source of satisfaction to the colonists who wanted retaliation for what they saw as a Māori atrocity at Wairau. The *Nelson Examiner* reported that *North Star* was ordered to 'show herself along the coast', but to take no action. While the *North Star* was in Nelson, the colonists petitioned her Captain (Sir Everard Home) to intervene by contrasting their self-perceived predicament as unprotected, tax-paying, law-obeying British subjects with 'the French nation at Akaroa, living in perfect security under the constant protection of a vessel of war'. In the aftermath of Home's refusal to act, the colonists asked Major Richmond the Resident Magistrate if he was agreeable to asking the French frigate for protection. Richmond refused, considering it '…a stain on the British arms'.[8]

It was in the north though that the French presence had its greatest impact. In April 1842 an open letter from the 'inhabitants of Kouorarika'(sic) was published, thanking Monsieur Le Commandant of the *L'Aube* for remaining on station after the massacre perpetrated by the 'natives'.[9] There was a pointed reference to this 'gallant officer of France' providing protection when Governor Hobson had not. Lavaud's written response (he gives his title as 'commanding the French Station at New Zealand') acknowledged the thanks while modestly saying that his actions were 'guided by a sentiment of humanity common to all civilised men'. It was a pointed, backhanded rebuke to Hobson and the

British colonial authorities as well as a reinforcement of the shared values of the European colonial powers.

Despite such gallantry, a less favourable French character was resurrected through innuendo and rumour during the Northern Wars. Hone Heke's war was not (as it is often erroneously described) a treasonous rebellion against a lawful sovereign authority, nor was it a foreign-inspired insurrection. The great northern chief was clearly his own man, although he sought counsel from many Pākehā of various nationalities as well as his own Māori confidants and advisors. Heke was trying to reclaim the mana he believed he had been tricked into ceding to the colonial government by the Protestant missionaries under the cover of the Treaty. Considerable commerce had been lost when the duplicitous Government had relocated the capital to Auckland soon after the Treaty was signed, thereby removing New Zealand's commercial hub from Heke's territory. The imposition of customs duties by Governor FitzRoy was seen by Heke as a further flouting of the Treaty with a consequent erosion of Heke's authority in his own land. Heke's war was a reassertion of his rights and authority as an essential step to rebuilding the severely damaged northern economy.[10]

Attributing Hone Heke's actions to external influencers belittled Heke and distracted from the substance of his grievances. It was simple for non-Māori to deliberately misrepresent Heke's symbolic act of felling the flagstaff as being motivated by 'some White of the beach-comber species…' rather than addressing his complaints on their merits.[11] In the colonists' narrative, Hone Heke is presented as a destructive, sulky and petulant child who was defying the Crown.

The Colonial Government attempted to deflect culpability for the resulting war from its own actions by blaming the French. Heke was quoted as saying that reports from the 'French and American people' that 'the English would enslave, ultimately, all the natives' had led to his 'little crime … of cutting down the flagstaff'.[12] Not only does this seem a highly unlikely verbatim quote, it also diminishes Heke's agency in this symbolic reassertion of his mana in his own land.

In his diary the Rev. Burrows similarly deflected attention from the substance of Heke's complaints by blaming those 'not of English birth' for telling Heke that the natives in other countries ruled by the British suffered ill-treatment and dispossession. Burrow's defence of the 'old missionaries' who had supported the Treaty relied on the need (as they saw it) to get control over the 'state of the Country' (presumably the disorder in the Bay of Islands) and to resist attempts by both 'the French and by the New Zealand Company to colonise'.[13] A Legislative Councillor (Dr Martin) also claimed that it was 'systematic opposition' from the French and the Americans to the Colonial Government that had inflamed native opinion by predicting slavery and alienation of Māori land.[14]

Heke's letter of grievance addressed to the Queen is described as being 'written, it was thought, in a French hand…'.[15] Whether this referred to the language of the original or the style is not clear and there is no supporting reference for the claim. Rev. Burrows also refers to a letter, written by Heke and forwarded by Burrows on Heke's behalf via Archdeacon Williams to FitzRoy. The tone of Burrows' comments suggests he was present at the drafting or at least aware of the content, but if so Burrows makes no mention of any overt or covert French advice or interference.[16] Probably 'Heke's French advisers' included Catholic mission members since they were the most significant and obvious French presence at Russell, but there is no evidence that their counsel was a malignant influence.[17]

On 16 September 1844, Governor FitzRoy wrote a detailed account of the northern situation for the Secretary of State.[18] FitzRoy predicted a 'disaster' due to the Colony's 'pernicious' customs regulation problems which would (FitzRoy claimed) be 'fatal to the prosperity of the colony … (and will) alienate from us a large portion of the Aborigines – would cause open opposition, indeed rebellion – and involve us not only in hostilities with the Native race – but possibly with France or America'. FitzRoy continued: 'the late disturbances at the Bay of Islands were caused chiefly by Americans – and Frenchmen, exciting the natives…'. Māori were being told they would be oppressed under the British flag and once the weight of numbers was with the settlers, the Māori population would be enslaved. FitzRoy blamed 'American traders' and 'some of the French'. The latter are identified as the twenty Roman Catholic missionaries who along with their bishop were allegedly inducing a 'bad feeling' towards the Protestants and the British in general, under the guise of spreading the 'written word'.

FitzRoy enclosed with this despatch a copy of *The Southern Cross* of 7 September 1844.[19] This featured a favourable account of FitzRoy's visit to the Bay of Islands accompanied by a transcript of FitzRoy's speech to the chiefs in which he described French outrages at Tahiti and linked these to the earlier French expeditions to New Zealand. The British had saved the locals from a fate such as befell Tahiti and the Marquesas (under French rule).[20] FitzRoy was quoted as saying that: 'Formerly European nations attacked and conquered countries inhabited by uncivilised men, and to their everlasting disgrace, killed numbers of men. But England acted differently…' England and William IV had protected the New Zealanders and 'would never allow these dreadful scenes'. To justify the Treaty, FitzRoy pointed out that in other countries the act of raising a local flag and proclaiming sovereignty as the Māori Declaration of Independence intended, had not saved their native populations from the French.

In his 29 September 1844 despatch FitzRoy was more circumspect. While still mentioning 'ill-disposed Americans and Europeans…' he was probably getting closer to the truth of the unrest when the chiefs are quoted as questioning the right of the Queen to stop vessels going to harbours other than government designated entry ports.[21] An accompanying supplementary report from George Clarke, the Chief Protector of Aborigines (dated 30 September 1844), detailed the outcome of Clarke's own visit to the north in response to the unrest.[22] Clarke had met with the chiefs at Waimate who informed Clarke that the disquiet was due to Europeans (unfortunately no nationality is specified in Clarke's report) 'continually telling them that they would be enslaved and the Government were their oppressors'. Moreover, the Treaty of Waitangi was blamed for Māori now being 'extremely poor'. The chiefs pointed out that they had not sided with Heke and they were determined to look after 'their Europeans'. (The term 'Europeans' is used generically rather than specifically referring to Continental Europeans.) Nevertheless, Russell was sacked shortly thereafter.[23]

Despite FitzRoy's inference of antagonistic Frenchmen located in the Bay of Islands, the evidence suggests that the French religious presence was apolitical. Bishop Pompallier remained an active participant in local civil affairs such as land purchasing, education and hospital admissions before and after the wars.[24] On 4 April 1845 Pompallier wrote to the Colonial Secretary to point out the obvious – it was not possible to give a return of Catholic numbers, churches and establishment owing to the disturbances.[25] This and other letters to and from the Governor and the Colonial Secretary before, after and during the time of the northern unrest are cordial and suggest routine cooperation with the Colonial Government. When Pompallier wrote to Captain Home of HMS *North Star* on 1 April 1845 to reject Home's offer of evacuation for himself and his missionaries, he noted that: 'As for myself Capt. and all the priests and catechists comprising my mission we have all left our homes forever (to) try to work in the salvation of New Zealand and the other Islands of Oceania. We have neither wives nor children…'[26]

These were not the phrases of an agitator who did not intend to maintain a permanent presence.

Despite this, the duplicity between official claims of French antagonism and local examples of civil interactions persisted. The French ship *Le Rhin* arrived at the Bay of Islands six weeks after the sacking of Kororāreka to offer aid and support to Pompallier and his priests. The visit was obviously cordial for the crew of *Le Rhin* joined their HMS *North Star* counterparts to celebrate the Queen's birthday.[27] In fact, while the British were maintaining a civil relationship in public, FitzRoy was petitioning London for authority to remove the French from New Zealand. Perhaps having positioned the French as a malignant influence he felt he had to follow through despite the evidence contradicting his original conclusion.

On 23 September 1845 the Under-Secretary to Colonial Secretary Lord Stanley wrote to his opposite number in the office of the Secretary of State (the Earl of Aberdeen) enclosing an extract from the previously cited confidential despatch of Governor FitzRoy concerning the causes of destruction at Russell under chiefs 'Heke and Rewiti' (sic).[28] Stanley's man noted that FitzRoy blamed the French and American presence for the unrest. He enclosed the previously quoted letter from Pompallier to Captain Home of HMS *North Star* and 'other papers'. FitzRoy had interpreted these as showing that Pompallier had 'mistaken his position' in assuming he was entitled to maintain neutrality between Government and 'those in arms against it, if he does not go further'. Stanley's Under-Secretary asks his opposite to tell Lord Aberdeen that Lord Stanley thought the Governor should have the power to remove foreigners who might be 'justly suspected' of breaking the 'tranquillity' of New Zealand. He asks for Lord Aberdeen's views on granting such powers.

On 10 October 1845 Aberdeen's Under-Secretary replied. While agreeing that the Government of New Zealand should have such power to remove any person so suspected, Aberdeen urged discretion especially with respect to the French missionaries. He pointed out to Stanley that 'our' missionaries were in the same position with the French authorities in Tahiti. It would be 'hazardous' for the British Government to be seen as complaining about the French authorities' treatment of British missionaries, if the British Government was simultaneously expelling the French missionaries from New Zealand. Sir George Grey, who had by then succeeded FitzRoy as Governor, was authorised to propose legislation for the removal of aliens but he was warned to '...observe the utmost caution, and circumspection in exercising such a power'.[29] This was one of the earliest examples of

New Zealand's immediate interests (whether they were worthy or not) being subordinated to the broader interests of the British Crown.

There is no evidence of either British Government disquiet or general public concern in New Zealand about French missionary activity even at the time of Heke's war, despite the reports of Heke being advised by the French. As far as the religious divide went, the official position that Church and State were separate entities is supported by the considerable records of routine, business-as-usual exchanges between the Colonial Government and the French Mission. The discrepancy arises only in the Governor's despatches to the Secretary of State in which undue influence by the French and the Americans is cited as a cause of the unrest. This was an attempt to deflect blame rather than a truthful summary of the causes of the Northern War.

The positive sentiments expressed in these reports needs to be assessed alongside the frequent and extremely negative news of French actions elsewhere. These usually related to the merits of France as a colonising state. Using the counterfactual 'what if' argument, the British were idealised as a colonial power, often by citing reports from French colonies by way of example. Algeria and Tahiti were common examples. One *Daily Southern Cross* article published in 1844 clearly had an undercurrent of strong support for the establishment of an independent government in New Zealand. The French counter-example was a by-product rather than the main message. The French in Tahiti were not contributing to the progressive civilisation of the world with all the benefits this should have for the Tahitians. Using particularly strong language, a negative side of French colonisation was highlighted: 'Who would have supposed that the countrymen of the glorious Lafayette, and the servants, the officers of the philosophical and learned Guizot, the justly distinguished author of the Civilization of Europe, would be the oppressors and destroyers of the innocent Tahitians?' The article goes on using words such as 'sickening' and 'disgusting' while asking:

> Could not the revolutionary demons of anarchy and bloodshed satiate their thirst on the blood red rivers of Algeria, without adding the innocent sons and daughters of Tahiti and the free and fearless savages of the Marquesas to the countless numbers of the sable sons of Africa, whom they have already so cruelly massacred.[30]

Via somewhat shaky logic the blame was assigned to the local colonial authorities. The French Government was assumed to disapprove of the action taken by their colonial authorities just as the British Government is assumed to be similarly disapproving of the '…deception practiced by Hobson and Shortland as regards New Zealand'. The conclusion drawn is that it is the governments of Europe, not the settlers, who are to blame for 'destroying' the indigenous populations. The concern is less with what the French or British settlers have done or might do and more about the role of the Home Governments who were interfering in their respective colonies through unsuitable political appointments. The theme was that all would be well, especially for the indigenous population, if the Home Government stopped interfering by sending misguided officials to run things. France was the chosen example, probably because using a British example such as India would have raised some uncomfortable comparisons directly critical of the Home Government and the role of British Colonial authorities elsewhere.

These extremely negative opinions did not always go unremarked. One letter to the editor (written from Tahiti) praised the infrastructure development being undertaken in Tahiti and claimed that the French had 'incurred much unmerited calumny from misrepresentation of our fellow countrymen…'.[31]

The interaction between Church and State – coinciding as it did with the British-Protestant/French-Catholic divide – nevertheless remained a fraught issue in early New Zealand. In June 1844 the Legislative Council debated the respective roles of Church and State as a result of a motion proposing an appropriation to support the Church of England's Bishop (Selwyn).[32] The Imperial Parliament had voted £600 for his salary 'to be increased by colonial vote'. The colonial government was instructed to meet his expenses. The Governor wanted an additional £200 for the 'Auckland minister'. This led to a discussion within the Council as to whether Church and State should be linked and whether using taxes to support a religion which some of the taxpayers did not believe in could be justified. While defending the bill, the Governor noted that the 'voluntary principle (of funding religious establishments) had been tried and failed'. There was nevertheless strong argument against state funding for one denomination in preference to others. The Council therefore opposed assisting 'the religious establishments in the colony'.

During the debate the Governor firmly rebutted the Attorney-General's claim that 'the colony was a Church of England colony'. As Council Member Dr Martin pointed out, '...New Zealand might (on the same basis) be called a Roman Catholic, or a French (colony) as a Church of England colony' since all these entities were present in New Zealand. Dr Martin went on to say that he believed 'Bishop Pompallier was supported by the Government of France, and that he could command the services of any French man of war on this coast, if he at any time required them...' but that did not make New Zealand 'a French or a Roman Catholic colony'. This view was not challenged. The Governor's proposal to supplement the Church of England Bishop's salary by £200 was lost by five votes to two.

At the highest level of Colonial Government, even in 1844, there was strong support for separating Church and State accompanied by a desire to avoid the rigid sectarianism existing elsewhere. Despite the assertion of the French religious mission being hand in glove with the French Navy there was neither rebuttal that such was the case nor an argument made that it could be countered by funding Protestant denominations. By 1844 the presence of French civilians and the French Navy in New Zealand was not seen as a serious threat to the British. Nevertheless, a shadow of doubt persisted. As late as 1878 the explorer and missionary James Buller was still hinting at a sectarian faultline that divided the French from the British. Speaking of the French Marist priests he wrote, 'As Frenchmen too, perhaps unconsciously, in their zeal, their influence was as adverse to the sovereignty of our Queen as to that of the saviour'.[33]

Despite his premature recall, the hapless FitzRoy continued to promote the French threat to explain his New Zealand failures. In one instance (published in the London *New Zealand Journal* in 1845) his claims of an antagonistic French presence in New Zealand provoked a correction of the 'misunderstanding'. The published correction affirmed that: 'all residents in New Zealand, acquainted with their character and conduct, describe Bishop Pompallier and his Priests as single-minded men, devoted to their calling, and as having abstained from in any way interfering with politics with a scrupulous care worthy of imitation.'[34]

It went unremarked that many Protestant missionaries had aligned with the British colonial establishment to protect their own locally acquired land and wealth, while their Wesleyans and Roman Catholic brethren possessed neither.[35]

PART II

The Threat Remains

> There was fear of French domination of the islands themselves, and also an acute awareness of the strength of France in the Pacific, the imperialistic attitude of her missionaries, the isolated position of New Zealand, and a corresponding desire to stop further French progress.
>
> J.A. Salmond, 'New Zealand and the New Hebrides'[1]

Anti-French attitudes persisted in New Zealand even though France had ceased to be a threat to British political domination. It would have been understandable if the sentiment had simply faded with the passing of the generations, but it did not because New Zealand remained a devoted member of an Empire that competed with France. Moreover, the irritating French presence in the Pacific continued as a prompt and a reminder – an aide-memoire – of past deceits from the early colonial days. It was only once the *entente cordiale* between France and Britain metamorphosed into a full military alliance in the early twentieth century that the traditional New Zealand dislike of France was put aside, albeit temporarily. Despite their geographic proximity in the Pacific, the French remained strangers owing to the minimal direct contact between the two populations. Most trade, cultural contacts and political exchanges were directed through Paris and London respectively in the eighty years prior to 1914. Maintaining this physical and cultural distance played an important part in perpetuating an anti-French bias in New Zealand.

It is easy to generalise about strangers in the absence of specific knowledge or first-hand experience.[2] Using terms such as 'they' and 'them' to group nationalities or races helps make sense of a complex world but in doing so the nuances of the individual and their circumstances are lost. Generalised characterisations can then be used to fill the knowledge void. The total number of French nationals present in New Zealand between 1892 and 1914 was only ever between six and seven hundred individuals. They constituted less than 0.1 per cent of the population, meaning less than one person in every one thousand identified as French. The gender bias in the statistics in favour of males was greater than that for the overall population, suggesting that amongst the few French nationals present in New Zealand, many were present in some capacity other than residency, be it as seamen, visitors, religious personnel or in other transient occupations requiring their temporary presence.[3] Less than 160 people (a minuscule 2.5 per cent) of all the foreigners who became New Zealand citizens in the same period were of French origin.[4] There were so few French citizens or former citizens resident in New Zealand that the probability of a local knowing a French man or woman on a personal basis was tiny. In any case, the thousand or so French residents in New Zealand were not a community. They had quickly 'merge(d) into the populace' by assuming a New Zealand identity.[5] By 1914 trade with France – another point of contact and a potential source of mutual knowledge – still comprised less than 1 per cent of New Zealand's direct imports and exports. Yet, despite the cultural distance and the absence of trade especially in primary produce exports, there was still news of France in the papers. French remained the most commonly taught second language in schools. There were higher-end, fashionable French goods freely available in the shops. These, along with historical perspectives, substituted for direct knowledge of the French as a race and of France as a political and economic entity.[6]

The geographic distance between Britain and Europe could not, however, be ignored by Britain, which was (and of course still is) an island nation in the North Atlantic with a clear view of continental France across the English Channel. New Zealand was not a British offshore island, as James Belich pointed out when he described the Pacific Ocean as an impediment between Britain and New Zealand.[7] The Anglophylic New Zealanders nevertheless distorted the distance by imagining that France was far away while Britain was close. Felicity Barnes neatly encapsulated the essence of it when she referred to London as New Zealand's metropolis.[8] Although cable communication was improving and modern shipping was getting faster and more efficient, a considerable distance still separated New Zealand from both France and Britain.[9]

It is not necessary to consider the full catalogue of events over the eighty years between 1840 and 1914 to find evidence of the continued dislike of the French. The tenacity and strength of feeling could still be seen, even in the two and a half decades immediately preceding World War I (1890–1914). Officially New Zealand had no direct political or diplomatic interactions with France or any other foreign power (apart from Britain) in the mainly colonial era of 1840–1914.[10] New Zealand's political relationship with France depended on the British because Prime Ministers Seddon, Ward and subsequently Massey chose to work within the imperial framework rather than challenging its authority by developing an independent foreign policy. An awkward three-way liaison between France, Britain and New Zealand therefore developed to accommodate this preference. Changes in the direct bilateral relationship between any two of the three countries inevitably influenced the third.

The Empire tie was so strong that New Zealand was prepared to put aside its own ambitions when these clashed with the Empire's priorities. New Zealand's self-assigned place was alongside Britain and if that meant accepting a French presence in the Pacific, New Zealand had to swallow hard and accede to Britain's policies. Any suggestion of official dissent was muted by the imperial structure. After Sir Joseph Ward's abortive effort during the 1911 Empire Conference to introduce a Round Table-like constitution (which would have given Empire members a greater voice), New Zealand did not attempt to influence imperial policy in any significant way. New Zealand clearly still had the desire for an independent Pacific policy but she lacked the will to challenge the British and implement it. Accepting this degree of British control had consequences.

Many pre-World War I New Zealanders saw their country as a significant Dominion within a coherent, culturally consistent and economically beneficial Empire that formed a '...tightly knit power resting on free association'.[11] The British Empire never existed in this form because it failed on both dimensions. Most scholarship now argues that New Zealand was not significant and the Empire was not tightly controlled.

> ...when we talk about the British Empire we are really referring to a loose and often accidental association of units, embodying in their disorganization the worst features of the feudal and federal systems.[12]

It has been said with at least the spirit of truth that the British Empire was founded in a fit of absence of mind, and that the largely ad hoc development of the overseas extensions of Britain owed more to traditional British pragmatism than to any master plan emanating from the corridors of Whitehall.[13]

The fundamental flaw was the lack of a primary purpose or reason to exist. There was therefore no overall plan to guide specific actions. The Empire was a loose association of interests with a variety of agendas beneath a tissue-paper thin skin of solidarity. Although the 'tightly knit power' version of the Empire was never true, the image certainly persisted in Australasia where New Zealand in particular clung to the myth long after the reality was exposed. This flaw became

New Zealand's inherited policy weakness for it concealed the absence of any coherent national plan.

The Empire was an ad hoc mix of British and local peoples with an uncertain moral purpose based on a partially free-trade inclined economic model. It was neither cohesive nor well-ordered, but it would be unreasonable to blame British governments of whatever political persuasion for that being the case. Some initiatives, such as pre-World War I colonisation in Africa, were planned but actions elsewhere were often opportunistic. Colonisation was just as likely to be the result of private enterprise (as was the case for New Zealand) or penal settlement (in the Australian example) or the pursuit of strategic defence interests, as it was to be part of a coherent plan.[14] Once this haphazard collection of historical sovereignty claims, private ventures and conquests from indigenous inhabitants was established, its reason for being were justified by a mix of emotive appeals and self-serving interests. Post hoc justifications for colonisation included social engineering, ridding Britain of her surplus population (as discussed in Part I) and protecting the local inhabitants in newly acquired territories, whether they were indigenous or colonists.[15] There was a vague assumption that Empire members would eventually achieve economic independence and become what Lord Roseberry called a '...commonwealth of nations'.[16] There were in the meantime many unanswered questions about the status of the members as far as nationality and allegiance were concerned. Especially concerning was the issue of whether the members could remain neutral in the event of war.[17]

The British countries and territories that made up the Empire were supposed to be a source of primary produce and raw materials to be used for manufacturing into finished goods at Home.[18] This created a pattern of inward and outward trade that can be imagined as numerous radii or spokes centred on a London hub. The physical and economic wealth of the world's greatest industrial and financial power flowed through these spokes. Attempts to retain this model included developing a British culture and character within the (white-ruled) dominions and colonies. There were organisations created for just this purpose.[19] As a result of these initiatives, intra-Empire trade and defence of the Empire became central concerns of British foreign policy. In that sense British diplomacy was not so much orientated towards achieving a specific goal as it was about preventing the collapse of the system. As New Zealand Premier Richard Seddon said, 'Our first duty was preservation of the Empire.'[20] The opposing foreign pressures for change were reactive. Externally there was envy and a desire to equal or exceed British power and prestige. Russia, France and particularly Germany were (at different times) so motivated. Internally the forces for change were potentially equally damaging for the Empire. There was domestic pressure at Home for social reform, wealth redistribution and universal suffrage. There were too many un-enfranchised subjects to make emigration a practical means of clearance. From 1867 to 1928 as the number of electors in the United Kingdom rose from 1.4 million to 28.5 million the rulers of Britain were forced to govern for the many, not the few.[21]

The increased domestic enfranchisement in Britain along with the influence of world events meant the United Kingdom gradually moved away from a parental role, against New Zealand's wishes. The problem was exemplified when the 1889 Naval Defence Act introduced the Two Power Standard as a strategic benchmark to assess British naval strength. This raised the issue as to whether or not the standard included the Empire and therefore whether the Empire was a de facto closely bound 'constructionist' Federation. The 'constructionist' viewpoint was of an Empire that was planned and directed as against a traditional, liberal, free trade model based simply on common moral values and bonds. The conflict in the history on these points arises because the argument was never clearly defined at the time and therefore went unresolved. The events of 1914 overtook the debate meaning it never had to be decided. By extension the impasse between the Liberal ideal of colonial (dominion) defence forces controlled by their domestic governments and the Federationalists' view – that central control was preferable – was in a continual state of flux.[22]

Arguably the only real threat to the British Empire between 1856 and 1918 had been the possible emergence of another 'Napoleonic superstate' in Europe. Keeping Europe quiet but unsettled became a British objective because a Continental power attempting to attack the peripheries of the British Empire would be vulnerable to invasion at home. This strategy meant the Royal Navy could secure both Home and Empire. The success is shown by the absence of any significant attack on British interests between 1814 and 1914.[23] This in turn led the British to believe that in foreign affairs – especially in their respective empire and colonisation projects – they were superior to the French.

The South African (Boer) War served as a test-run for the Empire's governance and defence arrangements. The general lessons the British learned from the Boer War and the reaction of New Zealand and the other Dominions to it were sobering. Firstly, the lack of intelligence in the military sense was a major shortcoming that needed to be urgently addressed.[24] This catastrophic failure was repeated at Gallipoli and in the trenches in France. Secondly, fighting wars in distant lands was costly and therefore a significant drain on the public purse.[25] This should have sounded a warning for New Zealand: if fighting in southern Africa was expensive for the British (and for New Zealand) then the cost for New Zealand of sending troops to Europe would be even more so. Thirdly, notwithstanding the Royal Navy's power, prestige and cost, the navy could not win against a land-based force. Fourthly, diplomacy was a necessary component of war if only to prevent other powers intervening.[26] Fifthly, the Dominions would help Britain by active participation but their assistance would be subject to their own circumstances.

After the Boer War the British establishment therefore had cause to reassess, despite the domestic delight within New Zealand at the favourable outcome. There was criticism of the British tactics but what little opposition there was in New Zealand was 'diverse and ineffective'. Isolated incidents of dissent, such as the exchange between Seddon and the Chief Hansard reporter who in his capacity as a private citizen questioned the legitimacy of New Zealand's role in the Boer War (as did the radical MP Tommy Taylor) were exceptional.[27] The Boer War seemed to confirm that New Zealand's interests were best served by preserving a strong 'Greater' (sic) Britain that would continue with the undefined imperial project. The Boer War also increased the colonial sense of self-importance as well as New Zealand's pride in the Empire. Seddon was 'profoundly moved' that the United Kingdom would commit to a war to defend a colony. Perhaps more importantly the Boer War established the precedent of New Zealand involvement in wars beyond the immediate national interest to '...uphold imperial power...'.[28]

The political relationship between France and Britain in the twenty years prior to World War I was shaped by a numerically small but highly influential power elite, over which New Zealand had virtually no influence. Only eleven British cabinet members served as British Foreign Secretary over nearly sixty years from 1856 to 1914.[29] By comparison France had fifteen Ministers of Foreign Affairs in just ten years between 1905 and 1916, leaving power effectively in the hands of senior French officials. Sensitive information was 'rarely' passed on to French cabinet ministers and sometimes not even the President was informed.[30] On the other side of the Channel, Sir Edward Grey was in office from 1905 to 1916 and so could largely dictate British Imperial foreign policy. With a small group of supporters and confidants he pursued his own course. All he required was the Prime Minister's approval and tacit Conservative support. Relations between the British Foreign and Colonial Offices were not intimate but nor were they distant. The two could work in tandem, thus extending Grey's influence.[31]

Chapter Four

The Fashoda Incident – an irrelevant influence?

In the aftermath of the 1860s' depression the great powers belatedly realised that their new colonies could be both a source of raw materials and a market for the excess production generated through industrialisation. This depended on the colonies having an adequate population with sufficient purchasing power to make a difference on the consumption side of the equation. While not usually a primary motivation, bolstering national prestige became in many cases a further reason for colonial acquisitions, if only to outshine competitors. Conquest followed by exploitation therefore became the colonialists' mantra in their attempts to increase support for imperial expansion and presumed prosperity at Home. With these aims came the task of fending off impudent imperial challengers who sought territories that Britain believed were hers to own and rule.[1] These characteristics were exposed when France challenged Britain in North Africa during the 1890s.

Although few New Zealanders would have seen any direct relevance, the French interest in Fashoda as a potential transit point for land passage between the French colonies in East and West Africa became a significant factor in foreign policy and New Zealand public opinion.[2] At issue was the conflict between British ambitions for an uninterrupted north–south route from Egypt to South Africa and French designs for an east–west pathway. Apart from Fashoda's importance as a staging post, the location was otherwise without immediate value for either country but the French occupation of this obscure North African fort was reported in New Zealand in great detail. It showed the New Zealanders by example how the British responded to a French threat and how imperialism was applied in practice. It also re-energised support for the Empire as a political model, while reigniting the New Zealand Liberal Government's own local attempts to develop a Pacific Empire.

The reason why the Fashoda incident became a potential cause for conflict is still debated by historians. One view holds that French colonial expansion into Africa and the consequential confrontation was the result of a failed policy of Gabriel Hanotaux, the French Foreign Minister. Hanotaux's initial confidence in new colonial ventures was based on his belief that the Franco-Russian alliance would preserve European peace and thus allow France to pursue her overseas ambitions.[3] This view attributes the Fashoda occupation to an ill-judged initiative resulting from the disarray in French foreign policy, rather than from a colonial venture based on sober reflection with a realistic objective. Whatever the reason, the opportunistic French occupation of Fashoda was easily thwarted by what was publicly presented as a coherent and adroit British response. The implied lesson was that confronting the British Empire was futile so the obvious solution for France was to simply withdraw.[4] A unilateral retreat would, however, have raised political difficulties in France since the government of the day depended on Colonial Party support. France was desperate to save face and so Germany was asked to back the French position. The German price was acceptance of the status quo in Alsace-Lorraine.[5] That was too much for any French government to accept. Under pressure from Britain the politically isolated French were therefore forced to order their mission leader (Marchand) to retire. Thereafter the French Colonial Party was less keen to confront the British and in that respect the door for the *entente cordiale* was opened, although the venture left the French with a sour taste of '…hostility towards Britain … (that) endued for most of the pre-war period'.[6]

An alternative view links this simplified narrative to the concurrent domestic turmoil in France caused by the Dreyfus affair (see next chapter). Out of the tangled strands of anti-Semitic, anti-Dreyfus sentiment and anti-British emotions, the Fashoda expedition leader (Marchand) emerged as a success, positioned in the French press as a victim whose withdrawal was simply a temporary setback on the path to eventual French colonial glory.[7] He was (in this version) a Napoleon-like hero who acted in the best interest of France without regard for his own fortunes. His retreat traversed Africa, thus avoiding the humiliation of retiring by boat down the Nile through British territory. He was eventually welcomed home, acclaimed as a victor and championed by both political right and left as a unifying distraction from the political turmoil surrounding the Dreyfus controversy.

The press in both France and Britain had an extensive part in developing their respective national interpretations of Fashoda. Victorian press commentators were not naive and had realised early on that the new telegraphic technology could spread lies as well as truth using newspaper reports. Aside from publishing their own version of very newsworthy stories that would be popular with their readers, the press narratives were themselves subject to manipulation by 'jingoes' and politicians.[8] Lord Kitchener's advance up the Nile towards Fashoda was followed by crews installing railway and telegraph lines. He therefore controlled the information flow: even the isolated Marchand depended as much on Kitchener's sources as he did on his own for intelligence. Kitchener in that respect held all the cards.[9] Although Kitchener found a well-resourced and confident Marchand at Fashoda, his reports stated the opposite – that he had found a demoralised expedition in a hopeless position that he then 'saved from massacre'. Kitchener was able to hand the French expedition some Paris newspapers filled with news of the 'terrible Dreyfus affair…'. Their isolation and demoralisation through the skilful use of propaganda was complete.[10] Fashoda was reported by the British as a vindication of Britain's territorial 'rights' in Africa, an exhibition of Britain's excellent colonising ability, and a demonstration of military superiority. The French withdrawal was a humiliating backdown.[11]

From French press viewpoint, the absence of first-hand reports left room for speculation, rehashed stories and opinion to fill the gaps in the local news. Without direct access it was possible for Marchand to be recast by the French newspapers as a hero in a country still desperate for a unifying figure. In the cultural vacuum between the revolutionary ideal of a nation of equals and the reality of individual achievement, Marchand assumed the 'mythic image' of a hero of French imperialism and glory.[12] He became the personification of France herself, just as Kitchener's image embodied all the self-assigned characteristics of the British. With hindsight it seems that the Fashoda incident assumed prominence in the press far beyond its minor place in bilateral diplomacy, for the disputed African claims were settled just four months after the immediate crisis had ended.[13]

The New Zealand press described the Fashoda incident through a rehashed selection of reports sourced from both British and French newspapers. The African location lent an exotic element enhanced by a dramatic plot with a hero (the British Army under Kitchener) and a villain (France). Moreover, since colonial and diplomatic actions in the late nineteenth and early twentieth centuries were generally interpreted as competitive (not unlike a representative sports event) the contenders were 'us' against 'them', without (in this case) local cost or sacrifice.[14] New Zealand was a partisan spectator supporting the winning team. The news content played on the prevalent anti-French bias of the New Zealand population by suggesting the French were inept in their execution of colonial politics, unable to successfully annex territory and lacking in the fortitude necessary to match the British. Because news editorials treated the New Zealand identity as synonymous with that of the British, the incident reinforced the common citizenship and protection found within the Empire.[15]

These news reports also reinforced the paradigms the Victorians and Edwardians used to view foreign colonisation, race and culture.[16] The evidence included descriptions of the treatment of local inhabitants in the occupied territories, the arguments used to denigrate competing colonial claims, displays of nationalism and military capability and claims that the 'others' were incompetent colonisers. Commercial interests further justified colonisation by claiming it was both inevitable and necessary for accessing primary resources and acquiring land for national living-space.[17] The argument was which nation was the better coloniser, a characteristic attributed to the self-perceived cultural and national-ethnic features of various (usually white) races. By implication the indigenous occupants of territories destined for colonisation would either have the good fortune to be colonised by the British or the misfortune for others to do the same using (often) brutal methods. In this case the French expedition came into direct conflict with the indigenous inhabitants. One article included the news that the natives of 'Ilasha' had defeated the French who were crossing the British hinterland.[18] French troops were reported as burning towns that were supposedly under British protection. The British claimed the native 'Shillooks' had helped the French in the mistaken belief that they were allied with the British.[19]

Such attitudes and uncertainty as to the identity and loyalties of native populations were substantiated by reports of callous (French) brutality. An editorial in the *Star* quoted extensively from a letter written by a French Army NCO serving in Africa. 'The author of the letter provided a graphic account of his own part in the brutal work (of the expedition)'. The quoted letter included comments such as '...it was difficult to slaughter everybody', not in the context of the inhumanity but owing to the logistics involved in so doing. The New Zealand editor commented that '...the unhappy natives have good reason to doubt the advantages of civilisation as they were exemplified by the adventurous citizens of the liberty-loving Republic'.[20] Another editorial in a similar vein referred sarcastically to the natives lapsing into cannibalism, '...in spite of the gentle influence of French civilisation shed by their leader'. This editorial collectively accused France, Germany and Belgium of annexation exemplified by 'deeds of the foulest tyranny and brutality…'.[21]

Armed struggle with the locals and general destruction of their property were not uncommon by-products of colonial ventures. That such a description could have been applied to any one of a number of British colonial adventures including the New Zealand Wars and the destruction of the Summer Palace in China in1860 was an inconsistency overlooked in the New Zealand reporting.[22] Moreover Kitchener did not, in French eyes, hold the moral high ground as he had 'mercilessly slaughtered 15,000 Islamic soldiers'.[23]

The New Zealand newspapers adopted a more aggressive tone than the British political leadership. It opens speculation as to which was leading and which was following. The New Zealand newspapers advocated British action without any local involvement or threat, for as far as foreign affairs were concerned the New Zealand newspapers saw New Zealand as part of a broader British nation, with a legitimate right to offer an opinion. French colonial interests in Africa were in direct conflict with Britain's claims (although the legitimacy of both was arguable) so any thwarting of British action led to domestic pressure for a response. The unquestioned threat of force against the French – albeit through a newspaper report – was a justifiable means for the British to achieve their ends, suggesting there was little doubt amongst the editorial writers about the righteousness of the British cause. As a consequence of the British failure to immediately intervene to stop the French expedition, 'Conservative organs' called for 'a policy of surrender to France' to stop.[24] Further comment stated that the French were expected to soon withdraw from Fashoda because it '…will not suit her [i.e. France] to enter into hostilities with the Mother Country…' The (New Zealand) *Daily Telegraph* said France had no right to Fashoda and her actions were 'inexplicable'.[25] The generally anti-establishment views of the *Telegraph* with regard to the concentration of land ownership in New Zealand were irrelevant as far as foreign affairs were concerned: there was neither room for another viewpoint nor for a more considered approach. Despite the bellicose stance in the local press, Balfour was reported to have made a speech mentioning negotiations with France over 'the Niger difficulty'.[26]

The intricacies were reported in detail but for the casual newspaper reader the overall message – that Britain was in the right and France was wrong – was unambiguous. Despite a more diplomatic stance at higher levels the public received a very adversarial account of the conflicting interests. National pride was inextricably linked to military prestige in a seemingly reckless fashion in these pre-World War I years, in order to build domestic support.

> Two great nations are running one of the strangest races of modern time. Its prize is the rule of a continent. England and France are the contestants, and whichever gets to Khartoum first will get possession of the great central portion of Africa. It is a race worthy of the prize, and six separate expeditions are engaged in it.[27]

In contrast, by September 1898 the Paris newspapers were exuberantly reporting Marchand's successful arrival at Fashoda.[28] These reports were understandably very nationalistic with military resistance suggested as likely at any suggestion of a threat to the French position through British action against Marchand.[29] In keeping with the characterisation of the French as an emotional people the French newspapers were described as being 'tremendously excited'. A *Daily Telegraph* report speculated that the Marchand expedition was a private venture, rather than government sanctioned, and therefore the incident could be treated as over-reaching by a single French subject (Captain Marchand). Although patronising in tone, it implied that France had an opportunity to withdraw without dishonour, because it was unlikely that a 'great nation' such as France would go to war just because of the action of one individual.[30] On the other hand, some of the New Zealand press treated denials of (French) Government involvement as 'sheer lying'.[31]

A war with France was consequently not beyond contemplation. One report, requoted in the *Star* from the London *Standard*, summarised a situation in Africa that local editorial opinion construed as preparing the (British) public for the possibility that Britain might have to dislodge the French from Fashoda by force. Fortunately, it was soon reported that the French expedition to Fashoda had 'failed', but just to be sure editorial comments still belittled the French by talking of 'greed and dishonesty' amongst their ruling elite.[32] Notably, despite the confrontation the Queen still made her annual visit to southern France, thus suggesting that the public received a significantly more adversarial interpretation of events than the socially elite and the political leadership believed or experienced.[33]

Once Kitchener entered the narrative the editorial comment inflated his abilities by claiming that it must be 'mortifying' for France to be confronted in Africa by such a figure. Kitchener reportedly gave Marchand an ultimatum to quit Fashoda, and by late September 1898 the British had garrisoned Fashoda without conflict. The French were reported as awaiting instructions from Paris.[34] The local press did not match the official diplomatic restraint: 'The success of the British army has caused a thrill of pride over the whole Empire, but the action of the French expedition, under Captain Marchand, at Fashoda has appeared to be ominous to a certain extent.'[35]

A British-sourced editorial stated that Kitchener's conquest of the 'Soudan' (sic), including Fashoda, had been a 'service' for the rest of the civilised world as well as for Egypt. While giving some credit to Marchand personally, this piece again mentioned the possibility that his actions might have provoked a war.[36] Under the byline 'France's Weakness at Fashoda' it was reported that '…the complications of France…' were under discussion within the Triple Alliance.[37] Obviously basking in the ease with which Fashoda had been occupied, another leader writer mused as to what the next colonial action of the

French would be, given the disturbed domestic situation that was characterised as being dogged by '...anti-Semitism and Army scandals'.[38] The smug tone reflected a belief in British invincibility backed by being in the right both morally and legally. New Zealand's resident imperialists reading such copy must have been impressed and proud. It seemed that wars in Africa were, if not bloodless, then apparently not difficult to win with the threat of British action seemingly sufficient to induce compliance if not supplication from opponents. Although the Boer War was still twelve months away, such enthusiastic reporting and editorial comments add credence to the idea that New Zealand was likely to be a willing participant in an Empire confrontation. One news item even lamented the settling of the Fashoda issue by diplomacy. If there was any British failing it was Lord Salisbury who was 'too honest' compared to the French and the Russians.[39]

The British and New Zealand press characterisation of the French as incompetent colonisers was a convenient fit with New Zealand's ambitions to override French claims in the Pacific. France had not exploited her colonial gains nor had she been capable of establishing 'true' colonies, according to popular opinion. With her population at best steady if not decreasing, France had no need for additional territory but still she harassed Britain in various places around the world while her South Seas possessions were a threat to Australia and Fiji.[40] Britain was the ultimate coloniser and with much of the world destined to come under British rule, the world would be all the better for it: 'Here are a few rectifications of the map that are waiting, and have long been waiting, for the next French war. For their sake the inevitable, when it comes, may even be welcomed.'[41] Although a war (with Britain over Fashoda) would have resulted in France losing her colonies, they were an 'intolerable burden' for the French. A defeat by Britain might result in a strong French leader emerging who could create a secure, workable, post-colonial, Continental France.[42]

It is difficult to determine within the complex interaction between the press, the public and the politicians of the three nations (France, New Zealand and Great Britain) who was leading and who was following. At the time of the Fashoda confrontation (the late nineteenth century) United Kingdom newspaper readership was skewed towards a middle to upper class voter cohort. It was reports written for this audience that were used as the basis for New Zealand newspaper articles. The New Zealand newspaper readers probably encompassed a broader, more enfranchised audience who assumed that what they read reflected the opinions of their social class equivalents in Britain, rather than the more elite stratum of British newspaper readers.

Although the views expressed in the local newspapers were presumably more or less aligned with public opinion (in order to be commercially successful), no single newspaper could claim to represent the entire population either geographically, demographically or politically. Moreover, the audience composition changed as newspapers became cheaper, more widely distributed and therefore more widely read. The politicians accordingly adapted their craft to use the press to develop, test and promote their own agendas with the public, as well as to put pressure on other politicians. Conversely, the 'public' (however defined) could now use the press to push a government to act.[43] In the early nineteenth century British politicians (and newspaper proprietors) took the view that the public were unaware of where the country's interests lay and as a result assumed it was their task to educate and inform, thus nudging the public towards making the right decisions.[44] Sharing information assumed that there was interest in the issue under debate and that an informed public would come to the correct conclusions. Cultivating relationships with journalists and selectively sharing information was therefore a common method of influencing the news and public opinion. Close, mutually influential personal relationships between journalists and politicians developed. Influential proprietors and journalists, such as Repington at *The Times* or Blatchford writing in the *Daily Mirror*, became an important element in political activity.[45] In some instances, information such as the Foreign Office *Blue Books* that should have been publicised were not, as government departments decided what was in the public interest.[46] In other cases confidential information was deliberately leaked to achieve some political end. All of these factors contribute to our current unquantifiable perception of what the public knew or believed.

The term 'Fashoda' occurs over six thousand times in the New Zealand Papers Past database across all content types.[47] Advertising mentioning Fashoda was about 12 per cent of this total and largely restricted to the years 1898–1900 inclusive. Since no illustrations accompanied any of the Fashoda news articles, public impressions created through advertising would have been extremely important because they augmented the readers' mental images.[48] The Fashoda name did not have an even cachet throughout New Zealand because its use was limited to the circulation areas of particular publications and advertisers, implying there was likely to have been uneven pockets of top of mind awareness.

The Fashoda name was used to draw readers' attention to advertising that associated a brand or product with the victorious Empire and British colonial values. More nuanced uses suggested a lucky or improbable outcome. When associated with French failure and British success these impressions would have supplemented the readers' image of the French national character. Some examples illustrate how the Fashoda incident was linked to reinforce these associations. The *New Zealand Herald* advertising featured a boarding house, including rooms to rent as offices, in Grey Street (Auckland). The name may have been intended as a metaphor for temporary occupation.[49]

This 'Fashoda' does not appear to have been a destination for those who could afford better. An advertisement from one tenant using the address read:

Jewish Widow would place daughter aged 13 with Jewish family; services in return for home and clothes – Mrs. Myers, Fashoda. Upper Union st [sic].[50]

One hundred and thirty-five of the 145 relevant 'hits' from the West Coast were advertisements in the *Grey River Argus* for the Lutz Brothers, butchers. Presumably of German extraction, the Lutz Brothers linked Fashoda and praise of the German Emperor with festive season meat sales. It seems that in their view the Emperor resolved the crisis. Apart from the Fashoda linkage the association with Germany was clearly not deemed as detrimental to sales.[51]

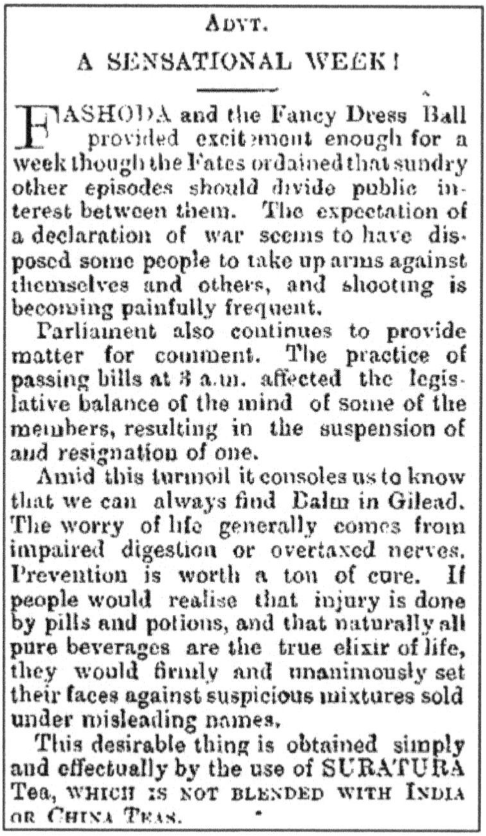

ADVT.

A SENSATIONAL WEEK!

FASHODA and the Fancy Dress Ball provided excitement enough for a week though the Fates ordained that sundry other episodes should divide public interest between them. The expectation of a declaration of war seems to have disposed some people to take up arms against themselves and others, and shooting is becoming painfully frequent.

Parliament also continues to provide matter for comment. The practice of passing bills at 3 a.m. affected the legislative balance of the mind of some of the members, resulting in the suspension of and resignation of one.

Amid this turmoil it consoles us to know that we can always find Balm in Gilead. The worry of life generally comes from impaired digestion or overtaxed nerves. Prevention is worth a ton of cure. If people would realise that injury is done by pills and potions, and that naturally all pure beverages are the true elixir of life, they would firmly and unanimously set their faces against suspicious mixtures sold under misleading names.

This desirable thing is obtained simply and effectually by the use of SURATURA Tea, WHICH IS NOT BLENDED WITH INDIA OR CHINA TEAS.

Figure 1 Use of 'advertorial' style promotion.

Advertising included use of an 'advertorial' style linking the news with branded product promotion was common at the time. Presumably the advertiser hoped that having attracted a reader's eye, the commercial message would be absorbed. Again, the link with Fashoda was positive, presumably based on the victorious British result.[52]

The use of the Fashoda name for a goldmining company is suggestive of a lucky strike or opportunistic gain.[53]

There were at least 154 results for Fashoda tea in the *Marlborough Express* between the selected dates. Often the advertising was in the context of four brands: Soudan, Fashoda, Khartoum and Omdurman. Prices were tiered from the cheapest (Soudan brand) to the most expensive (Omdurman). Presumably this was a reflection of the British prowess exhibited in each case with Omdurman the ultimate.[54]

APPLICATION FOR SPECIAL CLAIM.

Marlborough, December 13, 1898.
To the Warden at Havelock.

I HEREBY apply for a Special Claim for gold-mining purposes under the provisions of "The Mining Act, 1891," and amendments thereof, of the lands hereinafter described, which have been duly marked in accordance with the mining regulations.

Signature of Applicant:
LOUIS BRIGHT.

No. and date of Miner's Right:
36354

Name and address in full of applicant—Louis Bright.

Style under which it is intended to conduct the business—Fashoda Goldmining Company.

Locality where the land applied for is situated—On a spur between Top Valley and Arm Chair Creeks. On the west of the Trocadero claim, and north of the Albion claim.

Extent of land applied for—100 acres.

Amount of capital proposed to be invested—£20,000.

Proposed mode of working the land—Quartz Reefing.

Term for which license or special-claim grant is required—21 years.

General Remarks—Pegged out at 8 a.m. on the 10th December 1898. Pegs marked X X —.

Figure 2 Claim Application from the "Fashoda Goldmining Company". *Source*: *Marlborough Express*, 17 December 1898

WHARF—
THURSDAY, 10 p.m.

Tickets available for return by any of the Union Steam Ship Company's steamers via Picton.

FELL BROS. & CO.,
Agents, Blenheim.

OVERHEARD IN THE SOUDAN.

KHALIFA (to Lord KITCHENER): How did you get your men into such fine trim?

LORD K.: Why, we gave them Soudan Tea, of course, at 1/10!

MARCHAND: Oh, if we only had Fashoda at 2/-.

SPIRIT OF GORDON: I'll stick to Khartoum at 2/4.

KHALIFA (with a sigh): Omdurman did for me at 3/-.

LORD K.: Ha! ha! We infused it a bit strong for you. But they are all excellent Teas, and are packed by

THE
NELSON TEA
PACKING COMPANY,
AND SOLD BY ALL STOREKEEPERS.

Figure 3 Tea Brands' ranking by implied British military prowess

The unfortunate Marchand's performance was attributed to a lack of Fashoda tea for his men.[55]

By mid-November 1898 Lord Salisbury was quoted as saying French withdrawal from Fashoda had '…relieved Europe from a very dangerous and threatening storm'.[56] Chamberlain attributed the same result to a '...united nation'.[57] There had undoubtedly been a possibility of war between Britain and France into which New Zealand could have been drawn by the ties of Empire. Despite the suggested recourse to diplomacy amongst the political leadership on both sides of the channel, the New Zealand press wanted no part of a peaceful resolution for this was a good story that could be perpetuated with additional drama and suspense in the telling. Editorial opinion was firmly against allowing France or any other power a share in the spoils of North Africa. Nor would it permit any disruption to British aspirations for unbroken north to south intra-continental travel.

National pride similarly forced France to sanction Marchand's actions, perhaps aided by the opportunistic hope that his unofficial adventure might succeed with the side benefit of a major distraction from the Dreyfus affair and domestic unrest within France. British faith and confidence in the might of the Royal Navy had not been tested since Trafalgar, but the threat of its use in the latter part of the episode seemed to vindicate its perceived strength and invincibility. In the eyes of both the British and New Zealand public the failings of France as a coloniser, her shortcomings in national character, her insecurity and the lack of restraint in allowing continual aggravation of the British had all been exposed. A few (political and diplomatic) voices recognised that a stable, well led France could be an essential part of the British future. They were becoming aware that Britain's destiny might have more to do with Europe than with the Empire, the Dominions and especially inconsequential colonial competition in the Pacific region. These voices were in the minority and overwhelmed by the expressions of hubris from the opposing point of view that saw New Zealand as firmly placed within the Empire with France a significant Pacific colonial competitor.

The Fashoda incident became more than a casual warning when on Wednesday, 26 October 1898, the Defence Department announced that New Zealand was preparing for war between England and France. Having aroused public sentiment, the local press could now almost gleefully report that the population wanted visible signs that they would be defended. Men were ordered into the barracks, fortifications were manned and plans made to lay mines in Wellington Harbour. A heavy gun was to be placed on the hill above the Wellington Botanic Garden. The cable stations were kept open 'in case of emergency'.[58] While the placement of artillery in the Botanic Garden made little sense from a military point of view, the adverse view of the French created by and in the New Zealand press demanded a response, even if it was militarily ridiculous. The newspapers had arguably exacerbated the French threat, and then demanded a firm government response to the fears they had helped induce. The only clear loss in the Pacific was to the reputation of France, that then had to face renewed political hostility from the British nations as the result of sabre-rattling over a trivial fort in Africa.

Chapter Five

The Dreyfus Affair

> It is most difficult for people of our race to penetrate the secret springs of action that sway the collective mind of the French people.... somehow French public opinion has gone all wrong...
>
> Lead Article in the *Otago Daily Times*, September 1899[1]

The Dreyfus affair was a French political scandal that caused an acrimonious divide within France between the defenders and accusers of the main character, the French Army Captain Dreyfus. Although the scandal was essentially a French domestic matter of no relevance to New Zealand, it was described in great detail in the local press using syntax virtually indistinguishable from the original British reports. As was the case with Fashoda, the apparent flaws in the French national character and political system were endlessly contrasted with what was presented as a superior British system. The matter dragged on for five years from 1894 to 1899 with the volume of press reports ebbing and flowing as events evolved. The affair had some significance for Britain – given that it involved relations between France and Germany – but most attention in New Zealand centred on what was interpreted as yet another example of a catastrophic, military-related French failure.

Dreyfus related articles first appeared in the New Zealand news in late 1894. These reported that Captain Dreyfus (a French Army officer of Jewish heritage) had sold military secrets to Italy, Germany and Austria. Dreyfus was described as a traitor, swiftly court-martialled and convicted.[2] By the time Dreyfus' judicial appeals had been heard and he had been sentenced, his guilt had been accepted in most New Zealand reports. Controversy and doubt arose when, despite new evidence that showed his conviction had relied on forged documents, the French Government stubbornly maintained that Dreyfus was guilty. The British and New Zealand newspaper reports and editorials gleefully highlighted the apparent deficiencies in the French judiciary, culture and political system. Dreyfus was eventually exonerated only by Presidential pardon.[3]

The French leadership was unable to shut the matter down, notwithstanding the damage it caused both domestically and to what little remaining regard there was for France within the British world. In the New Zealand newspapers' narrative, an ugly faultline had opened in French society. Although mob condemnation of Dreyfus made supporting him difficult if not dangerous, several distinguished public figures openly took up his cause. For this extensively reported dissenting minority, the unfair treatment of Dreyfus validated the then fashionably positive views towards English values held by the French intelligentsia. This French clique believed that England would have handled the matter less clumsily and would never have allowed it to fester.[4]

For the French military establishment seeking to defend their position, Dreyfus exposed the external (German) and internal (subversive, Jewish) threats that the French nation faced, regardless of Dreyfus' personal culpability.[5] His conviction had to stand to vindicate these positions. The passionately supportive intellectual elite proved to be just as susceptible to maintaining inflexible positions as the mob, who were convinced of Dreyfus' treachery. Considerable public disquiet was displayed through social disorder, civil disobedience and political instability. Early practitioners of the emerging discipline of psychology sought answers in studies of crowd behaviour and what would now be commonly referred to as self-reinforcing 'group-think'.[6] The psychologists proved no more detached in their observations than did the lawyers, many of whom had their own opinion on the affair despite maintaining an air of legal indifference. The British Ambassador in Paris (Sir Edmund Monson) reported that the weakness of the legal case against Dreyfus was known within diplomatic circles in France but the French did not want to officially recognise the fact for fear of exacerbating civil unrest and anti-Semitic sentiments.[7]

The Dreyfus matter thereby became far bigger than the original event: it was presented as a struggle between conservative and progressive political forces in France with the potential for conflict between the civilian and military authorities for control. The affair ended the civilian-military status quo of the Third Republic but in so doing it created a new political climate in which the *entente cordiale* between France, Britain and the British Empire could exist. On the one side, the French military establishment's stubbornness led to a loss of moral authority as their actions were exposed as reactionary and their creed as pro-clerical. On the left, the Radicals benefited from Dreyfus and so emerged as a strongly anti-clerical 'decisive force'. By subsequently implementing an agenda of general social reform, the left achieved a secular Republic with strengthened civilian control. The anti-clerical laws passed post-1902 under the Combes Ministry were part of this push for separation of Church and State.[8]

These political changes gave Britain what was perceived to be a stronger, independent Continental partner who was less concerned with building a competitive Empire and more focussed on European affairs. It was hoped that this reinvigorated France would help Britain by counterbalancing growing German assertiveness. This was broadly the outcome that some had speculated would result if an Anglo-French confrontation (such as Fashoda) had forced France to reconsider where her national interests lay. The result therefore had consequences beyond France itself, for it affected the major European power alliances and had ripples that affected geographically peripheral nations like New Zealand.

Apart from the political consequences, the misfortunes of Captain Dreyfus developed into a fascinating, newsworthy story with sensation, intrigue, the French state as villain (again) and Mme Dreyfus as the heroine. It was a storyline ideally suited to regular updating and for this reason the newspapers had a strong motivation to keep it running and their readers engaged. The theme of idealised heroism with the innocent Dreyfus repeatedly pleading his case to a cold-hearted (French) state while stoically facing his many setbacks was a neat fit with the Victorian ideal of innocent heroes, popularised in events such as the charge at Balaclava (romanticised in Tennyson's famous poem) and Gordon's death at Khartoum.[9] Dreyfus was assigned the qualities of British self-sacrifice and heroism while the cold-hearted and callous French state was the antithesis. When reporting the obvious weakness of the French authorities' case the New Zealand newspapers clearly delighted in the conundrum created by the refusal of the French establishment to admit fault. France was a civilised nation that had failed and thereafter lapsed into political chaos. This was confirmation of the fiascos caused by the French state and judiciary, the flaws in the French character and the blessing for New Zealand of being a British Dominion safe within the institutions of Empire and Home. The persecution of Dreyfus was another example of all that was wrong with France.

With so many different views and constituencies involved, it was unclear which news reports were factual accounts and which were frivolous diversions and emotional appeals. The reporting did, however, add to New Zealand's overall anti-French bias by associating French Anglophobia and French Catholicism with Dreyfus' accusers. *The Times* adopted the conceited slant of the British way being best, a theme also prevalent in much of the New Zealand coverage. Anti-Semitism was another factor that *The Times* used to characterise France.[10] Local relevance was achieved by links, however tenuous, to

New Zealanders or the Pacific region. Although this suggests that the New Zealand press recognised the remoteness of the Dreyfus case and its lack of domestic consequences, it also meant that subtleties that may have softened the generic anti-French demeanour in the news were missed.

The New Zealand newspapers concluded that France self-evidently needed reforming because the French judicial system was unable to correct an obvious mistake while intellectual opinion was simply ignored or attempts made to suppress it.[11] This was based on the '...great doubts [that] exist amongst **Englishmen** [emphasis added] concerning the guilt of Dreyfus...'. Support for French jurisprudence from the French Press and public showed that neither had a sense of due legal process or 'decency'.[12] By comparison (as one article put it), '...we certainly manage this sort of thing better under English law...'.[13] The French system was derided as 'peculiar' and based on 'strange ideas of justice'.[14] The comparison between French and British justice implied a superiority that may not have stood closer scrutiny but was not subjected to such by the local newspapers.

The difficulties of resolving Dreyfus lay, it was claimed, in the nature of the French as a race. The Minister of War's assurances that there was no case was therefore described as 'absolutely Gallic'.[15] Another report hypothesised that France was due for one of its (periodic) revolutions. Public reaction to Dreyfus was sarcastically linked with the need to relieve the pressure induced by a surfeit of revolutionary activity. The cause was 'The poison in the blood...'.[16] Further commentary drew attention to the French, especially Parisians, 'jumping on a man when he is down...'.[17] No doubt this was meant to contrast the French reactions with the British sense of fair play. The problem of resolving Dreyfus' case lay in the 'unfortunate excitability and ingrained suspicion of the French race...'. The French Government was advised to be open and hold a public enquiry, despite the short-term discomfort such a course of action might involve.[18] 'It must always be remembered that Frenchmen love their army, and will see nothing evil in its doings. That is why crowds parade the streets of Paris crying: “Vive l’Armee, mort aux Juifs!”[19] The *Grey River Argus* helpfully explained that:

> …the French are a queer people. They are as susceptible to change as a column of mercury to the weather. The object of their devotion just now is the army and the abomination of their detestation of the Jews. But neither can for long possess a nation with public opinion so unstable.[20]

This editorial asserted that Frenchmen of ‘intelligence’ were collectively responsible for the Dreyfus debacle. Redemption through exoneration of Dreyfus was in their hands. This would require more than a (Gallic) shrug of the shoulders. France had been shamed and needed to wear ‘sackcloth and ashes for a while’.[21] On the other hand, French public opinion and the press were so absorbed by Dreyfus and his prominent defender Émile Zola (the well-known public intellectual, writer and advocate for the use of naturalism in literature) that they had no time to be ‘…bating [sic] England’ nor ‘…in lashing the public mind to frenzy over the aggressions of perfidious Albion…’ in Africa (presumably Fashoda was still recalled).[22]

While the French were described as ‘…honourable and chivalrous when not under the influence of passion…’ they had in this case ‘blundered terribly’. France was weak, her laws disgraced, and she was exposed to the contempt of the world, in contrast with the God-fearing and Emperor-loving Germans.[23] From a New Zealand perspective these reports reinforced a stereotypical view of the French people and nation. Even stronger comment referred to the ‘…lying, fraud, forgery, bribing, and general all-round rotteness [that] are about to be sheeted home…’, but to who is not clear. The French action was even likened to the inquisition for: ‘Without national Stability she (France) froths and bubbles up similarly to a geyser, down the orifice of which a foreign body has been dropped.’[24]

Under the headline ‘Turbulent France’ there was the claim that ‘[the French people] have a morbid craving for political excitement not unlike a diseased appetite engendered by powerful drugs'.[25] There were reports of a possible military coup.[26] Attempting some balance, a favourable comment on Madame Dreyfus noted that: '…we sometimes forget the ideal wife and mother may come from France…'.[27]

Anti-Semitism in France was a recurring theme. Although a 'hatred of the Jew' was described as a national characteristic of Russia, France and Austria, the Russian press campaign for a revision of the Dreyfus case was taken as evidence that anti-Semitism there was declining.[28] (In fact Russia was more concerned about the instability of her closest ally.) A boycott of French goods and services by the Jewish population of Broken Hill in September 1898 was reported in New Zealand.[29]

Another Pacific and New Zealand concern was introduced through news and comment from the captain of a supply ship who provided an account of the (reportedly) appalling conditions of Dreyfus' imprisonment.[30] This very detailed and sympathetic description of the suffering of Dreyfus while imprisoned on *île du Diable* would have reinforced New Zealand concerns about his treatment and the presence of such institutions in the Pacific. The Presbyterian Church had petitioned Gladstone in 1884 to block penal settlements in the New Hebrides and there are numerous pages of like-minded correspondence in the Appendices to the Journals of the House of Representatives in support of the widespread opposition in New Zealand to penal colonies.[31]

Dreyfus-related reporting, while emotional and passionate, still remained somewhat remote until a theatrical performance that included a scene based on Dreyfus' public humiliation toured New Zealand. Entitled *One of the Best*, the play was initially staged at the Princess Theatre in Dunedin.[32] It was well patronised with one review stating that the show was very popular, with people turned away.[33] This suggests that there was considerable ongoing local interest in Dreyfus. The publication of a sarcastic poem in the *Star* in 1898 summed up the tone:

To Dreyfus' guilt I pledged my word

A Frenchman's word, a trusty un!
Denial therefore is absurd,
And argument but fustian[34]

French visitors to New Zealand were understandably nonplussed by such strong local opinion that was based on highly prejudicial reporting. One officer from a French warship visiting Wellington took umbrage at a newspaper article that used 'poltroonism' and 'scoundrelism' to describe the French Government and Army. Despite demanding satisfaction, the French officer received none and was forced to leave by the departure of his ship, with his pride still injured. Locals saw the affair as amusing.[35]

More nuanced opinion was rare. The President of the French Literary Society, M. de Montalk, gave a 'careful exposition' of the Dreyfus affair following which there was discussion of the trials of Dreyfus and Zola.[36] Unfortunately the content was not reported. One particularly critical article was published in September 1898. Edith Searle Grossmann was a contemporary New Zealand scholar and her views were consistent with the concept of race-based national characteristics then in academic fashion as a framework for historical analyses.[37] *The American: In Peace and In War* was a review of two books, one written by an Englishman and the other by a Frenchman. Grossmann compared and contrasted the views each took of the American character. In Grossmann's view, 'disaster and crises' revealed a 'nation's soul'. To make her point she referred to the violence of the French revolutions, the Dreyfus affair and gave two other instances ('fire at the charity bazaar' and 'the sinking of … *Bourgogne*') as examples of French 'callous brutality'.[38]

An interview with Professor Louis Vigouroux, a visitor from the Musée Social, gave a native French point of view.[39] The Professor was apparently shocked by the tone of the New Zealand reporting on France and Dreyfus. He pointed out (correctly) that English views of the French were based on cable messages reported in the newspapers. These were misrepresentations as they were skewed by 'national bias'. He saw

England and France as having much in common beyond simply geographic proximity, and he blamed newspapers for the ill will between the two nations. Differences between nations were no more nor less than those between individuals within any one nation. The English newspaper reports (Vigouroux went on) inevitably tried to show British superiority whatever the subject. In the Antipodes he found much evidence that the locals were actually learning from foreigners (French wine-making was one of the examples pointedly given, textile manufacturing another) but editorials and lead articles in the same publications had nothing good to say of French virtue, honesty or freedom. Vigouroux drew attention to one article that he said misrepresented the nature of local government in France. In a gently chiding comment he said central government in France would not allow the 'tyranny' of a local board establishing prohibition. No doubt referring to the extreme stance of New Zealand temperance movements, he said '…the French are a temperate people and we don't require prohibition'. The irony appears to have been missed by the reporter.

Vigouroux also pointed out that invariably only Paris newspapers were quoted in the local press; the French provincial press with different views, was not.[40] He reflected the common elitist prejudice that diplomatic matters were far more complex than a few cables could explain and therefore were best left to well-informed statesmen rather than public whim. Vigouroux circumspectly did not offer an opinion on Dreyfus but he doubted the French military was biased to the extent claimed. Civil authority was not under the control of the military in France.[41]

There was also the opinion of Professor Albert Métin, another 'intelligent' Frenchman visiting to gather information about New Zealand's social and political legislation. He claimed the Dreyfus affair was political in nature and reflective of the divide between the Liberal and Radical factions ranged against the Catholic and Conservative wings in French politics. Métin claimed that the matter was a purely military affair. Oddly, after appearing to defend the conviction, Métin said the results of the new court-martial would be universally accepted, regardless of the result, but the result must be an acquittal. Métin also believed that the various political currents, particularly anti-Semitism, were 'magnified' in the New Zealand publications. France wanted neither a dictator nor to disturb the peace in Europe. These were simply misbeliefs of the English press.[42] Despite these opinions, there is no evidence that there was any reassessment of either the Dreyfus affair or any revisionist opinion of France in the press.

Although not an official communication, since New Zealand had no independent stance on foreign affairs, it was reported that all members of the New Zealand House of Representatives, with five exceptions (one of them being the Premier), signed a cable of sympathy addressed to Madame Dreyfus.[43] Curiously, given the enthusiasm with which the whole sorry Dreyfus affair had been covered by the press, the following note declining publication of a letter appeared in the *Wanganui Herald*:

> 'A Sympathiser of Dreyfus' –
> Your letter is declined, as we have no intention of opening our columns to a sectarian dispute, which would only lead to great bitterness of feeling.[44]

Were the cause of Dreyfus' release to be in any doubt the *Ohinemuri Gazette*, a Paeroa-based journal, was able to report that the nearby town of Te Aroha had '…put the climax on the job by burning the French flag'. As news of this brave act reached Paris, the *Gazette* sarcastically continued, Dreyfus was released post-haste. The *Gazette* facetiously claimed that the French nation was to henceforth voluntarily abstain from using the Te Aroha Sanatorium.[45] By late September the French Government was also trying to shut the matter down, with the Minister of War reportedly advising the President to grant Dreyfus clemency while the Army was ordered to consider the matter closed. There were to be no further reprisals, but Dreyfus still demanded that he be allowed to prove his innocence as a condition for accepting a pardon.[46]

Dreyfus related advertising appeared more frequently and over a longer timespan than was the case for Fashoda. The geographic spread was broadly reflective of population distribution and newspaper circulation, in contrast with the more localised Fashoda coverage. This suggests a nationwide carryover effect long after any direct impact had faded. Reminders of the relevant events, whether factually true or not, would have increased top of mind awareness and kept the memory of a French embarrassment alive.[47] While advertisements were common, illustrations were not. (One advertisement listed in the *Illustrated Press* of 7 September 1898 included 'Dreyfus' as a subject but the illustration could not be found.[48]) The following reproductions appeared in the *Auckland Star* of 5 November 1898. After all the vilification, the simple normality of the French visages may have surprised some readers.[49]

Figure 4 Main characters in the Dreyfus Affair, (from left) Mme Dreyfus, M. Mercier, and M. Billot. *Source*: PapersPast, *Auckland Star*, 5 November 1898

BOOKSELLERS.

UPTON & CO.

NOVELS OF THE YEAR.
NOVELS OF THE YEAR.

"ALICE OF OLD VINCENNES,"
"ALICE OF OLD VINCENNES,"

By

MAURICE THOMSON.

More original than "Richard Carvel," more vital than "Janice Meredith," more cohesive than "By Order of the Company," more dramatic, spontaneous, and artistic than any of its rivals. Such is Maurice Thomson's superb American Romance.—"Times."

2/6 Paper. 3/6 Cloth.

DREYFUS.
DREYFUS.

The vivid personal story of arrest, trial, degredation, imprisonment and suffering now for the first time told the world.

HIS OWN STORY.
HIS OWN STORY.

Containing the Diary kept at the Ile du Diable.

Many Unpublished Letters of his Wife.

FIVE YEARS OF MY LIFE.

"The 'Most Remarkable Book of the Year."

Price, 2/6.

UPTON & CO.

Figure 5 The published diary of Dreyfus containing letters from Mme Dreyfus. *Source*: PapersPast

Advertising for 'Five Years of My Life' by Captain Dreyfus.[50]

GLORIOUS Reign Record Number, London News, The Duke in Southern Isles 1s, The Dook's Visit, The Relief of Kumasi, The Career of a Beauty, The Lord of the Sea, Five Years of my Life (Dreyfus), The Column; cheap editions in great variety by popular authors—H M JONES

Figure 6 Further advertising for the Dreyfus story. *Source*: PapersPast

There were also examples of advertising that linked products (such as soap) to Dreyfus.[51] Presumably the advertiser hoped that the Dreyfus name would draw attention to the copy. The link between Dreyfus and soap is at best tenuous, but presumably would not have been used if the advertiser had not believed it would attract interest. There was clearly no concern that the negative aspects of the Dreyfus case would reflect upon presumed product quality.

Flora Soap.

THE DREYFUS affair has quite for a long time been the all-absorbing topic of foreign affairs. But to come to something nearer home that creates nearly as much interest it is the good qualities imprisoned in a cake of FLORA SOAP.

Flora Soap.

Figure 7 Dubious advertising associating Dreyfus with quality 'imprisoned' in soap. *Source*: PapersPast

One dilemma for the typesetters was layout. This sometimes resulted in the appearance of non-commercial material in advertising columns. In the following case the report is of a sermon, Dreyfus being the subject. Reference is made to both France having to 'answer to God' and to the 'character of the (French) nation'.[52]

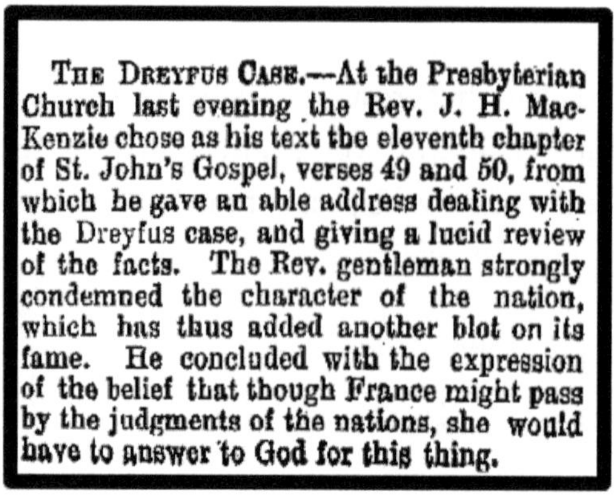

THE DREYFUS CASE.—At the Presbyterian Church last evening the Rev. J. H. MacKenzie chose as his text the eleventh chapter of St. John's Gospel, verses 49 and 50, from which he gave an able address dealing with the Dreyfus case, and giving a lucid review of the facts. The Rev. gentleman strongly condemned the character of the nation, which has thus added another blot on its fame. He concluded with the expression of the belief that though France might pass by the judgments of the nations, she would have to answer to God for this thing.

Figure 8 Dreyfus judged from a New Zealand pulpit. *Source*: PapersPast, 'Advertisements', *Colonist*, 28 September 1899, p.1.

When a Fuller's Waxwork Tableaux of the Dreyfus incident was exhibited in Dunedin the advertising suggested the Dreyfus affair was akin to a circus act or fairground attraction rather than a matter of serious political consequence.[53]

There were also reports of meetings and talks: unfortunately, as was often the case, the content of the talk was not recorded, nor were the credentials of the speaker(s).[54]

Despite the case being officially closed, Dreyfus related advertising still appeared 194 times between 1 January 1910 and 1 January 1939 (Fashoda was mentioned just sixteen times over the same period). The 'Martyrdom of Adolph Beck', who was described as the English Dreyfus, featured in 1910 cinema advertising.[55]

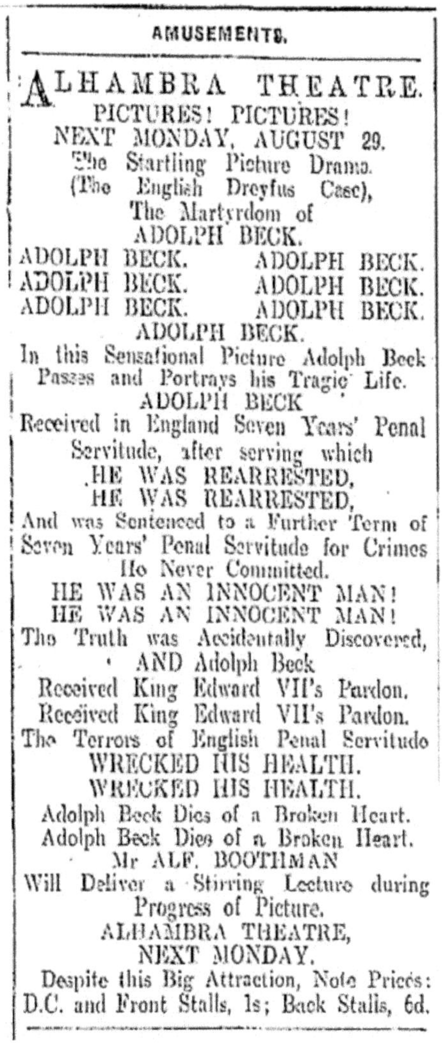

AMUSEMENTS.

ALHAMBRA THEATRE.
PICTURES! PICTURES!
NEXT MONDAY, AUGUST 29.
The Startling Picture Drama.
(The English Dreyfus Case),
The Martyrdom of
ADOLPH BECK.
ADOLPH BECK. ADOLPH BECK.
ADOLPH BECK. ADOLPH BECK.
ADOLPH BECK. ADOLPH BECK.
ADOLPH BECK.
In this Sensational Picture Adolph Beck Passes and Portrays his Tragic Life.
ADOLPH BECK
Received in England Seven Years' Penal Servitude, after serving which
HE WAS REARRESTED,
HE WAS REARRESTED,
And was Sentenced to a Further Term of Seven Years' Penal Servitude for Crimes He Never Committed.
HE WAS AN INNOCENT MAN!
HE WAS AN INNOCENT MAN!
The Truth was Accidentally Discovered,
AND Adolph Beck
Received King Edward VII's Pardon.
Received King Edward VII's Pardon.
The Terrors of English Penal Servitude
WRECKED HIS HEALTH.
WRECKED HIS HEALTH.
Adolph Beck Dies of a Broken Heart.
Adolph Beck Dies of a Broken Heart.
Mr ALF. BOOTHMAN
Will Deliver a Stirring Lecture during Progress of Picture.
ALHAMBRA THEATRE,
NEXT MONDAY.
Despite this Big Attraction, Note Prices:
D.C. and Front Stalls, 1s; Back Stalls, 6d.

Figure 9 Using the Dreyfus case as a metaphor. *Source*: PapersPast

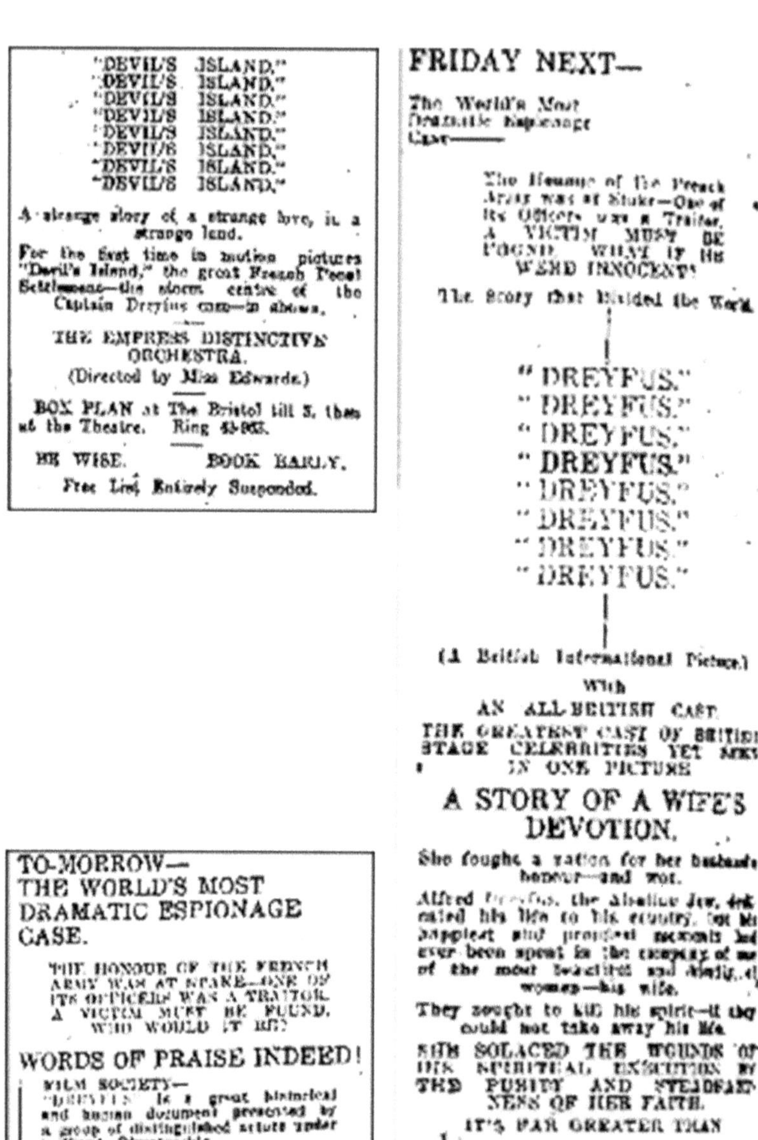

Figure 10 Advertisements for films set on Devil's Island (left) and about the Dreyfus Affair (right).

Dreyfus was the subject of a full motion picture set on Devil's Island (above left).[56] There was also a film directly about the Dreyfus Affair, with an 'all-British cast' (right).[57] The latter was extensively advertised from October 1931 before its 'run' started and then whilst it was screening until December 1932. Note the review from the British Film Society.[58]

The consequences of the Dreyfus affair thereby remained in the public consciousness long after the event.[59] Unlike the British triumph at Fashoda, Dreyfus was a human tragedy that could evoke personal sympathy while highlighting the failings of France at a national level. These flaws could not be easily forgotten, dismissed or ignored. Despite some evidence of dissent and alternative views, mainstream reporting had suggested that French society was in chaos and that establishing Dreyfus' guilt had considerable French public and establishment support, despite the obvious doubts. Under a perceived threat from Germany, the French establishment believed it needed to maintain both civil domestic coherence and the continued support of the Army. These requirements outweighed the risks of cutting off potential allies, Russia excepted, and have to be seen against a background in which French military planners assumed that another war with Britain rather than Germany was the most likely scenario. Planning for this possibility was only abandoned in 1907, three years after the *entente* came into being and four years after Germany had been identified as the most likely adversary.[60]

From the New Zealand point of view, even a superficial reading of the forgoing accounts leaves little doubt for the less engaged reader as to the flaws in the French character, military, justice system, government and race. The absence of alternative public opinion from the English political establishment suggests the British leadership was content to let the discomfort of an old enemy fester. Despite intense media reporting, the New Zealand Government and Parliament remained similarly aloof, consistent with New Zealand's stance of non-involvement in foreign affairs.[61] At a time when France was vulnerable and may have needed friends whether political, diplomatic or military, she had isolated herself from the British world on all grounds. There was no hint of a rapport with France developing, in fact quite the opposite from the New Zealand point of view.

There was a tone of smug superiority in the reporting that ignored the differing domestic agendas and international pressures a European nation might face. As a result of the Liberal reforms of the late nineteenth century and New Zealand's description as a social laboratory, it was easy to dismiss other viewpoints. Characterising the French as emotionally unstable and excitable, susceptible to a belief in conspiracies and collectively anti-Semitic was a simple way to explain Dreyfus, especially as New Zealand had no widespread anti-Jewish history on the scale of the local anti-Chinese sentiment.[62] The French politicians were apparently at loggerheads, a majority of the population seemed prepared to back the Army whatever the judicial merits of the Dreyfus verdict, and the very British ideal of 'fair play' was conspicuously absent. France was a failing state. 'France has been guilty of many dark deeds, but surely never fouler plot than that against Captain Dreyfus has been hatched in the darkest history of the great Republic.'[63]

Chapter Six

Reconciliation and the path to the entente cordiale

Prior to 1914 many New Zealanders enthusiastically accepted the need for Empire membership as an all-embracing political, defence and trade necessity, although this meant that nearly all of New Zealand's trade-based economic activity was dependent on Britain. Membership on these self-imposed conditions required the shipment of bulky, largely unrefined primary produce to the most distant market on the planet. New Zealand was therefore totally reliant on naval defence to protect the world's longest marine trade route, while hoping that Britain's economic strength and importing capacity would continue indefinitely. It followed that New Zealand's foreign policy interests were best served by contributing to the Empire's defence. This problem, when isolated from all the rhetoric and emotion, was met by New Zealand famously offering to contribute a dreadnought battleship to the Royal Navy.[1] Despite this contribution the (principally naval) defensive shield still required an extensive and expensive series of global bases where warships could be either reprovisioned or based permanently or on assignment. Strategic and diplomatic considerations as well as developments in resources, funding, technology and domestic politics meant that defence requirements were continually altering. Securing these bases and the Empire was therefore a 'constantly evolving' task.[2]

It had been assumed that a viable economic model could be developed to self-fund the occupation and exploitation of the many new territories that Britain and France (along with the other empire-building states) acquired. These territories were however often contained within arbitrarily defined borders established without regard for natural geographic features and barriers. Resistant local populations needed to be subdued while the territory was being defended from external threats. This was a significant challenge, especially for the geographically dispersed British Empire. The Royal Navy's 'command of the sea' therefore required not only protecting the United Kingdom but also defending trade routes to the Empire's peripheries as well as ensuring the security of the Dominions. Building infrastructure (such as the cable and telegraph network) in advance of the French and other competitors to support a common British identity came to be seen as an essential tool for developing a cohesive Empire culture and a sense of belonging. As telegraph and shipping technologies improved, the time required for the movement of messages and physical goods greatly decreased thus aiding this process. Meanwhile new metropoles such as Auckland and Sydney appeared that challenged the perceived necessity for a London-centric Empire hub within a clichéd 'shrinking world'.[3] The policy-makers in London had to take account of these factors while ensuring that defence and infrastructure costs did not consume resources to the point that they undercut the Empire's viability.[4]

Although the Royal Navy was the public showpiece for the Empire's defensive power and British prestige, settlements and agreements with the United States and Japan were needed to supplement the Royal Navy in the Pacific. These agreements were still insufficient to address the imbalance that the British felt existed between the Empire and the European powers, particularly as far as land power was concerned. The Empire therefore had to seek a defensive partnership with one or more European states if it was to have any chance of survival. France was the chosen partner and the *entente cordiale* was the backdoor means to achieve an alliance. But could New Zealand's cultural distaste for the

French be accommodated within an Empire now allied with the traditional enemy?

The mid-nineteenth century had been a period of '...crises, war scares and preparations for war on both sides…' of the Channel. The French loss of Alsace-Lorraine after the Franco-German War that ended with the defeat of Napoleon III in 1870 prompted some sympathy amongst the British, but an anti-French sentiment still prevailed.[5] For the *entente* to succeed, the significant emotional distance that had been deliberately constructed between the British and French nations as an everyday manifestation of the Victorian cultural difference model used to keep 'us and them' apart had to be closed.[6] The public unveiling of the *entente cordiale* between France, the United Kingdom and by extension New Zealand began with King Edward's state visit to Paris in 1903. Since the earlier reciprocal royal visits of 1843 and 1844 were exceptions rather than new beginnings, the visit marked the most significant political realignment in European foreign affairs in the decade prior to 1914. The geographic closeness of Britain and France as demonstrated by reciprocal Heads of State visits in 1903 was the first show of this emotional reconciliation.

> No British monarch of recent times came to the throne better equipped to play a constructive role in foreign affairs. The King was well travelled and well connected. He was accustomed to spend part of each year in Germany and France, and as King he continued to do so. He could speak in public in French and German. … The King's easy public manner made him a natural ambassador, though his ministers, accustomed perhaps to Victoria's hostility to public engagements, were slow to take advantage of this.[7]

Exactly what had prompted the initial diplomatic overtures is uncertain but it seems that Théophile Delcassé (French Foreign Minister for six years after the Fashoda incident) was a key actor.[8] He realised that Germany, not Britain, was the real threat to France because Germany's Naval Law of 1900 was a menace to both France's colonial aspirations and Britain's isolationist stance.[9] Delcassé also perceived that France and the United Kingdom could be friends despite their concurrent colonial rivalry. The diplomatic moves that followed were clearly signalled. Edward's public reception in Paris was described as 'tumultuous enthusiasm from enormous and eager crowds', 'a continuous ovation' with 'crowds ... similar to those in London on Coronation night', indicating that the King received a very warm public welcome.[10] King Edward duly praised France and talked of 'mutual prosperity' as well as 'friendship and admiration' between the two countries. Past rivalries and differences were to be forgotten through '...[an] advance together in the path of civilization and peace'.[11] One editorial said the King's remarks had been plainer than was normal for diplomatic language and they hinted at a 'practical issue' to be announced.[12] This appeared to be anticipating a Treaty or some other official communiqué arising from the visit.

The French President's return outing to London shortly after Edward's trip was astutely timed. It signalled that the diplomatic overtures were initiated on an equal and mutual footing. Citizens of both countries were able to see the public welcomes extended to their respective leaders. French visitors were in London in unprecedented numbers, ready for their President's visit.[13] Platitudinous speeches by the King and the President included the French President's woefully inaccurate prediction that the friendship would '...guarantee the peace of the world'.[14] French was spoken in the streets of London and used for day-to-day greetings as well as to order in restaurants. French hawkers sold French newspapers to the visitors.[15] Britain and France were now apparently as closely allied as their physical proximity permitted.

Following the King's visit, reports of an Anglo-French agreement being signed received generally favourable coverage in New Zealand. The friendship displayed during the Royal visit and other *entente*-related events had been prominently reported based on second-hand British news, but there was a struggle to provide local context and relevance.[16] Oddments such as 400 French Marines being permitted to sightsee in Singapore, the French garrison in Madagascar entertaining the crew of HMS *Fox* and the Australian Government sending a message of goodwill to New Caledonia were published as examples of colonial goodwill.[17] The British and French flags were raised in Australia, thereby signalling that President Loubet was a guest of the Empire, not just of Britain.[18] Editorial comment based on reports from Europe said that Loubet was '...exactly the sort of Frenchman to be popular with English people'. It was claimed that the French had lost most of their Anglophobia. The importance of cross channel trade (an issue of potential significance for New Zealand) was mentioned. Even the attitude of the French press during the South African War was now excused. Peace and goodwill existed between the '...two great powers of Western Europe'.[19]

Despite the recent Dreyfus and Fashoda publicity, the *entente* provoked little public objection, probably because there were no immediate consequences for New Zealand. A change in attitude on the part of the French Colonial Party with regard to competing colonial interests, it was hypothesised, would perhaps lead to a more favourable climate for peaceful settlement of conflicting Pacific colonial ambitions. Although some reports suggested war in Europe was a possible outcome from the *entente*, the New Zealand public did not seem – so far as can be seen from the newspaper reports of the day – unduly perturbed. The only competition in the future should be 'friendly' and restricted to trade and industrial rivalries.[20] In that respect Dominion indifference and dutiful acceptance was probably as favourable a reaction as the Home Government could have hoped for, given the past hostility and vilification of France.

Despite this generally favourable New Zealand coverage, there was an element of cynical disbelief that the diplomatic initiative was anything more than an uneasy truce. There was even some outright dissent, for *The Ashburton Guardian* found it necessary to rebut negative views of the Royal visit in what it described as the 'gutter press'.[21] The *Berlin Post* (requoted in the *Feilding Star*) said the *entente* would not last, as colonial competitiveness between France and Britain would lead to differences.[22] The *Oamaru Herald* was also less than effusive in welcoming the new friendship. It suggested French affection for the King was shallow and would be short lived as it was based on cynical commercial interests.[23] The *Free Lance* was critical of *The Times* for attaching significance to the Australian flag-raising act and more so for treating it as newsworthy enough to be cabled back to the Antipodes. This paper cast a particularly jaundiced eye over the visit and the theatrics involved.[24]

The local newspaper reader, if so inclined, would therefore have been well informed on the general implications of the *entente* for foreign relations.[25] One apparently well-informed correspondent said it was 'incorrect' to consider the *entente* an alliance, but nevertheless he welcomed the reduction in tension caused by a secular and peace-minded French Government. Mervyn J. Stewart noted that one consequence of the new relationship was the reduced threat of a German-Franco alliance against the British Empire. Stewart referred to the past hopes of the German Government for 'a successful war…' with England and need for counterbalancing defensive alliances to deter the threat.[26]

The French appeared to be open to the possibility of direct negotiation with New Zealand and other British dependencies in the Pacific to settle local differences by extending the spirit of the *entente* into the Pacific. An editorial, requoting from *Le Temps*, astutely noted that Anglo-French disputes were often related to colonial matters and were now complicated by the British colonies carrying 'more weight … in the policy-making of the Empire' owing to their increasing independence.[27] The *Press*, in summarising the various regions of conflict, drew attention to the New Hebrides as a territory that was of '… special interest to inhabitants of this (Antipodean) part of the world…'.[28] (The shared British-French administration of the New Hebrides was a constant irritant for activists in each country who wanted their opposites removed.) In the aftermath of Edward's tour, even Henri Lorin suggested that colonial differences between France and the British could be settled by direct contact between France and the relevant 'autonomous' colonies, thus bypassing the London-Empire channel. Moreover, the exiling of convicts to the Pacific could be conditionally ended if it was still an issue. There were other suggestions to settle old colonial disputes by negotiation.[29]

Britain believed she had achieved two objectives through the *entente*. Firstly, she had neutralised the eternal European power plays. On both sides of the channel there was talk of the *entente* progressing to a more formal agreement covering any outstanding matters while providing a framework for resolution of future (European) disputes. Britain could prosper and grow alongside her Empire, sheltered behind an understanding with France and the powerful defensive screen of her navy.[30] In fact, the *entente* entangled the Empire and thereby New Zealand in the fate of Europe. Secondly, the *entente* offered the possibility of resolving outstanding Anglo-Franco colonial disputes.[31] On several occasions during the so-called century of peace, war might have broken out with France over colonial matters, not just in Fashoda but also in Tahiti and Egypt. While with hindsight they were never enough to have justified the threat of a full-scale war, at the time this seemed possible.[32] The French knew they could not win such a war as long as Britain had the Royal Navy, so a settlement made sense. Peaceful coexistence meant trade, cultural exchanges, growth, tourism and of course mutual protection for the two western hemisphere powers.

Despite Britain's re-engagement with Europe an increasingly out-of-step Joseph Chamberlain continued to push his Empire-centric alternative. The *Southland Times* pointed out that even the *Paris Journal* had noted the inconsistency between Chamberlain's views and the spirit of *entente*.[33] In proposing tariffs on cheap foreign imports to preserve British jobs, Chamberlain's opinion was that there was nothing that the '… reserve of sons overseas' could not provide to England. His view went to the heart of the debate about the purpose of the Empire.

Was it to be a loose association of interests or an integrated economic federation as New Zealand desired? It could not be both.

The *entente* implicitly recognised the dominance of the Royal Navy as a force that trumped the land power of Russia and served as an extremely powerful military counterbalance to any German threat to France. The *entente* was therefore reinforced by a well-publicised confluence of the British and French navies.[34] Captioned illustrations of the British Fleet's visit to Brest included reference to 'A living demonstration of the "entente cordiale"', and 'A friendly invasion of Brest…'. The symbolic visit conditioned public opinion through an impressive demonstration of the combined strength of the two fleets and the willingness of the old enemies to work together. The show, which was more akin to a regatta, was repeated in Portsmouth shortly thereafter.[35]

The strength of the phrase *entente cordiale* lay in its vagueness since it could be interpreted as the user saw fit.[36] The *Oxford Dictionary* defines the term as 'A friendly understanding or informal alliance between states or factions'. For those in favour of an accommodation between the United Kingdom and France it meant an open-ended friendship. Frustratingly for opponents, it meant nothing more than a hint of cross-channel cooperation. The inherent imprecision removed the grounds for specific objections. At the national level an expression of non-hostile intent directed at France was as unobjectionable as doing the same with any other nation of a similarly non-threatening, Western-orientated disposition. The use of a French expression served a secondary purpose. In the lingua franca, the phrase *entente cordiale* became an expression meaning an unspoken understanding. The phrase entered the vernacular and was widely used beyond the British–French national relationship to describe agreement and harmony.[37] For the educated Francophiles in English society prominently led by the King, it was a signal that a competitive phase of Anglo-French relations had ended. Admiring French culture, custom and learning were no longer activities best kept within the upper social classes. For Francophobes the accord was an opportunity to end a long running hostility and, for the more opportunistic, a chance to consolidate English supremacy. Public demonstrations of military cooperation and political exchanges could be interpreted as demonstrating that France was under control.[38] A state of *entente* became normal.

The *entente* was neither fully explained nor justified to the New Zealand public, probably because there was no immediate security threat or trade implications and thus no need to reassess the relationship with France. The press reports suggest that initially the *entente* was seen as a more or less acceptable but benign development. Despite this, the new *entente* did not magically remove inter-empire tensions in the Pacific. The public mood gradually shifted from acquiescence to disquiet, as was shown when Prime Minister Massey spoke at a public meeting in Milton in mid-1913 alongside Sir James Allen, who was both Minister of Defence and of Education (Finance came later in his career).[39] Allen and Massey clearly needed to assuage concerns within Allen's Milton electorate. Dealing with public trepidations is an essential task in any democracy, but it was especially so in New Zealand where the electoral franchise was much broader than was the case in either Britain or France.[40] The reports suggest that Massey and Allen had to publicly justify a British Pacific defence policy that hinged on the 'slender thread' of the *entente cordiale.* Their comments made clear how unpalatable such an arrangement was for New Zealand.

Massey pointed out that the political price of the Empire's reliance on France was a constraint on the 'mother country' (and therefore New Zealand) from doing anything in the Pacific vis-à-vis French interests for fear of disrupting that relationship. As an alternative, New Zealand should be preparing for 'manhood' as a nation.[41] Massey's referral to a 'constraint' was probably a reference to Allen's quest in London to secure a coaling station on Rapa Island 'now held by the French'.[42] Allen went so far as to state that there were '...questions relating to the New Hebrides that could be faced ... without repudiating the *entente*'. Allen also said that '...the time has come when the statesmen of this

Dominion and of Australia must have something to say in regard to the diplomatic questions in the Pacific', an issue that frequently appeared on the London Colonial Conference agendas. Editorial comment referred to the unsatisfactory nature of relying on alliances owing to the unpredictability of the demands that might result and the tendency of the participants to 'neglect' their own defence. New Zealand therefore needed to do more than just paying the mother country to defend her.[43]

The consequences of the new alignment with another major power were therefore clearly outlined but, as with all the World War I protagonists, the potential obligations were understated. In public Allen and Massey still characterised defence as a burden for the Empire collectively. Defence was to be achieved through the power of the Royal Navy (including Ward's dreadnought) rather than defence being directed to the security of New Zealand as an isolated territory. This public stance conflicted with the position expressed privately in Allen's memo written prior to his United Kingdom visit. In this memo, Allen outlined an alternative, independent direction for New Zealand policy but the conclusion seemed to be that 'isolation' or what we would now call an independent foreign policy would be 'too costly'. It is significant that an alternative policy beyond the British Empire could be considered at Cabinet level, thus giving credence to the idea that New Zealand's choices were not believed to be of particular concern to the United Kingdom.[44]

Embracing defence as a joint obligation alongside the Empire assumed there was a potential threat to New Zealand (even if only indirectly), a circumstance that was clearly not immediate. The *Wairarapa Times* noted that Anglo-German alienation had occurred since the Boer War. Notwithstanding the ties of (royal) kinship and common ideals that previously existed with Germany, Britain had ended up in an alliance/*entente* with two nations (i.e. Russia and France) previously considered to be enemies and with which there was little in common '...racially and politically and temperamentally...'. The implications for Australasia were unclear. It was also pointed out that one unfortunate consequence of a complex British policy was the dependence in the Pacific on an alliance with Japan for imperial defence. This pointed to the need for New Zealand to one day have a greater say in foreign affairs. It would in the meantime be preferable to settle Pacific issues with France as a friend and work through the Home Government rather than upsetting the European balance of power. The message was clearly that New Zealand should consider the greater good. Allen's comment on the need to provide manpower to share in defence of the Empire was noted. Was Allen (in mid-1913) following his discussions overseas preparing the political ground for the possibility that the New Zealand population might have to fight in Europe to (supposedly) defend New Zealand's interests?[45]

Just why these reservations and nascent signs of independent thinking were not acted upon remains uncertain. Loyalty to the Empire was unquestionable, at least in public, but Germany, hitherto a friendly power, was no immediate threat while France was a non-hostile Pacific competitor. New Zealand was a global minnow and unlikely to be of any consequence numerically.[46] That could be interpreted as suggesting either that no defence arrangements were necessary or that the counter-argument applied and alignment with a great power was necessary since the country was unguarded. Even assuming the latter view, these were serious reservations for establishment figures to be raising in public.

Since the introduction of the *entente* to the New Zealand public had been so low-key compared to the effort in Britain, local reservations about any accommodation with the French remained. Moreover, New Zealand did not seize the opportunity to promote the *entente* and engage directly with France on regional Pacific matters or trade. Loyalty to the Empire overrode other concerns by default as long as there was no immediate threat to New Zealand's status quo. The broader issues could therefore be politically quarantined as Continental problems were for Britain to deal with. There was no immediate threat and whatever fighting there was would presumably be quickly dealt with by the Royal Navy in northern hemisphere waters.[47] There may have been small gains from repudiating the *entente* locally but there was a significant risk to New Zealand's position within the Empire if that course were chosen. Once World War I began the price to be paid for this flaccid policy stance was cruelly exposed.

PART III

Options and Opportunities 1918–1935

> 'Is it not the fact that with such friends there is an alluring prospect before us in respect of the future relations between France and New Zealand?'
>
> Report of the 'French Mission' requoted in the *Oamaru Mail,* 8 May 1920[1]

New Zealand attempted to put the national trauma of World War I in the past by simultaneously disengaging from Europe while meshing into the Empire, as if a nominally independent nation were a vassal state. Disengagement was a reflex rejection of all the horror that Europe had come to represent. It was a relatively easily implemented policy because it resurrected the old prejudices and dislikes of the French, supplemented by a propaganda-inspired dislike of Germany. It was a policy that repositioned the *entente* as a temporary accord, created solely to meet an immediate Anglo-French need.

Reinstating the cultural and social barriers between New Zealand and France while re-emphasising the geographic distance between New Zealand and Europe was critical to the disengagement process. It began with official resistance to repatriating bodies from the battlefields so as to lessen the period of close contact, along with compensatory haste in preparing local monuments to replicate the grander memorials being constructed in France. Thus, when France attempted to maintain contact with her erstwhile New Zealand ally through trade and diplomacy, the clear wish of New Zealand to re-identify as a British-dependent entity determined to put the war in the past was already under way.

Nevertheless, France remained (along with Britain) a significant global power, owing to the Versailles Treaty and post-war political and economic engagement. As a result, New Zealand was still drawn into interactions with France. While the other British Dominions chose a more independent path, New Zealand spurned the French offers of post-war friendship. Germany was already lost as a friend, and trading partner. New Zealand was left, by choice, diplomatically isolated while clinging culturally, economically and diplomatically to the remnants of a British Empire that had no need for her former colony.

Chapter Seven

Relics from France

> It is with astonishment that Frenchmen who visit Britain run up against a host of ancient prejudices which they thought were long extinct. Daily one hears of the ambitions of Louis XIV or Napoleon, for the British people are evidently not quite sure that the French have definitely renounced these ideas.
>
> André Siegfried, 1924, Geographer, philosopher and member of the 1918–19 Mission to New Zealand.[1]

The British dislike of the French that André Siegfried noted resulted from the reinstatement of the popular version of Anglo-French history that was rooted in the Revolution and the Napoleonic Wars. This version of France had successfully survived in colonial New Zealand despite the favourable presence of Frenchmen such as Captain Lavaud, Bishop Pompallier and their successors. It may have been forced into hibernation during the war, but New Zealand's version of French history was subsequently reset to exclude these early, positive first-hand experiences. This collective national amnesia meant that local politicians such as Harry Atmore (the Independent MP for Nelson) could by 1924 refer to France, the recent ally of New Zealand and Britain, as if it were a distant country with no recently shared connection:

> Suppose [Atmore said], while the Kaiser was butchering Belgium because she barred his way to that dinner he was going to eat in Paris in October, 1914, that France had said, 'England is my hereditary enemy; Henry the Fifth, and the Duke of Wellington, and sundry Plantagenets fought me'; and suppose England had said, 'I do not care much for France; Joan of Arc and Napoleon and sundry other French fought me'. Suppose they had sat nursing their ancient grudges like that? Well, the Kaiser would have dined in Paris according to his plan.[2]

Many other casual post-World War I references to France included similarly dubious comparisons which muddled current events with historical precedent and traditional antagonisms. This folklore had already been embedded within New Zealand's landscape through place names such as Wellington, Nelson, Picton et al. It was supported through historical tropes delivered via media such as books and films that defined France and the French from a British viewpoint. Formal teaching of French history and the frequently unfavourable tone adopted when reporting French current affairs continually refreshed such interpretations. This version of Anglo-French relations left a view of France as a geographically and culturally remote place in constant rivalry with the British. The post-war re-establishment of this natural order in New Zealand was helped by the patriotic sentiment which developed from being a member of a victorious Empire, alongside the primacy given to the idealised British rural way of life. It was a reversion that was relatively easily accomplished because most of the post-war contact that could have delivered favourable, counteracting views of France was restricted to intellectual circles within the local cultural elite and the polity.

During the nineteenth and early twentieth centuries the English had come to see themselves as a more 'harmonious and more stable' people than the 'others'. This opinion was inextricably linked to the image of a predominantly rural Britain – as the United Kingdom was still imagined to be by many New Zealanders. It was a powerful image but in truth it was a mirage. England was being extensively modified by the industrial development which had begun in Victorian times.[3] There was therefore a disconnect between the affectionately imagined pre-industrial, rural images of New Zealand's Britain and the landscapes experienced by the English masses during the early twentieth century.

The colonial New Zealanders' self-assigned task was to transform their local surroundings into a likeness of an idealised rural England, for if New Zealand came to resemble a bucolic England, Britain's cultural and historical roots would be revalidated as a legitimate template for New Zealand's own origins and cultural identity. Using the names of the British heroes who had defeated France to label New Zealand was part of the process. The renaming served to culturally annex the land which the British settlers had already physically appropriated. It reinforced the settlers' right of occupation through military conquest. Hence the City of Nelson with its Trafalgar Square and its Collingwood, Hardy, Nile and St Vincent Streets is a living monument to the Napoleonic Wars. Wellington's Waterloo Quay commemorates the city namesake's famous victory while Auckland has a Waterloo Quadrant. This colonial rechristening alienated the Māori place names and exiled them to locations far from the city centre while their British substitutes – many with scarcely hidden references to the evils of France – were placed directly in the New Zealanders' day-to-day lives.[4]

The presumed collective aspiration for a rural way of life in a replicated little England resulted in the offer to returning servicemen of a land settlement scheme. Rural settlement along with geographic and cultural isolation from the trauma of France would nurture the links with Home. There was, however, a disconnect between the image and the realities of wartime Britain. That had become apparent to Prime Minister Bill Massey's tourists (as the army volunteers were affectionately termed) when they visited the Old Country. The imagined and idealised rurally based economy of small-farm England was inconsistent with the reality of large tenanted estates owned by the

United Kingdom's aristocrats and gentry and newly monied industrialists. The Constable-like images existed alongside a crowded, industrial sprawl inhabited by the urban poor, all of which was still controlled within a rigid class structure. It was the French landscape (outside the immediate zone of conflict) that appeared to be a better fit, thus creating an awkward dissonance which was not easily resolved since Britain's anti-French heritage was so firmly implanted in the New Zealand mindset.

Evidence of the true nature of France was reinforced in New Zealand through historical fiction largely sourced from England. There were 'novels of the recent past' somewhere between history and the real experiences of the authors. Over one and a half thousand novels on the French wars were published in the United Kingdom, and according to British library records they were extensively read.[5] There was a '...cascade of popular biographies ... and historical novels ... exploring every imaginable angle of the revolutionary period between 1789 and Napoleon's downfall...'[6] Nelson and Trafalgar, Wellington and Waterloo made great material for novels and these were significant subjects in shaping Victorian and Edwardian images of manhood and national identity. Admirals, generals, battles, heroes and victories became part of Britain's national narrative. The genre is narrow in focus and understates both the global implications of the French Revolution and the involvement of the rest of Europe in the Napoleonic Wars.

A general review of books, published in the *Northern Advocate* in June 1925, suggests that literature featuring Napoleon and the Revolution was well known to New Zealand readers. The writer stated that 'goodness only knows' how many books had been written covering Napoleon and the Revolution. For the British and New Zealand reader, *A Tale of Two Cities* (Charles Dickens, 1858) delivered a metaphorical message of redemption, sacrifice and survival involving the traditional protagonist. The *Advocate* reported that a van was needed to deliver the 'hundreds of volumes' Dickens borrowed in preparation for writing *A Tale of Two Cities.* These came in turn from amongst the 'enormous' number Carlyle had amassed when writing his own history of the revolution.[7] The readers' perception that these were factually based, mainstream historical literature topics was reinforced by such reporting. The influence of popular authors such as Dickens was amplified through public readings. In some cases, these events were intended for an intellectual, highbrow audience. Monologue extracts from popular novels were read and then supplemented with expert comment from the lecturer on the authors' works, illustrated with verbatim quotations.[8] Even for those not attending, the newspaper reviews of these events created an impression that the works were based on authoritative and reliable historical sources. These public lectures continued even after the 'movies' became an accessible and regular recreation.

Through repetition in the available media the 'Terror' of the French Revolution became a metaphor for the French national character and by implication the English became a mirror image: of similar form but characteristically opposite. In London, Madame Tussaud's made extensive use of Napoleonic memorabilia (Napoleon Bonaparte's coach was one artefact on display) so that fiction and non-fiction were fused in the public mind through the use of real visual stimuli. It was as if seeing the objects made the story true, although the legitimacy of the subject could be undermined by tilting the balance away from the legend and towards the mortal man, thereby avoiding any suggestion of god-like status.[9] The exhibits could not of themselves tell the story. They depended on a narrative to give them meaning rather than, as the public may have assumed, the opposite being true. The illustration or model or representation therefore became evidence which implicitly proved the legend.[10] Even *sans* the physical evidence, reports that it existed added credence to the narrative. In a similar manner, the *Ashburton Guardian* felt it newsworthy to report (in June 1919) that one of Napoleon's 'silk stockings' had been sold for £50.[11] This was 'evidence' that Napoleon was real and that the British interpretation of him as a villainous ruler was correct.

Significantly, there was a break between (approximately) 1910 and 1920 in the displays in England of such memorabilia to allow for the *entente cordiale*. Unlike pre- or post-war civilian visitors, the New Zealand soldiers on leave could therefore visit England without being exposed to any overtly anti-French propaganda. Business as usual was resumed thereafter with the relevant exhibits restored to prime display spaces. In New Zealand the much-publicised vandalistic destruction of the bells in the Christchurch (German) Lutheran church to supposedly allay French sensitivities showed a similar degree of support for the French, but by 1925 the *Northern Advocate* was reporting that the Aldershot 'tatoo' (sic) again included a performance re-enacting the Battle of Waterloo. Trafalgar Day celebrations also resumed, signalling that a regression to the old attitudes was acceptable within seven years of World War I ending.[12] Through such devices the story of the French as a nation of revolution, 'crime and violence' was resuscitated and perpetuated despite the contrary evidence from the successful *entente* and the World War I alliance.[13]

The French goods available in England and New Zealand commonly consisted of luxuries – cognac and textiles being classic examples – that fuelled an image of '…elegant and easy living'. This raises speculation as to the dissonance thus created. The contradictory images could apparently coexist because they were simultaneously 'selective and generalised'.[14] In New Zealand these products were freely available alongside the printed word. They provided a substitute for first-hand experience of the artefacts, tombs and memorabilia. Together with the histories both factual and fictional, the cultural influences, the evidence painted on the street signs and the merchandise available in the shops, there was a sufficiency of anecdotal evidence to reinforce the British version of France in post-war New Zealand.

Newspaper publicity boosted post-war awareness of French-related movies and this concurrently increased interest in the Anglo-Saxon version of French history that was frequently used in literary classics. The silent movie version of *A Tale of Two Cities* was launched in New

Zealand in late 1917 and went on to achieve national distribution in 1918, supported by extensive print advertising. Presumably the United States Fox organisation saw little contradiction in distributing a movie implicitly critical of France even as the United States was being readied politically for joining (on 6 April 1917) the much-derided European War. While the frequent mentions in the newspapers pre- and post-1918 suggest that the novel mainly attracted the interest of the cognoscenti, it was the movie version that won over a broad audience after 1918 and was therefore influential in highlighting the Revolution in the same year that the war in France ended. There was an intersection between fact and fiction as the New Zealand public was confronted with the reality that the war had been fought to defend a nation responsible for a particularly bloody revolution.

This contradictory image of France, based on self-selected, popular sources, probably extended throughout society. A common trope in New Zealand's biographical political historiography is the description of the self-made success – often applied to politicians – who compensated for a lack of formal education through their own extensive reading.[15] This well-meant praise does not acknowledge the widely differing sources the self-schooled may have been exposed to, especially at a time when secondary education was far from universal. The resulting (predominantly British sourced) pre-war knowledge was consequently inconsistent and arguably historically inaccurate both in matters of fact and in interpretation when compared with recent French history scholarship. This was compounded by the diversity in New Zealand's political leadership. British and French politicians were commonly drawn from a small, formally educated elite, whereas New Zealand's pre-war and immediate post-war leadership was more broadly based. It included both locally born politicians and British immigrants from all social classes. Owing to their educational diversity and the disparity in their personal experiences, they did not share a common version of pre-war French history. The result was a leadership cohort whose knowledge and interpretation of France frequently differed from that of their European and British counterparts.[16]

The anti-French bias was further emphasised through the post-war school syllabus that highlighted the various factors had contributed to the Allied victory in the World War I.[17] While the superiority of the white races over all others was an inherent part of the mindset, it was the political coherence of the British and the Empire that had made the difference. Since so few of the pupils progressed beyond primary level these messages were necessarily targeted at a younger, impressionable cohort. During the war, a failure to openly accept oaths of loyalty, salute the flag or otherwise publicly demonstrate one's patriotism could lead to ostracism or even prosecution, at least until Ormond Burton's famous refusal to accept the oath led to change.[18] Remnants of this indoctrination still survive today in the military displays used to open significant sporting events on or near Anzac Day as well as through resistance to changing a national flag which still includes the Union Jack.[19] Although no longer recognised for their British origins, such ceremonies and symbols show how embedded the Empire became and how entangled the identity of Britishness was with being a New Zealander, to the necessary exclusion of the 'others'.

World War I was New Zealand's first direct, large-scale exposure to France since the initial competitive colonial period (approximately 1820–50). As we have seen, negative perceptions of the French had been sustained through the extensive reporting of the Dreyfus affair, the Fashoda incident and news of the brutal suppression of various indigenous populations by the French.[20] Entering a war in an alliance with the French was a jarring inconsistency with these sentiments. If the proposition had been presented to the New Zealand electorate without the background of the *entente cordiale* and the British link, it is questionable whether the public would have seen common cause with France. The 1914–18 wartime alliance was therefore a significant change. The experience that the New Zealanders acquired, both first hand and indirectly from the war, suggested that this created an irreconcilable dissonance between the France of the past and the present.

When the troops returned, the pre-war, often fictionally based versions of France had to be reconciled with real experiences in France. There are at least four distinct classes of narrative covering 1914–18 from a New Zealand viewpoint that contributed to this process. The first of these – the earliest 'real' accounts – were clearly meant for those who had not been to France and seen the war at first hand. They attempted to present a simple, factual account of events without interpretation. These apparently independent, unbiased and non-fictional government-sponsored histories did much to shore up the official version of the conflict. These versions were often treated as unchallengeable in the inter-war years.[21] A second genre came from the soldiers' own wartime correspondence which gave a more direct description of day-to-day events. In many cases these appeared less than forthright on the realities of the wartime conditions.[22] Third is the soldiers' edited wartime experiences as reinterpreted by later historians such as Glyn Harper, Jane Tolerton et al., but influenced by Paul Fussell who brought a raw, unromantic reality to the genre. Finally, there is the almost sacred first-hand family account, that of the taciturn, perhaps shell-shocked veteran and his kin who carried the memory-legend as an infrequently mentioned personal experience or second-hand account. This version was an acceptable part of the New Zealand stereotypical male as seen in Jock Phillips' *A man's country?* The Mark I New Zealand man of colonial settler heritage was expected to show stoic acceptance of difficult circumstances without complaint or rebellion. This image in particular was perpetuated through the collective World War I experience, as recounted by the returning soldiers.[23] All these versions had to be processed alongside the semi-fictional drama and movies that presented yet another view of the war from a more creative and artistic perspective.

The first of these versions – the official accounts produced in the immediate post-war years – attempted to give a factual interpretation of events in France while sometimes drawing on the first-hand experiences of their respective authors.[24] Although now seen to be of limited scope as secondary sources, these volumes have assumed close to primary source status in their own right as contemporary versions of military reporting. When they were first published they did receive some muted criticism. *The General History* dealing with the three campaigns of 'Gallipoli (including Egypt), France and Sinai-Palestine' was described as '…tolerant and fair, devoid of extravagance and criticism; they are plain, well written and accurate narratives that deserve a high place in the Dominion's literature'. Sir Guy Powles' contribution, *The Story of Two Campaigns* dealing with the events in Gallipoli-Egypt, received critical approval. The volume on France was, however, characterised as 'not an easy book to read', while *The Auckland Regiment* history caused outright discomfort. It was severely criticised for including Mr Burton's 'unjust criticism'. Descriptions of drunkenness, cowardice and incompetence amongst the troops were not considered appropriate subjects at the time of publication. These were 'harsh and irrelevant statements' according to the reviewer (J.H. Luxford), but the substance was not directly challenged.[25] Too much reality created a dilemma that was also evident in the Napoleonic War-based fiction. The factual account had to be adjusted to suit audience perceptions and sensitivities.

The second version was based on the first-hand personal accounts from the young men of New Zealand who volunteered in 1914. The enlistees had what would have seemed to be a one-off chance to tour the old world.[26] They were optimistic, as young people about to travel are, and they had widespread public support when they left. Many were sightseers disguised as soldiers – an example of military-led mass tourism.[27] Those who served in France brought with them an assimilated legacy – that set of beliefs and truths used to fill gaps in human knowledge – that while not overtly Francophobic did not extend to a collective embrace of the French nation.[28] It was their collective experience which was to shape their lives and to influence other New Zealanders' views of France in the inter-war years. As is the case with sightseers in general, the soldier-tourists had a firm idea of what they wanted to see when they set off and France was not the main attraction. Although the troops were initially sent to the Middle East, when they did travel on to Europe it was their idealised homeland, 'blighty', they really wanted to visit.[29] Some leave was taken in France, but the men looked forward to visiting the United Kingdom every eighteen months or so.[30] Many would still have had intergenerational relatives there, perhaps only once or twice removed. Parents and grandparents no doubt urged the young soldiers to visit an imagined and idealised Home.[31] France was therefore a lesser, local alternative; Britain was the main event.

The anecdotes, postcards, letters, memorabilia and selected images of the landscape sent home from France by the New Zealand soldiers included extensive reports on the individual writers' wellbeing and nostalgic discussion of memories from home. When the historians selected material from these writings, they naturally chose content associated with the progress of the war, the location of the sender and the soldiers' day-to-day wartime experiences. That is why much of New Zealand's World War I writing concerning France is about the conflict. *Just to let you know I'm still alive*, Glenn Reddiex's work on the use of the postcard format, contains '…examples of the type of postcards that were in circulation and used by New Zealanders during the First World War'.[32] If these are representative examples (rather than selections made by the author), then it seems virtually all the images were military related – uniforms, trenches and equipment predominate. The landscape, apart from military engineered structures and topographical features, was vague and indistinct. There are virtually no scenes of France or French people, urban or rural. The soldiers' immediate surroundings were apparently mud, trenches, barbed wire, trapped horses and guns. It could have been anywhere in the world. Cowan's written descriptions are similar. France is simply the setting for the war.[33] If the selected material used by historians today is representative of the soldiers' accounts from the war, then nearly all the soldiers and the initial recipients of their letters would have seen of France was a war zone.

Many of the war-themed accounts we read today are based on similar post hoc selections rather than a random selection of the soldiers' written and pictorial accounts. In fact, 'the front line' was a relatively narrow strip measured in yards not miles, bisecting a geographically huge country. Although the war images presumably heightened awareness that France was the setting for a catastrophic event, questions persist about the communication between the returning soldiers and those who remained at home. An exchange with the cruelly punished pacifist Archibald Baxter, a victim of Field Punishment No.1, exemplifies the lack of communication which probably influenced societal attitudes in the inter-war years:

'*And you were in France?*

Yes, I was in France

How lovely for you to get a chance to see all those places. I believe France is a very beautiful Country.

Yes, it was lovely for me'[34]

There was another version of France that helps explain this discrepancy. The postcards in Lieutenant Horopapera Karauti's collection – presumably pre-approved and mass produced –include some scenes of war-damaged, post-combat landscapes, but they also show well-fed and clothed soldiers inspecting the destruction.[35] There are no bodies or obvious wounds or fresh graves. The viewer is drawn to the conclusion that the French civil and religious infrastructure had been badly damaged by enemy activity with minimal human injury.[36] The reproductions are grainy black and white prints which imply reality and gravity. Another genre in Lieutenant Karauti's collection is labelled 'Boulogne-sur-mer'. These feature seaside scenes, including a gnarled looking fisherman (*Type de Pêcheur*) and a young woman in her Sunday best (*Une Boulonnaise Toilette de Ville*). There is no obvious evidence of war, nor is there any apparent distress. The viewer might easily believe that the sender had visited – perhaps while on leave – the

French seaside and seen holiday-makers and day-to-day French life much as it had always been. Some of these cards appear to have been photographed in black and white then coloured or tinted during the printing process to give a lighter touch, as was the practice before colour photography became common.

A third set of postcards in this collection straddles the first two. Whimsically labelled 'In the Field, Western Front, Somewhere in France' but with the telling subtitle 'Anniversaire' these are peaceful rural scenes. Typically, there are one or two trees in the foreground with flowers and green fields beyond; in the distance a faint reddish glow which may have represented the sunrise or the sunset or (more probably) a hint of an out of sight battle. No people are visible. The deliberate ambiguity leaves the interpretation to the viewer within the context of a generally peaceful, rural France. The dissonance between the current version of wartime France commonly displayed in pictorial war histories, and this contemporary version presented without commentary, provides a clue to the ambivalence surrounding France and the war and its consequences.

There is an important caveat to apply to the soldiers' contemporary writing (when comparisons are drawn with their later recollections). Douglas Wood's letters to his sister provide a robust illustration. Apparently bland and uninteresting, they include few mentions of France – apart from the weather – but they do contain detailed comments and advice on the domestic events that Wood had left behind. Perhaps less articulate than others, Wood would nonetheless have been alert to the strict admonishment on the envelopes to write only of 'private and family matters', and that is what he did.

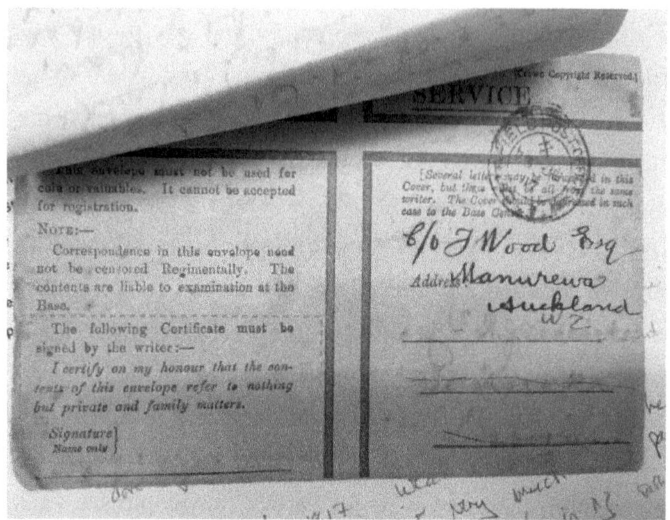

[Crown Copyright Reserved.]

SERVICE

... envelope must not be used for coin or valuables. It cannot be accepted for registration.

NOTE:—

Correspondence in this envelope need not be censored Regimentally. The contents are liable to examination at the Base.

The following Certificate must be signed by the writer:—

I certify on my honour that the contents of this envelope refer to nothing but private and family matters.

Signature (Name only)

[Several letters may be [illegible] in this Cover, but these [illegible] all from the same writer. The Cover [illegible] in such case to the Base [illegible]]

C/o J Wood Esq

Address Manurewa Auckland NZ

Figure 11 Declaration regarding soldiers' correspondence.

Given such a stern instruction enforced with the threat of military punishment and discipline as well as the difficulty for the less educated and articulate in describing a wholly new experience, it is unsurprising that many of the soldiers' private memoires say little about France the country. The vast majority of the private soldiers were not trained observers, historians or scholars and they probably wanted to convey as little as possible of their own privations while continuing an involvement in matters at a home to which they hoped to shortly return. The content of many of the letters are therefore a direct result of these motivations reinforced by orders to discuss only permitted topics.[37]

When the former Liberal Party politician W.P. Reeves gave his account of a visit across the channel during 1914 (the manuscript appears to have been subject to later editing as it includes the comment that this was 'early in the war' thus implying knowledge of later events), he commented upon the emptiness, the silence, the absence of young men and the apparent inactivity. The young and the old were continuing daily life by taking on work which neither had anticipated doing in normal circumstances at this stage of their lives. While many accounts from the serving soldiers mention activity, movement and social interaction, Reeves' writing suggests an empty countryside devoid of people and action.

Soldiers on manoeuvres (like sports teams) typically travel in readily identifiable, socially self-contained groups. They interact with outsiders collectively rather than as individuals. Their observations unconsciously record the manner in which the local populations react to the presence of what to the locals appears to be a large group of self-sufficient strangers. Reeves' observations reflect his intellect and education as well as a less intrusive civilian presence (to the extent he was in one incident suspected of being a spy). The influence from the bustle and disruption of massed troop movements are therefore absent from his observations. His comments give context to the soldiers' observations of French civilians or peasants going about their daily tasks with apparent disregard for the war.[38] Reading Reeves' account, it becomes apparent that the French civilians he saw were ineligible to serve by reason of age or gender. They were trying to maintain the domestic economy of a largely rural country as best they could. It was the soldiers who were the intruders. The soldiers' observations were those of the impromptu actor who stumbles on stage during a live performance without the self-awareness of the role they were inadvertently playing. In that context, the apparent indifference that the soldiers described was the day-to-day struggle for existence by a very stressed French civilian population who were probably resentful of any military disruption.

Revisionist World War I historians such as Professor Glyn Harper, Jane Tolerton et al. have created a new genre by reinterpreting a selection of the soldiers' first-hand accounts. These make up the third version of New Zealand's wartime history. Johnny Enzed, Professor Harper's fictional, composite soldier, was aware of – and recorded – his observations of the French countryside as did Cecil Malthus, his non-fictional contemporary. Of the two, it was Malthus who savoured the French connection, and was to return in a civilian capacity.[39] Harper's Johnny Enzed enjoyed his leave in France and was '…careful not to abuse it'.[40] Despite favourable comments on the *estaminets* where soldiers enjoyed convivial company with food, drink and socialising, Johnny Enzed remained a stranger in a foreign land. He picked up French phrases (Malthus was already fluent in French), but Enzed had difficulty communicating with the local civilians. When recalling individual acts of kindness and hospitality on the part of French civilians, the soldiers' descriptions imply that their warm welcome was unexpected and further suggests that they may have been anticipating an anti-New Zealand bias – perhaps based on their cultural identification with the British.[41] Predictably, those on leave in Paris visited the traditional tourist sites such as *la tour Eiffel*, *la Place de la Concorde* and *l'Hôtel National des Invalides*. Apart from visits to Paris, and patronage of local food and drink outlets, interactions with the French seem to have been occasional – and more often than not – accidental rather than deliberate. Some of these encounters resulted in misunderstandings or disruption to farming and other civilian activity. As one soldier put it, 'The French people were very good really – unless the troops did something silly'.[42]

There is a surprising paucity of comment on contacts with serving French soldiers. The British and French fought the same war on the same side but, as Roy Jenkins put it: 'The two sectors, due as much to the French taste for closed shutters as to British insularity, remained contiguous but almost hermetically sealed.' Sir Joseph Ward's claim that there was intermingling of the Allied troops which did much to bring the Allied nations into close association seems fanciful.[43] Accounts in letters home of interactions with the French are typically confined to civilian encounters on Sundays in town with beer, meals and girls; such carefree descriptions were presumably intended to make the front-line experience seem less traumatic. Writing from a war zone meant that these letters could only partially counter what Malthus refers to as the 'piffle' of the war correspondents. As both a participant and an observer he recognised that the letters were for domestic reassurance rather than intended as a historical record. The less than frank newspaper accounts further ameliorated the description of trench warfare to an unpleasant but acceptable experience, with the well-intentioned aim of easing concerns at home.[44] The soldiers' edited descriptions should therefore be treated with circumspection.

The fourth genre of the wartime history – the first-hand (usually verbal) accounts of the returned soldiers – was a self-edited adaptation of the personal experience. The returned soldiers were taciturn Kiwi 'blokes' who brought a new reality and a minimalist style to the trench warfare reality for family and close acquaintances.[45] One can understand the resentment of Johnny Enzed when told that the real heroes were those buried in France, not the soldiers returning home.[46] The recipients of this news were in the commonly accepted persona of the returned soldier unlikely to readily retell their own experiences anyway, but whether this was exaggerated by a wish to forget, or a perception that New Zealand people were not interested in hearing about the soldiers' real wartime experience, is unclear.

In sporting circles, New Zealand teams commonly share the adage that 'what goes on tour stays on tour' as an informal bond of confidentiality amongst the players. This perhaps partially explains the reticence of the returning soldiers to discuss details once they were home. When (former All Black) Chris Laidlaw interviewed one of his successors as the national team captain (Anton Oliver) both men related a common experience, namely that national sports teams performed for their mates, not for the brand or the flag or the anthem.[47] Anton Oliver linked his All Blacks experience to that of his war veteran grandfather who had described wartime sentiments in terms similar to those in the sports team narrative. Like the national game, combat was a shared personal experience of a few comrades fighting for their lives (or in sport, for the game) whatever the hue of the uniform.[48] Both interviewer and interviewee agreed that the public did not understand this truth in sport and war, because nationalistic propaganda and sports advertising suggested exactly the opposite. The heroic status accorded the amateur-era All Blacks in New Zealand culture sits awkwardly with the reality of their professional successors' financial motivation, because the official, commercialised version still draws on the image of a patriotic amateur player-soldier battling against professional opponents.

A similar sentiment – that the soldiers (at least in the early years) travelled to experience the world but then fought a very localised war of survival alongside their mates in France – was omitted from the official, patriotic legend of the returning soldiers. Just how much these sentiments influenced the children and grandchildren of that generation remains open to speculation. Equally questionable is the belief that the men understood the supposedly great cause for which they fought. Once in combat the men almost certainly fought for themselves and their companions' very survival.[49] It did not matter in what geography the war was fought, or what the geopolitical objective was. The war could have been fought anywhere from New Zealand's point of view with much the same strategic plan, namely winning through attrition. Both the location and the involvement of France are coincidental rather than fundamental.

The role of New Zealand in supporting Britain and their shared, almost sacred Empire heritage was nevertheless propagated in the everyday, public narrative as the cardinal reason for fighting battles in France. The soldiers' visits to the British tourist sites in the Empire's heart therefore became virtually obligatory pilgrimages. Britain was held in such regard that any discord with the idealised image attracted attention. At its most base level, the discovery that England had prostitution, poverty and a rigid class structure should not have come as a surprise.[50] Malthus noted the air pollution and crowding.[51] But if Britain was an idealised tourist destination and cultural museum, the French hinterland was the everyday weekend environment. France behind the lines was not a complete escape, but it was where one would expect to find food, drink and sexual adventure well away from England's imagined perfection, and even further from Johnny Enzed's memory of the 'frousy old wowsers' at home.[52] France was someone else's backyard to play in.

The tourists who returned to New Zealand from their regimented, packaged tour had seen – as soldiers do – much that they did not want to see; still less that they wanted to recall and retell. When the returnees remet those they had left behind, the common ground they returned to was their last mutually shared memory at the time of departing, as is the case for returning holiday-makers or expatriates when repatriated. There was a new reality and thereby a defining disconnect caused by separate experiences and growing apart. The suppression of memories in order to reintegrate into daily life became part of the identity of those who had first-hand knowledge of the conflict. In the absence of their account it was the physical memorials, the political platitudes and wishy-washy Anzac Day sentiment that filled the gap in the narrative. The questioning of returning servicemen followed a line of enquiry more appropriately directed to a returning holiday-maker: 'How was it?' Possibly because the ex-servicemen had acquired an image as men who drank and had seen 'vice', more detailed questions were not asked – or were only asked privately. This was nothing new; returned travellers have always edited their recollections to suit the audience. Many veterans simply wanted to get on with the rest of their lives. Their responses were consequently taciturn thus leaving an information deficit for those curious to know what had really happened 'overseas'.[53]

Overlaying these four accounts was the fictional genre typified by films set in wartime France. These added a layer of hyperbole to enhance the stories because the movie producers wanted to attract an audience and make a profit. Amongst these were some French-made films and other foreign productions but they all had only limited commercial appeal in New Zealand because they frequently relied on themes featuring war and plots that belittled Germany. Consequently, many were neither escapist enough on the one hand nor sufficiently relevant on the other to attract a broad post-war New Zealand audience. This presented a dilemma as the critics and reviewers sought to provide context and thereby a reason for cinemagoers to view them. *Le Figaro*'s announcement in August 1928 that *La Grande Épreuve* would be released and distributed in New Zealand (and other countries) through Paramount can be taken as a case study. The film was set in wartime France, although ten years had passed since the hostilities ended. The *New Zealand Herald* excitedly announced that it was produced with the full cooperation of the French Government, the participation of 20,000 troops and the use of the 'actual battlefields of Verdun, [and] the Marne…'. Local reviews were mixed and sometimes incoherent. The *Bay of Plenty Times* arranged fiction alongside hyperbole by claiming that: 'not one [picture] has shown the French nation's part in that great conflict and no matter what one thinks of war the mental outlook will undergo a change after seeing the "Soul of France"…' while saying little.[54]

The non-committal tone of other reviews suggests that the critic(s) relied on the publicity material and had not seen the movie as they do not seem to have realised that it was a comedy. The Bay of Plenty Times described it as 'a human document, real, vivid and dramatic'. By the time it was shown in Auckland it had been downgraded to a 'supporting feature'.

Figure 12 Movie promotion poster.

While not all French-related movies were about the war, many that were shown in post-war New Zealand were war-related or used the war as a background theme. *Hearts of the World* was dramatically described by the *Manawatu Standard* as:

> …mostly centreing [sic] around the war on the French front, and bringing home, in however minor a degree, the horrors and struggles of the terrible campaigns waged for so long over some of the finest country in Europe, now laying waste and desolate.

And further on in the review:

> …through the hideous war-scarred regions into which they have been transferred by the bestial brutality of the Hun invaders. It is a picture that will live in the memory for many a long day to come, for the cinematograph has been carried into the fighting line, and **faithfully** [*emphasis added*]

> produces some of the historic combats, with trench fighting, men going over the top, the great retreat of the Allies and their subsequent victorious advance, with tanks, pill boxes and murderous artillery outbursts, shrapnel barrages, the release of poison gas, bayonet charges, the surrender of Hun prisoners and other momentous happenings, including cavalry charges and infantry advances, with the recapture of the French village in which the story opens, the whole being cleverly woven together, and presenting the finest series of war pictures yet presented locally.[55]

A Soldier's Oath used a pre- and post-war French village setting; *The Firefly of France* featured an American aviator 'who foils the German's plots', while *The Brass Check*, set in a lunatic asylum, included an inmate in a padded cell who 'thinks he is the Kaiser and has dressed himself up grotesquely to aid his illusion'.[56] At the other extreme *The Better 'ole*, a movie adaptation of the stage musical, provided a light-hearted version of the war as seen through the experiences of the 'truthful types which are seen every day in our armies in the field'.[57] Although presumably filmed before the war ended and therefore released into a post-war market for which they were not intended, it is difficult to imagine a more inappropriate selection for developing a positive impression of modern France. Even movies using historical themes contributed to an image of France as a place of conflict, as the reviewers' summaries show.

There was one great truth about New Zealand's war that received scant attention for fear of exposing the desperate circumstances in the final phases. In 1917 France was desperately awaiting American intervention to save her (and her Allies) from potential defeat. The volatility and changeability of the French political circumstances – explained by the French historian Maurice Agulhon as the essence of being French even in a time of conflict – had erupted as a major threat to the war effort. The 1917 strikes and mutinies amongst the French seemed for some to be omens of another French Revolution. Agulhon justifies these rebellions as less than such because they did not take place in the front line. Likewise, the increasing number of French desertions were (in his view) simply typically Gallic demonstrativeness.[58] It is a distinction that no military force could accept in a time of war, and the uprisings were dealt with for what they were – mutiny. New Zealand's battlefield heroism in 1917, so often portrayed as a futile waste, was part of a desperately needed diversion to relieve the pressure until discipline was restored amongst the French. This version of history was a poor fit with the narrative of New Zealand's support for a heroic, besieged ally.

Commenting on these events, W.H. Triggs (a Member of the New Zealand Legislative Council from Canterbury who had visited post-war France) described the muddy morass where the New Zealanders had fought, notwithstanding that drought conditions prevailed during his trip. Even though Triggs was apparently letting the facts speak for themselves, he was adjusting his narrative to suit a received historical description which contradicted his personal observations. The muddy terrain explanation suited the World War I image of the battlefield conditions as a mitigating factor in the failure of the 1917 offensives, even as Triggs' own experience (obvious though it was) implied that an attack could have been advantageously delayed until the weather conditions improved. Moreover, the use of a Victorian-Edwardian narrative of futile but brave self-sacrifice helped divert attention from the point of the battle. Triggs lauded the New Zealanders' effort at Passchendaele and commented that although they had failed to achieve their primary objective, their action was 'absolutely essential' at the time because it relieved pressure on the French Front.[59] The significance of these comments does not appear to have been appreciated by the Legislative Council. Triggs' assessment seems to be the only public recognition in the immediate post-war New Zealand parliamentary record of just how close run the war's outcome had been owing to the lack of resolve within the army of the key protagonist, France. France owed much to the fortitude of her allies when her own will was ebbing.[60]

Had such been made explicit at the time, the post-war attitude of France's allies would presumably have assumed a very different tone, but the matter was successfully suppressed and left in abeyance, apart from this brief mention. Thus, New Zealand's France emerged from this version of the war with a largely unscathed military reputation. Nevertheless, although France was the victim, she remained an arm's-length ally because there was little or no meaningful connection between New Zealand and the French, whether military or civilian. In that respect the New Zealand soldiers replicated the standard tourist experience. The New Zealanders saw the sights (both the historical edifices and the battles in which they fought) but they did not experience France in the context of the political strain and disruption to local life beyond the weekend hospitality which was in any case adjusted to suit their needs. They do not appear to have understood the significance of the military engagements within the broader context of the war, nor did they interpret the war in its broader context within European affairs. The version of France they brought back to New Zealand was therefore easily assimilated into the existing histories.

What followed was an attempt to place France in the past and leave it enshrined as a sanitised place of memorial. First, however, the memories had to be dealt with. During their visits to England the New Zealanders had acquired some experience of the British class-based traditions and rituals used for post-conflict commemoration. They saw that burial within St Paul's Cathedral was reserved for the military leaders – Wellington and Nelson, most relevantly – not the common soldiers.[61] The example of honouring a common soldier was not unfamiliar in France, however. New Zealand readers of the *Evening Post* of 9 November 1929 would have seen a description of La Tour D'Auvergne, the soldier whose name is still called on ceremonial occasions by the Forty-sixth Regiment and whose heart is in the Chapel of St Gregory under the 'Dome of the Invalides' (sic) where Napoleon 'sleeps'.[62] In pre-World War I Britain – even where death and commemoration was concerned – there was unease regarding possible disturbance to the English class system if lower ranked participants were buried amongst the elite. Moreover, the bodies of those who died mutilated or wounded were depicted in a perfect image, such as that used for Captain Rundell Burgess in St Paul's who is represented as a near naked, classical figure. The usually male subjects appear with females in support or as angels alongside Britannia as a maternal figure.[63]

After access fees were finally abolished in 1851 (for the Great Exhibition) these images were more widely viewed. How many New Zealand soldiers saw them and the adjacent tombs of Wellington and Nelson in St Paul's and were thus influenced by the treatment of the elite in comparison with the French treatment of La Tour D'Auvergne and the dead from the British lower ranks remains speculative.[64] Whatever the case, the image of restored perfection after death became embedded in the post-war ideal through the neat rows of crosses prepared in France for those at home who never saw the battlefield realities. For years to come the ubiquity of service in France was likewise unpretentiously and seamlessly embedded in New Zealand's past.

OBITUARY

MR. WILLIAM MACKAY

(By Telegraph.—Press Association.)

CHRISTCHURCH, This Day

The death has occurred of Mr. William Mackay, aged 46, manager of the grain department of the Canterbury Seed Company. He was a prominent member of the Chamber of Commerce and treasurer of St. Paul's Presbyterian Church. He was born in Invercargill and served in France with the artillery.

Figure 13 Obituary Notice from 1935: *Evening Post*[65]

This cleansing isolated the war in France as if it had been a tragic and unavoidable event beyond local control, a task relatively easily achieved because the wartime contemporary newspaper reports, the soldiers' later accounts and the official post-war histories did not give a complete and frank account of the battlefield realities. Nor were the military problems France faced in 1917–18 acknowledged. Downplaying or ignoring the broader challenges that post-war France faced was part of a process which simplified the task of leaving France, but it necessarily restricted any broad post-war contemplation and reconsideration. New Zealand's world view was therefore blinkered and restricted within a corridor of limited options.

Chapter Eight

Reparation and repatriation – Versailles and beyond

New Zealand emerged from the war without a plan to guide the future relationship with France. This shortcoming was due to the lack of any clearly stated wartime objectives, apart from the tactical imperative of assisting the British. Without a strategic objective, any claims of victory or of a specific achievement were unverifiable. This gave credibility to those making the 'waste-and-futility' argument. Because the Massey Government was politically exposed in this respect, three interlocking post-war policies were developed to conceal the problem. These were aspirational rather than practical, they lacked clarity and they were frequently contradictory because they depended on Britain's own changing priorities. These post-war policies were never coherently and consistently articulated, so they can only be deduced from government actions and statements.

The first objective – typically described in generic phrases such as 'the war to end all wars' or 'never again' – was to symbolically leave Europe with all its apparently insoluble political problems by claiming the war had been won and the issues which led to it were resolved. It followed that France as the main location of the conflict could similarly be consigned to history, while due respect was given to those who had died there. This objective required sensitively curtailing the grieving and homage for the dead who remained in France. This was a delicate path to tread, for it required redirecting attention towards a future without France, while avoiding the appearance of insensitivity by implying the loss of life there had been pointless. The second objective was therefore to localise the commemoration and idealise the war by quickly erecting local replicas of the memorials being built in France. This (it was hoped) would symbolically distance France by placing it in the past rather than in the present, thereby avoiding continual retrospection, reassessment and pilgrimage.

The third objective was to reinforce New Zealand's self-assigned role as an essential producer of food for Britain. If the British economy came to rely on Empire-sourced food, as it had during the war (rather than relying on more conveniently obtained French or other European supplies), Britain would have an interest in New Zealand's future prosperity. The Empire could become a self-contained community and Britain would then have an interest in defending the ocean supply routes used to transport the produce, rather than bothering with Europe's problems. Quickly resettling the ex-soldiers on small (usually dairy) farms would also create a cohort of hard working, family orientated, small business-minded Reform Party voters (coincidentally the party of Prime Minister Massey). The emotional debt owed to the returned servicemen would be repaid while New Zealand's future as a primary produce-generating nation would be secured. The New Zealand Government's actions have been critically re-examined in this context.

The New Zealand histories of the war settlement conference and its immediate outcome typically bypass the broader international consequences of the peace process as if they were of little concern to New Zealand.[1] The Treaty of Versailles has instead been viewed as a redundant peculiarity with little apparent long-term local significance, except as the marker that formally ended World War I, and a document of unfulfilled promises which led to World War II (typically blamed on the failure of the United States to ratify the Treaty).[2] This last view merits a challenge. The scant mention of the Treaty in the general histories of New Zealand, and its absence from more recent multi-topic volumes such as the Rachael Bell edited volume *New Zealand Between the Wars* perpetuates the view that the 1919 Paris Peace Conference had little direct relevance for New Zealand. This is partly due to the apparently subservient posture adopted by New Zealand within the British Empire delegation at the time the Treaty was negotiated, alongside a general desire to rebuild a South Pacific British dependency, deliberately isolated from Europe's problems. Such sentiments were wishful thinking. The location of the 1919 Peace Conference in Paris demonstrated the extent of French global influence. A unique opportunity to shape events was recognised and then seized by France. Much of the world – not least the New Zealanders – ignored the implications, while metaphorically checking their timetables and glancing at their watches in anticipation of getting back into their home time zones, literally as well as in sentiment. The very fact of seeking independence and remaining free from international entanglements while continuing as an active participant in the British Empire was, however, a paradoxical quest.

From the extensive newspaper reporting related to Versailles it seems that contemporary New Zealand viewed the Versailles agreement as both a symbolic end to further direct involvement in European politics and – when the Anglo-French Guarantee Treaty of 1919 failed – the end of any obligation to support France.[3] It was, however, not that simple. Wartime objectives, the military outcome and the future of Europe were inseparable from issues surrounding the treatment of the returned soldiers, construction of memorials and graveyards, the future of the Empire, trade, and domestic political concerns in New Zealand's post-war years. Moreover, the societal and political differences that had been partially left in abeyance for the duration of the war re-emerged, in part because France sought to achieve her own post-war aims through the Versailles Treaty and its attendant security guarantees with the backing of New Zealand and the other Allies. These issues dominated New Zealand–French diplomacy in the immediate post-war years. The French position depended on maintaining a belligerent hostility towards Germany, a stance which left the Allies divided and in politically difficult positions. Punishment of – and extracting reparation payments from – Germany and her allies became the headline under which these differences were debated. The thousands of publications devoted to the reparations issue will not be re-examined here as the central issue is the New Zealand public's knowledge of events, and how the actions of France affected those perceptions as the topic ebbed and flowed in the local news.[4] New Zealand's seat alongside France on the victors' side of the table at Versailles presented a unique opportunity. Just what stance would most advantageously benefit New Zealand in the long term was less obvious. It seems that *carpe diem* was the chosen course.

Claims of victory when the war ended did not justify the hubris that followed, because New Zealand had not 'won' anything. Until America intervened in the later years of the war, France and her allies had been very close to defeat. New Zealand had been part of a coalition that had with American assistance achieved a position sufficiently dominant to temporarily thwart Germany, thus forcing an end to the fighting. Nothing was resolved as far as the traditional Franco-German antagonism was concerned. Evidence for the fragility of the victory claim was exposed when France made a determined effort to retain her wartime alliances, not least because an unallied France was in no condition to enter another conflict with Germany. Moreover, any hint that there was some legitimacy in Germany's pre-war stance or in her arguments against the imposed post-war conditions (it was not a mutual agreement as the word 'treaty' implies) exposed the weakness in France's post-war position and so were fiercely resisted.

This diversity in the New Zealand politicians' opinions shows that the point of the war was unclear. None of the following MPs' comments are necessarily contradictory – nor are they particularly controversial in isolation – but collectively they expose the differences of opinion and thus partially explain the lack of coherence in New Zealand's relationship with France once the war ended. J.P. Luke (Reform, Wellington North) had referred on 10 April 1918 to those who had survived Gallipoli and were now in France '…fighting for you and for me and for the cause of humanity', but what the 'cause of humanity' meant and what relevance conflict in France had to do with it was not explained. Two days later C.J. Parr (also Reform, Eden) referred to '…whether the Empire is to stand or fall is being debated tonight in bitter battle in the fields of France, and with it the issue of whether this little country is to maintain its independence and be a portion of that great Empire'.[5] In so doing he managed to assert both national independence and Empire membership, as if there was no contradiction between the two. Nor did he explain how winning battles in France could achieve either.

As late as 1919 Sir Joseph Ward was still struggling to articulate a trading policy which would on the one hand make it 'difficult' for former enemies – Germany being the case in point – to resume trading with New Zealand, but on the other would avoid placing New Zealand in a 'difficult' position once the mother country resumed trade with Germany. This was a foretaste of the post-war political bind that the New Zealand Government was in. As a result of various policies adopted during the war, such as New Zealand's concurrent support for the Empire, for France and for New Zealand's own commercial interests, a confusing array of contradictory international positions (affirming French security while supporting global disarmament being just two) had emerged. New Zealand having assumed independent, sovereign nation status by default when ratifying the Versailles Treaty had to reconcile these. When Sir Joseph Ward spoke in support of a resolution of appreciation and sympathy for the New Zealand servicemen he did say that the New Zealanders 'fought to maintain the freedom of this portion of the British Empire and other parts of the British Empire', although again the relevance of fighting in France against Germany went unexplained.[6] W.T. Jennings (Liberal, Waitomo) extended this to the 'right' of the men to aspire to freehold land, as this (he said) had been their reason for fighting 'so strenuously against the German hordes' in Belgium and France.[7]

Labour MPs, emboldened by their recent electoral gains, were not afraid to highlight these oddities and their vigorous rebuttals no doubt caused some squirming on the government benches. These inconsistent rationales undermine the consensus view that New Zealand's war was to support the British and the Empire, for if this were so why did so few politicians not simply say so without qualification? Presumably such a stance would have opened a political debate as to whether Britain and the Empire really were at risk and even if they were, how fighting a war in Europe to save the 'froggies' would help to save either. The political Centre-Right did not want to debate with the Labour-Left over this political ground, and even less over why Germany – previously a friendly and important trading partner – had been designated without qualification as the enemy.

Further complications with broader, longer-term consequences soon became apparent. Speaking during the debate held in response to yet another invitation for the Prime Minister to attend a forthcoming Imperial Conference, the Labour Party Opposition Leader H.E. (Harry) Holland laid down some important 'markers', one of which was to push Prime Minister Massey to seek self-determination for the peoples of India and Egypt. This was (as Holland pointed out) the original reason British statesmen had given for the war in France; to preserve the independence of other nations such as Belgium. Holland also reminded the House that the United Kingdom had rejected Ward's 1911 proposal for an Imperial Parliament because it would remove the power of the Home (i.e. British) Government to declare war without the consent of the Dominions.[8] These positions may have been somewhat consistent with the right of independence for Belgium, France and New Zealand, yet the Empire project was an explicit rejection of such rights for other nations. By 17 March 1921 Holland was certain enough of his political support to assert that while the New Zealand men had been told they were fighting for the defence of small nationalities, the big powers were secretly dividing the world up amongst themselves.[9] Colonel W.E. Collins speaking in the Legislative Council in 1922 neatly summed up the problems when he stated: 'It is now nearly four years since the Great War ended, and one cannot help asking what benefit any one has derived from the unparalleled loss of life…'[10]

In the immediate post-war years, the Allies had the option of either neutering Germany politically and economically and thereby creating what France assumed would be an impoverished non-threatening neighbour, or they could help Germany establish a functioning state in the image of the other Western democratic powers (the United Kingdom, France and the United States) and thereby achieve the same aim: turn Germany into a non-threatening force. The first option was the essence of the French policy while the latter alternative was advocated by the United States, Keynes and other progressive economists who foresaw the consequences of humiliating and subjugating Germany. The Allies – New Zealand included (with France being the exception) – lacked the will to execute the first approach which would have required force. On the other hand, they could not face their voters with an alternative which appeared to ignore the great personal losses and the promises to punish German aggression.[11]

The anti-German spirit aroused amongst the New Zealand public had heightened patriotic support for the war, but it was a contrived sentiment stimulated by propaganda, rather than a reawakening of any latent cultural bias. Pre-war Germany, with its significant ties to the United Kingdom through royalty, culture and trade, had been a supplier of high-end, specialist manufactured goods to New Zealand. Prime Minister Massey therefore had a difficult path through the Versailles process as he needed to adhere to the pro-French British policy of punishing Germany while simultaneously winning compensation for New Zealand's wartime losses, maintaining New Zealand's preferential trading position with the United Kingdom and dealing with French opposition to New Zealand's aspirations for British rule over the New Hebrides.[12]

This diversity of views and lack of a common post-war objective became obvious to the New Zealand public almost as soon as the war ended and the peace negotiations began.[13] The punitive French approach held that German participation in the new post-war world order was to be a reward for submitting to the French conditions. A 'leading French authority' argued that German membership of the League of Nations should be conditional on Germany meeting the provisions of the Versailles Treaty. The proposed exclusion of Germany rather missed the point because if, as the quoted expert M. Burgecix (probably Léon-Victor-Auguste *Bourgeois*, later to be an active supporter of the League) claimed, the two main functions of the League were to be arms limitation and imposition of penalties for infringements, removing Germany from the League's jurisdiction also removed her from any voluntary reason to comply with the former without removing the latter.[14]

It was in this unsettled mood that direct post-war diplomatic exchanges with France began through the General Pau led French Mission's Australasian visit of late 1918 to early 1919. The Mission was a direct extension of the Clemenceau Government's single-minded drive for victory which was to be followed by punishing Germany.[15] The message for New Zealand and Australia was direct, consistent and unambiguous. General Pau praised the Australasian troops and their leadership while placing the collective hopes of the Allies in a future of 'fraternity, greater liberties and greater civilization'. In so doing he echoed the French revolutionary motto of *liberté, égalité, fraternité*. Such a reconciliatory spirit was not, however, to be extended to Germany. As Pau put it, 'no punishment for Germany would be complete until she was defeated on German soil…'[16] He accepted that considerable resources would be needed to do so.

There is a consensus in the academic literature that Germany's unwillingness to accept the peace conditions arose because Germany – as far as her public could see – was neither demonstrably broken militarily nor economically damaged when the war ended. Therefore, when Germany signed the armistice without substantive evidence by way of invasion or conquest to show that Germany had been defeated, the 'stabbed-in-the back' narrative gained currency with the German public. Germany remained the most powerful state in Europe while the term 'armistice' suggested a temporary ceasefire rather than a surrender.[17] The point that Germany had not herself experienced the horrors of war was a consistent theme from the French. For that reason (the French believed), notwithstanding the repudiation and disgrace of the former German leaders, German aspirations remained. General Pau repeatedly used quasi-religious idioms to reiterate that France and Britain had had God on their side, thus implying that the proposed punitive action (Germany 'must be quickly and strongly punished') was morally legitimate. Germany's crimes included aspiring to acquire material wealth from the rest of the world (i.e. possessing an empire) and her overblown pride. (A cynical observer could claim that neither characteristic was in short supply from the French or the British in the first days after victory.) While stressing the need for fairness, Pau did say that Germany must pay for the war damage and give a warranty against future wars.

New Zealand was anxious for those serving to return home, a subject of greater concern than invading Germany or hearing praise for the dead from visiting Frenchmen. After all, if the Allies had won why was any further military action needed? Invasion and occupation of Germany was too much to ask of the New Zealand soldiers still in Europe. The newspapers reflected this view with their frequent references to repatriation plans. New Zealand was therefore understandably disinclined to contribute to the considerable resources that General Pau accepted France would need to invade Germany. The few New Zealand soldiers who did cross into Germany were met with sullen disapproval and resentment which contrasted with their understandably more welcoming reception in Northern France. Despite this, once in Germany the New Zealanders fraternised, shared their supplies in return for favours, and patronised the prostitutes, just as invading armies have always done. One soldier (Bert Stokes) recalling his time in Germany said that the New Zealanders had '…much more affinity with them [the German public] than the French. We didn't like the French very much…' This seemed to have been based on the suspicion and resentment that arose from the soldiers observing French farmers going about their day-to-day activities close to the lines, within range of the guns where New Zealanders were dying.[18]

Germany's post-war opinions were extensively reported in the New Zealand press. As early as January 1919, articles based on reports from German correspondents were unequivocally of the view that the peace as proposed would prevent Germany from rebuilding economically, while occupation of the vital mining areas would lead to a 'slow and painful death'. Germany would be better not to sign, as the German state would simply collapse under the imposed terms while German workers became the 'slaves' of the French. Strikes and disruption since the end of the war had already made the indemnity load extremely burdensome. Annexation of the Saar, loss of her colonies and dispossession of 'Dantzig' (sic) made it nearly impossible for Germany to meet the imposed indemnity payments.[19]

While recognition had to be given to the war dead and French political concerns, it was the survivors and New Zealand's immediate future which concerned Prime Minister Massey. Fixated on his dairy-centric small farming plan, he pushed the international issues aside and ignored alternatives. His post-war objective of retaining New Zealand's place within the Empire by turning New Zealand into Britain's main supplier of dairy produce was easily explained to the public and appeared simple to execute. All that was needed was the acquisition of land suitable for subdivision, followed by conversion to higher quality dairy pasture using a reliable and cheap source of phosphate-based fertiliser. Additional farmers could be recruited from the ranks of ex-servicemen, supplemented with British immigrants. The sea routes essential for exporting the resulting produce would be defended by the Royal Navy.[20] Matters concerning France and European stability and trade in non-dairy products from the wool and meat industries were distractions and Massey did his best to avoid involvement with them.[21] Massey also deliberately overlooked the implications for New Zealand of Britain's evolving role in global affairs, her changing relationship with France and the important domestic changes occurring within the United Kingdom which would affect trade policy. New Zealand could not, however, seal itself off within the Empire as long as the United Kingdom remained a free-market trader and a globally engaged world power. Despite these contradictions Massey, who showed an astute appreciation of the public mood throughout his political career, probably accurately reflected the sentiment within the New Zealand electorate.

Massey's conduct at Versailles nevertheless tends to be portrayed as that of an unsophisticated and bumpkinesque character (with his small moustache and hat his visage is vaguely suggestive of Charlie Chaplin's screen image) intent only on securing mandates over the Pacific territories of interest to New Zealand.[22] Massey did foresee the uncertainty for the French resulting from the untested, experimental nature of so many of the Versailles proposals. He also appreciated that French fears about German intentions were not unreasonable, especially if France did not occupy the left bank of the Rhine. Above all, the complexities of the Treaty and the many difficult issues that were left for later settlement were certain to lead to discontent. The Allies had motivated their citizens through a combination of patriotism and appeals to the righteousness of their cause in response to the injustices of the enemy. They could not then ignore the payback implied by the public investment in the war. Lloyd George had contested and won the 1918 election in the United Kingdom by promising to punish German 'war criminals' (revenge for lost lives), gain compensation through reparation payments (material reward for wartime sacrifice) and all the while protect the domestic British market from product dumping (implying a better, economically secure future for the social classes who had provided most of the fighting manpower). These promises restricted Lloyd George's room for compromise during the Versailles negotiations, and by extension also constrained New Zealand's position.

The weight of New Zealand public opinion in general – and that of the troops in particular – was strongly anti-German and would have punished a softer line. The New Zealand soldiers were convinced – as Cecil Malthus explained – that Germany's invasion of France was the primary cause of the war. Any subsequent suggestion that the war was wrong was due to the appalling casualties and the conflict's duration, not because the war was seen as unjust.[23] France neither trusted Germany nor saw that France had done anything wrong, views which are difficult to refute. The British did recognise that German nationalism and living space demands had some legitimacy, given the awkward truth that Germany's broader aspirations were not dissimilar to those of Britain and France. Even the French left-wing newspaper *L'Humanité* foresaw trouble within an empire-colonial paradigm by noting that 'a large overpopulated country is, without discussion, deprived of all its colonies'.[24] Moreover, Britain seemed to tacitly concede that Germany did not and would not accept that she was solely to blame for a war which she did not in any case believe she had lost. Whether Britain eventually accepted that an economically strong Germany would ultimately safeguard European security (as was implied after the premiership of Lloyd George ended) remains uncertain but that position is accepted by some scholars.[25]

Both sides of the argument were clearly explained and cogently argued in the New Zealand newspapers, making the public well aware of these views and the possible consequences. As early as February 1919 the *Dominion* was presenting the German view that payment of reparations in labour or goods in lieu of gold would damage the Allied economies; that forced mining of Germany's mineral resources under duress would be 'humiliating and unprofitable;' and that intergenerational issues would arise.[26] Clemenceau was not backward in putting the French case. His language (the war had been won but this was simply a 'lull in the storm') conveys both the ongoing nature of the France–German rivalry and his urgency in pushing for French demands to be met. He raised fears that Germany could still ally with Russia despite the Allies' assurances they would assist France if this eventuated. Clemenceau's claim that Germany had attempted to destroy the French economy – hence the destruction in the northern *Departments* while German factories remained undamaged and usable – was a telling point. Reciprocating with punitive economic damage would neuter a traditional foe, with the side benefit of revenge.[27]

While Massey has been criticised for his stance at Versailles, a mutually acceptable resolution was beyond the capabilities of the best political leadership the world had to offer. The German Premier Scheidemann (who was just as subject as the Allies to domestic opinion) claimed that Germany was in a struggle for life, not nationalism or prestige, against the peace terms. He declared the Treaty unacceptable to 'cheering' from the House. In the same news item Belgium raised her claim for more African territory, a view which was consistent with the alliance partners' intent to treat large and small nations equally.[28] Possible grounds for settling the stalemate were nonetheless becoming clearer by May 1919, even if they were no more acceptable to either side than the earlier proposals. Germany would reluctantly make reparation payments but would not accept the designation of any payments as indemnity (punitive) levies. The urge to accept what was on offer and get home reflected the mood of the New Zealand population who wanted to return to an imagined, better past. Moreover, the distribution of a major prize, the German territories in the Pacific, had already been agreed. As *L'Humanité* put it:

> ...the great colonial states will keep their overseas possessions, which they will continue to exploit according to the savage methods of capitalist colonialism. ... This is the first act of the Peace Law! In the previous day, German colonies of the Pacific (New Guinea, etc.) were occupied by the British Dominions of Australia and New Zealand.[29]

and

> We must take advantage of the presence in Paris … of the British Dominions' representatives to resolve the issue of settlements … that the Allies share like thieves.[30]

New Zealand may have seemed to be better off than the European nations, but this was not the same as being as well as off as the public imagined New Zealand would have been without the war, especially given the appalling casualty rates.[31]

New Zealand was therefore drawn into the slipstream of French and British enthusiasm for punishing Germany by Prime Minister Massey's opinion being more or less in alignment with that of Lloyd George.[32] Ignoring Keynes' warnings of the potential consequences, Massey and Ward joined the rush to endorse the peace terms demanded by Britain and France. In a remarkable act of good faith, loyalty and patriotism, the initial discussion of the Versailles Peace Treaty in the New Zealand Parliament was held without any MPs – apart from Massey and the Leader of the Opposition – having copies to hand. Massey brushed this concern aside by claiming that the indexed version in *The Times* was better.[33] By way of an introduction to the ratification debate, Massey said 'several telegrams' from the Imperial Government had asked for Parliamentary approval, thus suggesting both a constitutional imperative and urgency to meet Imperial demands and complete the formalities.

During his speech Massey made a number of points that were subsequently contradicted – in some cases by Massey himself. By signing the Treaty in their own right, the Dominions (Massey claimed) ceased to be dependencies and became partners within the Empire. Taken at face value this interpretation permitted New Zealand as an equal partner to interact with France or any other country as freely as Great Britain herself, if she so wished, even without Britain's consent. Secondly, Massey repeated that Germany's burden as a result of the Versailles Treaty was not disproportionate to her crimes, a position maintained by France for many years to come. Whether this was so or not, the claim was contrary to expert opinion (Keynes' being the most notable example at the time) and it was not accepted by Germany.[34] Thirdly, although acknowledging the damage caused by Germany's destruction of French property and industrial capacity in the war occupied *Departments*, Massey nevertheless mentioned the opportunity that German now had to become a 'very successful competitor' in goods formerly produced by France, Britain and America. He went even further when he admitted that in some areas of production Germany was better than Britain. Despite this acknowledgement of the possibilities for New Zealand as a free-trading nation, Massey (frustratingly) did not allow himself to draw the obvious conclusion which his remarks presaged. Fourthly, while noting French representation on the proposed Council of the Great Powers (of the League of Nations) Massey claimed that the only guarantee of peace could come from the United States, the United Kingdom and France acting in unity (i.e. being in sole charge of world affairs). Despite this, Massey conceded that such a structure for maintaining world peace was not possible. He concluded with approbation for the French Army and people. These sentiments would prove to be the political high-water mark in New Zealand's support for France.[35] Thereafter the pro-French political tide slowly ebbed as the inconsistencies in these positions became clear.[36]

New Zealand signed and ratified the agreement as an independent state, notwithstanding the apparent constitutional contradiction in so doing while claiming to be an equal 'partner' within the Empire. New Zealand had therefore – at Britain's request – formally assumed a legal status under which she could take independent action, sign treaties, and therefore negotiate with France or any other country over her trading arrangements. The probable explanation for the British enthusiasm to obtain one signature per Dominion lies in the one-country/one-vote principle which Hall-Jones remarked upon. If the Empire was recast as a group of independent sovereign states it achieved increased leverage in any one vote per nation forum such as the new League of Nations.[37]

This simple rationale downplayed the constitutional significance of signing the Versailles agreement as a sovereign state, for New Zealand's definition of loyalty was now redefined. The test was no longer one of obedience to British/Empire direction(s). The elected government was now obliged to act in the first instance in the interests of its own citizens. Its most pointed implication came in the potential involvement of the Dominions in future wars.[38] Under Massey's own interpretation of the ratification motion, any Imperial edict ordering participation was voided. Only the Dominions' respective legislatures could grant the necessary authority. The requirement for the Dominions' consent through their respective sovereign parliaments was legislated through the United Kingdom's Anglo-French Treaty (Defence of France) Act, 1919.

On the other hand, nothing except emotion now prohibited New Zealand from developing a direct relationship with the French. To the contrary, if there was benefit for New Zealand in doing so, it followed that as a sovereign nation there was an implicit obligation to follow that course. It was the able and perceptive William Downie Stewart representing Dunedin West for Reform (speaking during the Peace Conference valedictory debate on a motion wishing Ward and Massey well on their mission to Europe/United Kingdom) who pointed out an obvious if emotive truth which arises from this interpretation:

> 'Ever since this Dominion was founded we have been under the protecting wing of Great Britain. She has guarded our shores... All that spirit has been removed by the rude shock of this war. We have seen that we cannot dissociate ourselves from world politics, however remote we may be…'[39]

Although Massey wanted to move away from involvement with France, the new global political order intervened as France attempted to ensure her allies both honoured their promises and did not forget Germany's culpability or perfidy. From a New Zealand perspective, parts of France were now a New Zealand cemetery and therefore de facto consecrated New Zealand soil. There was no possibility that France and the war could simply be forgotten. What then was to be the place of France in New Zealand's future? New Zealand presumptions of a vaguely defined but somehow better post-war world included a politically unified France committed to establishing a peaceful Europe. Arguably none of these conditions had existed since the French Revolution, nor had Versailles created them. Despite this, the reasons for the unsettled French political climate in the post-war years and the French inability to move on from the war seemed beyond the comprehension of the New Zealand politicians, as their subsequent actions reveal.

Chapter Nine

Return and remembrance

The unsatisfactory nature of the unratified Versailles settlement left the authorities to reconcile the hagiographic imagery of a noble death for a great cause with the realities of post-war politics. Any questioning of the war's purpose reflected doubt on the motivation of those who had ordered the troops to fight and by implication on the reason for the heroism and sacrifice shown by those who had died. Moreover, the messy practicalities of disposing of thousands of decaying (in some cases hurriedly interred) corpses had to be aligned with public expectations of appropriate treatment for the heroic dead. An obvious solution for the families was to exhume the soldiers' remains for ceremonial reburial in New Zealand. Such requests were obviously anticipated, for in a little publicised agreement the removal of any bodies, apart from those to be relocated to designated graveyards in France, was proscribed. This agreement was signed under French and British authority on 26 November 1918 just fifteen days after the armistice.[1]

> Article 3.
> Bodies buried in cemeteries or in military graves shall not be exhumed for transport to the United Kingdom or to another part of the British Empire without the approval of the Imperial War Graves Commission; the French Government undertakes to instruct the prefects to refuse all applications for

> permission for the removal of bodies unless preferred though the Commission.[2]

This decision blocked any hopes of locating, exhuming, identifying, embalming, and transporting the dead back to New Zealand. (It also sidestepped the issue of dealing with incomplete body parts.) The task would have been immensely resource intensive by requiring labour and financing over an indefinite period, as the discovery and exhumation of corpses a century later has shown.[3] A tortuously prolonged grieving period would also have kept the debate on the war's purpose active in the public discourse.

When the Liberal MP W.T. Jennings (who had himself lost two sons) raised the issue of exhumation and repatriation, Prime Minister Massey ducked behind the Imperial Authorities who were against this solution because it would lead to 'chaos'. His answer was not incorrect, but he must have been aware that mass repatriation was never a possibility. Massey did assure the House that the graves were being taken care of.[4] The following year a petition was presented on behalf of Haami Tutu requesting the exhumation and return of his son's remains at his expense. Again, the Defence Department advised that all such requests were being refused. The most likely reasons for this intransigence – aside from the outlined practicalities and fiscal issues – was the risk of exposing the relatives to the chaotic battlefield archaeology. To paraphrase Paul Fussell, the image of the dead being gently laid to rest was often far removed from the reality of their mode of demise and burial. Initially the French Government resisted similar requests from French parents for reinternments in village cemeteries but a 'right to a free annual visit' was eventually granted and then on 28 September 1920 the French Government 'gave in' and allowed repatriation of bodies at the state's expense.[5] New Zealand parents may have become aware of this change, but if so there is no evidence of a further push for New Zealand reburials.

If exhumation and repatriation was denied then perhaps one soldier could be symbolically re-interred in New Zealand. Massey (probably unintentionally) raised that possibility when he read to the House a cablegram detailing arrangements for the re-interment in Westminster Abbey of an unknown warrior 'taken from amongst those buried in France'.[6] A similar re-interment for a New Zealand soldier did not take place until 2004, possibly because one repatriation may have established a precedent for all, or perhaps because one British soldier buried in New Zealand's metropolis at the heart of the Empire was judged to be representative.[7] For the New Zealanders who wanted the bodies returned, France became a place where the dead were held in eternal exile. As if to permanently extinguish the possibility of disinterment and reburial in New Zealand, the battle exhumations were declared completed in November 1921, after what was described as six systematic searches.[8]

Traditionally sailors and soldiers had been buried where they fell (whether at sea or on land) with exceptions made for the admirals and generals. After the battle of Waterloo, the dead were interred in mass graves while after Trafalgar it was Nelson's corpse that was returned to England. A common soldier (or sailor's) identity was thereby incorporated into a collective loss. Mass interments made the burial/battlefield sites worthy of mass visits while assuming the features of pilgrimages. David Lloyd has identified three characteristics that transform what otherwise might be considered a site visit into a pilgrimage: firstly, the scale (of the losses); secondly the spiritual nature of the struggle (with a quasi-religious sacrifice of the innocents and the promise of redemption), and thirdly the sanctification of the ground, rather like the Gettysburg battle site of Lincoln fame.[9] All three conditions could be met through visits to places of mass interment in France.

British sources reported pilgrimages to France for the poor. These included descriptions of prayer and the 'great comfort' for those participating. Appropriate though these visits were for less well-off

British residents, similar expeditions were beyond the resources of many families or the New Zealand exchequer. Visits such as that organised by 'Bienvenue française' for 200 female teachers from Canada and New Zealand and other Empire countries (the visit seemed to be restricted to British Empire participants despite the headline), to see the battlefields and the sites of Paris were more exclusive and were obviously organised to further French interests ('these initiatives which can only serve our cause with our friends'). Nonetheless, they were still described as pilgrimages.[10]

Sir James Allen (now the New Zealand High Commissioner in London) accepted that journeys such as those described by the Rev. Mullineux MC during a London lecture (attended by Allen who lost a son at Gallipoli) were all but impossible for many New Zealanders to contemplate, but Allen did note 'the intention to try and place before relatives some impression of what the completed cemeteries were like'.[11] Consequently, with no possibility of mass visits or of repatriation of the New Zealand remains, the care of the graves in France assumed additional significance as did their replication in New Zealand. The need for the goodwill of the French locals was essential, especially in the months before formal war cemetery construction began. In this context, the Westland MP T.E.Y. Seddon (Liberal and son of the famous 'King' Dick) asked for the publication in both British and French newspapers of the various resolutions of appreciation and sympathy passed by the House. He had letters from people in France who were unofficially caring for graves and he felt it appropriate that New Zealand's appreciation was expressed. J.G. (Gordon) Coates made a similar point.[12]

Following debate in the United Kingdom parliament a policy of individual, uniform headstones for the war graves was adopted, rather than allowing relatives to choose their own designs. The rationale was that individual headstones would not be completed in the foreseeable future whereas standardised versions could be finished and installed within ten years. The War Graves Commission thought these headstones would last a hundred years. Churchill at his eloquent best promised additional memorials inscribed with all the names at each of the battle sites, ready within ten years and built to last 3000 years.[13] Even this was not without controversy for Churchill had originally proposed leaving the site(s) largely untouched, rather than restoring the landscape and erecting the ordered headstones and grand monuments which are visible today.[14] On 10 October 1919 Sir James Allen announced to the New Zealand House of Representatives that under the authority given to the Battle Exploits Memorials Committee (a highly suggestive name) in the United Kingdom, sites in Belgium at Messines and Gravenstafel had been approved for purchase with the intent of erecting such memorials and formal cemeteries for the New Zealander soldiers.[15] This formalised the adoption of these slivers of European soil as New Zealand cemeteries alongside the French burial sites. The following year the Minister of Defence (Sir Robert Heaton Rhodes) informed the House that the graves were now under the care of the Imperial War Graves Commission. The sites included land at Gallipoli which had been granted by treaty. After a visit to France, Rhodes assured the House that the graves were being cared for. Although Allied re-interments to date totalled 128,577 there was still much to be done since New Zealand bodies were scattered throughout France. (Seddon Jnr had previously asked that the task of memorial construction be completed by next Anzac Day commemoration, clearly an impossible deadline.)[16]

Meanwhile, public lectures provided a first-hand, sanitised experience which diverted attention from the graphic reality of clearing the battlefields. Themes of recall and remembrance were also propagated through written war histories. Importantly and unlike the histories of earlier wars, these included stories of the 'men' not just those of the generals or admirals. The reverence with which the war losses (and by juxtaposition France as a graveyard) were treated was promoted through the work of Samuel Seager the official war memorial architect, who toured New Zealand in 1927 with his 250 lantern-slides showing the places of memorial in France and Gallipoli.[17] An advertorial column in the *Marlborough Express* advised readers that Chaplain-Captain Burridge would give a talk on his war experience in Gallipoli and France, covering the '"stunts" in Flanders' which would be 'interspersed with many anecdotes of incidents of active service both humorous and pathetic'.[18] Similar lectures in the United Kingdom were reported in the New Zealand newspapers. A description of a talk titled 'Mr Philip Gibbs dispatches [sic]' at Tottenham was greeted with 'warm cheers'. Gibbs' account (he was described as a war correspondent for *The Chronicle*) was a 'moving story of those thousands of Tommy Atkins who were the men who really won the war'. As with similar raconteurs, Gibbs used a mix of trench warfare 'realities' interspersed with 'humorous' incidents of day-to-day life at the front to engage his audience.[19]

When it came to erecting permanent memorials in France and Belgium, Lochhead says that there was an avoidance of 'skiting' and an aversion to 'historical styles' while taking care to avoid offending the defeated.[20] In other words, victory was understated as was the role of the enemy while official recognition of the graves gave validation and status to the loss of life. Thus, E. Newman MP (Reform, Manawatu) referred to Sir James Allen (by then High Commissioner in London) as not wasting time while visiting the Continent. He was visiting war graves and attending the League of Nations.[21] These visits became an obligatory ritual when government representatives – such as Sir James – visited. The visits were reported in France as were reciprocal visits by official French visitors to the New Zealand memorials.[22] The visual manifestations and their officially sanctioned, complementary narratives were made accessible through local reproductions in New Zealand. The designs used in New Zealand were British in origin and copied from the originals. Exploring such themes, Katie Pickles has observed: 'The stories of all historical figures are products of their times. They are then re-told and re-presented by successive generations, being constantly adapted to new conditions. And when the stories are no longer relevant they are forgotten.'[23]

Figure 14 Nurse Cavell Lane, Paparoa

Katie Pickles (using the case of the executed Nurse Edith Cavell) pointed out that while the 'markers' are often still present they are no longer commonly recognised as commemorating the individual.[24] This seems to be so for the 'No Exit' side road at Paparoa in northern New Zealand, named in Edith Cavell's honour.

A similar fate may await the New Zealand memorials in France and their New Zealand proxies. The War Memorial of the now defunct Newmarket Borough Council hangs in the Auckland City Council Archives – perhaps (ironically) a more appropriate setting than intended when it was first placed there – for it is located in the basement of the Auckland Central City Library building, down three flights of stairs from ground level at 44–46 Lorne Street. It is physically distant from the dead it commemorates (who are presumably in overseas World War I graveyards, although the inscription does not record where they are interred). The memorial is removed from the sight of their descendants and the community who once mourned them.

Figure 15 'Lest we forget': Newmarket war memorial[25]

Fred Waite gave early impetus to the narrative of heroism at Gallipoli, a process which without apparent official intent or any malice was to displace the primacy of the New Zealanders' service in France in the public mind.[26] This theme gained early currency, supported by claims such as Massey's reference during the later Chanak Crisis to the Turkish occupation of the Gallipoli Peninsula: 'It would not have troubled us so much but for the fact that on Gallipoli lie thousands of the best and bravest men the British Empire ever produce who – including New-Zealanders – left their bones there.'[27]

Somewhat cynically *Le Figaro* opined that Lloyd George was exploiting the 'self-esteem' the ANZACs derived from their earlier exploits at Gallipoli.[28] If that was Lloyd George's intent, it was fulfilled. New Zealand's support for Britain during the Chanak Crisis was based on raw emotion rather than any military imperative. Even without formal graveyards, the Gallipoli battle sites became if not consecrated ground then at least the revered equivalent in the public mind. But in France there was also sacred ground containing New Zealand graveyards, thereby creating a similar, enduring but arm's-length tie between New Zealand and France. Thus, when Sir T. Mackenzie speaking in the Legislative Council recalled the 17,000 'fine young men lying on the fields of France and other countries' or W.E. (Bill) Parry (Labour, Auckland Central) evoked the events that had 'moistened the earth with tears of women and children, and fertilised the fields of Flanders with the dead remains of human beings', they were evoking sentiments similar to those applied at Gallipoli. By implication, the status given to Gallipoli should have been extended to France. Moreover, if consistency was applied there was a similar obligation to defend the French sites.

During the same Parliamentary session Massey referred to the £35,387 set aside for war graves ... and battlefield memorials in France.[29] Preservation of the gravesites and the construction of memorials made little sense, however, if they went unseen by the families. Understandably there were requests for financial assistance for relatives to visit, once individual body identification had been completed and grave monuments erected. The potential volume of such requests, the support required, and the likely costs raised significant issues for the authorities and, in any case, what was the purpose of such visits?[30] When Dr H.T.J. Thacker (Liberal, Christchurch East) asked whether assisted visits to graves for the poorest widows and mothers were possible, Massey demurred by saying no decision had been reached. Sir James Allen answered a similar question by confronting the issue of cost head on. He pointed out that large-scale access funded from the public purse was impractical.[31] G. Witty (Liberal, Riccarton) also asked about the need for 'permission' for visits to the graves in the United Kingdom, and was told (perhaps to his surprise) by G.J. Anderson (Minister of Internal Affairs) that no one could enter the United Kingdom without a passport and this needed to be 'vised' (sic) by the French Consular Officer for visits to France.[32] During the same Question Time W.H. Field (Otaki) asked for a reduction in the 'enormous rates' for passages to visit war graves.[33] Jennings (Liberal, Waitomo) plaintively asked how overseas relatives could see the war graves given these barriers. He pointed out that while there was assisted passage for migrants, fares were still expensive for those wanting to make the reverse journey to visit the battlefields. William Nosworthy (Reform, Minister of Immigration) stalled by saying there was no funding.[34] The remoteness of France, and the impossibility of financially constrained families ever seeing the graves, must have seemed a harsh outcome since so much had been spent on creating appropriate individual burials. The descriptions and photographs of the battlefield left the imagination to create an unedifying vista. By extension it would have been unlikely to present an image of France as an appropriate place for permanent interment of one's relatives.

Rhoda Howden received two stark black and white photographs of her husband's grave. Both appear equally forlorn, and to the untrained eye they do not appear to be the same grave as the backgrounds are dissimilar. The accompanying printed slip records that 'it is possible that errors may have occurred...' The condolence letters (he was the 'whitest and best of men') addressed to Mrs Howden include a description which omits any hint of suffering (Howden had died in hospital ten days after a gas attack). Rhoda Howden's image of France was a sanitised version of her husband's demise, a good character reference and two black and white images which could have been photographed anywhere that a selection of wooden crosses were available.[35]

Figure 16 Rhoda Howden: memorial correspondence

Figure 17 Paeroa war memorial, Paeroa, New Zealand[36] and New Zealand memorial, Longue-val, France

If mass burials were no longer acceptable, more or less the same outcome could be achieved using uniform, individual grave markers. The identical, stylised headstones in France depersonalised the losses and made them of equal value while transforming the site into a sacred place of collective hurt and memory. Memorials similar to those proposed by Churchill were constructed in a more modest form throughout New Zealand, thereby symbolically transplanting the graves. These artificial, local sites possessed neither the bodies nor the original location but they had the advantage of being non-specific. Such sites were acceptable memorials for all the battlefields, for all the war dead, and therefore an appropriate place for all the locals to grieve. They were also a symbolic repatriation of individual souls. Private commemoration could be undertaken locally, even when conducted in proximity to or concurrent with the public ceremonies.

The process culminated in suggestions for a shared national memorial where the whole nation could grieve. Despite general agreement, the specifications for a national memorial aroused intense debate between those favouring utilitarian structures such as halls and parks and those who felt more grandiose structures were appropriate (perhaps more in a style of Queen Victoria's monument for Prince Albert).[37] The latter view was championed by Sir James Allen who wanted 'beautiful, statuary, emblematic' structures such as 'monuments like the Champs Elysee, the Nelson Monument in Trafalgar Square and the Statue of Liberty'.[38] All these examples had a French connection although the association seems to have been inadvertent. It would be difficult to think of a more inappropriate archetype than Nelson's column given the recent alliance with France. When the discussion resumed approximately a year and one election later, the House was no more cohesive; ideas ranged from scholarship funding, to the purely functional, or simply an artistic monument. Prime Minister Massey, perhaps still enthralled by imperial glory and New Zealand's own modest aspirations in the Pacific, favoured a national monument (the Arc de Triomphe and the Statue of Liberty were again mentioned) in a style similar to those used by France to commemorate her victories.[39] Massey was attempting to associate the New Zealand losses with the positive outcome of victory and in so doing he drew on French rather than British icons. Perhaps in his own way he was trying to validate France as an appropriate place of burial for the corpses and the memories.

One result was the structure at the bottom of Bowen Street, Wellington. It rarely attracts more than a glance from the busy commuters hurrying to and from the Railway Station, unless when used as a de facto windbreak. The blandness reflected in the cenotaph inscription is exaggerated through the absence of punctuation and the misphrasing applied to Rupert Brookes' anodyne phrases from *The Red Sweet Wine of Youth:*

> These laid the world away
> Poured out the red Sweet wine of youth gave up the
> years to be of work and joy and that
> unhoped serene that men call age and
> those who would have been their sons

they gave their immortality[40]

Another manifestation was the plethora of public amenities including swimming pools, libraries, gardens, park benches, band rotundas, statues, flagpoles and public buildings, all displaying the prefix 'War Memorial'.[41] Their proliferation diluted the impact to the point that the poignancy of the personal losses they supposedly commemorated was lost, just as the profusion of events in 2018 similarly diluted the 1918 war centennial commemorations.

With the bodies sequestered in France, it was important that the survivors were resettled and given an appropriate future rather than left to brood and grieve. No public figure – regardless of their political disposition – wanted to be seen as insensitive to the needs of the repatriated soldiers. Validation of the war effort required that the Government show that those who served were coming home to a better place and that their interests would be protected. The political opposition had to remain sympathetic to these views while arguing that more could or should be done. Less well considered was the form of resettlement to be used and how to ensure it succeeded.

There was a general presumption that the returning soldiers would want to farm and that small-scale pastoral farming would be appropriate and economically viable. This view probably owed as much to the imagined English ideal, as discussed earlier, as it did to New Zealand conditions. There is no indication that the soldiers' opinions were sought, apart from anecdotal comments gathered by politicians when visiting the troops.[42] Although there was some provision for alternative vocational employment and university scholarships, the possibility of some ex-soldiers who were otherwise disinclined to farm being induced to do so by the lack of alternatives or by the seemingly generous financial incentives does not seem to have been seriously considered.[43] Moreover, despite the assumption that the New Zealand 'bloke' and his equally dependable and practical wife were resilient rural dwellers, the inexorable demographic transition towards an urban society was expanding the opportunities for those interested in urban-based occupations. On the one hand, there was a financial inducement to adopt farming as a profession and, on the other, a lack of practical experience and understanding on the part of some participants as to what this might entail. These factors, alongside a dearth of alternative rehabilitation programmes, meant rural settlement became a self-fulfilling outcome. Problems soon became apparent. On 8 August 1923 G. McKay (Hawkes Bay) reminded MPs that warnings of the dangers of placing inexperienced returned soldiers on highly priced or overvalued land were not based on hindsight but had been raised at the time the land settlement scheme was mooted. Massey was quoted by McKay as having promised the servicemen land at favourable prices, but Massey's Government had not only raised land prices by competing to buy blocks for settlement, it had also ignored calls for the inexperienced men to be given practical hands-on training.[44]

Later it would be claimed that the success rate of the settlement scheme had been inflated by those whose survival depended on off-farm income sources or who had retained possession while defaulting on rent (or lease) payments. In his analysis refuting this view, Michael Roche correctly pointed out that there is a continuum rather than a dichotomy between complete success and outright failure, and that neither can be objectively diagnosed based solely on the length of time the land was occupied. Using off-farm income to retain the land made economic sense in some cases.[45] Moreover, land settlement matched the constant refrain for development of the Dominions, a key component of the Empire's ethos. In the broader context, the lesson of population stagnation and the resultant inability of France to defend itself without British assistance made the New Zealand case for intensified land use as part of a broader Empire model appear obvious. It was also a good fit with Massey's ambitious scheme to make New Zealand a significant supplier of agricultural – especially dairy – produce to Britain. The promotion of farming – appropriately described by Roche as '...rooted in a nineteenth-century yeomanry' – incorporated the idea of populating the so-called waste land and encouraging development through rural population increases.[46] Population growth also ameliorated fears of demographic oblivion, particularly the dread of being overtaken in the Pacific by the numerically superior 'others' of Asian heritage.

French agriculture was often used as a reference point when these matters were discussed, but why? Admittedly, both New Zealand and France had important rural sectors – both were predominantly rural countries – and owing to the geographical diversity there were inevitably regions that shared similar climate, soils and topography. Beyond that, there appears to have still been an assumption that the New Zealand servicemen would be familiar with small-scale intensive French farming, and this would be an appropriate template for New Zealand. Kaiapoi's Liberal MP David Buddo correctly pointed out that there was 'no comparison' between France and New Zealand agriculture owing to the latter's enormous volume of primary production in relation to population, but this was an argument too general to be sustained across the many different types of agriculture in each country.[47] There seemed nevertheless to have been an underlying assumption that French farming methods would be relevant to New Zealand circumstances.

The cultural, political and economic differences were in truth so great that any parallels were coincidental, even in cases where there were physical similarities. Hence when the Timaru-based Member of the Legislative Council J. Craigie repeated the perennial Liberal shibboleth in praise of small farms: 'Our boys in France have seen what can be done with small holdings. I have seen many of their letters, which show a realisation that it is not necessary to have 1,000 acres, or even 100 acres, to make a living. Those boys have seen prosperous families on small areas', he was relying on the size of the holdings to validate his comparison. In a later Parliamentary session even W.T. Jennings (Taumarunui) speaking to the Land Laws Amendment Bill raised the use of small areas for intensive cultivation in France and Flanders as an example for settlement of ex-servicemen. The 'infamous bridge to nowhere' (spanning the Mangapurua Stream in the Whanganui National Park) that survives within his former electorate's hilly hinterland demonstrates the fantasy of such aspirations. The difference between Northern France where many New Zealanders served and the notoriously difficult landscapes and soils of the central North Island defies any meaningful agronomic equivalence. Only a few MPs showed some foresight as to the potentially disastrous mismatch between aspiration and economic reality for some of the inexperienced and undercapitalised ex-soldiers. John-Pearce Luke (Reform, Wellington North) cautioned against sending the 'boys' onto bushland. Others, such as J. Bitchener (Reform, Waitaki) rejected possible hardship. His rebuttal to those criticising the purchase of the Hakataramea Estate for resettlement was to claim that the snowfall there would be little in comparison with how the settlement men had suffered in France.[48] That may have been climatically true but was irrelevant to their wellbeing as small farmers. More significantly, it was France that was referred to in these debates rather than the idealised countryside of Home, which still included the large hereditary estates of the aristocracy and the gentry.

> Memories change with the demands of each generation, from those who lived the events, to the generations who grew up hearing about them, and ultimately to those who only inherited some version of the narrative.
>
> Nigel Hunt[49]

With the dead buried, their graves marked, the returned servicemen resettled and appropriate memorials erected in New Zealand – their primary purpose seemingly to commemorate the Gallipoli landings – France could perhaps finally be put aside.[50] France was destined to become a New Zealand graveyard on uncontested soil. In the immediate post-war decade, however, the French connection could not be completely renounced because France still influenced New Zealand's international relationships and was a continuing background presence in day-to-day life. Moreover, many news reports of deaths apparently due to natural causes were linked with post-war trauma (tubercular disease was often mixed with wartime gas-related respiratory ailments). Cases of individual hardship (sons and fathers who were ineligible for assistance, widows and children who lacked support or private means) and the casually understated biographical notes which recorded that deceased had once served in France provided continuous reminders which conflicted with the urge to forget and move on.

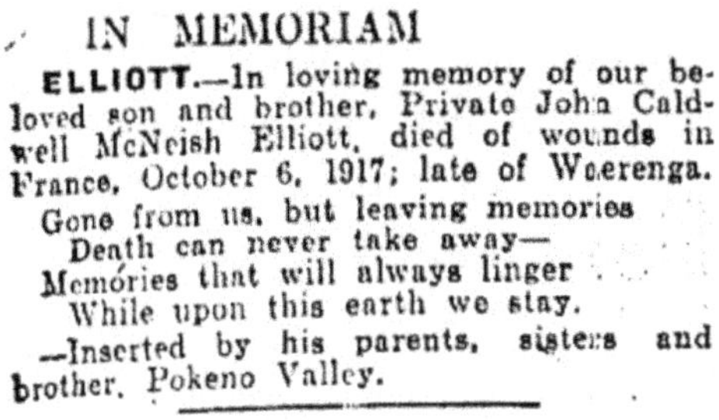

IN MEMORIAM

ELLIOTT.—In loving memory of our beloved son and brother, Private John Caldwell McNeish Elliott, died of wounds in France, October 6, 1917; late of Waerenga.

Gone from us, but leaving memories
Death can never take away—
Memories that will always linger
While upon this earth we stay.

—Inserted by his parents, sisters and brother, Pokeno Valley.

Figure 18 In Memoriam Notice published in 1933[51]

New Zealand's attempt to disengage culturally and politically from France implied that France was to some degree the cause of New Zealand's losses rather than simply being the venue. In a 1919 letter to British Colonial Secretary Long written at Massey's instigation by the New Zealand High Commissioner (Thomas Mackenzie), attention was drawn to the 1917 notification received by the Imperial War Conference under which France's 'generous action' in allotting gravesites in perpetuity was noted with 'deep appreciation'. Despite this, Massey's use of the French example to push during the Paris Peace Conference for Turkey to be forced to cede equivalent rights at Gallipoli implied the Dardanelle graves were in the New Zealand psyche already as important as those in France.[52] These attempts – if not downplaying France and all that happened there – were at least deliberately raising Gallipoli to a similar level emotionally. Whether this was the primary reason for the status of Gallipoli rising, or whether the ready acquiescence of France in ceding the necessary land to the War Graves Commission led to the single-minded pursuit of similar cemeteries in the less than friendly Gallipoli territory is unclear. The implied equivalence did, however, conflict with the more significant part in world affairs that France had (and would continue to have) for New Zealand.

Resettlement of ex-servicemen came to mean more than repatriation; it was a symbolic expunging of the past through a new beginning. Of all the claims made, one that cannot be sustained was that the returned servicemen were ignored.[53] The evidence from the political dialogue and the news indicates that at least in the immediate aftermath of the war considerable attention was paid to both their collective good and the many deserving individual cases. About 23,000 ex-servicemen were assisted in some way to purchase their own homes, farms or businesses.[54] Although the rural resettlement model was based at least in part on a misrepresented, idealised and therefore inappropriate (for New Zealand conditions) French ideal, some very influential parliamentarians believed that the intensive, small-scale farming that the ex-servicemen had seen in France could be appropriated for use in New Zealand.

The issues that arose from Versailles became a theme constantly revisited, never settled and even with hindsight clearly beyond any workable political resolution which could reconcile economic reality and public expectations. As with the economic problems, there was no obvious way of ameliorating the personal losses from the war, particularly as cultural conventions were so closely linked with the grieving process. For many servicemen the glimpses of French civilian rural life in very close physical proximity to the war zones must have evoked memories of a rural homeland in New Zealand (whether the soldiers were from a rural or urban location mattered less when viewed from such a distance) and appeared as an aspiration which was at the polar opposite both geographically and emotionally from their wartime circumstances.[55] Whether the small-scale French farmers owned the land or rented it and, whether they prospered or struggled at a subsistence level, would not have been immediately obvious to the passing observer. They appeared relatively content while simultaneously symbolising a peaceful home and a break from the wartime experience of France. The urge within the polity to replicate a France-like countryside interspersed with memorials and populated by contented small farmers is therefore understandable.

Chapter Ten

Trade and engage or disconnect and forget?

> Men would always struggle on economic grounds, and when these struggles reached an acute form the only way out was war.
>
> General Pau, Leader of French Mission to New Zealand 1918–19.[1]

Despite New Zealand's constitutional status as a post-colonial state, the country continued to identify after 1918 as a culturally British, agrarian-dependent nation. Any expectations that the post-war national interests could be better met by adopting a more autonomous position were quickly quashed with little consideration given to the longer-term consequences. While New Zealand assumed that British protection and trade were essential, there were alternatives – even within the limitations of 1918 agricultural technology. The decision to remain Britain-dependent also ignored the obvious evidence that however stable global trade might appear to be, the lengthy sea routes to Britain were susceptible to unexpected disruptions, especially in time of war. By 1927 this policy morphed into what was assumed to be an unchangeable destiny, so that in 1927 Prime Minister Gordon Coates would claim that 'Our natural market is Great Britain, and many of our troubles in New Zealand are due to the fact that Great Britain has been passing through a parlous period. We have no desire to change our principal market…'[2]

New Zealand's trade plan presumed that any exported produce would suit consumer preferences at Home and therefore would be of such importance to Britain that defence of the shipping routes and material investment in the supporting infrastructure would be obvious and justifiable. The concurrent reliance on Britain as a redistribution hub for any excess produce destined for Europe further exposed New Zealand's trade base, because it depended on Britain continuing a free-trade policy. Moreover, relying on the British market to serve New Zealand's re-export interests while transmitting Continental end-user preferences back to the local primary producers was a fragile foundation on which to build a national economy. Re-exporters will sell whatever is available at a price that serves their financial interest, with little concern given to the producers.

British intervention through the purchase of New Zealand commodities in support of the war effort had been the most obvious constraint on developing alternative products and markets. As meat (March 1915), cheese (November 1916), wool (December 1916) and finally butter (November 1917) were added to the wartime requisition regime, New Zealand became even more dependent on shipping a small range of commodities using one shipping route to one market protected by one navy. The inherent risk in this approach became obvious when a shortage of shipping caused serious delays. Departures fell from ninety-nine sailings in 1914, to seventy-eight in 1916 down to sixty-two in 1917. Shipments of meat decreased from 8.8 million carcasses to 5.6 million between 1914 and 1917.[3] Although historians have pointed out the benefits (for the seller) of stability through price fixing, and (for the purchaser) of continuity of supply and availability, exclusive supply agreements can produce serious distortions in commodity markets in the medium to long term by dampening or totally removing consumer feedback.[4] The benefit for New Zealand of Britain buying more or less whatever New Zealand produced meant that sales activity (such as it was) could be restricted to supplying raw, unprocessed low cost produce to one customer. Innovation was therefore concentrated on technical improvements to increase the volume and efficiency of production of these undifferentiated commodities (wool, butter, cheddar cheese) rather than measuring consumer preference and then adapting the end product to suit. Despite various marketing suggestions and the later introduction of producer boards, the solution to low market prices was usually to lower the cost of production. In the economists' language, producing more using the same capital base along with cheaper inputs lowered the marginal cost per unit so that prices could be reduced. As with any market condition, once this pattern was in place it was difficult to consider alternatives since by definition the system worked. It was this economic orthodoxy, bolstered by wartime patriotism and loyalty to the Empire, that France had to crack in order to establish a direct trade-based relationship with New Zealand.

When M. Leon Hippeau was appointed French Vice-Consul in New Zealand in late 1916, he replaced an Honorary Consul as the highest-ranking French diplomat in New Zealand. As an experienced professional Hippeau would have been aware of diplomatic protocols and unlikely to act outside his brief.[5] In March 1917 at least nine articles were published in various newspapers under the auspices of local French consular offices inviting New Zealand firms that wished to import French goods in lieu of their German equivalents to apply via the consulate to the *Office National du Commerce Extérieur* in Paris for the names of suitable suppliers.[6] This seemingly unremarkable initiative caused considerable disquiet. Why the issue of trade with France should raise such a concern at this time is not clear, particularly as in one of his regular updates to Prime Minister Massey just six months earlier Sir James Allen had noted that the Paris Office of the British Chamber of Commerce had suggested via the Colonial Office that Australia, New Zealand and South Africa appoint their own Trade Commissioners to visit the main trade centres in France.[7]

Once they were aware of Hippeau's enterprising approach, the Colonial Office in London asked the British Ambassador to France (Lord Bertie) to raise with the French Government the activities of the 'French Vice-Consul at Auckland' who had been 'addressing the New Zealand Government direct on questions which are considered outside his legitimate sphere'. The Colonial Office noted that 'the Dominions have not complete independence in external affairs and three of the four subjects mentioned in the French note are outside purely internal business...' Lord Bertie was requested to 'approach the French Government on the subject in such manner as you may think best suited to the circumstances with the view of discontinuance of the practice to which the Governor General calls attention'.[8] Lord Bertie wrote to the French Government to explain that Hippeau had been in direct contact with the New Zealand Governor-General regarding:

> ...questions of a general political order, such as the development of commercial relations between France and New Zealand, the sequestration of a number of bells in the belfry of a German church at Christchurch and which were cast from cannon captured by the Germans in the war 1870-71, the establishment of a French Consular Agency at Apia, Samoa, and the question of claims respecting private interests in enemy territory.[9]

Despite Lord Bertie's diplomatic wording, it was made clear to the French Government that French representations on such matters were to be made through the 'usual diplomatic channels ... [thereby] avoiding duplications and possible confusion'.[10]

Hippeau did not give up. In April 1918 he forwarded another notice, this time to the New Zealand Minister of Internal Affairs (Hon. C.W. Russell) rather than to the Governor-General, advising of trade opportunities. Hippeau requested publication of this notice in the *New Zealand Gazette*, presumably to imply official sanction. The covering letter makes it clear that the request for (albeit passive) government recognition of M. Hippeau's trade initiatives was seen by France as an extension of the 'bonds of friendship ... started on the common battlefields', and it also makes clear that this was an initiative of the *Office National du Commerce Extérieur.*[11] Unlike the newspaper notice, this version asked for communication with Paris via the local consulate(s). Joe Heenan, a senior civil servant, nevertheless wrote to the Under-Secretary at the Colonial Office in April 1918 to inform him and the Secretary of State of this fresh initiative and to seek further instruction. Heenan and his Minister saw the latest action as that of the vice-Consul 'acting almost in a diplomatic capacity'. They were especially piqued by the reference to strengthening bonds which could be interpreted as a Dominion giving diplomatic standing to the Vice-Consul's actions.[12] In response, the New Zealand Government was again instructed not to participate in making trade arrangements with France. Foreign policy remained the responsibility of the imperial authorities since even the fact of dealing with such a minor matter through the Vice-Consul might have implications for foreign relations beyond the brief of a Dominion government.

Despite this rejection France tried once again, this time through the 1918–19 visit of the French trade and diplomatic mission led by the retired General Pau.[13] The Mission's original brief included 'proper development of the world economy', so this was not just a goodwill visit. As the New Zealand leg took place after the armistice was signed, any additional morale-boosting component could be put aside while promotion of both trade and French post-war policy assumed additional significance. Amongst the mix of sightseeing and goodwill-boosting speeches, there were structured public statements on French policy towards Germany and trade that suggest that even if the details of the New Zealand itinerary were ad hoc, the diplomatic substance was not.

The precise objectives of the Mission were lost when the original leader – the scholar Emile Albert Métin – died in San Francisco on 16 August 1918 while en route to Australia.[14] The Mission's General Secretary, André Siegfried, assumed de facto leadership and took responsibility for that part of Métin's role associated with trade and economic development, leaving General Pau as titular head.[15] Métin had received verbal instructions before the mission departed from France, but he did not share these with his colleagues. This suggests that behind the Mission's official brief there were more sensitive objectives which had been restricted to a one-on-one verbal briefing. The mission's typewritten report notes that:

> In addition [to] Mr. Métin's more authoritative handling of the economic and political questions … he knew better than we [i.e. the other mission members], having prepared for the mission in personal conversations with the Minister.
>
> We judged ourselves to be cautious [...] on a number of issues that were not explicitly addressed in our instructions and on which Mr. Métin had certainly received verbal guidance from interested government departments.[16]

Métin's colleagues therefore decided that:

> Inspired by our written instructions which, in the absence of Mr. Métin, could serve us as a guide, we set ourselves the task(s):
>
> 1. to do work of French propaganda [To speak of France everywhere and to all was the essential thing]
>
> 2. to investigate various political, military, economic, social [matters]
>
> 3. to prepare for, through conversations with the Australian Government, such economic or political negotiations in which the French Government may eventually wish to engage with Australia.[17]

The New Zealand Government's involvement during the visit appeared strangely restrained.[18] By all accounts the Mission was well received and there was no shortage of crowds attending the public welcomes, even though the visit coincided with the aftermath of the influenza epidemic.[19] Since the visit took place during the traditional Christmas holiday break while Massey and Ward were again in the northern hemisphere, it was left to Acting Prime Minister Sir James Allen to represent the National (United-Reform coalition) Government. Allen, however, remained in the South Island when the mission was welcomed in Auckland. He did travel to Wellington to formally welcome the delegation when they arrived in the capital, and then travelled south with them to Christchurch where they met with the Governor-General, Lord Liverpool.

General Pau's preliminary report (telegraphed from Auckland to Paris by the Vice-Consul) succinctly summarised the political circumstances in New Zealand. In the absence of Massey and Ward, no one in authority was authorised to implement any initiatives or to make decisions, even those related to matters involving the 'simple execution [of] current affairs'. Official contacts were therefore restricted to what Pau diplomatically called 'useful conversations'. Discussion of matters related to the peace treaty and imperial conference or any consequential decision making was impossible. Pau's accurate assessment was that New Zealand would follow British policy, and 'does not appear to me to have any claim to an independent policy'. Pau obviously understood the domestic political nuances as he stated that the coalition Ministry would only survive in its current form until the next election.[20]

The news reports suggest that displaying the Mission as if it were a public curiosity took precedence in New Zealand eyes over the commercial priorities, probably because the Mission was effectively redirected to this end by local interests. Pau referred to a 'blood bond' linking the two countries, the contrition required of Germany to achieve forgiveness (rather like an absolution) and the praiseworthy service of the French priesthood during hostilities. He directly associated the French clergy and their Christian values with fighting for the 'laws of humanity', while the Germans did the opposite.[21] In the official report of the Mission the New Zealand war sacrifice is acknowledged through extravagant descriptions such as 'pulses thrilled for the great principles they [the soldiers] were upholding' and 'many of them now lie sleeping their last sleep on French soil'.[22]

General Pau had little faith in the proposed society of nations (i.e. League of Nations) and he did not in any case consider the Germans were fit to be included. The alternative was to reconfigure the Anglo-

French-based alliance that had been so successful during the war as a trade partnership.[23] In another report of what seems to be the same speech there was an even greater emphasis on the control of German trade. In Pau's view, the fear of German dumping would have to be thwarted by removing German control over both her merchant shipping and her seaports. On the other hand, Germany would have to pay reparations so she had to be allowed some degree of economic recovery. The self-evident contradiction between these policies was not addressed by Pau. Nevertheless, Pau said the Allies needed to act to 'reap the full fruits of victory'. He reminded his audience(s) of Germany breaking her word to Napoleon I (referenced to the 1807 Treaty of Tilsit) when she exceeded an army strength of 43,000 men.[24] The General's statements summarised with remarkable foresight the contradictions and missteps that were to disrupt the post-war world and the historical biases which influenced the underlying policies. These French policies and warnings were not publicly challenged while the Mission was in New Zealand.

Based on the newspaper reports, Pau's uncompromising advocacy of the French post-war attitude towards Germany was well publicised and succeeded in creating an understanding of – and sympathy for – the French position. Despite this, the Pacific territorial issues so important to New Zealand's own colonial aspirations went unresolved. Thus, the broader long-term implications for New Zealand's Pacific policy were unclear as was the issue of converting the trade opportunities suggested by the Mission into action. Meeting with Prime Minister Massey in Paris upon his return, Pau publicly praised New Zealand's treatment of the 'natives' and lauded the shared New Zealand–French battlefield sacrifice. Massey in turn 'hoped' that Britain and France would remain allies, that Germany would pay for the war, and that those who had caused the war would be punished, all of which were themes the Mission had reiterated while in New Zealand.[25] M. Hippeau's report (telegraphed to Paris immediately after the Mission's departure) stressed the goodwill generated by the visit and specifically referred to the interest shown by both the metropolitan population and the 'indigenes'. Hippeau made the point that the enthusiastic reception and overall positive reaction to the visit was even more of a triumph owing to the mix of sentiment at the time, coinciding as the visit did with the war's end, the influenza epidemic, the summer holiday season, and the uncertainty over rising post-war prices.[26] The contemporary newspaper reports suggest that the Mission conditioned the New Zealand public to accept a strongly anti-German, punitive post-war posture, in accord with Massey's own views and those of the Lloyd George Government.[27]

The Mission's Report was mainly concerned with the commercial and cultural aspects of the visit, rather than two matters clearly of greater importance to the New Zealanders: sightseeing for the visitors and reconciling a closer relationship with France with Empire membership. As was the case for the soldiers who travelled and existed within their own portable cultural tent while in France, the Mission members mistook the welcoming crowds and the temporary friendship extended to them in New Zealand as evidence of a permanent change in New Zealand's disposition towards France. The French visitors were often greeted in the spirit of fellow victors or seen as tourists who were there to be impressed, rather than as potential trade partners.[28] The Acting Prime Minister (Allen) apparently assumed that Siegfried was in New Zealand to study and would again be writing about New Zealand's social conditions, rather than recognising his leading role within the trade delegation.[29] The Mission's report concluded that mutual goodwill would be necessary to develop the commercial opportunities within the sectors identified as having the best prospects. In the cliché, trade would follow the flag. Maintaining direct communications would be of great assistance as would a continued interest from universities and intellectual circles in French language and culture. There was also a passing reference to the desirability of French missionaries continuing to visit New Zealand.

The Mission correctly viewed New Zealand as an independent self-governing nation with the legal right to develop direct trade if she so wished. The French noted that New Zealand controlled its own tariffs and had the right to make independent commercial arrangements – a basic legal requirement for any nation claiming independence. The commercial possibilities were not however pursued by New Zealand since the cultural realities conflicted with mercantile interests.[30] These views are consistent with those expressed in the New Zealand Parliament regarding New Zealand's sovereign status when the Versailles Treaty was ratified.

When meeting with the Auckland Chamber of Commerce, Dr Siegfried, M. Mathieu and M. Leclerq-Motte noted the complementary product range of each country. New Zealand's strengths in primary produce and French expertise in manufactured goods that could replace German supplies made a reciprocal trade agreement a logical step.[31] One problem from New Zealand's point of view was shipping. The use of non-British vessels to transport goods to foreign destinations would remove an essential component of the Empire's perceived economic strength and undermine the rationale for New Zealand's place in the Empire and the symbolism inherent in her defence by the Royal Navy. For this reason – and for those of cultural dissonance previously discussed – the offer of trade that the Mission ostensibly promoted was rejected by neglect. This was possibly influenced by the London colonial authorities' earlier quashing of the French Vice-Consul's local initiatives on the grounds that the Dominions could not make their own trade-related decisions, but the final outcome was determined by indifference. As Sir James Allen insipidly noted when updating Massey – who was still in Europe – 'I have nothing particular to say about them'.[32] Although Allen did give Massey some detail of the visit, it seems the significance of an offer of a direct commercial relationship was dismissed, probably because Massey and his deputy remained fixated along with the rest of the nation on trading with Britain by developing the dairy industry. Therefore, from a New Zealand domestic political perspective the Mission proved to be a sustained political propaganda campaign which reinforced Massey's uncomplicated public stance at Versailles. The proposed trade, which was of just as much interest to France as any political support, was not pursued by New Zealand.

The wool trade especially could have been of great benefit for the New Zealand producers who would have gained direct market access, with French support. From the French point of view, direct access to a supply of unprocessed New Zealand fleeces would have reduced supplies on the world market and thereby limited the options for Belgium, Germany and the British who were the main wool textile competitors of the French mills. It would also have extended (by default) the wartime alliance as a further protection against German aggression, for when trade was of mutual benefit both parties would wish to preserve and defend it.

In addition, developing the direct wool trade overcame the weaknesses of relying on Britain as a hub for Continental re-exports. This aspect was not concealed and in fact was openly discussed at the time. Because wool was non-perishable and easily handled and stored in bales, it was the only New Zealand commodity re-exported from Britain in any significant quantity (about £2 million out of total wool exports of £8,165,408) in 1913. Most of this was consigned to 'the manufacturing centres of Belgium, northern France, and Germany'.[33] Unlike the pre-war exports to Germany, direct exports to France from New Zealand were too insignificant to justify a separate line-item in the main statistics. Once the war began, the 1915 *New Zealand Official Yearbook* factually if somewhat drily recorded that, 'the proportion of exports shipped to the Motherland has become of overwhelming importance…'.[34] Direct exports to France did increase fourfold by value between 1914 and 1918 (from a paltry £227,027 to £810,007) but this did not fully compensate for the overall decline in re-exports to Europe.

Although New Zealand's direct exports of wool to France were minuscule, as much as a quarter of the New Zealand wool consigned to the United Kingdom was being re-exported to Europe (as noted earlier). Prime Minister Massey was aware that France and Germany were the main buyers as during debate on the Finance Bill (10 November 1920) he expressed concern about the forthcoming wool sales owing to the destruction of French and Belgian mills.

> '...some of our best customers for wool before the war – France and Belgium in particular – are not now able to manufacture, and therefore not able to buy. They did not come here to buy much before the war, but they did take a good deal of our wool, buying it in England.'[35]

Opposition Leader Holland interjected (possibly intending to embarrass Massey) to say that, 'A lot of your wool went to Germany before the war.' Massey replied:

> 'I know that. The Germans are getting to work now, but they are not doing much up to the present. The other countries – France and Belgium – will not get up to full production for years to come, and consequently they are not ready to commence to buy our wool in large quantities.'[36]

Although Massey was correct in his recognition of the short-term constraints on opportunities for exports of raw wool to Europe, he was wrong in his prediction of a lengthy delay before the French trade recovered.

Massey had other reasons for downplaying the opportunities for wool. Recognition of the potential for an expanded Continental wool trade would have undermined Massey's favoured intensive dairying model by encouraging investment in extensive sheep farming, possibly resulting in a restriction on the dairy industry and the necessary refrigerated freight capacity to the United Kingdom.[37] Fortunately Massey did not have to confront this dilemma because the shipping shortage in the post-war period conspired with British acquisition of the wool clip to prevent any immediate prospects for an expanded direct trade in raw wool with France. Moreover, the New Zealand sheep industry faced another challenge, as a reduction in the high levels of frozen meat imports by France was likely, given France's stated aim of post-war self-sufficiency.[38] The French offer to buy more wool could have perhaps been met by a counter-offer of further wool sales subject to retention of the meat trade but instead the French Mission was informed that all meat exports were now destined for the British market because New Zealand wished to retain her privileged market position there. Regardless of the political objectives, this was a gross intervention in the market that distorted market demand.

The paralysis in decision making owing to the absence of the all-controlling Massey (shadowed by his coalition deputy Ward) is apparent in General Pau's initial report. Although Pau believed that New Zealand wanted to develop wool exports to France (Pau uses the word 'eager') and that local opinion was favourable to such a course, his remarks suggest that some form of state control would continue. The responsible Ministers did inform Pau that with Massey absent they could not even make a **recommendation** (emphasis added) to the Inter-Allied Committee in London on the distribution of New Zealand's wool to France during the post-war transitional period. The situation was ludicrous. A New Zealand Cabinet could do no more than seek instruction from London in response to a request from a visiting French delegation who wanted to buy New Zealand wool for delivery to what was Britain's closest ally and cross-channel neighbour from stocks already available in England. Allen would do no more than telegraph Massey to request a policy statement, and Massey's reply (as reported by Pau) was that no decision had been made. The 'competent' Minister suggested that France needed to specify her needs in quantity and quality, but this was an obvious holding tactic as no decision about future supply was imminent. Moreover, the Mission was informed that despite France having been informed from London in September that 60,000 bales were available, the New Zealand Government had received 'instructions' on 21 December 1918 that all the wool previously allocated to France was now to be retained in England. Pau reported that the New Zealand Government claimed they were unaware of the reason for this counter-order.[39] There were clearly significant opportunities for exports of New Zealand produce to France (direct or via the United Kingdom) but these were not encouraged. Moreover, such being the case it was little wonder that Massey was able to tell Parliament that the French wool industry was still 'not doing much up to the present'.

The French share of New Zealand's exports duly fell from 3 per cent by value in 1918 to less than 1 per cent in 1919. France was not to reappear as a reported export destination with more than a one percentage point share until 1923. Virtually all the exports to France over this period consisted of raw wool although, as the 1921–22 *Yearbook* noted, there was much concealed behind the headline statistics:

> The forwarding trade of New Zealand has never at any time been of great significance, and, prior to 1914, on only one occasion (in 1907) did the amount exceed a quarter of a million sterling. Since 1913, however, this amount has rapidly increased until in 1920 it reached the comparatively huge figure of £813,072.[40]

By June 1919 the British Government had accumulated 'huge Colonial stocks' of wool and it was public knowledge that disposal sales had been 'unsuccessful'.[41] These distortions in the wool trade as a result of wartime market regulation meant that competition – such as it was – could only exist within the government-controlled trade. When surplus stock was auctioned there was strong demand for certain types, as reports suggested that the topmakers (producers of scoured and combed 'tops' or long fibres, suitable for spinning) would be beaten by manufacturers who could pay higher prices. The problem was not in a lack of demand. It was due to a deliberate distortion of market signals.

Supply chain problems had resulted in twenty-one cargoes destined for the May sales having to be reshipped or landed en route to the United Kingdom, thus further restricting supply. As a correspondent noted, 'Whenever the State interferes (in shipping in this case) there is usually a muddle'. Re-export of semi-manufactured wools such as 'noils' (the shorter fibres), still required a War Trade Department Licence and this would only be issued if the buyer had a recommendation from the French authorities. All this was still in place five months after the armistice was signed, and the reason for any Continental blockade – at least as far as France went – was long gone. Costs of transport by rail from London to Bradford were well above pre-war levels. The only means of easing prices was casually identified as 'raw material dropping (in price)'.[42] Clearly this was untrue as direct trading would have reduced double-handling in the United Kingdom, transshipping costs, internal freight charges and sales commissions. With all supplies directed to one market the reversion to the role of price taker for New Zealand growers was an easy answer when manufacturers' margins tightened.

French activity on the open market in response is apparent in the newspaper record.[43] A February 1920 article included a report dated 11 December 1919 that described French buyers as 'less active' due to an unfavourable exchange rate. Despite this, the correspondent was 'amazed' at the recovery of the French textile trade. While there was no apparent shortage of wool, the industry still had spare manufacturing capacity. Another item within the same report included news of 'very high prices' for West Australian merino wools – a clear market signal in favour of fine wools rather than the predominantly coarser New Zealand cross-bred product. Meanwhile the British Government was intent on bringing wool 'home' and selling it 'to the relief of the British Exchequer'. The (presumably) British writer described the British Government as the 'custodian for the colonies' as far as the wool clip went, thus highlighting the parent–child nature of the Anglo-New Zealand relationship.[44] By March 1920 the *Press* was reporting that 'French wool buyers were operating freely' on the London market while over 12,000 bales of Australian and New Zealand wool were on sale at Antwerp on 28 February, although it is not clear whether these were shipped direct or via London.[45] Similarly positive reports of French wool buying occurred up until 1924.

Unlike many other primary products, knowledgeable wool market participants from farmers (producers) to the end users (retail customers) can assess the quality of the material by inspecting the fineness of the fibre (softness), its lustre and its staple length. Fine wool was therefore easily identified. It could be manufactured into high-end fabric for the trend-setting French fashion industry; women everywhere 'submit ... to the dictates of the Parisian designer' as the *Otago Daily Times* reported in reference to French woollen garment designs.[46] Other primary commodities such as dairy or meat products rely on branding and trademarking to convey quality and thereby build consumer discrimination.[47] Hence wool is an ideal commodity for speculative trading.

Only about two-thirds of the raw wool available in the United Kingdom whether grown locally or directly imported was consumed locally (spun or weaved, resold as yarn or as finished cloth).[48] Some locally grown British wools were exported, while imported supplies better suited for domestic use were processed in the United Kingdom. Because the United Kingdom functioned as a clearing house for the Continental wool trade, a considerable quantity of raw wool was sent to France for scouring before reimportation into the United Kingdom for manufacture. Therefore, although the United Kingdom justified control of the wool trade by wartime imperatives, in practice this meant much of the extremely lucrative New Zealand wool trade was in the hands of British and French merchants and traders who profited through handling and dealing, not through producing or manufacturing.[49]

While the general pattern within the wool trade is clear, the movement of individual consignments is less so. As early as 1920 there were reports of French agents actively competing for New Zealand wools in the United Kingdom market, although there were still regulatory hurdles such as licensing controls as well as an adverse exchange rate to overcome. By 1921 the New Zealand High Commissioner was reporting 'fair competition' from France and Germany as a 'sharp recovery' in the French textile industry resulted in demand for raw wool increasing. French textiles again became available in England while Germany remained a potential market for raw wool, given the favourable exchange rate. The British Government's involvement through the commandeer system remained a concern. As United Kingdom post-war wool imports rose, surplus commandeered wool was sold outside the public auction system, leaving the Home Government vulnerable to allegation of profiteering through the (mis-)use of the stabilisation regulations.[50]

This situation had arisen because New Zealand and Australian wools were excluded when wartime restrictions on the sale and distribution of most goods covered by the General Security Act were lifted in April 1919.[51] This was a missed opportunity for New Zealand as far as developing direct trade with France was concerned. In addition, as Dr Thacker MP pointed out, buyers and profiteers in the old country were getting the returns. William Downie Stewart raised the alternative argument – that New Zealand imports of textiles sourced from France and elsewhere on the Continent were 'serious competitors to Britain from time to time' – but this assumed Britain could produce and supply the desired end product in competition with the fashionable French, clearly an arguable assumption.[52]

On 15 August 1922, the Minister of Agriculture (William Nosworthy) told Parliament that in the pre-war years 25 per cent of New Zealand's cross-bred wool had been sold to Germany and that 'a tremendous quantity of wool went on to Germany within the last seven to nine months'. Earlier the then Leader of the Opposition (Wilford) claimed to have been astonished that large quantities of the wool sent Home had been re-exported to Germany and that Germany was already purchasing (presumably cross-bred) wools directly from New Zealand. This, it was alleged, resulted in large quantities of wool being transshipped to Poland and Russia via Germany. In addition, there was active demand for fine, long wool cross-bred fleeces from Continental buyers, including France.[53] By favouring the British market while relying on wartime prejudices to dictate trade policy, New Zealand was forgoing significant opportunities for direct trade and bypassing important market signals.

As a result of shortfalls in post-war European supply the New Zealand wool industry had (as noted) attracted particular attention during General Pau's Trade Mission. While in Otago the Mission visited Port Chalmers and the Roslyn Woollen Mills (accompanied by various local dignitaries). The French industrial specialists were willing to forgo sightseeing opportunities in order to inspect the woollen mills more closely.[54] The Mission members were well aware that direct French imports of New Zealand wool were minuscule (as noted, less than 1 per cent of New Zealand's wool exports went directly to France) and that British wartime acquisition of the clip was a political and economic decision as much as it was a wartime imperative.[55] They were also aware that a large portion of the clip was on-sold to France via the United Kingdom. The Mission accepted there was 'no prospect' for change in the near future and that the practice of consignment through the United Kingdom reflected New Zealand links and reliance on the United Kingdom. Still, while on a global scale New Zealand remained a very small market participant, the Mission members showed keen interest in this potential source of supply.[56]

The Dunedin French Consulate records include numerous receipts dated from 1919 onwards for payments received when issuing a 'Certificate d'Origin' for wool destined for France.[57] The records are in some cases for hundreds of bales, but unfortunately they do not record the specific destination or the type of wool beyond the generic description 'laine'. Given the location (southern South Island) it seems likely that this was a high value, non-generic trade, almost certainly of speciality fine wool from merino or merino-cross sheep (such as Corriedales) whose fleeces were deemed worthy of identification as being from New Zealand (if not from a specific farm). By late 1924 there was such strong demand from French buyers for good quality wool that manufacturers had to rely on the 140,000-bale carryover stock from previous seasons. New Zealand production was increasing

(Australia's was lagging at the time owing to drought) but nearly all (90 per cent) of the Australasian clip was now bypassing London and being sold direct to buyers in the purchasing country. A 1926 Dunedin wool sale was reported as having a full bench of buyers including agents from France, Bradford (UK), America and Germany.[58]

The vagaries of supply and demand in primary produce markets have always been an issue for New Zealand. Changes in volume and type can take years to implement and by the time they are in place the level of demand has often changed. In the mid-1920s *Le Figaro* was reporting a dramatic increase in global wool production compared to the pre-war years. This was attributed to imports by manufacturing countries exceeding their immediate needs. Wool that had been stockpiled in Britain during the war and immediately thereafter was being relocated to replenish lower stocks elsewhere in anticipation of demand exceeding pre-war levels as consumer confidence recovered. The situation was complicated by complaints from the United Kingdom that exports of woollen textiles from France had risen from 2.3 million yards in 1920 to 9.5 million yards in 1922. *Le Figaro* tartly responded that English girls were now well-clothed, thanks to this trend, even though wool production within the United Kingdom had fallen. In fact, the United Kingdom's own exports of woollen products were also expanding, thanks to wool imported from (mainly) Australia and New Zealand. Counter-intuitively it was England's re-exports of raw wool to the Continent that assisted in driving up the United Kingdom's wool imports.[59]

The French woollen industry was aware of these inefficiencies and attempted to resolve them. In September 1924 French wool trade representatives met with those of the principal producer nations (Australia, New Zealand and South Africa) at Bradford. A key issue was the shortage of appropriate classes of wool. As *Le Figaro* pointed out, (from the French point of view) the Romney rams used in New Zealand were siring progeny that were ideal for meat but not for producing the fine wools which France wanted. South Africa blamed imported Australian breeds for lowering the quality of the South African clip, as if this was beyond local control. Other peripheral issues included contamination through the use of tar for branding (possibly treatment of shearing cuts was fouling fleeces in the 'shed' or perhaps tar-marked producer brands on the bales were contaminating the wool), fluctuating exchange rates leading to uncertainty in price and the perennial complaint of wool fibre spinners and weavers regarding the use of jute bales, the fibres of which can contaminate the wool yarn and cause flaws in the woven cloth. The suggestion of an umbrella industry association did not receive a response so again a French overture in the interests of developing a trading relationship was left in abeyance with the New Zealand Government showing little or no interest, despite local agitation over wool pricing and industry structure.[60]

The meat industry suffered even more government interference, prompted by the unsubstantiated threat of the American Meat Trusts.[61] This resulted in the Massey Government's introduction of the Meat Export Control Bill to establish partial industry regulation through a body to be jointly managed by producers and Government. During the debate on the bill in the Legislative Council, Sir William Hall-Jones discussed his experiences when trying to establish a trade in New Zealand meat with France.[62] Hall-Jones recalled the 1911 Roubaix exhibition where lower priced New Zealand meat was showcased to French housewives. Hall-Jones implied this may have influenced subsequent riotous demands for cheap meat. Although the circumstances therefore seemed to be favourable for imports of cheaper, frozen New Zealand-sourced meat, there was no infrastructure (cold storage, specialist meat railway wagons and so on) available and whole carcasses were not allowed into France without the internal organs *in situ*.[63] Hall-Jones attempted to get a trial shipment of 10,000 carcasses into France. With support from the British Chamber of Commerce in Paris he had arranged the infrastructure (cold store, cartage and a French firm to underwrite the venture) but he could get neither government support nor the meat companies' agreement to prepare the carcasses in accordance with French law. Hall-Jones explained to the Council that in the meantime Argentina had negotiated a lower duty on meat. Hall-Jones obtained French Government agreement to offer the same conditions for New Zealand but he could go no further as High Commissioner. Follow-up action was required from the (British) Foreign Office and the New Zealand Government but nothing was done. As Hall-Jones explained: 'I believe there is a big field to be opened up in France with regard to frozen meat, they [are] using more mutton and lamb than other countries in Europe...'[64] The possibility of French consumers accepting frozen meat was borne out by the *Herald*'s special correspondent who at about the same time reported that six years of war and rising prices were a powerful influence on the French public's preferences.[65]

In the immediate post-war years France was open to developing a trading relationship with New Zealand (although New Zealand chose not to take the opportunity). The case for this proposition is based on three factors. Firstly, any vestiges of pre-war dislike had been ameliorated at least temporarily by the sacrifice of New Zealand lives in defence of French independence against German aggression. Moreover, New Zealand was part of a coalition broadly sympathetic with the French position on the post-war treatment of Germany. Secondly, France had taken the initiative to visit New Zealand and investigate possible sources to help overcome shortfalls in supply. Thirdly, France had acquiesced in New Zealand's participation as a separate nation at the Versailles Conference and accepted her aspirations for territorial acquisitions in the Pacific both for immediate economic gain (in the case of Nauru phosphate) and to meet nascent colonial ambitions (in the case of German Samoa). By the time the final wool shipment left New Zealand under the commandeer arrangement in September 1922 the opportunity was almost gone. As the French Mission had somewhat wistfully noted, genuine free trade was unlikely with protective tariffs still in place (and there was no move from New

Zealand to end these).[66] The first French effort to reward the sacrifice and continue the wartime goodwill had been rebuffed.

In January 1923, the French battlecruiser *Jules Michelet* (named after the famed French historian of Renaissance expertise) visited Auckland and Wellington on her journey from Australia to New Caledonia. The Mission Leader (Admiral Gilly) highlighted the goodwill and gratitude of the French people, but the *Auckland Star* in particular was either naïve or feigning innocence in observing that 'behind its military aspect there was the penetrating shrewdness of the commerce of France'. The ship was equipped with a fixed display described as a '*Salon du Goutes Francais*' (sic) supported by four commercial representatives from the Departments of Commerce and Industries, Public Works, Foreign Affairs and Colonies.[67] The New Zealand hosts again seemed intent on arranging sightseeing tours for the commercial visitors rather than engaging in trade negotiations. The obvious French objective – to strengthen commercial ties with 'the great Dominions allied to France' – was all but politely ignored by a Government which apparently took little active part, aside from reciprocal set piece visits involving Prime Minister Massey while the vessel was in Wellington. M. Petrequin, one of the commercial representatives, stated that France could potentially buy more butter, frozen meat, and wool from New Zealand.[68] He repeated the practical observation that appointing trade agents would avoid delays in dealing through London. Moreover, direct shipping would stimulate trade volumes. During one interview in which he expressed these views the reporter succinctly summed up the New Zealand approach: 'And what do you think of the surrounding district of Palmerston North?' was the reporter's first question following Petrequin's statement.[69]

A month after this visit the New Zealand Industrial Corporation met. Within a lengthy report it was comfortingly concluded that none of the French products would compete with New Zealand's own secondary industries. The French exhibits were interpreted as a sign that New Zealand should develop her own manufacturing.[70] More reasoned opinion was offered by some press commentators. The *Bay of Plenty Times* accepted that the visit was 'principally' to further commerce and that there were 'bright' prospects for trade. Mission member M. Petrequin had correctly pointed out the low levels of commerce and the potential for French oils, wines and manufactured goods including machinery. France 'would like to take the place which Germany occupied before the war'.[71] Petrequin had yet again pointed out that France bought large quantities of New Zealand wool and he urged direct trade and closer relations in the vein of the Pau mission's earlier advocacy. While accepting that it was 'natural' for New Zealand to look to Great Britain, France would still like to be next in the order of suppliers.[72]

Clearly post-war New Zealand had significant market-led (as opposed to production-driven) export opportunities with Continental Europe in general and especially with France. The General Pau-led Mission suggested an alternative trade strategy in both wool and sheep meats in part to recognise the sacrifice and friendship of the war years. There was certainly an element of self-interest on the part of the French, who wished to secure the immediate support of their wartime ally and to extend the arrangement into a longer-term interaction which would bind New Zealand through mutual trade to a French-centred Europe. It was nonetheless a future better suited to post-war commercial realities even if it contradicted the old Empire order. New Zealand greeted the visitors politely, showed them the sights, and took nothing in return. The French offer of a toehold in the French market received the proverbial cold shoulder. Any inclination to exploit these opportunities was suppressed by an overdeveloped propensity to remain firmly in the British trading bloc, reinforced by the extended wartime commandeer, the shortage of shipping and a wish to develop a British-centric dairy industry. New Zealand greeted the opportunity by retreating into the Empire's failing United Kingdom-centred trading model.

'Trade' suggests a two-way exchange with each party supplying goods and services from product categories in which they have a competitive advantage. Manufactured goods and higher end consumer products such as brandy, perfume, clothing, cars and so on could presumably have been sourced from France. This required stimulating consumer demand in the case of high-end retail products while encouraging major commercial purchases by Government or private industry of French machinery, tools and equipment to displace formerly German-supplied products. Stimulating consumer demand required advertising, a point made in the Pau report.[73] The Papers Past advertising content is the best available data source to see whether this was attempted. Only 4 per cent of national advertising volume between 1919 and 1924 including some reference to France or French.[74] Clothing was the most frequently advertised category.[75]

Advertising of consumer goods is typically instigated by manufacturers and local retailers. In this case a diverse collection of non-perishable products (ranging from cornets and binoculars to French doors and French windows), as well as higher-end consumables such as brandy and tobacco were included. Haute couture items – millinery, gloves and gowns in particular – were prominent. The volume of education-related advertising – such as vacancies for teachers with expertise in French tutoring and language – remained stable, suggesting that there was no increased interest in the French language or culture in post-war New Zealand. Any halo effect extending from the time of the Mission's visit quickly faded, since despite a general increase in total advertising volume in the immediate post-war years there was a significant decline in French-related copy after 1920.

General Pau's report mentioned the issue of tariffs and the possibility of obtaining a preferential rate for France but, as was the case with other policy matters, the New Zealand Ministers had demurred owing to Massey's absence. The thought that France might be considered as a special case did not appear to have been considered. Despite the talk of industrial products and the supply of both machine tools and automobiles, the only immediate opportunity identified at the time was the provision of equipment for the major hydro-electric developments which New Zealand was planning. Pau did note that Switzerland was the most recent supplier of such electrical and related equipment.[76]

Hippeau pointedly remarked in his summary of the Mission's visit 'that the information obtained by the mission is about the same as the information collected by the Vice Consulate in recent years'.[77] He expressed with some force – just as Hall-Jones had expressed in relation to New Zealand meat exports to France – his frustration with the French traders' failure to seize the moment. The goodwill evident during the Pau visit would not last indefinitely, so it was incumbent on the traders to act before the opportunities were lost to American and Japanese interests. Even if trade did not start immediately, it was essential to maintain the relationships in anticipation of future business. Moreover, despite the official approbation that Hippeau had experienced as a result of his own initiatives, many enquiries from New Zealand traders had not been acknowledged by the French suppliers. The discouraged New Zealand traders had looked elsewhere. In plain language Hippeau made it clear that there was little point in promoting French goods if the exporters were unwilling to engage and it was up to them to act. The reasons given in the official Mission report for their tardiness – the small size of the New Zealand market and the not unrelated problem of direct shipping – are the most probable reasons for the failure to tackle the bigger issues of imperial preference, tariffs and non-specific trade barriers. Unsurprisingly, direct exports from France to New Zealand in 1925 were valued at just £918,600 sterling while direct exports from New Zealand to France were a similarly insignificant £600,800.

Acting Prime Minister James Allen either completely missed or simply dismissed the trade opportunities on offer when Pau visited. Massey's New Zealand seemed content with continuing the wartime trading arrangements whereby the British purchased New Zealand product on the assumption that this arrangement could continue in perpetuity. When difficulties arose, exporters appeared to simply hope that the British policy of free trade would be replaced by imperial preference. This proved short-sighted for not only were the wartime trading arrangements terminated by the British, there was also active resistance to them especially within some sectors of the rural industry. With France snubbed and memories of the Pau Mission fading, the public's relationship with official France lapsed into a mix of cultural and sporting contacts, supplemented by arm's-length interest in French-related commerce, transport and technology. Even as New Zealand neglected opportunities to engage with France, economic and political developments were changing the world and challenging what New Zealand saw as the Empire's hegemony.

Prime Minister George Forbes' statement prior to the 1930 Imperial Conference indicated how disconnected New Zealand remained from changing trade realities. His words were reminiscent of those used by his predecessor, Gordon Coates. 'We in New Zealand are in a happy position in our geographical isolation from the problems of the Old World and in our very complete economic affiliation to the United Kingdom.' Forbes claimed that New Zealand could concentrate on domestic problems without concern for 'international friction'. Forbes hoped that he could negotiate trade agreements with Canada and France while overseas, an objective which contradicted the previous points regarding New Zealand's isolation and economic security.[78]

A year later the Great Depression bit. The policy of reliance on the United Kingdom was finally questioned, sometimes bluntly. In 1931 W.P. (Bill) Endean MP (Reform, Parnell) described Britain as a third-rate economic power of indeterminate military status. Endean said an unnamed French economist had observed that the United Kingdom had 'changed over' from being the workshop of the world based on coal and iron (i.e. industrially based) to a service and trade-based economy reliant on insurance, banking and shipping. New Zealand was consequently suffering in her main market while the British could not compete with the other European countries owing to higher domestic labour costs. Were there any fault, it was as usual implied to be beyond local control for Endean stated that if France was 'amenable to reason' with respect to global debt, the economic situation could be restored.[79]

Despite the introduction of producer boards and attempts to control and direct trade activity through them, significant flaws remained in New Zealand's trade strategy. These were observed but ignored. In 1932 Robert Masters (then Minister of Industries and Commerce in the United-Reform Coalition Government) told Parliament that the Boards had no control or detailed knowledge of the £8 million of New Zealand produce re-exported to Europe by the United Kingdom. Masters was unequivocal in his declaration that the producer boards should be in closer touch with foreign governments and it was up to New Zealand to develop her own marketing efforts outside the United Kingdom. Well ahead of contemporary ideas, he pointed out that the various producer boards were too focussed on production in New Zealand rather than marketing. He mused:

> The thought has occurred to me at times whether the Boards are at the right end of the world – whether they should be in New Zealand or in London. Because after all, we may produce the finest possible article; but unless it is marketed properly, we do not get the true value of our products.[80]

W.H. Field MP (Reform, Otaki) similarly observed that the marketing of New Zealand wool was still 'entirely in the hands of Bradford' and that competitive purchasing from Japanese, German and French buyers had been 'our only saving' as far as price went.[81] In 1934 it seemed inconceivable that these three developing markets – of which New Zealand knew so little – would soon to be at war, leaving New Zealand even more dependent on the United Kingdom. New Zealand neither led nor followed, but rather chose to accept a trade trajectory set by Massey over fifteen years earlier, while blaming any adverse consequences on the policies of others.

Chapter Eleven

Post-war choices – independence, Empire citizen or membre de la Société des Nations?

Although New Zealand exited World War I as an independent country, it was no closer to defining a distinct national identity than it had been in 1914. If anything, the conflict proved that a strong emotional engagement with Britain and its imperial capital, London, remained. It followed that if New Zealand's London was a constant (as Felicity Barnes has argued) then so too was New Zealand's version of France, the traditional rival of the British.[1] Leaving France emotionally as well as physically was therefore not only a repudiation of the direct consequences of the war but also a logical outcome of Britain's rejection of a closer post-war engagement with France and the French people. The rationale was simple. Despite the confusion about the aims of the war, in the New Zealand narrative the British Empire had obviously 'worked'. The Dominions had rallied to the cause by mustering bodies to fight and by delivering essential supplies to sustain life at Home, while the French Empire had demonstrably failed, because it needed to be saved by the British. Judged on the tone of the early post-war intra-empire meetings and conferences as well as the international meetings at which the Empire appeared to act en bloc, the post-war British Empire was a successful political entity. Inarguably, though, once the common enemy had been defeated cracks appeared within the Empire, as well as between the Empire and France.

It therefore seems doubtful that there is sufficient evidence to support the commonly expressed contention that the war 'undermined … imperial ties' from New Zealand's point of view.[2] The continued close cultural and economic engagement with the Crown and Empire provides evidence of New Zealand's determination to remain a British nation in character and constitution, in contradiction with later assertions that a new mood favouring national independence emerged.[3] If there had been such a mood, some evidence would surely have been apparent as the relationship with Britain ruptured. An obvious post-war case existed in the Dominion of Ireland. The sovereign status of that Dominion conflicted with a nationalist movement desiring independence.[4] Discord, not necessarily evidenced by armed revolt, would surely have been similarly evident if New Zealand had been determined to discard her post-colonial garb and shape a separate path as a truly independent nation. Instead, New Zealand remained firmly attached to Britain's flank.

Political scientist Miles Kahler proposed a model that appears appropriate for explaining New Zealand's international façade as it may have appeared to France. Kahler identified four modes by which Empires embed themselves within a possessed nation, namely: in the 'political parties and [their] ideology', through 'economic actors' such as industry lobby groups, by creating 'populations of the Empire' whether indigenous or immigrant colonisers and through the presence of the 'state' including the colonial administration and staff. Although Kahler was describing later decolonisation, all four elements were recognisable in the supposedly post-colonial New Zealand of 1918–35.[5] Politically the Empire was championed in New Zealand by the United and Reform Parties, although it was generally treated circumspectly (at best) by Labour and the more radical left, at least until another war threatened. The early economic actors were business enterprises, not dissimilar to franchisees, who were either formally or informally licensed to exploit a territory or business sector. These largely British owned consortiums (the meat processing companies being one example) occupied the economic territory of New Zealand on behalf of the colonising state and profited by trading more or less exclusively with the British market.[6] Furthermore, New Zealand devoted considerable effort to ensuring that most immigrants were of British racial stock while actively discouraging the 'others', thereby embedding the Empire's presence through racial conformity.[7] Finally, the Governor-General, even if officially disempowered, retained his hollowed-out role as a constitutional reminder of the presence of the British state. British disengagement, even if only from the largely symbolic vice-regal control of the Dominion, would have been seen as an existential threat by New Zealand's political Right with its British-centric foreign policy. Collectively these factors made explicit to the French what was implicit for much of New Zealand: New Zealand was a British-dependent state with limited autonomy.

At the beginning of the twentieth century the scholar and intellectual (Sir) Richard Jebb suggested that the British Empire would remain cohesive only as long as the (predominantly) white Dominions were not forced to choose between federation and complete independence.[8] In other words, the existence of the Empire depended on maintaining an equivocal constitutional status. While Balfour's reference during the 1926 Imperial Conference to the 'rapid evolution' of the Dominions was describing a process that appeared natural, undeniably progressive and all embracing, it was not welcomed without qualification in New Zealand by Prime Minister Gordon Coates since progress would disrupt the current equilibrium.[9] Having staked New Zealand's economic future on Empire membership, Britain's renewed post-war interest in economic gain and diplomatic interactions elsewhere was far from reassuring since this raised the possibility of Britain metaphorically leaving the existing mature Empire and abandoning her 'much petted sons'.[10] Although Britain needed to change as the world situation altered, attempts to maintain the Empire's structure through actions such as securing peace in Europe, defending that vital eastern route to the Pacific through the Suez Canal and the construction of the Singapore naval base would have been a comfort to New Zealand.[11]

Despite this, the attention and resources of the British Government were being redeployed to other geographies where there were opportunities for direct material exploitation, driven in part by the disinclination of the British-taxpaying public to continue financial backing for the Dominions. As the New Zealand politician William Hall-Jones had observed, the other British Dominions were concurrently ignoring or actively discarding the implied necessity of Empire unity as they assumed a more independent and active part in shaping their own foreign affairs. The imperial infrastructure that remained was neither capable of developing a collective foreign policy for the Dominions nor was it effective as a body for cultivating trade relationships on their behalf.[12] Post-war New Zealand therefore had three coexisting, interchangeable identities: it was simultaneously a nominally independent nation, a member of the League of Nations and an Empire affiliate. The motivation for government action or inaction, whether it be over trade with France, or supporting Britain during the Chanak Crisis (a post-war dispute between Britain and Turkey) can be used to assess whether New Zealand was making decisions as an independent country or as a show of obsequious subservience to British Empire policy. Some decisions could even be interpreted as implementation of League policy, consistent with some vaguely defined universal interest. Since national governments are rightly held to account based on their ability to meet the collective interests of their citizens (rather than those of another sovereign authority) the motivation matters.

The evidence suggests that the delineation was unclear and that this manifested as uncertainty as to where New Zealand's interests lay and therefore how New Zealand should act in relation to France. Prime Minister Massey clearly saw Empire citizenship as the ideal position for New Zealand. The Labour Opposition Leader (Holland) imagined –

as far as can be judged of a politician who never had to implement his policy – that the appropriate position was that of a non-aligned, League member. New Zealand's imaginary and transient constitutional location ebbed and flowed between these two points between 1918 and 1935. Because the same ebb and flow applied to other nations including Great Britain and France, New Zealand's position was continually readjusted by the political shuffling and economic jostling. The aspiration of eventually achieving economic continuity and political stability was illusory.

Once the French offer to trade had been rejected, it was unclear to France which position New Zealand occupied. The decline in French interest in developing a deeper relationship was a reaction to this confusion. Given negligible direct trade, the founding of the League of Nations to resolve inter-country disputes and the continuation of an Empire structure to manage the bilateral Anglo-French relationship, there was neither a need for a direct association nor for supplementary diplomatic initiatives from the French viewpoint. Likewise, New Zealand simply bundled France with the 'others' until some matter of consequence arose. The status most appropriate for the situation was then adopted. The French could see that this was so, and it ultimately led to satirical derision of New Zealand in the French press. Diplomatically marooned, a supposedly post-colonial New Zealand was left desperately clinging to the remnants of a disintegrating pre-war Dominion model which was dependent on a restrictive trade strategy guided by an unnecessarily Franco-sceptic foreign policy.

The debate over possession of the New Hebrides exposed these incompatible positions. The persistence of the Presbyterian missionaries in pressing for full British control of these islands had been an issue since New Zealand was first recognised as a British colony. There had been suggestions of New Zealand and/or Australian stewardship over various islands in the Pacific, and successive New Zealand governments, including those of Seddon and Ward, had been vociferous in their public support for British sovereignty in place of the 'condominium', an arrangement that divided the New Hebridean governorship between France and Great Britain. Britain was, however, reluctant to press the French to alter this arrangement even when it was the loyal New Zealanders who demanded change.

One of the objectives of the 1918–19 French Mission was to 'facilitate resolution' of issues in Oceania (including the New Hebrides).[13] This was an attempt to engage directly with New Zealand on a matter of mutual interest. The British were not involved, at least in the preliminary stages. When General Pau and the French Mission departed New Zealand in February 1919, the Vice-Consul Lionel Hippeau when summarising Pau's visit noted that:

> With regard to the New Hebrides – with the exception of the Protestant missionaries whose attitude is known to you, there is little discussion of the New Hebrides, which is considered to be a rather influential zone for Australia. Although appearing to prefer the British Empire, it would probably raise no difficulty in the event of an assignment to the French Republic. Mr. Allen, Acting Prime Minister, declares that if England and Australia are in agreement, the Dominion Government would have **no objection to the cession of the New Hebrides to France**[14] [emphasis added]

Given that elsewhere in the telegram the paralysis in local decision making is apparent ('The ministers have always said that because of the absence of the Prime Minister and the circumstances, no orientation can be decided before the peace treaty and the imperial conference') it seems improbable that this offer was made by Allen – assuming it was not a misunderstanding or a misquote – without authority. Allen understood the issues as he had lobbied for the removal of French control during his 1913 visit to London.[15] The offer was therefore a remarkably uncharacteristic concession to France, despite the qualification requiring Australian and British agreement. From New Zealand's point of view, the reasons for this stance, its timing and the desired outcome are unclear. The offer (if valid) was not followed up and it understandably received no public airing as it was a significant deviation from the Empire's existing policy.

During the Versailles negotiations (that began in January 1919 while the French Mission was still in New Zealand and hence Ward and Massey were absent) the British Foreign Secretary (Arthur Balfour) told Massey that the New Hebrides had nothing to do with the peace negotiations and so it was not to be raised in conference.[16] Perhaps this was the reason that Allen was then told in some as yet undiscovered correspondence that New Zealand would no longer pursue the New Hebridean issue and that the French visitors could be so informed. If so, it was only a temporary respite. In 1921 a petition from local advocates for British control was commended to the Government for 'favourable consideration' (strong parliamentary language from a petitions committee) and immediate transmission to the imperial authorities for action.[17] Perhaps this stiffened New Zealand's resolve, for by the time the 1921 Imperial Conference met Massey was again raising the perennial Australasian complaint regarding the unsatisfactory nature of the New Hebrides arrangement.

On balance, while Allen's position as quoted by Hippeau was probably a correct reflection of the Government's private view, it was presumably not meant to be shared beyond the French delegation. The New Zealand Government may have seen no value in British colonial occupation of the New Hebrides, but publicly advocating for removal of the French was a political necessity to placate New Zealand's southern Presbyterian voters. These voters saw it as a matter of national importance and worthy of a challenge to the British policy of co-governance. The issue was an ongoing political irritant for the Massey Government because the thought of closer engagement with France was politically unpalatable while the French had a significant presence in the New Hebrides. Given Balfour's instruction at Versailles, New Zealand could perhaps have ceded her claim if given the political cover of United Kingdom and Australian agreement to assuage local disquiet. With the New Hebrides issue neutralised the way would have been cleared for a direct trade relationship with France that was obviously in the national interest.

New Zealand had fought a war to support the British policy of defending France, but would the British reciprocate and help New Zealand in the Pacific? That presumption that an emotional debt existed was being tested in an unforeseen manner through New Zealand's disagreement with France over the New Hebrides. The question was resolved in the negative as shown in the British version of events documented in the Annual Reports submitted to the British Foreign Secretary by successive British Ambassadors to France. (These reports were copied and forwarded annually to New Zealand.) Two paragraphs in the 1926 Ambassador's Report describe enquiries in Paris instigated as a result of the partition suggestion raised during the 1926 Imperial Conference. The French response was predictably negative. The French were informed that a commission representing Australia, New Zealand and Great Britain would visit the New Hebrides to investigate 'any disadvantages' the British settlers were experiencing. Subsequent notes in the Ambassadors' annual reports (copied to New Zealand and now filed in the National Archives) trace a downgrading of the issue until by 1932 in paragraph 115 under 'Miscellaneous' the relevant entry reads 'nil'.[18] There was never any serious post-war attempt by the British to meet New Zealand's demands. Successive New Zealand governments were made aware of that at prime ministerial level according to these British records supplied at the time, but no public statement resulted. None of the available New Zealand postures – an extremely limited independence, loyal Empire membership or League of Nations membership – gave New Zealand any leverage in the Quai d'Orsay offices. Despite this, New Zealand still did not fully embrace the demeanour, political structures or policies of a post-colonial nation, but instead continued in the role of Empire adherent, exhibited through rejection of a closer involvement in global affairs even within the League of Nations.

By the early to mid-1920s the British Empire was, as far as the Dominions were concerned, a non-prescriptive organisation, not dissimilar to a family supervised by an indulgent parent seeking domestic unity by accommodating the members' diverging needs.[19] Thus, the Empire's character eventually became so broad that it was little more than a series of generalised wishes. Even so, in New Zealand's view adhering more or less consistently to Empire policies (insofar as they could be determined) precluded embracing and developing a fully independent national identity as a self-governing member of the League. In part this was due to there being few matters of national policy – whether nominally domestic or international – which the League of Nations as it was first envisaged could not claim as being within the scope of its Covenant. Consequently, as a significant portion of the prescriptive membership requirements impinged on what might otherwise have been assumed to be the internal affairs of member states, New Zealand along with many other nations resisted wholeheartedly adopting the League's ideals.

Moreover, the League members – including New Zealand and France – expected the League to deliver immediate gratification consistent with their own national interests. If a favourable resolution was not forthcoming on a matter of substance it was met with either petulant withdrawal or simply ignored. If an issue or dispute seemed to be unrelated to the affairs of the relevant nation(s) it was treated with indifference. The members knew what was right for all the other nations, but they hypocritically resisted application of the same rules when they did not suit. As a result, League members would often fail to conform with League decisions while still expecting the League to enforce decisions consistent with their national interests.

Although a common opinion holds that the League of Nations failed due to its structure, it was this failure of the League members to place justice, human rights, international peace and fairness for all nations ahead of national interest which was at fault.[20] Just as various populations were expected to bend to suit newly defined post-war boundaries decided by the winners, so too was the League coerced into conforming with nationalistic agendas. As a literal translation of the suggestive name *La Société des Nations* implies, the League was treated as if it were a society or club, but one whose rules the most influential members obeyed or ignored as their circumstances required.[21] The immediate failure was blamed on the absence of the United States, for without American support the Allies could neither enforce the Paris peace terms nor unconditionally underwrite French territorial security using the threat of force.[22] New Zealand and the other Dominions shared the blame, because they would not support Austen Chamberlain's policy of guaranteeing French borders nor would they occupy Germany.[23] The apparently costless alternative – universal disarmament with any disputes to be resolved using the League of Nations – failed because France had no confidence in the League as a means of delivering national security, but given Woodrow Wilson's enthusiasm for the project, France could not ignore the League's establishment as a pre-condition for reaching an otherwise sympathetic resolution at Versailles.

Despite these shortcomings, membership of the League of Nations permitted New Zealand in the post-war years to engage as an equal with other non-Empire League members. The League was therefore one of the few venues where there was direct and regular contact with France. New Zealand could observe the continued influence of France amongst the great powers, yet even when both New Zealand and France were present, interactions were kept at arm's length, not only by the disparity in size, language and culture but also by New Zealand's continued identity as a British Empire member.

When the First League Assembly convened, the New Zealanders acted in lockstep with the British.[24] New Zealand's High Commissioner in London (Sir James Allen) acted as the leader of New Zealand's League delegation. His behaviour in this role was consistent with his time as acting-Prime Minister during Massey and Ward's lengthy absences in London. If there was no specified policy Sir James faithfully reported events back to Wellington but he did not initiate action. He was clearly not a political innovator nor did he prove to be a proactive diplomat, but given Massey's loyalty to the Empire and lukewarm, sceptical attitude towards the League, this was probably exactly what Massey wanted.[25] Prime Minister Massey did not expedite the publication of either Allen's reports or the League minutes when they were received, perhaps because he viewed such as an endorsement. By the time these were officially published the events described therein had long been determined and publicised elsewhere. Four years before the official record was finally published in the 1925 New Zealand *Appendices to the Journals of the House of Representatives*, a 1920 *Le Figaro* report had detailed the settlement of the New Zealand mandate ('Samoa assigned to New Zealand') and the protocols for the management of the mandated territories.

Nothing of direct consequence for New Zealand in relation to France was noted in Allen's first report, but in his second report Allen included considerable discussion on the French objections to the League's involvement in the regulation of trafficking in women and children. Typically, Allen seemed to miss the point, as he could see no reason for these objections apart from French 'jealousy' over another country leading the initiative, or perhaps concerns that the administrative function would not be in France.[26] The continued insistence by France that issues related to women's rights – apart from international trafficking of women for prostitution – were a domestic policy concern has several possible explanations.[27] One that should have raised concerns for all the colonial powers was the appalling treatment of indigenous workers – including women and children – working in slave-like circumstances, particularly in Africa. Presumably these colonial possessions could have been viewed as 'domestic' territories within an imperial structure. Another concern may have been French fears of a broader debate drawing unwelcome attention to women's suffrage in France. France had been the subject of scathing criticism in the British press which seemed to delight in the apparently illogical

French intransigence on the issue. This embarrassment may have been the principal French concern.[28]

The significance for New Zealand is less in the substance of French objections than in Allen's apparent growing irritation with the French, and his failure as New Zealand's leading diplomat to determine the basis of their objections. French views and their associated justifications had been debated with some force in both *Le Figaro* and *L'Humanité* so the discussion points were presumably available to diplomats – such as Allen – as well as the public. Immediately after the war ended the French press had argued that not only was it a 'disgrace' to deny the vote to women who had suffered alongside the menfolk but the sacrifice of women was of itself an affirmation that they should be treated equally. The French Senate's attitude was contrasted with the views held in Belgium and New Zealand, amongst others. A demographically tenuous but politically astute point was the claimed link between lower infant mortality and universal suffrage, a particularly sensitive issue for France given the continued concern with the low birth rate compared to that of Germany. New Zealand's lower infant mortality was used as an example. It seems incredible that Allen was either unaware of this debate or if he was aware, that he failed to connect the politically contentious domestic suffrage issue with the French stance on women's rights and, moreover, that he failed to report the reason for the French attitude.[29]

New Zealand had three principal delegates at the Third Assembly: Allen, Sir Francis Bell who was coincidentally in London and apparently offered to go along to assist, and Sir Arthur Steel-Maitland.[30] Already (in 1922, barely four years since the war ended) Allen accepted that post-war hopes for disarmament were 'inconceivable'. As Allen explained, the French had to consider Germany and (possibly) Russia as threats but both were outside the League and therefore outside whatever nominal control or influence the League may have. Allen's report did not include the qualification that Germany's exclusion was a French precondition for the formation of the League though he probably felt he did not need to. The development of aircraft technology and its military application was already a threat to stability and peace while concurrently rendering earlier discussions on conventional weapons redundant.[31] Allen observed that although France had been opposed to disarmament in 1921, current financial pressures meant that option might now be considered under a Treaty of Mutual Guarantee. Before disarming, France wanted very strict and exact security assurances. No doubt with an eye on their own situation the British (Allen reported) were not unfavourable but were most reluctant to give any firm assurances that could be seen in the United Kingdom as simply underwriting French defence. Fisher (for the United Kingdom) was therefore hesitant to even put this proposal to his Government for further work on the detail. Typically, Allen had no suggestions or recommendations and so New Zealand's position became that of the British by default.

The comfortable stance of acquiescing to British policy positions was replaced with action when New Zealand's interests came directly into question during the Third Assembly's review of the mandated territories. Overriding all was the self-interested display of sovereignty and independence which New Zealand was prepared to assume when it suited. Captain Mousley, a lawyer experienced in international diplomacy who had assisted Massey at Versailles, provided additional gravitas and expertise to the New Zealand delegation.[32] As Captain Mousley's report makes clear, the League's Mandate Committee was showing a rarely displayed interest in the wellbeing of the Nauru Islanders. Confronted with a matter of great importance for both the country and the personal prestige of Massey, New Zealand adopted the stance of an independent sovereign state and used the legal provisions of the Nauru Island mandate to resist any interference from the League. Without any apparent irony the inconvenient rights of this hapless, small Pacific nation were dismissed as internal matters, for New Zealand to adjudicate.[33]

New Zealand's representation at the Fourth Assembly held in 1923 reverted to a delegation of Allen, his private secretary and a departmental officer. Attention had turned again to initiating a Treaty of Mutual Assistance to bypass the apparently irreconcilable differences over disarmament. This suggestion from the Temporary Mixed Commission resurrected one of the earliest post-war security proposals. The French response was disarmingly pragmatic and simply proposed the abolition of the Temporary Mixed Commission (eminent persons' group) responsible for generating disarmament proposals. Lord Robert Cecil for Britain was opposed.[34] The whole point of the eminent persons' group was generating ideas for the Disarmament Commission independently from government control, and it was therefore a potentially useful mechanism for producing options unconstrained by the direct political consequences of its recommendations. It was for exactly these reasons that it had attracted strong French opposition. As a compromise, a temporary reprieve was negotiated for the Commission.

Allen's detachment during these discussions was palpable, both in tone and in fact when he reported that neither he nor his secretary were present. He had clearly become exasperated by the naysaying of the French for, as he noted without any apparent irony, they always opposed League involvement in matters of immediate concern to France. The dysfunction of the League was apparent to Allen in other ways, as shown when the worth of a resolution in favour of unresolved disputes being passed up to the League Council was undermined by the conspicuous absence of the United States, Russia and Germany. The same problem occurred when the new International Court was proposed. Litigants had to agree to take a case to the court so its function was in fact arbitration rather than delivering 'justice'. Exceptions were to be allowed for existing treaties and conventions. As this exception applied to the Treaty of Versailles, the court's efficacy was questionable.

In his address to the 1923 Imperial Conference, Stanley Baldwin had backtracked on Lloyd George's 1921 claim that the reparation and disarmament issues were settled. Solving French budgetary problems by making 'the *Boche* pay' was an illusion which could only underpin general political stability in France as long as it was allowed to persist. In the British view, once this fiscal mirage evaporated France would lapse into her default state of domestic political disharmony and dispute. Baldwin in his comments seemed to be aware that the United Kingdom could be accused of prevaricating, but any failed attempt at mediation (rather than adjudication) could be interpreted as dithering if the mediation failed.[35] France nevertheless continued to criticise Germany in an attempt to perpetuate Germany's status as the wrong-doing World War I protagonist. In an article dated 10 July 1923, *Le Figaro* reported examples of English opinion favouring the Ruhr occupation. The piece was obviously meant to bolster the impression that there was general support amongst the wartime Allies for the French position. *Le Figaro* was only able to provide one comment from New Zealand, and its authenticity is questionable because it is from an unnamed source(s).

> The last that has come down to us is particularly significant, since it comes from the antipodes. An Englishman of distinction, who lives in New Zealand, the city of Dunedin, capital of the rich auriferous province of Otago, asserts in his letter sentiments of the whole English colony in favor of France.[36]

This selected report was not representative of the general tone of the New Zealand press articles which tended to adhere to the British view of frustration with French obstinacy.

The contortions required for the League to operate alongside – rather than above – the existing European political structures were self-evident. Whatever sentiments New Zealand may have expressed to the contrary regarding the use of the League protocols in the European peace process, exactly the same problems existed when it came to the

Pacific because intra-Empire views were diverging. Reporting on the House of Commons debate on funding a naval base in Singapore, *Le Figaro* approvingly requoted the New Zealand Prime Minister as saying that:

> 'You say that your government [i.e. the British Government] is in favour of international cooperation through the enlarged and strengthened League of Nations. I think I have to answer that. One might come to regret the very existence of the League of Nations if the defence of the Empire depends only on that organization; the existence of the Empire depends on the Imperial Navy.'[37]

Like their French counterparts, the New Zealand Government had little confidence in the League as a means of protection, whether through disarmament or as a guarantor of mutual security. New Zealand believed that the Royal Navy operating from a safe regional base in Singapore was the best defensive option for New Zealand (and by implication British) interests in the Pacific. The same issue arose when the (Geneva) 'Protocol For The Pacific Settlement Of International Disputes' was proposed. New Zealand's objections to League involvement were more or less the same as those repeatedly expressed by the French. The prospect of disarmament and relying on the League and its associated bodies for protection left both countries feeling very insecure.[38]

Alignment between New Zealand and France became exceptional rather than normal as petty disagreements between France and her allies increased. In one case, intellectual property sharing became embroiled in national sentiment. When Professor Gilbert Murray (a university academic and prominent supporter of the League of Nations, described by *Le Figaro* as a British Empire delegate) presented his very positive report on the work of the Committee on Intellectual Cooperation, the French delegate (M. Cassin) associated the work of intellectual cooperation with the ideals for which the war had been fought. *Le Figaro* noted that the Australian delegate (a Mr Charlton) was an 'irreducible opponent, not of the International Institute, but of its seat at Paris'. Sir James Allen disagreed as he thought that the gift from France of intellectual property and a headquarters location should be accepted because the guarantees given for maintaining the international character of the Institute were sufficient.[39] That the ANZAC countries and France would dispute such a matter in an international forum would have seemed impossible six years earlier, but such was symptomatic of League and Empire dysfunction.

By the time the Sixth Assembly met (7–26 September 1925), Allen's criticisms extended to the use of the French language, because insufficient time was allowed for translation into English. A French proposal to exclude discussion of Allied debts and reparations from a forthcoming international conference seemed incredible to Allen. (France had also proposed regulation of private enterprise to ameliorate the mid-decade economic slump, a further point of antagonism.) Suggestions on security and conflict avoidance remained a touchstone because the League was aware that failure to deliver on these would undercut the whole point of an international body. In Allen's (correct) view, arbitration, security and disarmament needed to be inseparable components of any agreement.[40] The failure of the delegates' efforts in this regard had already doomed the Pacific Regional Treaty proposal.

It would be unreasonable to blame all of New Zealand's disaffection with the League on French actions. It could, however, be argued that in supporting what later came to be seen as unreasonable French views, New Zealand unintentionally undermined France's post-war position as the wronged party. When the League Council considered the recommendation of the Standing Committee on Warrants in 1926, authors of petitions from mandated territories wanted to appear before the Council to make verbal submissions. Chamberlain and Briand protested on the grounds of interference in the administration of their mandated territories. Briand in particular feared playing into the 'hands of trouble-makers'. *Le Figaro* related that: 'The representatives of New Zealand and South Africa present at the table of the Council associated themselves with Mr Briand's reservations, and it appeared that the Council would not follow the suggestions of the Commission in that direction'. Countries that ruled others through League-licensed mandates regarded the territories so granted as being within their own fiefdoms to control as they wished, without any direct means of protest or appeal being available to those under their jurisdiction.[41] Information for the League was to come solely from the occupying powers and in that matter New Zealand aligned with France.

Had she so chosen, post-war France could have used her moral authority and carte blanche to move towards a more internationalist position, but from New Zealand's viewpoint France seemed to be attending solely to her own interests. While not an unreasonable rationale in the context of the times, it was unlikely to bolster New Zealand's faith in internationally based solutions, nor in France as an example worth emulating, and even less in France as a potential partner in the Pacific. From the French viewpoint, New Zealand was doing more or less the same. The League was effectively dead as it was neither a useful forum for resolving disputes nor a venue suitable for developing a relationship with France. Unsurprisingly, little else involving both France and New Zealand was reported from League meetings after 1925.

Defence issues provided the starkest backdrop to New Zealand's post-war national identity debate, and in particular whether independent nationhood, cooperative Empire membership or mutual disarmament facilitated through the League of Nations was the most efficacious. As early as June 1921 *Le Figaro* had observed that the British commitment to disarm was qualified by the need to protect her Empire and specifically to defend Australia and New Zealand using the Royal Navy. It followed *ipso facto* that Britain would not disarm, although when reporting (in August 1921) on the outcome of the Dominion Premiers' Conference, *Le Figaro* indicated that the defence burden was now to be shared between Britain and her satellites.[42] *Le Figaro* reminded readers of this decision when reporting a year later that only

New Zealand and South Africa were planning to maintain their very small fleets, Australia was proposing a large reduction and Canada wanted to completely disarm.[43] *Le Figaro* reported that the British were 'alarmed' because they would have to replace these ships with others from the Home fleet and British taxpayers would thereby assume the burden of Empire defence.

Defending the Dominions and retaining British and New Zealand colonial territory in the Pacific at the expense of the British taxpayer carried the inherent assumption that the region had some economic benefit and presumably would reciprocate with manpower and financial support if there was another European conflict. Debate in the British Parliament concerning Egypt and the Suez Canal substantiates this view. *Le Figaro* noted Lloyd George's observation that over a million soldiers had been transported to France via the canal. It was in the interests of the French to retain ready access to these allies who were apparently prepared to support French interests by fighting wars in Europe while the British subsidised the cost.[44] There appears to be no publicly available record in New Zealand suggesting that the cost-benefit of occupying the canal zone and maintaining the canal was debated in either Britain or France. The Dominion governments – especially New Zealand's – had every reason to support the policy as it facilitated co-dependence through trade between the Pacific and Britain.

Protecting British interests within the Pacific presupposed a naval intervention by a capital fleet whether permanently based in Singapore or on temporary deployment there. New Zealand in particular had placed much faith in Singapore both as a symbol of British commitment in the Pacific and as a practical exhibition of British power. The public debate surrounding the issue was complicated by the uncertainty as to whether the base would contravene the terms of the Washington Treaty. *Le Figaro* opined that uncertainty over the Singapore investment was due to a period of reflection during which many of Britain's Empire dreams had been or were being abandoned. Britain was overly anxious and withdrawn in the application of her foreign policy, or so *Le Figaro* claimed.[45] Already the *Times* had observed – according to a *Le Figaro* report – that 'the world respects few who are not prepared to defend their legitimate interests'.[46] If the war with Germany resumed, support for France from the Pacific Dominions would be less certain if they were left undefended. *Le Figaro* therefore approvingly reported that a squadron of British cruisers visited the Pacific in 1923–24 in what *Le Figaro* interpreted as an effective counteracting propaganda initiative.

> The bâtiments [vessels or ships] visited a very large number of ports, above all in the Dominions ... the main goal was to exhibit [shine or burnish] the Navy in all parts of the Empire, thus contributing to strengthening ties between these scattered nations, and (finally) to create a favourable atmosphere for increased subsidies that the Dominions provide for the maintenance of the fleet.[47]

The message from Admiral Field's expedition was clear according to *Le Figaro*: the Dominions needed to support the Royal Navy and contribute towards its upkeep. The fleet's reception was, however, inconsistent (according to *Le Figaro*), varying as it did from Australian and New Zealand enthusiasm to a less motivated South African reception and outright controversy in the Canadian press *('...et surtout qu'au Canada, où elle a donné lieu à une polémique de presse')*. France, with its own interest in the French-Canadian community, had its reasons for viewing Canada as an exception amongst the Dominions, but nonetheless the lack of consistency and enthusiasm for collective defence from within the Empire-Commonwealth was obvious and concerning because a unified British Empire would have been of most use to France.

British Cabinet minutes indicate that the diverse views over Singapore and the implications for conciliation, peaceful resolution of disputes and limitation of arms were carefully considered before the British Prime Minister wrote to the French Prime Minister M. Poincaré (on 21 February 1924) stating that: 'Our task meanwhile must be to establish confidence, and this task can only be achieved by allaying the international suspicions and anxieties that exist today.'[48]

The Singapore base was postponed although neither France nor New Zealand wanted construction halted since the proposed base would have met the needs of both, largely at British expense. New Zealand especially had attached the greatest importance and symbolism to Singapore and the attendant naval strategy.[49] Cancellation put Britain's less aggressive stance towards any potentially competitive states at odds with New Zealand's policy of Empire loyalty and a *faux* independence, secured by the Royal Navy.

The 1924 Imperial Exhibition opened shortly after the Commons voted to defer construction of the Singapore base. The exhibition was an opportunity to counteract perceptions that the British Empire was weakening but who the exhibition was aimed at and to what end was less obvious. The most likely intent was a rekindling of British public support that was so essential for the Empire project, while encouraging intra-Empire trade and impressing if not deterring competitors. The primary wealth of the Empire was on display for the importers and manufacturers of England while the British public could view the produce available and replications of the diverse Empire scenery. Whether the visitors were supposed to provide financial support through taxation, buy Empire produce, migrate or visit as tourists was unclear.

Le Figaro described the exhibits and praised the replication of the Empire through the scale version of the Empire's idealised economy, within which raw materials were shipped to the United Kingdom for manufacture and then re-exported as finished goods.[50] *Le Figaro* noted the obvious conflict with the Dominions' ambitions to develop their own manufacturing capabilities. While it was apparent that the British Empire had size, diversity and development to its credit, if the colonies and Dominions were developing the industrial characteristics of the mother country rather than taking their rightful place as primary producers and developers of extractive industries, the British Empire's economic plan would fail. The reluctance of the United Kingdom to grant intra-Empire preferential tariffs was another omnipresent challenge, because the United States was in reserve as a potential alternative market for its Pacific neighbours Australia, New Zealand and Canada. The exchange rate of the British pound was encouraging the colonies and Dominions to import manufactured goods from non-British suppliers in Germany and Italy. The article concluded that there were lessons for France as she prepared for her own exhibition scheduled for 1927.

Le Figaro may have been certain about the primary purpose of the exhibition, but New Zealand apparently was not, for New Zealand's contribution appeared to reflect the vagueness and hesitancy of an uncertain national identity and purpose. One newspaper noted that the exhibition office was receiving some queries '...from people from Continental countries who are primarily interested from the trade viewpoint'. France was mentioned as one such but no detail is given.[51] The intent was clearly to sell more to Britain rather than to France or other Continental customers.[52]

When explaining the educational purpose of the exhibition, *Le Figaro* drew attention to the retrospection if not outright nostalgia reflected in the displays. The crowd was attentive and serious rather than entertained and amused as a play (or diorama) showed the Empire's formation with scenes of Cook's discovery of New Zealand, Nelson's victory at Trafalgar and similar significant events used to reinforce the British version of history and the pre-eminence of the resulting Empire. 'It is truly a beautiful show that is a fitting addition to the Wembley Imperial Exhibition, a monument to British power, wealth and pride.'[53]

The same correspondent provided a critical analysis of trade patterns within the Empire. Imports by Britain from the Empire posed no particular difficulties but the inconsistency in the British share of individual Empire members' imports was problematic. While 70 per cent of New Zealand's imports were sourced from Britain, India obtained only 40 per cent from the same source and Canada 60 per cent. *Le Figaro* asked hypothetically whether these percentages could be increased, to compensate for Britain's burden of defending these territories. The answer lay within the relatively less populous Dominions. Even if their citizens were loyal purchasers, there were insufficient individuals to significantly increase the proportion (quoted as four-tenths) of Britain's exports to Empire countries. Britain needed to expand her markets but, as noted, the Empire members wished to produce more of their own industrial requirements. The correspondent (Thomazi) concluded that it was impossible to predict how this situation would 'unfold'.[54]

Those in favour of the Empire therefore attempted to twist the statistical information to bolster their case. The following graph illustrates the expenditure per head on British goods across selected countries using published contemporary data. These have been multiplied by the omitted 1924 population counts. Although the average spend on British goods per New Zealand citizen was nearly thirteen times that of the average French citizen (£15-1-10 versus £1-3-9) loyalty could not overcome the disproportionate size of the two populations. Measured by value, France as an importer was worth nearly two and a half times as much to the United Kingdom as New Zealand.

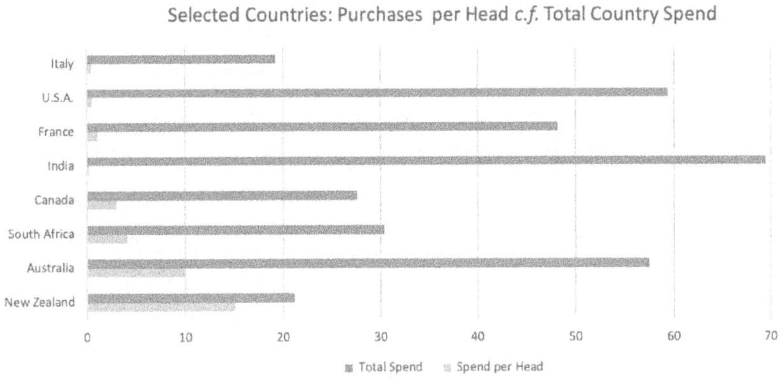

Figure 19 Selected countries' purchasing power (£ millions)[55]

If New Zealand was to have a future as an economy of significance within a British-centric Empire, it had to import an even greater volume of manufactured goods from Britain or become a more or less exclusive supplier of a product which offered an otherwise unobtainable benefit. The former would require rapid population growth. In New Zealand's case the potential demographic pool was severely restricted by the self-imposed preference for white, ideally British, migrants. As an undifferentiated supplier of bulk commodities with significant shipping costs, the supply-side opportunities were subject to severe competition from Danish and French dairy produce, Argentinian meat, Australian wool and so forth.[56] Sustaining and developing New Zealand within the Empire therefore required British subsidies which in turn depended on indoctrination and education of the next generation of Home voters.[57]

Arguably the increasing cultural and political divergence within the Empire was a more immediate problem. Not unexpectedly the French press tended to identify these differences rather than the consistencies, but the former were obvious and foreshadowed serious rifts that Empire Conferences, local politics and the New Zealand press could not conceal indefinitely. Jacques Chastenet, the prominent historian, lawyer, diplomat and intellectual, pointed out that despite the unwavering loyalty of Australia and New Zealand, South Africa wanted a Boer inspired flag without any Union Jack, Ireland claimed the right to independent representation at the League of Nations and Canada had recently forced the recall of Governor-General Lord Byng of Vimy, with future appointees being subject to Canadian approval. Britain, the article concluded, was now but '*primus inter pares*'. All these developments indicated that there was no longer any certainty about the Empire's fate, with Baldwin's Government in danger of falling over the trade issue and doubts arising as to whether the Dominions would ever again come to the assistance of Britain as they had during the Great War. 'Has the hour of decadence, which rings sooner or later for nations as for men, sounded for Albion? The immediate future will tell.'[58]

The impression that the Kingdom was no longer united was supported by the historian and journalist Jacques Bainville, who claimed that the defeat of the Unionists and the independence of Ireland placed the concept of the United Kingdom in the past tense. 'The Kingdom is no longer "united".'[59] Despite an apparent role for Ireland as (yet another) supplier of produce for industrialised Britain, doubts were raised by Bainville as to whether Ireland would even remain neutral during a war involving Britain. In Bainville's opinion, the 'beautiful [Dominion] unity' of 1914 was no longer a certainty. The Empire was undergoing an as yet incomplete evolution to a 'community of free nations' released from the 'bonds from which the Dominions have sought to free themselves'.[60] In the same issue *Le Figaro* published a brief summary of the recent Imperial Conference. Far from the laudatory accounts received in New Zealand, the piece exposed the contradictions and face-saving required to achieve a common denominator low enough to allow a claim of consensus. Hence peace and security through the League (*Le Figaro* reported) was supported as was a reduction in armaments, although this was apparently contradicted by the need to maintain the Royal Navy on at least '…an equal footing with the most powerful foreign navy'.[61]

Four days later *Le Figaro* published a scathing article under the authorship of W. Morton Fullerton.[62] In flowery prose Fullerton announced that the 1926 Imperial Conference was the 'death knell' of the British Empire. He sarcastically described Balfour's summary as if it were a papal announcement.[63] In Fullerton's interpretation, if the King was no longer King of a United Kingdom there was no longer an Empire. Moreover, the Empire or Commonwealth now existed only as an imprecise concept because – in Balfour's requoted words – it defied definition through being 'dissimilar to any political organization presently existing, or ever experienced, [and so] it is impossible to find an analogy or label for it'. Fullerton claimed that the concept of an Empire was by this admission a deception rather than a reality. The now independent states made their own policy and so England could no longer count upon their support. Fullerton interpreted this new order as leading to the obvious conclusion that England must now realise she was as 'an integral part of Europe … in spite of herself...'. While the Empire members endorsed the efforts of Austen Chamberlain to secure peace they were, Fullerton claimed, careful to avoid any commitment to aid the mother country or to give a guarantee to protect France or Belgium against Germany.

Fullerton did warn that this was two-sided. The Dominions might renounce any obligations to Europe but:

> if the Dominions wash their hands of any responsibility for the London initiatives, London is relieved of responsibility for a lot of problems, such as those that the future of the Pacific may have on the horizon [for] Australia and New Zealand ... This is true, despite the hitherto carefully concealed agreements on Singapore and the whole problem of defending the Empire![64]

This was New Zealand's worst fear. Despite protestations of loyalty and filial piety to Britain, New Zealand was slowly adapting her domestic policies to align with these truths. The inability of export dependent New Zealand to view the world from a vantage point broader than British-centric self-interest needed to be challenged.

Although intended as a lighthearted jibe at the expense of King George V and the Empire-Commonwealth, *Le Figaro*'s recipe for 1927 Xmas fare included a pointed reference to the produce of the various Dominions and territories. The clichéd reference to the British pudding becomes a 'dig' at the British Empire so popular – the poem says – with the 'old lords' who loved the (colonial) recipe. The poem thereby becomes a critical reflection on British colonisation and the aristocracy. The ditty says (satirically) that every European country has to think and get inspired by this British concoction. The poem includes a word play on the 'Société des Rations' (alluding to the 'Société des Nations') and the post-World War I hope of international cooperation through the League of Nations. The imagined pudding ingredients include contributions from the various British territories and colonies. New Zealand's offering contains a barbed reference within an ironic truth:

...And the sheep
Playing his role, he's in command
The fat in New Zealand
(Anyone else feels the ooze [or grease] they say)[65]

Perhaps New Zealand was led by sheep and the grease or ooze could imply an over-fawning obsequiousness towards the mother country as well as the fattiness of the carcass?

New Zealand had not entered the League of Nations intent on embracing the institution and its high-minded ideal. The aim was to secure mandated territory while participating as an Empire supernumerary with minimal emotional and financial investment. The League was viewed as a transactional forum wherein repeated transgressions were countered with claims of unavoidable exceptions. New Zealand's use of part-time representatives who were more akin to *rapporteurs* than diplomats supports this interpretation. When a transaction of importance required it, New Zealand's representation was significantly upgraded before lapsing into indifference once the immediate goal was attained. New Zealand's periods of intense interaction with the League of Nations were a product of self-interest. In any case, when the needs of one nation impinged on the 'rights' of another, a third uncivilised territory often bore the consequences of the settlement. Labour in opposition under Holland's leadership – along with leftish opinion in general – did recognise the League's potential as a global forum for collectively assuring the security of all nations. Any pretence that it would become an institution for peacekeeping through arbitration or a forum for progressing disarmament was, however, lost through the absence of Germany and America, the former at French insistence. Reinterpretation of the Washington Conference protocols allowed the Singapore Naval Base to be considered as a redevelopment of an existing military establishment, thereby excluding it from whatever limitations were agreed for such establishments in the Pacific.

Lest there be any doubt, there was Massey's explicit warning to Ramsay MacDonald's Government that it would be futile to rely on the League to maintain peace. New Zealand and France were equally complicit in this misuse of the League; they were 'sisters under their skins'.[66]

Finance and economics – using or misusing the French example?

> She [France] was much less dependent than the United Kingdom or Germany upon foreign trade and it was not until 1931 that she seriously began to feel the pinch.[1]
>
> J.P.T. Bury

The century between the downfall of Napoleon I in 1815 and the start of World War I was one of relative global stability, but it was neither consistently prosperous nor continually peaceful for either France or New Zealand. Nevertheless, despite the lives lost during the war, post-war nostalgia stirred a desire to reconstruct what Paul Einzig has called the 'Good Old Days'.[2] This fictional place never existed in the same perfect form as its imagined ideal because pre-war conditions were determined by individual experience and subjective assessment. Moreover, the broader issue of whether recreating the past is achievable or even a worthy aim for the population collectively is rarely considered. A return to the 'Good Old Days' presumed that change was diadvantageous, economic transformation was reversible, and that the good elements of the past could be reinstated without the bad. Relying in part on the selective use of France as an example, New Zealand attempted to re-establish an imagined better past before the dream was finally abandoning in favour of dealing with reality.

The ambition of reinstating New Zealand's pre-war condition had to be assessed within the context of the changed post-war world, the place New Zealand would have within it and how a British-dependent economy once restored to its pre-war state could interact with post-war Europe. New Zealand's Empire-centric policies relied on Britain to provide solutions for international economic problems within a regime of arbitrary financial rules or conventions based on moral righteousness, imperial pride and tradition. As New Zealand's economic problems worsened during the late 1920s, some New Zealand politicians turned to French policies in search of a remedy. Because the economic structure of the two nations was so different the comparison was inappropriate, yet the process did provoke a reassessment of New Zealand's economic strategy as traditional solutions failed. For all the criticism of the French, it became obvious to the New Zealand politicians that France was guided by French interests and so France was prepared to try alternatives when other solutions failed. New Zealand's continued loyalty to Britain along with her faith in the failing Empire model bemused the French as much as it came to baffle many on the New Zealand political Left who believed there were alternatives.

Recreating the past could not be achieved in isolation. It depended on the stance of the other nations with which New Zealand had to interact. France clearly did not want to return to a pre-war world in which Germany had been a threat. France was obviously strongly motivated to resist any moves that might restore the pre-war European political and economic environment and with it Germany's financial muscle and military strength. Britain in turn did not want a renewed commitment to assisting France, while New Zealand needed Britain to expand as an export market to preserve New Zealand's nominally independent status. That in turn depended on Britain and France accepting a recovered Germany as a trading partner within an (expanding) world economy so that Germany could meet its reparation obligations. No realistic attempt was made in New Zealand's economic plans to reconcile the disparities between the imagined Good Old Days and these post-war financial and political realities.

The clear wish of the troops to return to New Zealand from France as quickly as possible was facilitated through Massey's post-war strategy of rural resettlement. Far from restoring New Zealand to its pre-war state, this implicitly aimed to intensify and expand the British-dependent agricultural economy. Britain's control of New Zealand's primary produce exports during World War I had led the Massey Government and its successors to believe that New Zealand had a moral right of unrestricted access to the British market (justified by the wartime contribution) for as long as New Zealand fulfilled its self-assigned role within the Empire's economic model. The British were therefore expected to import or otherwise dispose of more or less all of the resulting increased dairy production, while a commensurate reduction in wool exports would lessen the trade opportunities with France and Germany. The plan therefore assumed that a significant economic expansion was possible while relying on a narrow product portfolio. Increasing primary production was a self-evidently necessary requirement since both policy and investment favoured this result. New Zealand was thereby locked into the role of a loyal primary produce supplier with only minimal secondary and light industry to create additional employment, while becoming even more dependent on the British export market. This was not a return to the Good Old Days.

These irreconcilable contradictions became obvious during the Great Depression. It was generally accepted that New Zealand had to operate within the economic conventions of the nation's main trading and financial partner, Great Britain. This limited the adoption of radically new ideas because it was assumed that if New Zealand did not conform there was a risk of being economically ostracised. The common interpretation of this decision suggests that during the depression years the United-Reform Governments did nothing apart from cutting government expenditure in the interests of lowering costs for the benefit of farmers and exporters to the detriment of the labouring classes.[3] Far from doing nothing, the United-Reform Government was acting to maintain farmer viability because the alternative appeared to be allowing the one significant foreign exchange earning sector that New Zealand possessed to collapse. Moreover, despite the obvious personal hardships of 1928–35, the United-Reform policies inspired in part by the British example had broad electoral support in New Zealand, albeit in some cases owing to the vagaries of the first-past-the-post (FPTP) system. When considered from this perspective, the changes that were introduced by the right-leaning governments of the early 1930s – inspired in part by French examples – were far-reaching and ground-breaking. The apparently more radical government that followed was gifted a base of macro-economic policies which could be extended in support of Labour's headline-grabbing social reform programmes. Labour reaped the electoral rewards accordingly.

As Malcolm McKinnon has pointed out, between December 1930 and 1932 the Government 'scrambled' for new policies.[4] This is somewhat distant from the common assertion that the Government simply cut expenditure and hoped for an improvement. The broader problem was finding equivalent national circumstances, whether from within or outside the British-centric world, which might offer policy alternatives. The newspaper reports and parliamentary debates suggest that France was a prominent if inappropriate model amongst the available examples. By any objective assessment be it political, geographic, cultural, economic or demographic, France was as dissimilar to New Zealand as could be imagined. Even a cursory investigation would have suggested that France was not an environment familiar to the general population nor was it strictly relevant from an economic management perspective, but these were desperate times. Why then was France even considered in the debate?

The initial empathy probably arose from the wartime narrative which had presented France as an innocent victim of German aggression. This scenario was used to encourage charitable fundraising for civilian relief in France and Belgium alongside general support for the war. As the war progressed, the victim mentality became entangled in the public mind with similar fundraising initiatives on behalf of those New Zealanders killed or wounded while serving in France. German oppression and destruction were commonly blamed for these deprivations. A theme of shared suffering developed.[5] This resulted in an awkward dissonance when the post-war French economy recovered surprisingly quickly.[6] It appeared as if Britain (and by implication her allies) were left with the debts and the dead. Meanwhile, France prospered by receiving reparation payments while concurrently failing to repay her debts.[7] On the other hand, if war-ravaged France could recover quickly, perhaps undamaged New Zealand could copy her example.

> Let us think of the advice the President of France gave to the French people only a few weeks ago, for it seems quite as applicable to this country as it is to France. He pointed out that it was not in the power of the Government of France to remove the difficulties and to restore to the country the conditions which existed previous to 1914. He said to the people, 'You must produce more and consume less.'[8]
>
> H.L. Michel (New Zealand Legislative Council), 15 March 1921

The French President's blunt but realistic assessment of government limitations and his prescription of less consumption and harder work was advice that few New Zealanders who had experienced the war years would have welcomed. Nevertheless, it was a policy widely adopted in the immediate post-war years.

As with all memories, the wartime images of France had persisted only until overwritten by new experiences. The images therefore became dated and were only sustained by the personal experiences along with anecdotes, books, diaries and films based on the war years. These were adapted and requoted as needed within the political process. The radical Labour MP John A. Lee was a leading practitioner of this technique. He interleaved memories based on his first-hand wartime observations from France with political opinion. The most memorable is his reference to seeing 'innumerable cases of women dragging harrows across the fields' in France. Lee's comment was made after the publication (in the Labour Party magazine *The Elector*) of the famous Depression-era image of New Zealand men apparently pulling harrows across a field in Petone.[9] French civilian hardship during the war was thereby linked by Lee with the Depression despite the passing of some twelve years.

When the Coinage Bill was debated in 1933 it was Lee who argued – based on his wartime experiences of municipalities in France issuing their own currency – that local coin should have been introduced once New Zealand stopped using (British produced) cash. This system had worked for him and for Gordon Coates (a 'dig' at a fellow returned soldier, now Minister of Finance). Lee's first-hand experience was however from fifteen years ago.[10]

Figure 20 French women (top, *source: Alamy*) and New Zealand men (bottom, *source: National Library Collection*) working as draught horses

In one sense these and other more credible wartime recollections were unchallengeable, validated as they were by the memorials, photographs, war histories and family legends. Their relevance was nevertheless questionable, because the first-hand knowledge of France was more about the past than the future. France was changing and so was the demographic profile of the New Zealand population. A disconnect developed between the population and those MPs who were using a wartime version of France that relied on redundant memories. Both world and local events had moved on, and a new set of problems had arisen by the mid-1920s into the early 1930s. The servicemen's generation were in mid-life and in some cases facing considerable financial difficulties. The next generation included the under twenty-year-olds who had not served in France.[11] This cohort probably recognised a familial obligation towards the truths of the preceding generation, but they had their own problems and challenges to deal with and they did not see the relevance of policies based on events of which they had no direct experience. No coherent case was presented to explain why France was a relevant source of policy options for New Zealand's contemporary circumstances.

The following chart shows the age distribution of MPs elected to serve in the 24th Parliament (1931–35). Since all were male, this has been compared with the cohort of male voters aged twenty-one years or older at the time of the 1936 census, the nearest available data point.

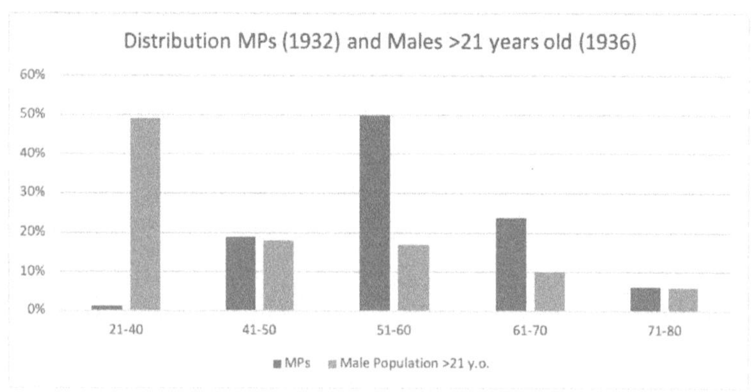

Figure 21 Age profile of MPs cf. male population aged 21 years or older.

Aside from the obvious gender bias, the profile varies markedly between the two groups. Just under half of the male voters were aged between twenty-one and thirty-nine. The oldest amongst this cohort would have been at most twenty-one years old in 1918 and although eligible for military service, many would have been younger and therefore could not have been balloted to serve. By contrast, in 1932 half of the MPs were between fifty and sixty years old. Even the youngest MPs would have experienced the war years as adults aged over twenty-one.[12] In addition, although there is no directly comparable New Zealand study, it seems likely – based on a sample of newspaper articles – that the trend in New Zealand was similar to that in the United Kingdom where reporting on parliamentary events as a matter of factual record was in decline.[13] New Zealand newspaper reports from France covered contemporary matters of foreign affairs and inter-government relations, not the war years. Because the parliamentary debates referred to an unfamiliar France of wartime experience, it was impossible for younger voters to validate the politicians' evidence or reasoning, assuming they were even aware of either.

The adoption of broadly British-centric economic policies in post-war New Zealand was motivated by Massey and Ward's desire to remain within Britain's embrace. New Zealand tried to implement conventional monetary and fiscal policies that Massey and his conservatively inclined successors believed would find favour in London and ingratiate New Zealand sufficiently to win favourable treatment in matters such as borrowing and market access. This was a necessary adjunct to an economic policy which presupposed there was consumer preference in Britain for New Zealand's produce. Britain had, however, already reached her apogee as a free trading, mercantile power by the time World War I began. London was steadily losing financial business to New York, British naval dominance was ending, the American merchant fleet was expanding and Britain's manufacturing advantage was fading as industries in which Britain excelled – such as textiles – were displaced by new businesses and competitors.[14] This process simultaneously undermined the perception that the Empire was a force for mutual financial benefit between Britain and her satellites and specifically undercut Massey's favoured model for post-war New Zealand as Britain's dairy farm.[15] While free trade was still important to Britain in the post-war decades, the divergence in the interests of the Dominions as discussed earlier precluded the possibility of a unitary intra-empire trading policy.

Even without additional colonies the post-war British Empire was fatally undermined as an economic construct. In part this was because it had never existed as a unified and self-sufficient financial entity. This truth is inadvertently exposed in the actions and statements of Massey and many of his Dominion contemporaries. While professing loyalty to and affection for the Empire, when it came to trade they were talking of Britain as a market for their exports. As mentioned earlier, Massey's solution to limited demand in the United Kingdom was for the 'Empire' – meaning Britain – to develop new markets.[16] New Zealand's post-war trade policy assumed that as a quasi-independent nation within the Empire, there was a right of access to United Kingdom markets in perpetuity and to Britain's adjunct trade partners on a selective basis. New Zealand appears not to have considered that the non-Empire markets might not reciprocate, nor that other suppliers might compete for access to the United Kingdom's markets. This left the status of France uncertain. Was France a possible market either directly or via the United Kingdom, or was France a competing supplier?

In many New Zealand histories the fiscal missteps within the larger economies that contributed to the Great Depression of the 1930s go unremarked or are treated as if they could not have been foreseen.[17] This view implicitly perpetuates the common explanation that New Zealand's post-war economic woes leading into the Great Depression resulted from the Versailles settlement, the unpaid war debts of the Great Powers, the reintroduction of fixed exchange rates, and production imbalances in the world economy. Just as the consequences of the punitive French-led fiscal pathway from Versailles to 1935 can be interpreted as a regrettable but unavoidable consequence of international post-war political attitudes, so too can New Zealand's economic difficulties be viewed as the result of ill-conceived British policies which were related to the world's economic problems. One authoritative albeit non-New Zealand analysis from 1935 neatly summarises the tone of the mainstream New Zealand view: 'The world learns through trial and error, and it would be unfair to condemn statesmen, bankers and economists for not having possessed in 1920 a knowledge of 1935'.[18] Such conclusions ignored the alternative views expressed at the time.

The famous economist John Keynes had argued – well before the Great Depression – that the post-war economic policy settings were wrong. He was not alone in expressing this widely publicised opinion. Keynes' critique suggested that French post-war demands were usurious and unnecessarily punitive. This positioned France within the Anglophile world as a convenient scapegoat for the later economic problems while ignoring the Allies' collective complicity in acceding to the French demands. As early as 1920 the concerns of various British notables and intellectuals that squeezing Germany too hard would be counter-productive were being reprinted in New Zealand newspapers.[19] With the support of New Zealand (amongst others) France appeared to be insisting on policies that were deleterious to Germany and while arguably beneficial for France in the short term, were of little discernible assistance to New Zealand. The New Zealand Government was briefed by the British on these issues and their consequences at the time.[20] Policies such as requisitioning and partially destroying the German merchant fleet removed the means for Germany to export goods and earn foreign exchange to pay reparations. But this enforced redundancy also removed aged vessels from the German navy, so that when Germany rebuilt her fleet the domestic economy was stimulated and modern maritime technology was introduced.[21]

As an exporting nation New Zealand could not avoid indirect links to these apparently European problems. In 1930 Bill (W.J.) Jordan MP (Labour, Manukau) wanted the Government to obtain lower interest rates on borrowing by asking the Home Government to guarantee New Zealand's loans, as he claimed the United Kingdom had done for Belgium and France.[22] New Zealand required access to credit because the country was perpetually running or deliberately creating a deficit (Ward's 1928 borrowing promises being a famous example). It was assumed that the London capital markets would offer preferential and favourable terms, but this in turn depended upon Great Britain Incorporated generating a surplus of funds to invest. This was at least partly dependent on the ability of France to repay her wartime borrowing to Britain. France dared not do so without the assurance of continued German reparation payments, for if France could make debt repayments without reparation instalments from Germany it exposed the reparations regime as punitive rather than compensatory. Hence the liquidity of the London capital markets and New Zealand's access to credit was indirectly influenced by French foreign policy.

Britain's advantage within a free-trading regime had been based on importing competitively priced raw materials such as wool, cotton and flax and using her manufacturing efficiencies to export the finished goods at a profit. Textiles were a traditional speciality but economic growth in the post war-years also occurred through the manufacture of capital goods such as machinery, machine tools, motor vehicles and electrical equipment. Other countries were outperforming the United Kingdom in these industries.[23] The new textile mills built in Belgium and France after the war had the 'very latest machinery and labour-saving devices'. British manufacturers were saddled with redundant technology and were thus at a severe cost disadvantage. As Paul Crouzet makes clear, no amount of protectionism or Empire grandstanding could change these facts.[24]

New Zealand assumed that Britain had a limitless appetite for imported primary produce. When difficult times came, the supporters of trade preference argued strenuously in favour of retention and extension of market share in the United Kingdom as they saw the problem as one of restricting access for competing suppliers. Less supply meant higher prices for the remaining sellers. New Zealand's strategy was therefore unsustainable because it ignored two intertwined truths. On the one hand the domestic market of the United Kingdom was not a source of unlimited growth, even assuming that British consumers preferred to buy New Zealand produce (or whatever the United Kingdom manufacturers could manufacture from New Zealand produce). Even more problematically, British consumers of the inter-war period had limited financial means and so wanted the lowest prices. New Zealand's plaintive litany (from many MPs including the United MP C.H. Clinkard who is paraphrased here) was to repeat the flawed argument that New Zealand was Great Britain's best customer per head of population, whereas French imports from Britain were only 10s per head.[25] In his book published in 1924 after he had visited New Zealand, André Siegfried neatly summarised this attitude:

> The industries most interested in Imperial preference are those which supply the Imperial market. Not too sure of their footing, they are less concerned with conquering new foreign markets than with preserving by means of special privileges the ground already won in the markets of the Empire.[26]

Considered in aggregate, it is apparent that the Empire was neither self-sufficient nor was it possessed (based on the trends in trade with non-empire nations) of a collective desire to be so. The other Dominions realised the problem and acted unilaterally. The Empire's external trade with non-empire countries grew before and even after the Ottawa conference. In New Zealand as early as 1921, George Mitchell MP (Independent Liberal, Wellington South) had argued that New Zealand should look for market opportunities in France and other European countries not just in England. Such alternative voices were rarely heard or taken seriously.[27] Given these circumstances, why was France used as a point of comparison by New Zealand and which economic policies were considered relevant? This question can be answered by considering the interrelated issues of unemployment, creating deflation through a deliberate constriction of the volume of currency in circulation, the use of gold to measure and store wealth, exchange rates, and the commensurate obsession with inflation even while the economy was clearly in a self-induced deflationary cycle.

Many politicians assumed that the quasi-subsistence scale farms observed in France during the war years were responsible for the low rates of unemployment in France despite the current austerity. Frequent repetition in the New Zealand Parliament (at least prior to 1930) of this war era-related interpretation of the French economy created the impression that the claim was both correct and a valid point of comparison for post-war New Zealand. The claim was not vigorously scrutinised until the Great Depression deepened. Although the New Zealand parliamentary debates suggest that unemployment rates in France were of interest and relevant, the general news coverage had few articles on the topic and most of the mentions were peripheral to the state of France.

The general tone was similar to the comprehensive if self-serving 1930 contribution from the President of the Employers Federation (T. Shailer Weston, a Member of the Legislative Council). Shailer Weston forecast deflationary pressure across all sectors of the economy in line with falling prices for primary produce. His remedies consisted of job redundancy and wage cuts in line with the orthodox conservative solutions of the Depression years. Cuts and reductions in Belgium and France – where he said there was no unemployment until recently – were due to the French citizens' habit of saving, thus limiting unproductive expenditure. The article is a lengthy and complex justification for the conservative-employer case which held that there was no alternative to austerity.[28] It did not directly suggest that France was a desirable example for the New Zealand electorate to follow.

The debate was frustrated by both the quality of the data and its use or misuse for political purposes. In October 1930 it was claimed that 'prostrated' France still had only 942 unemployed and therefore no need for an unemployment relief scheme (i.e. dole payments). When this was repeated in 1931, one MP countered that France (and others) reported lower unemployment rates than New Zealand because none of them had an unemployment scheme(s).[29] Hence, there was no reason for the unemployed to identify as such and register. The argument was validated by observing that the reported total of unemployed in New Zealand rapidly increased after the introduction of an unemployment scheme that required registration. The Labour Opposition Leader (Holland) appeared incredulous when he heard the claim and challenged the assumption that this was the reason for low French unemployment.[30] In this one exchange two potential flaws in the use of France as a comparative example were exposed, for not only was it questionable on the grounds of relevance, but the information was suspect.

By the time of the April–May 1931 parliamentary sitting, Sir James Allen was telling the Legislative Council that registered French applicants seeking work had in fact risen from 23,879 to 177,294 between 1930 and 1931. When Sir William Hall-Jones questioned the applicability of comparisons with unemployment rates in France and other larger nations owing to New Zealand's small population, he opened the question of why comparisons were being made with France. This line of reasoning was not pursued.[31] It was not until 1935 that S.G. Smith, the Minister of Education in the Coalition Ministry, was able to argue that to the contrary it was New Zealand's unemployment rate that was falling while other Continental nations including France were still recording increases.[32]

Deflationary monetary policies were another point of contention. Massey and his successors wanted the New Zealand economy to grow by selling more and/or increasing prices for New Zealand produce in the United Kingdom. This implicitly assumed increased demand in the United Kingdom, presumably through market growth, or by New Zealand producers displacing competitors, or by raising prices, or some combination thereof. Whatever the assumptions were, the demand side was clearly not thought through or if it was, it was not publicly articulated. Despite assumptions that there would be economic growth in Britain after the war, the British leadership tried to reduce prices to their pre-war level, consistent with a return to an imagined better past. Such an action implied a macro-economic contraction that was directly counter to the expansion Massey was planning for New Zealand's export-led economy.

The confounding issue was the overarching New Zealand urge to implement the British monetary prescription despite the obvious structural differences between the two economies. In mid-1920, Massey attempted to explain the necessity for post-war deflation to Parliament. Issuing paper money to fund a war, Massey explained, was not uncommon. The United States had done so after the Civil War as well as after the War of Independence. Britain had used the same device after the Napoleonic Wars while France used paper money to devalue the franc on an unspecified 'previous occasion'. The New Zealand Prime Minister was probably restating positions he had heard in England when he claimed that there was therefore a surplus of currency in the world financial system. As Massey correctly predicted, deflation would result if gold coins were removed from circulation and smelted down into bullion.[33] Despite removing gold from the financial system Massey precluded the issue of additional paper currency as a replacement by decreeing that 'surplus' paper money also had to be redeemed and removed from circulation. The Prime Minister implied that deflation by this method was 'normal' because the process had already started in the United Kingdom, and the surplus currency therefore had to be removed to maintain the gold standard. Both New Zealand and its principal export market were then locked into a deflationary cycle. The New Zealand politicians came uncannily close at times to identifying the underlying causes of this financial problem and how it might be resolved. They were diverted by orthodox interpretations and a desire to act 'normal(-ly)' through mirroring the deflationary monetary policies of the United Kingdom while ignoring the apparent prosperity and growing markets in France.[34]

As Andre Siegfried had explained, restoration of the pound to its pre-war value was a 'deliberate policy' which had the acceptance of both industrialists and the public. It was not treated as an economic question, but rather as a matter of national prestige.[35] Trying to restore pre-war parities made the Allies' war debts unpayable.[36] One review of the Great Depression – completed before World War II – held that governments had inflated their currencies during the Great War and then ignored the consequences.

> The attitude of statesmen towards the problem of the public debt was characterised by an utter lack in a sense of realities. Great Britain was not the only country to expect to restore the monetary unit to pre-war parity, and thus to increase considerably the real burden of the debt. There was not one single Government which was able to face the fact that in the long run the burden of public debt could not be borne unless it was dramatically reduced by a reduction in the value of the monetary unit in which the debt had been contracted.[37]

The quoted authority (Einzig) was wrong on this point because France ignored economic convention and devalued well before Einzig published in 1935. Using gold and bullion to back local currencies and facilitate international transfers gave gold an apparently unimpeachable status as a measure of wealth and financial security. A more relevant question was whether gold reserves allowed the state to provide for its citizens' wellbeing and if not, what point was there in holding bullion?

Frank Langstone was one MP who perceptively pointed out the obvious discrepancy between gold reserves and prosperity. He stated that huge reserves of gold were apparently no protection against unemployment.[38] D.G. (Dan) Sullivan MP (Labour, Avon) adopted a similar theme. Gold sent to America and France to meet reparation obligations, debt repayment and to fund purchases of goods was effectively removed from circulation. This process, referred to in the vernacular as 'sterilisation', meant that the countries sending the gold suffered a contraction of credit.[39] These perceptive observations went unremarked. For countries with low bullion reserves, accumulation of gold and its sequestering turned from a symbol of prosperity to one of selfish hoarding. It was reported from the 1933 Monetary and Economic Conference that the French delegates had emphasised the need for constancy, but the insistence of the European countries (including France) on retaining the gold standard in the interests of stability had 'brought the work of the conference to a standstill'.[40]

During the 1930s, it became evident to some New Zealand politicians that the management of the French economy was not bound by the same conventions as those used by the British, particularly in regard to exchange rates. France was holding huge quantities of bullion apparently without any moral compunction to maintain a fixed exchange rate for the franc against gold, as was the case for sterling. If the state of France had been considered holistically, rather than through selected and arbitrary examples, the benefits and shortcomings of French policy may have become apparent to New Zealand. The New Zealand political debate instead often reverted to using measures of economic performance – including exchange rates – as proxies for national prestige (as Einzig and Siegfried had explained) rather than as useful assessments of the wellbeing of the population. This explains the shocked reaction when France devalued while having huge gold reserves. Frank Langstone MP correctly observed that returns for investors in French war loans denominated in francs would be 'wiped out'. British investors in French financial instruments were understandably 'riled' by the devaluation and wanted recompense.[41]

The United Kingdom and New Zealand had done the opposite (i.e. effectively revalued) so that New Zealand's foreign debt burden increased in value while export prices were raised, making them even less competitive. Despite applying this conservative and apparently obvious economic solution, New Zealand's economy did not recover whereas France was doing the opposite and prospering. With France distanced, it was easy to develop a counter-narrative that blamed France for vigorously exporting using an undervalued currency. It was assumed that this was part of the reason for France's success. French gold reserves were being (unfairly) increased with negative consequences for other nations. Another interpretation attributed the successful recovery of France to common-sense (or underhand, depending on the point of view) exchange rate adjustments. Massey had noted devaluations of the German and French currencies (presumably against the pound) but he interpreted this as the cause of 'trouble and difficulty' because German and French goods became cheaper. Then Opposition Leader Thomas Wilford had agreed.[42] Obviously France did have a lesson for New Zealand, namely to ignore the conventions and adjust the exchange rate, but it was not applied. Rather than adopting the implied remedy of devaluing as France (and Germany) had done, it was inferred that devaluation was unfair. This was a self-imposed moral constraint, not an economic one.

New Zealand's agricultural produce, especially meat and dairy products (wool was an obvious exception), had a limited shelf-life but even frozen and non-perishable goods had to be brought to market to generate some income. Therefore, as long as the volume supplied to the depressed British market continued and the exchange rate was fixed there were limited alternatives, apart from a lowering of market prices. It was not until the night of Thursday, 20 January 1933 that common sense prevailed and the New Zealand exchange rate was reset at NZ £125 to Stg £100. Imports that previously cost £1 would now cost 25 per cent more while exporters would receive NZ £125 for every Stg £100 earned in Britain. Although New Zealand exports could now be sold at a lower price for the same return in New Zealand currency, devaluing also increased import costs. This appeared to be against the conventions of the political Right which had previously insisted that lowering input prices was the only solution that would ameliorate the farmers' plight. It was a policy that therefore appeared to work against the interests of both urban voters and the Government's rural base, despite the more favourable exchange rate.

The courage of this policy adjustment gets less praise than it should, for a hitherto orthodox, conservative Government paid a significant political price for its boldness. It lost one of its most capable administrators, the widely respected Finance Minister William Downie Stewart who resigned in protest, while simultaneously alienating substantial parts of the conservative press and traditional government supporters. The move gave the Labour Party Opposition – who opposed the resulting increases in domestic prices – additional grounds to criticise the Government.[43] New Zealand was, however, finally acting in her own interest by breaking with (British-inspired) conventions that had implicitly precluded earlier action. In short, New Zealand was making an adjustment that in spirit seemed more akin to the self-interested actions of the French. It was consistent with an independent nation acting in its own interests rather than blindly following British (Empire) policy prescriptions.

While it was obvious that New Zealand had to import from many countries as well as from the United Kingdom, it was left to Alexander Harris MP (Independent, Waitemata) to finally break with convention and claim that United Kingdom firms that could not exist even with a 10 per cent tariff preference did not deserve to survive. New Zealand's interests would be better served by reducing the British preference and encouraging as quid pro quo open markets for fresh produce in the likes of South America, France and Holland, all of which had potential.[44] With these changes in place, new possibilities for economic growth opened. As a clearly frustrated former Prime Minister George Forbes was to exclaim once he left office: '…makes me wonder why we had to struggle in the bog, when there was such an easy way out…'[45]

In the lead-up to 1935 general election the Labour Party began to consistently make the case for reinflating the economy, alongside other more moderate policies which countered the less coherent, radical and contradictory responses they had previously used. Despite this, inflation – the great fear of the political Right – remained a significant if self-imagined block to change. The main objection from the political Right to rectifying the deflationary cycle by increasing credit and the volume of money in circulation, as the Left advocated, was the risk of uncontrolled inflation. This risk was dogmatically repeated by the conservative parties until it became a mantra. W.J. Polson MP (Stratford, Independent) was one politician who pointed out the deleterious effect of inflation on savings by claiming that French savers had lost four-fifths of the value of their wealth due to inflation. On the other hand, the Westland Labour MP James O'Brien said that by inflating her currency (i.e. devaluing) France had transferred 80 per cent of her war debt to holders of French bonds. Austria and Germany had done the same, whereas Britain increased the value of her war debts by revaluing. These points were all correct, but given the burden of unpayable debt that the world had created as a result of the war and the Versailles settlement, a day of reckoning had to come, even for Britain.

As late as 1932 the Labour MP Rev. Carr was still making the point that governments were deterred from creating credit by exaggerated threats of inflation. In fairness, reports of hyperinflation in Europe had been well publicised and fears raised that the same could happen elsewhere. Malcolm McKinnon has argued that urban New Zealand was not opposed to inflation per se. In his view, the dispute was about the means to do so without damaging the economy, because expert opinion suggested a devaluation would dampen urban economic activity. McKinnon also argues that the establishment of common ground on this issue led to Labour interests aligning with those of the urban elite.[46] The adverse reaction to the 1933 devaluation was therefore a backlash of urban dwellers against the presumed beneficiaries, the farmers. McKinnon's case on this point is not compelling. Labour had caused a good deal of confusion in the public mind through their selective use of examples from France and elsewhere, as well as by the imprecise language used to describe their many inconsistent policy suggestions. More importantly, any change in monetary policy such as in interest rates or exchange rates is arbitrary and will therefore result in uneven outcomes depending on the financial circumstances of the individual at that point in time, be they debtors or creditors, employed or out of work. The urban elite included importers and exporters, many of whom would have also had some dependence –

even if only indirectly – on the rural sector. The case for and against inflating the economy was therefore, at least in the early stages, far from clear cut. Labour exploited this confusion to play on generalised fears that devaluation would negatively impact the economy, despite knowing full well that the outcome would be uneven.

The electoral success of United-Reform in the early 1930s suggests that until the devaluation of 1933, the conservative Coalition's arguments against economic expansion by increasing the money supply had held sway with the voting public. H.G. Dickie MP (Reform, Patea) had mocked the idea of inflating the economy by printing money because (he said) the problems in the United Kingdom were due to France, Germany and others inflating their economies in this way and then dumping goods on the British market. The tone was again one of moral disapproval and unfairness, rather than claiming that such policies had not worked to the benefit of France.[47]

As uncertainties grew, so too did suspicion as to the true conditions in, and relevance of, France as an economic example. A great deal of attention on both sides of the ideological divide was given to identifying New Zealand's problems, such as the French gold reserves or French currency manipulation or French obsessions with reparation payments, as offshore issues while insufficient consideration was given to matters New Zealand could control and influence. New Zealand was trying to manage a domestic economy that was dependent on overseas trade using a conservative political prescription within a moral framework derived from being British. With the alternatives restricted by these views and blame assigned to France and elsewhere, New Zealand was left brooding over global circumstances which were beyond local influence or control. This distracted attention from possible adjustments to domestic settings such as exchange rates, gold reserves, cost cutting and import-export controls. Nevertheless, it is true that many of the macro-economic solutions were beyond the control of a smallish, export-dependent economy. Rev. Carr MP pointed out that the large nations (such as America and France) could move off the gold standard and depreciate their currency, but when a New Zealand local body tried to pay interest on loans using New Zealand currency rather than sterling, the London Stock Exchange had delisted the securities. Carr said the New Zealand Government was prepared to 'aid and abet this bullying' of a loyal member of the Commonwealth although there was little the New Zealand Government could do. The broader point stood: the large nations acted in their own interests while even a loyal nation such as New Zealand had more limited scope to take independent action.[48]

When citing France to support their policy positions, the New Zealand MPs ignored the chronic domestic political instability of France during the inter-war years. If France in the 1920s had appeared to be at the pinnacle of her colonial prowess, the image soon regressed to a nation conflicted by a left–right divide which did not fit the New Zealand narrative of French success.[49] After his re-election in 1928, Poincaré had tried to achieve stability by fixing the value of the franc at 65.5 mg of gold and settling on a revised schedule of repayments to the United States. This remained contingent on Germany continuing to pay reparations. Initially it seemed that France had escaped the worst of 'Black Thursday' (14 October 1929) but problems arose with international payments in June 1931. Although adjustments had been made, it became obvious that Germany could not pay further reparations to France. Despite President Hoover's moratorium on all international payments, no French Government could persuade the United States to link repayment of French debt to America with German reparation payments. Both the French and United States politicians would have faced extremely adverse voter reaction had they tried to renounce these positions or even acknowledged the likelihood that the debtors might default. The New Zealand politicians lacked direction on the issue, and by appearing economically helpless contributed to an expedient aura of blamelessness.[50]

Lest it appear that New Zealand's view of France was an overly simplistic distortion, the reciprocal view – that of New Zealand from

France – would have appeared similarly immoderate and unbalanced. *Le Figaro* reported on 11 January 1932 that 'hundreds of unemployed people have been deprived of bread and have attempted to loot one of the largest grocery stores in the city [of Dunedin]'.[51] Reports of riots in Auckland followed. It was claimed that some New Zealand newspapers blamed Communist agitators. Forbes was quoted in *Le Figaro* as saying that 'the government is ready to act in the face of any eventuality, and it will not allow [itself] to be dominated by the forces of disorder'.[52] None of this was untrue but when reported without context it suggested chronic anarchy in New Zealand, just as C.H. Chapman MP (Wellington North, Labour) reinforced the impression of French unrest by saying that 'in France the political cauldron seethes and bubbles with uncertainty'.[53]

If the political Right was at fault for failing to recognise alternatives and adapt when the current policy solutions were so obviously failing, so too was the Left by insisting on positioning their solutions within a Marxist-socialist paradigm that appeared to lack relevance and applicability for day-to-day life within New Zealand's mixed economy. When one of the most progressive policies associated with France – the establishment of the Reserve Bank of New Zealand – was introduced the two sides had a rare moment of policy overlap, even if it went unremarked as such.[54] Introducing the relevant Bill, Gordon Coates the Minister of Finance quoted the precedent established in England and France of central government appropriating profits (or losses) on the reserves of gold when these were taken over by the state: 'Furthermore, it is a recognized principle that the value of the monetary unit, and, in fact, monetary policy generally, are entirely matters to be determined by the State, which must stand all losses involved and should take all profits accruing therefrom.'[55]

This was far from the traditional, right-wing hands-off view of economic policy and could easily have come from a left-leaning politician, for New Zealand now had the mechanism to control her own currency, a key element of sovereignty and nationhood. When Coates cited France, Belgium, Norway, Sweden and Italy as examples where central banks had helped tide over financial predicaments, Daniel Sullivan MP (Labour, Avon) refuted this with the astonishingly erroneous claim that France had not had to face a post-war financial crisis. William Polson MP (Independent) more realistically pointed out that when Britain went off the gold standard the French Government had bailed out the Bank of France even though it was under private shareholder control. His point was that ultimately it was the State that had to deal with any catastrophe so it was appropriate that the state should have control of the Bank.[56] The French Government's rescue of the Bank of France confirmed that with a national bank in place the Government was the ultimate backstop of the financial system.[57] It also reaffirmed the coincident uncertainty of using gold reserves to assess wealth.

With the United-Reform Government having accepted devaluation and adopted the concept of a central bank, attention turned to macro-economic policy. Much of the debate remained within conventional parameters, although interpretations of the proffered solutions within these boundaries varied and showed some eccentricities. Sir James Parr (Council) was one who seemed to grasp the broader possibilities for New Zealand now the new Reserve Bank was in operation. He pointed out that more than twenty-two countries including France now had a central banking system. New Zealand's new bank could trade in bullion, foreign exchange and general securities including those of France and the other large powers. Clinkard was another MP who was more aware than many of his contemporaries that sovereign nations could change their financial settings rather than adopting the stance of hapless victims. If the financial system of the world could not take the load Clinkard said, new measures could be taken. He again pointed out that France and the other larger nations had depreciated their currency when altered post-war circumstances required it.[58]

Even Sir James Allen came to the view that New Zealand was part of a global economy not just a British subsidiary. When it was suggested that the newly proposed Bank for International Settlements would include France amongst its shareholders (who were mainly countries using the gold standard), Allen hoped this would expand. He believed there was a case for a world economic organisation. James Hargest foresaw the need for greater flexibility as he quoted currency depreciations implemented by various countries including France while pointing out that New Zealand had no hope of maintaining her currency at its existing levels.[59]

Sir James Parr, when commenting on the 26 September 1936 League of Nations meeting, said that the crumbling of the European gold standard followed by the devaluations of the United Kingdom, United States and French currencies respectively was to be 'welcomed' as a portent of better economic times to come. Sir James contrasted this with the comments at the equivalent meeting in September 1931 when the Second Committee of the Assembly had 'felt sympathy' with Great Britain which had been 'obliged' to abandon the gold standard.[60] The stance in favour of national control of currency and exchange rates still had an awkward boundary with the free market, non-tariff economic model as Clinkard's suggestion that currency regulation should be under non-political control showed. This idea was still well ahead of the then accepted role of a Reserve Bank, as was the idea of an Empire-wide common currency that recalled the earlier British dream. This would have to wait, because it would only be viable within a common market free of trade and production controls.[61]

It was therefore not the case that successive New Zealand governments between 1918 and 1935 wilfully ignored obvious solutions which had been empirically proven elsewhere. As Sir James Allen had pointed out to the Legislative Council, even the gold committee of the League of Nations could not agree on the cause(s) of the economic crisis. A minority on that committee (Allen said) believed the cause was monetary difficulties. A majority, including the French and United States representatives as well as German and Italian delegates, had not revealed their opinion but they did not agree that monetary difficulties (i.e. interest rates and the supply of money) was the cause. As if to confirm this point, Reform's Bill (W.D.) Endean MP spoke against untested remedies, especially the use of inflation which had in the past caused chaos and led to wars. These were not unrealistic fears, especially given the huge debts that had been created by French demands for German reparation payments. Endean unfortunately undermined his argument by reverting to emotional appeals. He said there was a need to keep the Empire on a 'sound basis' as he referred to the thin red line at Waterloo when Britain faced the flower of the French army. British troops saved Europe then and a century later Britain had done the same thing as Britain engaged in an economic war.[62] This comment, made in 1932, was out of context but it comfortingly reinstated New Zealand's wartime ally France as Britain's economic enemy.

Einzig's view that little serious consideration was given in the immediate post-war period to facilitating repayment of war-related debts has attracted little academic attention in New Zealand. Reparations payments were never going to be a significant factor in the New Zealand financial plan, but French demands for payment had repercussions for the New Zealand economy far beyond the immediate fiscal impact.[63] Understandably, the attitudes amongst the victors' publics meant a less punitive attitude was unacceptable in the immediate post-war period but France made every effort to prolong this phase and New Zealand acquiesced even after Massey's admission that it was unlikely German reparation payments would ever reach New Zealand. That is not to say that the topic was ignored at the time. Keynes' explicit and very public airing of the unreconciled dissonance between economic recovery and punishment of Germany is evidence of that.[64] Those owed money were, as Einzig said, 'vaguely aware' that the debts could only be paid by the debtors (starting with Germany) running a surplus but this problem was observed rather than addressed. No means of support was offered to help those nations deemed to owe money to repay it.[65] There was little public criticism of either the United

Kingdom or France on this point so New Zealand simply adopted Lloyd George's policy of colluding with France to stifle a German recovery. As long as Massey remained Prime Minister and Ward (who finally left office in 1930) was politically active this largely remained the case, even as the British/Empire's stance on the issue softened. The indirect implications for New Zealand were not considered.

European economic policies were aimed at achieving easy political 'wins' and re-energising national pride rather than restoring financial wellbeing. The blame was shared: economists tended to ignore the political implications of their policy prescriptions while the politicians' rhetoric reflected voter sentiment rather than longer-term economic realities. When the MP A.S. Malcolm (Reform, Clutha) attempted to do both by advocating the economically sound and reasonable policy of offering cheap or free commodities to speed the recovery of Germany and the other 'impoverished countries of Europe', his inclusion of the point that 'Britain has proposed it in the case of France' disregarded the political implications of juxtaposing enemy and ally.[66] Nevertheless, at least some local politicians accepted the importance of aiding European recovery through the supply of cheap or free goods (i.e. credit in another guise), and that the recovery of both France and Germany would be an important factor in Britain's and therefore New Zealand's future prosperity and stability.

As the image of France as a devastated victim of malicious German aggression started to fade it was a financially recovered France of full employment and enormous gold reserves which had replaced it in the political imagination and news reporting. The adoption of radical economic policies by France once her conventional policies failed not only confounded New Zealand's British-inspired belief that doing the right thing would produce the correct outcome, but perversely reinforced perceptions of French unfairness, volatility and inconsistency. Nevertheless, once despair set in, New Zealand's own attitudes towards management of the economy underwent a radical transformation under the United-Reform Government(s), inspired in part by the selective use of French policies. Arbitrary changes to the exchange rate and the use of a Reserve Bank while not unprecedented were ground-breaking for New Zealand for they opened the path to what was previously considered heretical economic intervention.

The partial displacement of Britain's views and conventional financial orthodoxies was demonstrably under way before the first Labour Government took office. The public became familiar with the new, radical policy options and interventions introduced by United-Reform. Most importantly, although still constrained by the national fixation on primary production, the principle of New Zealand governments acting in the interests of New Zealand – just as the French did – was established. Labour would use these options in 1935–39 to enhance the subsequent economic recovery and build a welfare state. Far-reaching as Labour's changes were, other more fundamental questions about New Zealand's overall direction and the economic conundrum posed by introducing a French-styled small-farm economy went unaddressed.

Chapter Thirteen

Maintaining contact: sport and recreation, communication and technology

> The explicit use by the British Government of the press, newsreels and cinema to disseminate propaganda received critical impetus from the Great War…
>
> Chandrika Kaul[1]

Newer technologies (particularly in audio and pictorial transmissions) may have helped communicate and therefore perpetuate a façade of intra-Empire unity, but they also enabled the diffusion of counter-narratives.[2] Theoretically these could have been excluded through deliberate blocking, by omission or through audience rejection, but none of these were realistic options so the New Zealand public was exposed to an increasing volume of alternative, non-Empire, cultural influences and ideas. Despite this, there is no evidence to suggest that overall interest in or cultural exchanges with France increased after 1918, and nothing suggests that a closer understanding and relationship developed between the general publics of France and New Zealand.[3]

The New Zealand and French publics were not motivated to engage, notwithstanding their shared interest in innovative or unusual technologies, scientific developments, and sports – especially tennis and rugby. Domestic news from or about France (particularly after 1925) was reported in New Zealand in an unimaginative or bemused manner which did little to arouse reader interest. Reports covering legacy issues or matters of international statecraft were still predominantly drawn from secondary sources – principally via the United Kingdom – and this suggested there were few implications for New Zealand. Even when increasing discomfort with the continued British dominance in the administration of rugby coincided with the controversy over the 1926 Māori rugby team's tour to France, the shadow of Empire won. A French suggestion of an informal French-New Zealand challenge to the replication of the Empire's structure within the rugby world was therefore ignored. The cinema was potentially a more important influence than sport for extending knowledge of the 'others', but in that respect the French efforts were overshadowed by those of America. As a consequence, post-war New Zealand collectively learned little more about contemporary France and its people, leaving New Zealand's France metaphorically in the past.

A significant local French presence – whether through immigrants or leading figures – might have stimulated interest and helped overcome the 'othering' evident in the relationship, but there is no evidence of either in the newspapers. The redoubtable missioner Mother Aubert was an exceptionally well-known French identity, but she had to fit within the local culture to be effective. Her reputation in New Zealand was therefore a product of her local activity rather than her French nationality.[4] Between 1923 and 1938 immigration from France was too insignificant to warrant even a line-item mention in the relevant statistics whereas just seven immigrants from Switzerland were documented.[5] The absence of a significant French presence was not due to transport limitations since transfer of goods and people between France and New Zealand via the United States and points in between was routinely available. From mid-1925 onwards at least one company – the American Southern Pacific Lines railway company – regularly advertised a passenger and freight service to the South Pacific via New York and San Francisco.

Figure 22 Travel advertisement[6]

The reverse path to Europe for New Zealanders seeking a career in the arts, humanities, sciences and technology still passed through England but it often ended there with forays to the Continent as interludes. New Zealand writers and artists domiciled in France attempted to blend into their adopted environment by assuming the demeanour of the locals without perhaps realising – as was the case for the uniformed soldiers before them – that their presence as foreigners influenced the behaviours they observed. They were local in the sense of being semi-permanent residents, but still strangers – isolated within their own 'set'. This is not to deny the merits and consequent prominence of these New Zealand writers and artists, but news from them and of the French writers and distinguished intellectuals who visited New Zealand was occasional and exceptional.[7] Even while resident in France, most of the now famous New Zealanders recorded little of the local circumstances or environment beyond the climate, their immediate personal situation and their physical surroundings. Few if any offers were apparently extended to French interest groups to undertake visits to New Zealand. Whatever nascent post-war connections there had been were largely expunged, thereby leaving cultural France isolated and remote from the general newspaper reading public.

In the greater Pacific region the French – in common with the British – had shifted their empire and colonial attention to a more exploitative stance. French Indo-China and China itself assumed greater importance because – as Robert Aldrich noted – the Pacific region had not developed as was originally anticipated.[8] The Panama Canal could neither negate the awkward realities of a tropical climate nor overcome the uneconomic scale resulting from primary production spread over a few scattered archipelagos. The South Pacific was therefore neither an economically significant producer (apart from some extractive enterprises) nor a sizeable market. Moreover, as more efficient oil-fired ships replaced coal-fuelled vessels, the size and number of bunkering facilities and ports was greatly reduced while wireless and improved cable communications lessened the need for land-based relay stations. Without substantive trade, New Zealand declined in its significance for France which therefore became a distant European country with only indirect relevance. European political and economic affairs were treated by the New Zealand newspapers as if they could be confined within Europe, a stance which contradicted the experience of the previous three decades and ran counter to the increasing opportunities that opened as communication and travel developed.[9]

Reports from the 'costume and personal appearance' sections of the newspapers suggest that a perception of France as a female-gendered beauty and fashion orientated space developed during the 1930s to fill the cultural gap. This perception of a feminised, post-war France replaced the earlier version of the more pragmatic and combative France of political and economic significance.[10] Reports of frilly, exotic and titillating, *risqué* femininity demanded a counteracting, no nonsense, masculine-heavy disparagement from the imagined traditional New Zealand wife who was a more practical mate in both fashion-sense and work for the rugby playing man 'on the land'.

The *Sun* published a detailed description of the beauty school managed by Cleo de Merode (probably Cléopatra Diane de Mérode or an impersonator thereof, 'the most enchanting woman in France'). The article explained that Mlle Mérode had been 'requested' to train the girls of Parisian society using a regime including milk baths and dancing. For a peaches and cream skin, the girls slept between black silk sheets.[11] Less erotically but no less exotically, ladies in French-themed costumes inevitably featured during local social occasions. French costumed *mademoiselles* attended fancy-dress balls – a popular entertainment in the 1920s and 1930s – to reassert the sophistication and femininity of New Zealand women. Fashion accessories of French origin such as flowers, lace, ribbons, shoes, hosiery and gloves were worn at significant social events such as society weddings and were dutifully identified as symbols of upper-class refinement in the society columns.[12] These suggest that French imagery was associated with a Cinderella-like opportunity to escape the drudgery of everyday life and the farm – at least for one evening. The New Zealand department stores' histories indicate that while French fashion was an influence, this did not extend to everyday clothing. The need for practical garments for daily wear and the wish to follow the Home fashions probably restricted the market for more stylish French fabrics and garments, although expressions such as 'Paris models', 'crêpe de chine' and 'georgette' (crêpe Georgette) indicates that French fashion was of interest.[13]

Despite this marketing, 80 per cent of the goods sold by the Farmers retail chain store were still sourced from Home or the United States, as was the case in the pre-war era. The fragility of supply from Europe together with the post-war economic downturn and subsequent credit squeeze of the 1920s did, however, lead to one major change in Farmers' business model. Buying offices were established in New York and London to avoid any repetition of the difficulty experienced in sourcing European goods during the war, a theme consistent with the wish to stay clear of mainland Europe and any future trading problems.[14] Nonetheless, there was a clear desire to promote overseas styles and trends. Advertising from James Smith's, George Court's and the DIC frequently mentioned higher end Parisian fashion items alongside those of Vienna, London and New York. Buyers visited these trend-setting centres and local 'experts' were employed to promote the latest styles.[15] The dispersion of advertising suggests there was no collaborative effort to promote any particular country's fashion. While effusive in praising French products, the copy suggests exclusivity was targeted at the higher-end user.

Les femmes de France were not always associated with high fashion or morality. The use of makeup – described as being as necessary in France as 'bread and meat' – complemented reports of immodestly dressed French brides who required the temporary use of a shawl the local priest had purchased for that purpose. The story of a French actress who used fake jewellery also served to bring French women back into a flawed, morally suspect, everyday context. A seer purportedly described King Edward's mistress Lily Langtry as being as beautiful as 'La France roses', thereby neatly co-locating suspect French morality, beauty and royalty within the behavioural standards of the British upper classes.[16] Any hint of French cultural superiority or sophistication seemed to demand some belittling counter-narrative in the man's country, rather than the advancement of a superlative case.

In a broader context there is little evidence to suggest that the feminised French culture and themes extended into mainstream New Zealand life, notwithstanding the exposure through broadcasts, news and film. Searching the Papers Past database for common French words that might have entered the vernacular such as *vin*, *fromage* or even *haute couture* yields few results. Only one news item between 1925 and 1938 specifically referred to 'vin' and 'French' but even this was within a fictional item. *Fromage* appears in the Papers Past database just ninety-two times between 1918 and 1935, and then mainly in descriptions of imagined Continental menus. The term *fromage* suggests an adventurous French inspired menu rather than the addition of what was probably a simple cheddar. Recipes such as '*oeufs brouilles au fromage*', '*bananas gratinees au fromage*', and (it seems) nearly any other foodstuff that could be served '*au fromage*' were featured. The term '*haute couture*' received sixty-four mentions, mainly within the

Auckland Star's 'Fashion Notes'. One reprinted article captioned as 'Titles Don't Count' (culinary adventures were obviously treated as an exception) took particular delight in the disparagement of titled, previously well-off and/or older French women attempting to become models as a desperate response to the Great Depression.[17] French femininity was titillating, sexualised and exotic with more than a hint of moral ignominy.

If an overtly feminised France suggested a degree of post-war sophistication, it was the shared interest in rugby and tennis that provided a masculine counterweight. Results mentioning New Zealand were often reported in France even when there was no direct French involvement, although the opposite was again less customary. Themes that reflected broader political attitudes and concerns which might otherwise have been beyond what is usually assumed to be the apolitical world of sport were apparent. Hence *Le Figaro* repeatedly explained to readers that the international tennis rankings used in the Davis Cup competition had altered because New Zealand had been reclassified as an independent nation. This suggests that the two Australasian national identities which New Zealanders might have supposed to be well known were indistinct to the casual French reader. Matter-of-fact racial stereotypes were frequently used in New Zealand reports to explain sporting outcomes. These usually assumed that the New Zealanders were normal and without fault; thus, if the French Davis Cup team was 'brilliant but erratic', by default 'we' (presumably British-New Zealanders) were not.[18]

Rugby aroused particularly strong emotions. The internal politics of the game's administration were of as much interest to French rugby followers as it was to their New Zealand opposites. In rugby circles a distinctly New Zealand identity was clearly delineated from Australia's. Early post-war New Zealand reports described the success of the New Zealand Services' sporting teams ('our boys') winning competitions, including the inter-Allied football championships held in 'England and France'. This link between France, the armed services and the All Blacks is still evident at the time of writing.[19] Expectations were always high: a 'crushing' of the English team was anticipated when the New Zealand rugby team toured England in late 1924, but just to be sure the two matches against France were moved until after the England test match (scheduled for 3 January 1925).[20]

The Māori rugby team's 1926 tour of France was arguably of greater significance in the formation of a distinctly New Zealand national sporting identity for both New Zealand and French enthusiasts. The Māori players had been informed before their French visit that they would not be selected for the South African tour. The decision was excused by the Rugby Union Chair (Stan Dean) as being in the interests of the players:

> Native players sent there (i.e. to South Africa) with a football team would only be exposed to the risk of insult and to the contempt of the people, who were, unhappily, not educated to New Zealand's broad views on the colour question. Long before the tour was definitely arranged the New Zealand Rugby Union had discussed the subject with the Māori Advisory Board and had ascertained its feelings; and before the Māori team left last year on its trip to France the players had been specifically informed that they would not be eligible for the South African tour.[21]

French newspapers reported that while in France the Māori team acquitted themselves extremely well both on and off the field. Prime Minister Gordon Coates appeared and made a presentation in the best traditions of politicians associating themselves with sporting success but beneath the image of a happy Māori touring team there was a national divide.[22] Ron Palenski's account confirms that there was a 'tacit understanding' that this trip was compensation for the exclusion of Māori players from the South African tour, but nonetheless the tour was a humiliating second-tier option for Māori. George Nepia is quoted as saying that 'the whole of New Zealand was highly indignant', but Palenski notes there were alternative views aired in the press. In Palenski's words, 'the tour of South Africa in 1928 was a Rubicon for

New Zealand in terms of supinely acquiescing to the racist dictates of South Africa – however noble the motivation…'[23] Whatever the New Zealand national mindset, it is impossible to ignore the implications for Empire unity. No matter how well the Māori players were treated and respected in France, rugby fans saw that New Zealand had chosen to select a supposedly nationally representative All Blacks team on a racial basis to avoid offending a fellow Empire member while the 'others' (i.e. Māori in this case) were relegated to touring France – in this case clearly used as a second-best option – as compensation.

The New Zealand actions could be interpreted as a necessary sacrifice in the interests of Empire unity or they could be seen as one sporting code acting out of self-interest to the detriment of others, even at the cost of demeaning the national character. Little consideration appears to have been given to the significance of the impression created by New Zealand's selection of France as the non-Empire nation offering the best alternative for Māori. Greg Buckley pointed out in his thesis that there was ambivalence in South Africa over the Empire project owing to the distinct divisions within the racially divided white population. Even so, Buckley also says that 'the view of New Zealand political elites in relation to New Zealand and South African rugby tours remained imperialist'.[24] If so, this may explain why France was selected as the destination for the tour rather than another Empire country such as Australia or one of the Home nations. Although no direct evidence has been found on this point, there may have been a fear that touring another Empire member could have opened additional intra-Empire divisions over the Empire's treatment of its non-white races. Empire unity was perhaps bought for the price of acquiescing to racial discrimination within New Zealand's national sport.

New Zealand's reluctance to side with France in order to break the British stranglehold on inter-war rugby administration is consistent with a theory of Empire unity taking precedence. It particularly rankled with the French that the Home Union delegates were collectively described as an 'international' Board. In 1920 *Le Figaro* reported that a 'sportsman' was suggesting the formation of a rebel International Rugby organisation involving Romania, the United States, South Africa, Australia, New Zealand and France. England would thereafter be 'obliged' to join. The real reason for not admitting France to full International Rugby Board membership – according to a 1921 *Le Figaro* comment – was the likelihood that this would also open the door for all the southern hemisphere nations to join, thus giving them numerical superiority over the Home Unions. In 1926 *Le Figaro* reported that New Zealand had finally acted by refusing to accept representation on a committee considering changes to the laws of the game without concurrent admission to full Board membership. As *Le Figaro* explained:

> The Dominions of New Zealand and South Africa repeatedly demanded, without success, direct representation at the International Board. Now New Zealand is protesting again, refusing to allow its two delegates to sit at a consultative conference to be held in London, with the aim of unifying the rules of rugby, because the agenda does not [include a] proposal to form a rugby committee of the British Empire.[25]

The New Zealand concept of international representation still existed within the constraints of the Empire, in *Le Figaro*'s view.

Other apparently largely unreciprocated New Zealand interest in French sports extended to horse racing and boxing, two distinctly male-identified activities. The death of Joseph Oller the inventor of the 'Pari-Mutuel' or totalisator betting system was noted by the *Auckland Star*. Elsewhere it was conceded – in typically New Zealand fashion – that French horses were fast but there were no racecourses in England or France to rival the 'beauty or ideal racing' available at Ellerslie.[26] The exploits of Tom Heeney the New Zealand heavyweight boxing champion were reported by *Le Figaro* until he became Gene Tunney's 'last victim', although Heeney aspired to return to New York to avenge the defeat.[27] This contrasts with the prominence given in French reports to the New Zealand athletes at the Paris Olympic Games. Although understandable given the location, the detailed coverage of the New Zealand competitors during the 1924 Paris Olympics was in part due to the many excellent performances of Arthur Porritt, later to become New Zealand's first New Zealand born Governor-General.[28] France appeared to have had a more balanced view of New Zealand's place in the sporting world than did New Zealand of France, for New Zealand required a direct link to success to give legitimacy to sports reporting and thereby justify the national sense of self-worth. Consequently, some items were reported in New Zealand out of proportion to their wider significance for either country. The French press, on the other hand, showed interest in international events even when there was no direct French involvement, while concurrently demonstrating a greater awareness of the broader implications for the British Empire when Empire members assessed their self-esteem through sport.

Apart from these sporting exchanges the French version of post-war New Zealand as it appeared in the press regressed through the phases of social laboratory, wartime ally and then potential trading partner into just another (British-possessed) South Seas archipelago. This trend is typified by the treatment of New Zealand objects and collectors' pieces acquired and then traded in France as mementos of an earlier time. Once separated from their original setting and everyday context, their symbolic importance or the utility of their original function was lost. Two examples from the French press – the trade in postage stamps and Māori artefacts – are illustrative.

Collection of and trading in postage stamps became commonplace as international postage evolved. In many cases these items assumed additional value as collectors' pieces far beyond their original face value, but it is not clear what if any impression of New Zealand they conveyed to the traders and collectors. In addition, jade (nephrite, greenstone, pounamu) items apparently of New Zealand Māori origin also featured in traders' catalogues. Descriptions such as 'un "Tiki" en néphrite, verte, Nouvelle-Zélande, 5.000 francs; un casse-tête en nephrite verte, Nouvelle-Zélande, 9.000 francs' are typical of these listings. Portrayals of the items were not always clear, nor was it obvious whether the interest was artistic or simply for titillation and amusement.

> [possibly a] doorpost or lintel of woodwork, two coupled figures mounted [possibly meaning sexually joined or an upright figure] (New Zealand), 5,200 francs; a Hei-Tiki pendant in nephrite (New Zealand), 3,600 francs; a nephrite Hei-Tiki of rare translucency (New Zealand), 3,250 francs; a standing female Tiki, in gray stone (Marquesas Islands), 5,300 francs.[29]

Removed from their original setting and listed in advertisements alongside other exotic artefacts it seems unlikely that such items conveyed any meaning to the French reader or owner, beyond their obvious aesthetic or novelty qualities.

New Zealand was and still is a minor entertainment market owing to its relatively small population. Little of the received output from any source was therefore tailored to suit local tastes or circumstances. Increased exposure to American culture was one consequence of the war-enforced hiatus in British and European movie-making from which the Continental industry appeared slow to recover. The mediocre alternatives that were eventually produced in Europe resulted from a post-war misreading of the public mood by British, French, German and other Continental filmmakers. The lack of competitive British or foreign films assisted American marketing by default, although New Zealand audiences were subjected to aggressive promotions.[30] American movies delivered entertaining fictional storylines using superior production techniques whereas the old-world films often showed 'foreigners' – including the French – in less escapist stories which were embedded within British cultural parameters.[31] The latter seemed less relevant to a younger generation of post-war, post-colonial New Zealanders. Since the cinema was the only opportunity for much of the audience to see the 'others' in their natural setting these impressions mattered, even if it was implicit that a movie was no more than a staged contrivance. Consequently, at the same time as the United

States was withdrawing from active participation in various international forums (the decision not to join the League of Nations being the most publicised) American cultural indoctrination was increasing.

When the United States entered the war, cinema technology was employed to reinforce the new pro-Allied policy. Any stigma that American movies might have attracted if the United States' neutrality had persisted was consequently neutralised. The disarmingly flexible approach of the American industry became apparent when the film stars were (re-)presented to their American audience as enthusiastic, and patriotic (although many such as Charlie Chaplin were not American natives) supporters of a war that had previously been portrayed as solely a European concern. In part this was necessary for self-preservation because the international Hollywood community had significant European representation from both sides of the wartime divide.

Contrasting examples show the pivot in attitudes required to move from a neutral isolationist stance to full-blooded support for the American soldiers. In *The Little American* Canadian-born Gladys Louise Smith – known professionally as Mary Pickford – played a character who chose a German suitor in preference to a French Count. Two months later Pickford was starring in a fiercely patriotic short film, *One Hundred Percent American*.[32] English-born Charlie Chaplin announced that he, Pickford and Fairbanks had 'four weeks' hard work ahead on the Third Liberty Loan drive'.[33] A gossip columnist described with approval Eleonora de Cisneros' protest 'against any revival of German music in Uncle Sam's Land – at any rate for a good while to come'.[34] The tone made a virtue of any French connections and an evil of the German equivalent. In that respect the American movie industry was, in sporting parlance, 'on side'.

At the war's end the American industry was quick to adapt by producing films of an escapist genre that coincidentally promoted American culture as an unobjectionable background. British nationhood within the Empire was thereby confronted with a threat far greater and less manageable than politicians, intellectuals and the cultural elite could have imagined. The new technologies that the pro-Empire theoreticians and political actors had assumed would be used to reinforce the Empire were guilelessly utilised to relentlessly undermine British culture. The ready post-war availability of foreign, mainly American films using escapist themes confounded the British producers who were seemingly fixated on reviving familiar pre-war cultural habits through the portrayal of a socially conservative, hierarchical society. Although consistent with the theme of returning to 'normal', these appeared to be attempting to reset the social order to pre-war conditions (as was done for instance after the Great Plague through the sumptuary laws). It also (re-)established old cultural themes such as a renewal of the British elite's affection for the French alongside the lower classes' disdain for the same. Many New Zealand servicemen had seen the British class system in action within the British Army in France, as well as in the United Kingdom in its civilian guise when the soldiers were on leave. Many had been disconcerted by this cultural reality of Home. They instinctively rejected the class system as they planned their return to an idealised pre-1914 egalitarian New Zealand society. Once home, few therefore presumably desired to see European and British movies – whether depicting the war or using pre-war class themes – that reinforced British societal structures.

The British producers were apparently constrained by the constructs of Empire, cultural legacies, wartime sentiment, and post-war politics, perhaps because this was the culture of the winners.[35] If so, they badly misread the change in the public mood. As the prominent British film producer Sir Oswald Stoll (requoted in *New Zealand Truth* in 1920) said more in hope than reality:

> Public taste is becoming more insistent upon the exhibition of British films of super-excellence, and these films can probably be better produced in Great Britain than in any other country, taking into account the great Variety [sic] of scenery, the opportunities for picturesque and historical background, the proximity of the Continent of Europe for occasional

> international effects, and the imaginative talent of British authors and actors.[36]

Stoll's statement missed the point; where and how films were made did not matter because the very purpose of filmmaking is to create an illusion. Portrayals of France did not have to be made on location, they simply needed to depict France – truthfully or otherwise – through representation or by implication.

As interest in wartime induced patriotic themes declined, the entertainment value and quality of the plot rather than the cultural theme became the deciding factor in the selections of the movie-going public. Mr C. D'Arcy Allen (who was described as the managing director of the British and Continental Feature Film Co. Ltd) explained that British filmmaking was to be based on dramatising 'well-known' books and that as a result English film production was 'steadily forging ahead'. He badly misunderstood the local mood when he predicted that with the 'pick of the Continental output' his company's films would be of interest to the public. One of the Stoll films released by the British and Continental Feature Film Co. Ltd in New Zealand typifies the disconnect. *The Four Feathers* was a 1921 filmed adaptation of the A.E.W. Mason book of the same name. The complex plot and sub-plots involved an English girl, a Frenchman from Fashoda and a French journalist. The Gallic connection included references to the presence of the competing colonial powers in the Sudan region and the French-constructed Suez Canal.[37] It thus integrated virtually all the elements and themes of the uneasy pre-*entente* Anglo-French relationship. The film was an undisguised reassertion of the British class structure, moral superiority and imperialism located in conquered North Africa using a traditionally negative depiction of the French.[38]

Such productions were not attractive, even to the British public. A July 1925 column from the *Auckland Star* reported that Stoll Pictures lost £46,639 in 1924 with costs 'greatly in excess' of forecast revenues. The article plaintively noted that the company had sufficient new inventory ready 'when and if' there was a resurgence in 'taste' for the genre of film the British were producing. Films that reinforced stereotypical images of a class-based society within a British nation becalmed in a self-created sea of historical nostalgia were of little interest to New Zealand audiences. Without any acknowledgement of this shortcoming, the lamentations on the state of the British film industry appeared platitudinous and lacking in substance.

The Dominions attempted to retain the relevance of the Empire by excluding the 'others'. During the 1926 Imperial Conference the Canadian Prime Minister (Mackenzie) referred to the importance of films in maintaining the Empire's cultural identity. The Australian Prime Minister Stanley Bruce commented that 'the propaganda value of the film with its universal appeal cannot be overemphasized'. He went on to decry the lack of films showing British customs and trade without apparently realising the contradiction in his own position, namely that if the content was of interest, audience demand would result in additional productions. The *New Zealand Herald* pointed out that the Conference's own sub-committee report had noted that any official action would be useless unless films were '...of real and competitive exhibition value'.[39]

Not all movie-making subjects were as trivial as the advertising and reviews suggest. There were attempts to use the medium to increase understanding between nations and countries beyond crude cultural or racial dramatisation. Desley Deacon credits the producer Walter Wagner with developing the idea that film could be used to overcome the public's uncertainty or fear of foreigners by seeing the 'others' in their (supposedly) home setting through 'natural drama(s)'. While the images were obviously staged and stylised they were nonetheless an opportunity for cross-cultural sharing as the audience saw the others eating, working and carrying out everyday tasks.[40] The genre was not a commercial success for Paramount Pictures because it overlooked the most important role of the cinema especially in difficult times, namely to indulge the audience by allowing a brief period of escape into a fantasy world. Post-war depression – both economic and emotional – had led the middle American mass market towards entertainment genres that escaped, rather than featured, reality. The traditional theatrical themes of fantasy, romance, fortune and conflict predominated. These presented to the rest of the world a misleadingly positive America that appeared to be very different from day-to-day experiences elsewhere.[41]

Despite a purportedly 'open door' policy, the United States film industry had official assistance via the various restrictions imposed on foreign productions by a heavily lobbied Congress. It was accordingly difficult for French and other European films to penetrate the American mass market even though America was able to export its own culture, apparently confident that it was America's moral right to use its financial clout in order to demonstrate American superiority. This led to the paradox of American political isolationism coexisting with American cultural expansion. In many cases the movie moguls driving this trend were themselves immigrants from Europe who deliberately 'Americanised' their movies using nativist themes. This shift to popular American subjects was also evident in New Zealand.[42]

Perversely, the French-sourced or French-related films screened in New Zealand seem to have exacerbated the otherness of the French rather than creating a common understanding. What was perceived as a somewhat snobbish intellectual culture operated through film societies and the like to associate French and other Continental productions with rather highbrow, sophisticated tastes which were better suited to the intellectual classes. These societies unconsciously replicated the British upper-class affection for French culture that contrasted with the lower classes' disdain for the 'froggies'. Sigley quotes various Gordon Miriams authored articles published in the *New Zealand Listener* that could have introduced such productions to a broader audience, assuming that Miriams' columns were read by the general public. Miriams developed the theme of French films being distinctive and what now might be termed 'arty' without the simplicity, glamour or celebrity element. Sigley notes that Miriams tried to avoid being snobby or intellectual when 'nudging' his presumably more high-brow readers towards this different genre of films. Nevertheless, the intellectuals were just one segment of the *Listener*'s readership and of the movie going community. The commercial reality was that the *Listener* had to be aware of the 'common-sense' reader just as the New Zealand film industry had to be conscious of the movie-going equivalent. Such content was therefore limited.[43]

There were insufficient New Zealand productions of whatever character to displace the huge volume of imported content necessary to feed the growing demand for movie entertainment. Aside from distance and technology the nascent New Zealand film industry – as with any enterprise dependent on scale – was and still is limited by the size of the domestic market. Local films have to balance domestic tastes against possible foreign appeal and sales. Depictions of the New Zealanders' involvement in France through fictional films therefore appear to have been limited to a small number of pioneering local productions.[44] In his oral history, Rudall Hayward, the innovative New Zealand film entrepreneur, described the production of the patriotic war film, *Just as the Sun Went Down*, and explained that the war scenes were filmed in New Zealand at Narrow Neck, Devonport during army manoeuvres, rather than on location.[45] This seems to be the one of the few war-period local productions with a specifically French-associated wartime setting and only one advertisement for this feature has been located. Two other mentions of the film in the *Northern Gazette* on the 4th and 5th of February 1915 have been found, but there are no reviews, suggesting that the film had very limited commercial success.

BRITANNIA THEATRE

J. L. BENWELL & SONS, PROPRIETORS. (Formerly Queen's)

TO-NIGHT ! TO-NIGHT !

JUST AS THE SUN WENT DOWN

Auckland's First Photo. Play in Two Parts.

A War Drama, including Scenes of the Departure of the New Zealand Troops.

EGYPT AND ITS DEFENDERS.

A Fine War Picture, depicting the land to which the New Zealand Troops have gone.

AND FULL PROGRAMME.

Figure 23 Promotional advertising *Just as the Sun Went Down*[46]

Whether filmed locally or *in situ*, the representations of France available to New Zealand cinema audiences would – in the absence of an alternative narrative – have probably added to the impression that France had become a badly damaged battlefield, consistent with the wartime propaganda.[47] Without movies that showed a distinct New Zealand presence in France during the conflict, the New Zealand experience became blurred with that of other Allied troops. New Zealand's military identity, fused with that of the ANZAC contingent, was subsumed within the Empire's presence in France. Despite the individual diaries, photos and memories, New Zealand's war – as far as its dramatised presence in France was concerned – was not that of an independent country. Not only did the New Zealanders have little direct interaction with the French public, they also apparently served as

Empire soldiers in a distant, badly damaged and very unforgiving climatic and geographical environment.

Since the British identity was dependent on public goodwill towards the monarchy, cultivating an appropriate public image was – as the Prince of Wales' private secretary put it with a pointed reference to France – 'better than a guillotine in the yard of Buckingham Palace'.[48] The oblique reference to the fate of the French monarchy alongside a rise in politically Left-leaning philosophies was an explicit acknowledgement of the fears of the British ruling elite that they too could face the wrath of the mob. Staged production techniques were already being used when filming the Prince of Wales' 1920 tour of Australasia to counter this threat. On the one hand, the promotion of a youthful and apparently vigorous heir-apparent was a blatant appeal to the ideal of a progressive Empire, while on the other it was an assertion of the ascendancy of the 'whiteman' and an attempt to pull 'the Dominions firmly back into the imperial fold'.[49] Journalism and filmmaking skills were a crucial part of the process. Awareness of camera angles and differing points of view – as seen by the viewer in the edited output – were necessary to project appropriate images likely to stimulate sympathetic reactions towards the Prince amongst the audience. Through film and news reels the media was becoming a significant influence on the popularity and therefore the survival of the British royals and the Empire. Despite ready access to arguably the best and most patriotic of Empire themes, the contest for British cultural dominance in New Zealand was nonetheless being lost. Film quota legislation and royal propaganda were a desperate attempt to stem the tide of popular choice. The French efforts, misclassified in some cases and too 'arty' in others, failed to gain any significant mainstream influence for French culture in New Zealand.[50]

New Zealand and France shared an interest in the technical innovations that were constantly improving communication, the transport of goods and personal travel. The news reports show that advances in transport were usually judged by improvements in speed and range rather than safety or comfort. There was a particular fascination with land speed records in 1918–35, although there was obviously no functional purpose for travel between New Zealand and France. New Zealand was often the venue for record attempts rather than providing the innovator or a participant.[51] Progress in aviation assessed by speed and height was also keenly reported in the French press with endurance records often featuring new routes in the Pacific.[52] Given the topography of the globe, the need for long flat surfaces and the significant oceans between the continents any improvements in the speed of land travel faced significant limitations that did not apply to aviation. Could these developments be exploited to bring France and other northern hemisphere countries closer to New Zealand? An early suggestion of using airships to improve communication between Britain and the Dominions exposed the lack of common purpose within the Empire owing to the Dominions' geographic dispersion. After discussing the technical difficulties *Le Figaro* realistically concluded that, 'Obviously, the practical difficulties are very serious'. Both South Africa and New Zealand declined to participate in 'un service aérien par dirigeables au travers de l'Empire britannique', apparently owing to their respective financial situations. Nonetheless, air travel was rapidly establishing a commercial base, for in 1930 *Le Figaro* announced that 'New Zealand's first scheduled air service from New Plymouth to Wellington has just been inaugurated'.[53]

As *L'Humanité* observed, wireless technology supplemented by improved cable services was making a more connected world possible, even when travel was difficult:

> While waiting for the large Soviet post which will be heard throughout Europe with a current receiver, another method is offered for the wide dissemination of programs. Imagine a normal station at the moment, such as that of Moscow (RDW), which would be relayed every thousand kilometers for example by other stations the range [of which] would extend over the whole earth…

L'Humanité appreciated the political possibilities – presumably since the dream of a worldwide socialist regime was still alive – but as the paper observed it was the British who were introducing such a system so that 'English propaganda will soon cover the whole earth'. *L'Humanité* also noted that 'In Sydney, Australia, a radio service has just been created to relay the transmissions of the United States and Europe and distribute it to New Zealand, Tasmania, Western Australia, North Queensland and the Islands of Oceania'.[54]

As was often the case, it was the novelty of the new innovations that had first attracted attention. A report that 'A famous artist from New Zealand has just married…' with guests apparently participating through the airwaves using the services of T.S.F. (probably *télégraphe sans fil*) went on to explain that 'The rites were accomplished one by one, without the distant guests losing anything. They had attended the wedding'.[55] In 1928 a weekend telegram service – presumably aiming to utilise off-peak capacity – was launched linking France with New Zealand and other southern locations. A similar service had already been instigated between France and America.[56] By 1932 *Le Figaro* was able to publish details of the fee structure agreed between the United Kingdom and French Governments for international telephone charges. Prices applicable for calls to New Zealand and other Pacific locations were included.[57]

The 1932 Christmas message from the King was the first to be broadcast simultaneously to the British colonies, Dominions and territories. It was (*Le Figaro* noted) intended that the 'message would unite all the British people in a single thought'. A follow-up item confirmed the success of the broadcast, and pointed out to readers the different climate and time zones that the Empire-wide audience would have experienced (it was dawn in New Zealand) at the moment the King was broadcasting from Sandringham (3pm local time).[58] Hence, by the early 1930s a common British-based identity could be relatively easily shared within the Empire in real time.

These observations are distinguished by their almost exclusively French sources. This suggests that French readers had a broad interest in these topics even when France was not directly involved. Conversely, New Zealand readers heard little of innovations in France or those involving the French in general, unless New Zealand or perhaps the Empire was directly involved. This hints at exclusion of such news as a local phenomenon. It also confirms that a less outward-looking, Empire-centric society existed in New Zealand. Maintaining that status relied in part upon excluding – not necessarily with malicious intent – messages that did not reinforce the relevance of Empire or the close links with the United Kingdom rather than exclusion owing to technical limitations. The unofficial diplomatic discourse of 1918–19 between Paris and Auckland at the time of the Pau visit showed that telegraph and telegram were already being used to transmit messages and facilitate travel arrangements while letters between Paris, London and Wellington were still literally in the post.

The earliest French visitors to New Zealand had assessed and recorded potential sites for possible future settlement, evaluated the natural resources and – in the early twentieth century – investigated and studied social and democratic innovations.[59] Despite New Zealand's self-assumed reputation as an innovative nation, there is little evidence that the French still saw New Zealand as such in 1918–35. The earlier social laboratory legislation phase of the innovative Liberal Government had passed. When there was comment from the 1918–35 period in the French press, it usually related to agriculture or to New Zealand as the site of scientific observation rather than New Zealand as a social innovator. If anything, it was New Zealand that was looking to France for new ideas.[60] Perhaps because France had such a well-deserved reputation as a nation of science, *L'Humanité* was scathing in its post-war protest at the lack of scientific study and the neglect of the science education as far afield as New Zealand, in favour of military research and spending on memorials.

> While the government maintains armies of nearly a million men, pays generals generously, subsidises activities intended to maintain in the new generation the spirit of war and revenge, our researchers are doomed [voués] to indifference, contempt, and misery.
> Lately we have witnessed the scandalous fact of an expedition to study, in New Zealand, one of the most important questions for the development of our knowledge, without a French representative. The pretext, it required 200,000 francs. Ah, if it had been to celebrate a great battle.[61]

The French newspapers' fascination with natural phenomena such as earthquakes and thermal activity was heightened by the science fiction writing of authors such as Jules Verne. The 1931 Napier earthquake was reported as if it were a predestined climax to earlier reports of geophysical activity.[62] This fitted with a narrative of colonisation as a project that imposed a familiar landscape on a foreign environment, as if the geography as well as the people had to be tamed to fit a predefined image of a civilised nation.[63]

Agricultural development in the Pacific was seen by New Zealand as a necessity to earn a national income and remain relevant to Britain, whereas for France it was a means of justifying colonisation. Hence the use of agricultural science and technology in cropping systems, the interest in the impact of refrigeration and the need to protect (by patent) inventions and inventors, all of which were noted by *Le Figaro*. New Zealand's use of parasites as a biological control for rampant 'blackberry brambles' was noted as was the possibility of pest control through 'the use of insecticidal powders … by airplanes flying at height'.[64] Such innovations became a necessity when attempting to establish an exotic ecosystem in a foreign environment whilst simultaneously (and paradoxically) battling weeds and pests which were imported with the foreign ecosystem.

New Zealand's active participation in agricultural conferences contrasts with an obvious indifference to participation in other world forums because this was one matter in which the Empire and Britain could not represent local interests. Curiously one *Le Figaro* article lamented the poor presentation ('packaging and presentation deplorable') of fresh food exports from France. It referred to a talk by 'M. Serre, Consul of France in New Zealand, on the conservation of fruits by the cold.'[65] Such reports obscured the broader issues. Both France and the United Kingdom were attempting to implant European-based agricultural systems to justify the occupation of their territories on the other side of the world, in many instances within unsuitable physical environments.

Figure 24 New Zealand hill country[66]

If New Zealand identified by choice as a British nation located in the South Pacific, the use of European style agriculture provided an economic justification for its existence. This was not dissimilar to the French colonies in the Pacific, for in both cases agriculture became the excuse for occupation and the reason for territorial retention within their respective Empires.[67] The incongruity is apparent in the physical separation between two of the world's largest economies, with their complementary range of primary and secondary industries, by a mere thirty-one miles of English Channel.

Cultural exchanges obviously require a means of transmission, but there must also be a relevant message sent to a receptive audience. Given the earlier rejections and the lack of significant inter-country exchanges, there was little more that France could say or do to penetrate New Zealand's thick crust of Empire-centric, anti-French culture. The misleading narrative of a small, isolated, British-dependent agricultural country became a self-assumed and therefore self-perpetuating characteristic within the New Zealand identity. The more this theme was repeated the more it was assumed to be correct and as a consequence the more it was used. This ingrained self-image assumed that the main conduit to world trade and wisdom ran through London. Return communications had the obligatory veneer of anti-French bias applied before transmission. The technology had not failed, but the received messages were being voluntarily censored and reinterpreted. The infrequent, unanswered and ignored messages from France eventually eased in their frequency and depth of content so that by 1935 it was American culture – employing popular messages and escapist, appealing themes – that forced its way past this barrier, in part through repetition and volume. It would be unfair to blame this on a lack of direct and relevant messaging from France. France – the place where the New Zealand sacrifice had been most evident – failed to gain a local cultural presence because New Zealand chose to be unreceptive. The main reason the messaging failed or went unreceived was the distorted, negative view of France that was accepted as an inseparable part of New Zealand's post-colonial British identity.

Paradigmes déplacés: leçons de Français pour la Nouvelle-Zélande (1918–1935)

We are in France. After months of waiting we step on hallowed soil.

John Moloney, War Diary[1]

The British colonists' attempt to replicate an old world in a new one required transporting the English view of France to Aotearoa New Zealand alongside the rest of their cultural baggage. The adoption of a simplistic, adverse view of France as the site of revolution and regicide was therefore a reflexive action that conveniently overlooked the irony of Britain having once experienced similar events. The arrival of the French in New Zealand led to competitive religious and territorial interactions, as well as contradictions between the inherited version of France and first-hand experience. The image of the British heroes who had saved Europe and the world by defeating Napoleon were nevertheless given a final fictional polish in their adopted home and were then permanently displayed in place names, to be commemorated annually during Trafalgar and Empire Day, lest we forget. These experiences were selectively reinterpreted through the biases brought from Home, thereby helping to sustain a negative predisposition towards France, despite evidence that France was ultimately a benevolent presence.[2] Moreover, these events tested the utility of using the experience from an inherited historical narrative as a paradigm for defining an independent foreign policy. They also tested the bonds of Empire against a more utilitarian, independent, nation-state alternative.

A relationship with France – whether adversarial or cooperative – was (perversely) both a part of being British as well as a requirement for an independent post-war New Zealand. Achieving the latter status required ignoring or minimising the pre-World War I anti-French heritage in order to adopt a more constructive post-war relationship, but so too did the former as Britain engaged with the world beyond the Empire. In either case, Britain's traditional views of the French had become so embedded in the preceding 100 years that a complete repudiation was impossible. So, when the French made official visits to New Zealand as allies and potential trade partners, or when New Zealand and French politicians met during peace negotiations, commemoration events, or during conferences, the dissonance between an inherited pre-war Napoleonic/revolutionary view of France still had to be reconciled with France the post-war ally. New Zealand had discovered at first hand that Napoleon really was dead and France was a different country from that of 1790–1815. There was a clear dissonance between past and present.

The new France could be accepted for what it was – an ally and potential European partner – or the old prejudices could be kept alive and the ancient memories nurtured in the tradition of pre-*entente* Britain. There was an absence of leadership on the issue from the New Zealand politicians and what nowadays might be termed the local highbrows or intelligentsia. Both cliques had been educated, whether informally or formally, in an era when the local culture was a version of British culture, permeated with France the enemy of the public and the favourite of the elite. Pre-war references at imperial conferences and in selected titbits published in the newspapers provided evidence of quirky French behaviour. Historical fiction, Trafalgar Day celebrations and the names on signposts warned New Zealand to be wary of abandoning the anti-France ethos of the British, even as Britain was embracing the *entente cordiale*. It was easier to generalise and revert to mischaracterising the 'others' as a foreign, irrelevant group when contact was kept to a minimum. From a distance, the post-war reality of modern France – as seen through personal contacts with Frenchmen such as Clemenceau, Siegfried and Pau who were living in the present and dealing with the issues of the day – could be overlooked.

One of the key themes in the New Zealand identity that emerged was that of a 'small' or inconsequential nation. 'Small' is the essence of New Zealand's defining myth which sits alongside the isolation notion to form the basis of much of the self-assumed national character. New Zealand is not a small country by land area when compared to many other sovereign nations and if it is small in population it is by choice not capacity. Assisted by the cartographers' predilection for using a north–south global orientation, New Zealand is typically drawn in the lower right-hand corner of the globe. Despite the realities of comparative land area, close proximity to Australia (Auckland is closer to Sydney than London is to New York) and a Pacific location within easy reach of populous South East Asia, the myths of size and isolation have become embedded, essential interpretations of the national self. It is a theme that has been nurtured and sustained as an indispensable element in constructing both a sense of powerless dependency and the 'punching above our weight' myth, a useful fiction whenever an individual New Zealander exceeds the nation's deliberately understated expectations.[3] But this construed, self-conceived isolation only exists if the datum or reference point is assumed to be in Britain. The annual national rituals of Anzac Day and Waitangi Day reinforce this interpretation by placing New Zealand's role within a British context while simultaneously downplaying the nation's exposure to other nations and the opportunities forgone by ignoring them. On both anniversaries, the celebrations draw attention to a deep link with the British Crown, either by Treaty or by military alliance. These themes and the adjacent terminology perpetuate the myth of Britain as the centre of the world. This imagined cartography overlooks Europe and France even though both are adjacent to the United Kingdom geographically and politically.

Colonisation proved to be an unstoppable Anglicising process, no matter how much London or Māori tried to temper settler enthusiasm. The isolation myth led to the narrative of a distinctly British national identity which was implanted and nurtured in a new land. As politicians and historians have adapted and repeated this story, it has evolved into the legend of a nation developed and funded through agricultural enterprises that utilised the lush, green pasture grown in a rural hinterland of the great metropolis of London. Agricultural output boomed in response to an assumed demand from British consumers without regard for market requirements or environmental consequences.[4] Technology such as refrigeration and steamships was enlisted to provide more efficient transport, pleas for expanded market access to dispose of the increased supply resulted, requests for capital funding to produce yet more followed, and demands increased for Britain to defend the whole fragile structure from unidentified 'others'. This message of continuity and limited options could only be sustained if the alternatives were ignored. The conflation of loyalty, trade and Empire membership made New Zealand's relationship with Britain predictably self-fulfilling, but in so doing it limited interactions with the 'others' for both entities, even when the 'others' were geographically or economically more proximate.[5]

Breaking out of an existing national or empire perspective requires reconsideration of the role of the writers of history in the development and migration of ideas from their original national or empire-based narratives. The first step is to reconsider how the role of non-Empire participants in the New Zealand history of 1918–35 has been presented. The relationship between New Zealand and France in particular has been presented as a series of discrete topics, as the result of a perceived need to write histories based on evidence of direct contact. Examples such as the military histories of the Great War, General Pau's visit, the French presence in the New Hebrides, the teaching of the French language in schools, colonial France in the Pacific, stories from and about the New Zealand artists and writers who lived in France, the French religious missions, colonisation at Akaroa and so on, abound. Physical contact and direct influence are usually taken as foundation evidence. These topics have then been corralled within the artificial borders of specialised knowledge, time periods, geography and so on with the net result that the collective French influence in New Zealand's history between 1918 and 1935 has been understated.

It is no surprise that a significant theme identified by this reassessment is the persistence of the tripartite link between Great Britain, France and New Zealand. For all the uncertainty and worry expressed by the French, when Britain was forced to choose she decided to support France in the two world wars of the twentieth century. Similarly, the uncertainty evident at times in reconciling New Zealand's loyalty to Britain with a distaste for the French, while concurrently claiming a degree of independence, melted when a war in support of Britain (as a recruitment agent for France) required it. New Zealand therefore proved to be a loyal and useful adjunct provider of manpower and primary produce during both world wars, to the advantage of the French. In the interregnum of 1918–35 the British – whether by design or coincidence – maintained New Zealand in reserve through the Royal Navy's protection of New Zealand's sea routes, lending money when required, accepting New Zealand's exports in more or less whatever unrefined form New Zealand chose to export them (raw wool of variable quality, fatty sheep and beef carcasses, semi-processed yellow dairy fats) and by managing New Zealand ambitions in the New Hebrides. New Zealand reciprocated with manpower and food in times of adversity.

Dividing memories of France, the nation of revolution, Napoleonic heritage and political instability from the France of World War I experience had appeared to be relatively easy at first glance. It was as if there were two adjacent but self-contained versions of France in New Zealand's post-war memory. One was the wartime ally, the fellow victim, in a land known for muddy bogs, trenches, rest periods for the troops in the *estaminets*, occasional sightseeing in Paris and infrequent contacts with French locals who saw the soldiers as a collective disruption in their own struggle to survive. This France included the idealised small family farms set in an appealing rural landscape; it seemed more like 'us' than the pre-war 'others' had been, for the earlier 'other' France was based on a now apparently redundant image of a traditional enemy of the British. It seemed in the immediate post-war years that this version could finally be set aside. Whether motivated by military design or a genuine urge for a better world, France tried to ease this transition using diplomatic engagement that attempted to overwrite the pre-war history with the wartime alliance experience and a new cooperation.

New Zealand's case for rejecting France and retreating into the Empire's clinch seemed inarguable, for if the war had been fought (in the British interpretation) to preserve the independence of smaller nations such as Belgium, it was the British Empire rather than the French equivalent that had demonstrably saved them. New Zealand's subsequent self-imposed censorship restricted post-war knowledge of France to an eclectic mix of newspaper articles, formal academic study of language and pre-war history, alongside literature from a genre of what is now termed historical fiction, films, and myths about the French character, all rooted in the assumption that cultural differences were racially based. These were supplemented with experiences – both first-hand and retold – from the war. The evidence suggests that much of this knowledge was wrong or at best misleading, especially in the case of agriculture.

France had no more interest in addressing New Zealand's concerns through the League of Nations – provided their respective territorial and economic interests were not in conflict – than did New Zealand in directly supporting France. As far as any bilateral contacts between

New Zealand and France went, the League was a superfluous appendage of the post-war settlement. Any nation could potentially be a victim or an aggressor – or in some circumstances viewed as both – so few trusted the League to protect their interests. There was no single universal formula which would be completely acceptable in all conceivable circumstances. There was little that suggested the League could be an efficacious body through which to establish additional ties with France. Moreover, the apparently illogical positions taken by France – such as those relating to women's rights and use of the French language – were not treated as indicators requiring explanation but rather as inconsequential examples of the vagaries of the French character that reinforced the perception that the French were the 'others'. From the viewpoint of France, still facing a powerful Germany and dealing with the other great powers of Europe, New Zealand's supposedly independent views must have seemed an odd, self-selected assortment of semi-independent stances underpinned with an adherence to British policies of questionable relevance for an emerging independent nation in the South Pacific.

Post-war New Zealand became part of the 'others' for the French, just as France regressed to a similar classification from the New Zealand viewpoint. Some of the best evidence for this reversion comes from the shrewd and perceptive observations made of New Zealand in the French press. Because it is impossible to imagine ourselves exactly as the others see us, these newspaper opinions assume extra significance as an external historical source when assessing New Zealand's world status between 1919 and 1935. Moreover, because the imagined self is close to perfection and so does not readily accept fault, any criticism comes as a surprise and reflexively invites denial. Positive national characteristics are taken as obvious whereas the negatives are proscribed, thus setting boundaries defined by what we are not. Our strengths are seen in the reflected weaknesses or flaws of the 'others' and are taken as obvious.

The French newspaper reporting suggested that Britain's post-war Empire was faltering and New Zealand was constitutionally adrift. New Zealand's repudiation of a continued role as a French ally and trade partner meant further interactions would be limited. Within the French news reports, lengthy critiques of the British Empire model, doubts about the future of New Zealand within it and the changes in British security arrangements crudely exposed these vulnerabilities in New Zealand's assumed position as an Empire member. Britain aspired to remain apart from the interdependent states of Europe, but the two-way flow of ideas and goods within the Empire and the very fact of the Empire's existence made Britain part of the world, and thereby so too New Zealand. Although nations can be useful political units, they are never completely independent. By clinging to the ambivalent concept of an independent Dominion within the Empire, New Zealand delayed an inevitably critical and awkward examination of its own history of colonial conquest and subjugation of Māori which full independence would demand.

Such matters were not of concern to a France that was in any case not keen to reassess its own colonising adventures. Moreover, despite New Zealand's apparent rejection of French overtures and the Empire's shortcomings, France still had an interest in Britain maintaining her Empire, at least where it was not directly competitive. As long as the British Empire's constituent countries including New Zealand remained as such, they were potential allies and a possible source of military manpower. New Zealand, having believed it had no need of France or at least only a limited need for any non-British military or economic relationship, now saw that the British Empire was facing a conundrum on both dimensions. New Zealand's hopes had largely been hitched to an Empire that was dissolving because it was unsustainable. New Zealand had failed to anticipate the change in the public mood in Britain and the highly consequential political and economic changes that resulted, for the British public now placed less faith in the Dominions' status than did the New Zealand electorate.

New Zealand's economic management until circa 1932 assumed British actions had a benevolent moral motivation. This opinion implicitly interpreted the policies of the others as self-interested. Having placed Britain and British values on a moral plinth at the pinnacle of civilisation, it followed that Britain was right and those who did otherwise were misguided or morally at fault. Views on devaluation, inflation, or on deficits – both in external trade and internal budgets, adherence to the gold standard and the treatment of the unemployed were subjected to a moral examination rather than being read agnostically as economic indicators. It followed that transgressing nations such as France were morally wrong when they ignored the British solutions. The economic prescriptions that resulted, especially those of the conservative Right, meant evidence of success using alternative policies had to be contradicted or invalidated. There was a naivety in the faithful assuming that acting correctly would deliver a good outcome in the face of mounting evidence that other nations – eventually including the British as well as the French – would ultimately act in what they saw as their own national interests. As New Zealand vainly pursued its ill-fated economic policies, it was left in an economic bypass by both Britain and France. Using lessons from France such as the need for a central bank, the adoption of a looser money supply to inflate a depressed economy and the acceptance that sovereign nations could adjust exchange rates regardless of their gold reserves suggested that flexibility and a willingness to adapt were not necessarily faults in the others but might even be strengths.

Britain's history still provides the base for much of New Zealand's non-Māori colonial and post-colonial history but the significance of France within Britain's story cannot be overlooked. Europe and European powers were an obviously important part of New Zealand's past. It would therefore be neglectful to restrict by omission the influence of say Napoleon Bonaparte or the French Revolution to specialised studies of France, just as the same could equally be true for neglecting the global significance of the American War of

Independence or the Russian Revolution. The importance of France in international affairs, trade and historical background is worthy of acknowledgement as an influence in the formation of New Zealand's national identity, for New Zealand has not been an unfortunate victim of events. The decisions on who New Zealand would engage with, what was to be grown or produced here, where that produce was to be exported and what cultural traditions would prevail were matters of choice rather than circumstance or obligation.

About the Author

After an extensive career in Asia, Dr Alistair Watts returned to his native New Zealand to study and write about his home country from an outsider's perspective. Using comprehensive archival and newspaper sources, he has re-investigated the origins of the New Zealand nation state from a fresh perspective that moves beyond the traditional bicultural view prevalent in the current New Zealand historiography. Dr Watts holds a PhD in history and qualifications in agricultural science and business. He lives in Auckland, New Zealand.

Contact: https://www.facebook.com/alistairwattsauthor/

Bibliography

Primary Sources and Manuscripts

Alexander Turnbull Library Wellington, NZ:

ATL 09-270 Australian Administration *Foreign Relationships: 1922–1936.*

ATL 11535-073 J C Beaglehole *Letters from England His Parents: 10 Jul–23 Dec 1928.*

ATL 92-166-01 Michael Bellam *Collection South Pacific French Imperialism: 1969–1975*

ATL 2189 William Biddell Birdwood, Baron, *Letters to Sir Godfrey Williams: 1916–1918.*

ATL 1346-212 (Dr) Ada Paterson *Inward Personal Correspondence: 1925–1935*

ATL 1504 Rhoda Howden *Correspondence, Re Illness and Death of Her Husband: 1917*

ATL 90-234-16/04 George Jackson *France in perspective and other topics: n.s.*

ATL 1846 Archibald Roderick *Jensen Recollections: 1895–1981*

ATL 8456-31 Horopapera Karauti *French Post Cards: 1917–1918.*

ATL 90-389-2/16 Reuel Anson Lochore *French and English Word Lists: 1928–1986*

ATL 1194 John Keith Moloney *War Diary: 1915–1917*

ATL 9608-48 (Sir) Arthur Espie Porritt *Letters to His Father: 1924*

ATL 0129-33 William Pember Reeves *Account of a Visit to France During World War One: ca 1919*

ATL 9000606/15/16 Frederick Lloyd Whitfeld Wood *Notes on French History: n.s.*

ATL 8911-2 Patrick Douglas Wood, *Letters from Douglas Wood Letters to His Sister, Evelyn: Jan–June 1917*

Archives Nationales (France), Pierrefitte-sur-Seine:

Commerce Et Industrie (1921-Vers 1962): *Réponses Des Agents Diplomatiques In Elimination de la concurrence austro-allemande des marchés étrangers: 1914–15.*

F/12/6741-F/12/10289 Ch. Schmidt, R. Marichal, Ph. Du Verdier. *'Honorary Distinctions – Legion of Honor – Individual Files. 1890 to 1939.' Trade and Industry Trade and Industry.*

Archives of the Ministry of Foreign Affairs (MAE), Centre of Diplomatic Archives of La Courneuve *Political and commercial correspondence called 'New series' (1896–1918)*:

Oceania, 2nd new series, New Zealand:

186CPCOM / 1: General file, 1899–1912, June

186CPCOM / 2: ditto, 1912, July – 1917

186CPCOM / 3: Economy, 1896–1917.

Political and Trade Correspondence, Series E – Asia, Subseries 'Australia', 1918–1940:

31CPCOM / 9: French Mission to Australia

31CPCOM / 10: ditto

31CPCOM / 11: idem: report

Archives New Zealand, Wellington, NZ:

Proclamations. 1840 Blue Book of Statistics. (see also: *New Zealand Advertiser and Bay of Islands Gazette).*

R22319675, Allen and WF Massey correspondence: *Miscellaneous files and papers.*

C 361 197, Allen, J. *Ministerial Files – English Trip 1913, Notes of Interviews*, 1913.

(R222319686 Allen, James. *Minister of Defence – Naval Defence Matters – Memoranda from Hon. James Allen to Ministers)*, 1912.

R24547991, Anglo–French Treaty (Defence of France) Act, 1919.

R17708971, British War Graves in France in Countries – United Kingdom – External Relations – France: 1922–1930.

R 2 607 010, Grey, Stanley. Ordinary Inwards Despatches from the Secretary of State – 24 January –23 July 1845.

C583 303, Liverpool to Long. *Overseas Representation in New Zealand – France– Powers of French Consuls 1918–1942.* Archives New Zealand.

G30 7, Pompallier to Colonial Secretary. Duplicate Outwards Despatches to the Secretary of State 1 January – 7 September 1845. Wellington.

G30, Fitzroy to Secretary of State. Duplicate Outwards Despatches to the Secretary of State 1840–1861. Wellington.

External Relations Files:
R17709260 France – Economic Affairs – Currency.
R17709262 France – Foreign Policy – General.
R17709174 France – External Relations – Germany.
R17708909 France – External Relations – Saar.
R17709125 France – General – Annual Reports.
R17709173 France – Political Affairs – General.
R17709249 United Kingdom – External Relations – France.
R18870366 Overseas Representation in New Zealand – France – *Powers of French Consuls 1918–1942.*
R18874438 Versailles Peace Treaty (1919).
British Library, London, UK:
MSS Eur D686 Papers of Field-Marshal Lord Birdwood, Indian Army; C-in-C, India 1925–30: India Office Records and Private Papers: 1883–1949.
Hocken Collection, Dunedin, NZ:
AG-514 Consulat de France, Dunedin *Records:* 1876–1938.
AG-200-11/04/1953 Documents related to the French Mission Luncheon with the Otago Harbour Board.
AG-514-03, AG-514-04, AG-514-06 Consular Receipts 1920–1924, 1924–1926.
(The) National Archives London, UK:
CO 5360 Colonial Office and Predecessor *New Zealand Original Correspondence* in Records of the Colonial Office, Commonwealth and Foreign and Commonwealth Offices: 1830–1922.
CO 61622 Records of the Colonial Office, Commonwealth and Foreign and Commonwealth Offices, Empire Marketing Board, and Related Bodies.
CO 537 Colonial Office *Colonies general supplementary original correspondence*, 1759–1955.
CO 694 Colonies General register of Secret Correspondence, 1865–1938.
CAB/24/172 Imperial Defence Committee *Report Made by Imperial Defence Committee Recommending to the UK Government Not to Ratify the Geneva Protocol*: 1925.

Office, Cabinet. Draft Telegram to 5 Dominions. Cabinet Meetings and Papers. The National Archives, Kew. http://filestore.nationalarchives.gov.uk/pdfs/large/cab-23-47.pdf.

Yale University Library Online:

William Morton Fullerton *William Morton Fullerton Papers:* 1865–1952.

Significant Published Government Documents

Armistice Between Germany and the Allied Powers (Detailed Terms of) 1918.

Commission, Electoral. *General Election Results 1890–1993.* Wellington 2013.

Election Results 1890–1993. Wellington 2013.

'Second Referendum on the New Zealand Flag: Final Result.' Updated 30 March 2016.

Confederation and Annexation. New Hebrides Group and French Convicts. Wellington: Appendix to the Journals of the House of Representative, New Zealand Government, Session I, A-03f, 1884.

Conference of Prime Ministers and Representatives of the United Kingdom, the Dominions, and India (Summary of Proceedings and Documents of the), Held in June, July, and August, 1921, at London: Appendix to the Journals of the House of Representatives, 1921.

Despatches from the Secretary of State for the Colonies to the Governor-General of New Zealand. Appendix to the Journals of the House of Representatives.

Despatches from The Governor (later Governor General) Of New Zealand To the Secretary of State for The Colonies (later Dominion Affairs). Appendix to the Journals of the House of Representatives.

Kellogg-Briand Pact.

New Zealand Parliamentary Debates (Hansard), Financial Statements presented to the House.

Departmental Reports: Agriculture, Defence, Education, Industries and Commerce, Lands and Survey, 1918–1939.

Government, New Zealand. 'Census Results.' New Zealand Government.

———. *Correspondence between the Rt. Hon. The Premier and the Chief Hansard Reporter. Relative to Letters Written by the Latter Commenting on the Despatch of Contingents to the Transvaal.* Wellington: Appendix to the Journals of the House of Representatives, 1900 Session I, H-29, 1900, 1900.

———. *Imperial Naval Conference (Proceedings of Informal Meeting of Members of the House of Representatives on the Question of the Representation of New Zealand at the).* Wellington: Appendix to the Journals of the House of Representatives, 1909 Session I, A-05, 1909.

———. 'New Zealand Official Yearbook.' Wellington, 1915.

High Commissioner for New Zealand (Annual Reports).

Imperial Conferences, Minutes. Appendices to the Journals of the House of Representatives.

Imperial Economic Conference 1924 and Ottawa 1932.

London Naval Treaty 1930.

Monetary and Economic Conference, Convened by the League of Nations, London 1933.

New Zealand Yearbooks 1919–1939: Statistics New Zealand:

'New Zealand Long Term Data Series (LTDS) Title: *Consolidated Population by Age and Sex.*' 2018.

Patriotic Funds. Tables Showing Details of the Various Patriotic Funds in New Zealand from the Outbreak of War to the 31st March, 1918: Appendix to the Journals of the House of Representatives. 1918.

Protocol for The Pacific Settlement of International Disputes: Correspondence Relating to The Position of The Dominions, 1925.

Reports from the New Zealand Representatives to the League of Nations.

The Great War, 1914–1918. New Zealand Expeditionary Force. Roll of Honour. Wellington: Government Printer, 1924.

Treaty for The Limitation of Naval Armament. Signed in London, On 25th March, 1936.

United Kingdom Parliamentary Record: Commons Sitting (Hansard).

United States Proposal for The Renunciation of War (Correspondence Respecting The), 1928.

Waitangi Tribunal. *Rekohu: A Report on Moriori and Ngati Mutunga Claims in the Chatham Islands.*

Audiovisual Material

Jackson, Peter. *They Shall Not Grow Old*, 2018.

Oliver, Anton. 'Anton Oliver.' In *Sunday Morning*, edited by Chris Laidlaw. Radio NZ Website, 2008.

Tolerton, Jane. *The Armistice and Afterwards. New Zealand soldiers on the Western Front gradually heard that the Armistice had been signed*: Radio New Zealand.

Walter Harris. *Early Cinema in New Zealand – [Interview with] Rudall Hayward.* Archives New Zealand: National Film Unit. R24349834.

'What Do We Know About Australia's Unknown Soldier?', Updated 11 Nov 2013, 3:44pm, 2013, accessed 04 July 2017, http://www.abc.net.au/news/2013-11-11/what-do-we-know-about-australias-unknown-soldier/5081574.

Books

Agulhon, M. *The French Republic, 1879–1992* (English ed.). Oxford: B. Blackwell, 1993.

Aldrich, Robert. *The French Presence in the South Pacific, 1842–1940.* Basingstoke: Macmillan, 1990.

Andrew, Christopher M. *Théophile Delcassé and the Making of the Entente Cordiale: a reappraisal of French foreign policy 1898–1905.* London: Macmillan, 1968.

Andrew, Christopher, and Paul Vallet. 'The German Threat.' In *Cross Channel Currents: 100 years of the Entente Cordiale*, edited by Richard Mayne, Douglas Johnson and Robert Tombs, 23–32. London: Routledge, 2004.

Bagnall, Nicholas. *Newspaper Language. Journalism Media Manual.* Oxford: Focal Press, 1993.

Ballantyne, Tony. *Orientalism and Race: Aryanism in the British Empire, Cambridge imperial and post-colonial studies series.* New York: Palgrave, 2002.

———. *Webs of Empire: locating new zealand's colonial past.* Wellington: Bridget Williams Books, 2012.

Barnes, Felicity. *New Zealand's London: a colony and its metropolis.* Auckland, NZ: Auckland University Press, 2012.

Bassett, Michael. *Sir Joseph Ward: a political biography.* Auckland, NZ: Auckland University Press, 1993.

Becker, Jean-Jacques. *The Great War and the French People.* Translated by Arnold Pomerans. Oxford: Berg Publishers, 1985.

Belich, James. *Making Peoples: a history of the New Zealanders from Polynesian discovery to the end of the nineteenth century.* Penguin Random House New Zealand, 2007.

———. *Paradise Reforged: a history of the New Zealanders from the 1880s to the year 2000.* Auckland, NZ: Penguin Press, 2001. books.google.co.nz.

———. *Replenishing the Earth: the settler revolution and the rise of the Angloworld.* Oxford Scholarship Online, 2011.

Bell, Leonard, and Diana Morrow. *Jewish Lives in New Zealand: a history.* Auckland, NZ: Godwit, 2012.

Binney, Judith, Judith Bassett, Erik Olssen, and Tim Galloway. *The People and the Land = Te tangata me te whenua: an illustrated history of New Zealand, 1820–1920.* Wellington, NZ: Bridget Williams Books, 1993.

Black, Jeremy. *Natural and Necessary Enemies: Anglo–French relations in the eighteenth century.* London: Duckworth, 1986.

Bloch, Marc Léopold Benjamin, and Etienne Bloch. *Apologie pour l'histoire, ou, Métier d'historien.* critique préparée par Etienne Bloch. ed. Paris: A. Colin, 1993.

———. Peter Putnam, and Joseph R. Strayer. *The Historian's Craft.* Manchester: Manchester University Press, 1954.

Blosseville, Jules de. *A Proposal for a Penal Colony in New Zealand.* Translated by Martin L Purdy. Bilingual, French/English / ed. [Canberra]: ANU, 1986.

Brooking, Tom. *Richard Seddon: King of God's Own – the life and times of New Zealand's longest-serving prime minister.* Auckland: Penguin, 2014.

Buick, T.L. *New Zealand's First War: Or, the Rebellion of Hone Heke.* Cambridge University Press, 2011.

———. *The Treaty of Waitangi: how New Zealand became a British colony.* Cambridge: Cambridge University Press, 1933.

Buller, J. *Forty Years in New Zealand.* Hodder and Stoughton, 1878.

Burrows, R. *Extracts from a Diary Kept by the Rev. R. Burrows During Heke's War in the North in 1845.* Upton, 1886.

Bury, J.P.T. *France, 1814–1940.* Methuen, 1969.

Chaudron, Gerald. *New Zealand in the League of Nations: the beginnings of an independent foreign policy, 1919–1939.* McFarland, North Carolina, 2012.

Clark, A., E. Haddow, and C. Wright. *Resonant Histories: Pacific artefacts and the voyages of the HMS Royalist 1890–1893.* Sidestone Press, 2018.

Clark, Christopher. *The Sleepwalkers: how Europe went to war in 1914*. New York: Harper Perennial, 2014.

Clarke, Stephen. *After the War: the RSA in New Zealand.* New Zealand: Penguin, 2016.

Clifford, Andrew, and David Galt. *New Zealand Trading Banks and Early Paper Currency*. Auckland, New Zealand: New Zealand Banknote Guild, 2017.

Cook, James. *Captain Cook's Journal During His First Voyage Round the World Made in H. M. Bark 'Endeavour', 1768–71.* Edited by W.J. L. Wharton. London: Elliot Stock.

Cowan, James, and New Zealand Maori Regimental Committee. *The Maoris in the Great War: a history of the New Zealand Native Contingent and Pioneer Battalion, Gallipoli, 1915 France and Flanders, 1916–1918*. Uckfield: Naval & Military Press, 2006.

Crawford, J., & McGibbon, I.C. (eds). *New Zealand's Great War: New Zealand, the Allies and the First World War*. Auckland, NZ: Exisle Pub., 2007.

Crouzet, François. *Britain Ascendant: comparative studies in Franco-British economic history*. Paris: Editions de la Maison des sciences de l'homme, 1990.

Davis, Lance E., Huttenback, Robert A. *Mammon and the Pursuit of Empire: the political economy of British imperialism, 1860–1912.* Online ed. Cambridge: Cambridge University Press, 2015.

Dawson, R. M. *Development of Dominion Status 1900–1936* (2006 ed.). Oxon: Routledge, 1965.

Doyle, William. *Aristocracy and its Enemies in the Age of Revolution.* Oxford: Oxford University Press, 2009. Downloaded 26 September

2018 from:
http://www.oxfordscholarship.com.ezproxy.massey.ac.nz/view/10.1093/acprof:oso/9780199559855.001.0001/acprof-9780199559855-chapter-1

Dummitt, C., and M. Dawson. *Contesting Clio's Craft: new directions and debates in Canadian history*: Institute for the Study of the Americas, University of London, 2009.

Dunmore, J. *Aventures Dans Le Pacifique: from the accounts of French voyagers to the Pacific, Australia, and New Zealand*. A.H. & A.W. Reed, 1967.

Eamon, Ross. *The a to Z of Journalism (No. 117)*. The a to Z Guide Series. Lanham: Scarecrow Press, 2009.

Einzig, Paul. *World Finance since 1914, Routledge library editions. Banking & finance; v. 12*. London: Routledge, 2012.

Fairlie, Helen A. *Revaluing British Boys' Story Papers, 1918–1939 (Critical Approaches to Children's Literature)*: Palgrave Macmillan, 2014.

Falloon, Malcolm. *To Plough or to Preach: mission strategies in New Zealand during the 1820s*. London: Latimer Trust, 2010.

Fenby, Jonathan. *The History of Modern France: from the Revolution to the War on Terror*. London: Simon and Schuster, 2015.

Fieldhouse, D.K. *The Colonial Empires: a comparative survey from the 18th century.* Weidenfeld and Nicolson, 1966.

Frame, Janet. *The Envoy from Mirror City*. Auckland: Vintage, 2000.

Franks, Peter, and Jim McAloon. *Labour: the New Zealand Labour Party, 1916–2016*. Wellington: Victoria University Press, 2016.

Fraser, Lyndon, and Angela McCarthy. *Far from 'Home': the English in New Zealand*. Dunedin, NZ: Otago Univ Press, 2012.

Fussell, P. *Abroad: British literary traveling between the wars*. New York: Oxford University Press, 1980.

———. *Doing Battle: the making of a skeptic* (1st ed.). Boston: Little Brown and Co., 1996.

———. *The Boy Scout Handbook and Other Observations*. New York: Oxford University Press, 1982.

———. *The Great War and Modern Memory*. New York: Oxford University Press, 1975.

Gabriel, Richard A. *Scipio Africanus: Rome's greatest general.* Washington, DC: University of Nebraska Press, 2008.

Gaunt, Philip. *Choosing the News: the profit factor in news selection, Contributions to the study of mass media and communications, no. 16.* New York: Greenwood Press, 1990.

Geary, Cecilie. *Celebrating 125 Years, 1880–2005: Smith + Caughey's.* [Auckland, NZ]: Smith & Caughey Limited, 2005.

Gildea, R. *The Past in French History.* New Haven: Yale University Press, 1994.

Goldman, Lazarus Morris. *The History of the Jews in New Zealand.* Wellington: Reed, 1958.

Goulter, Mary Catherine. *Sons of France: a forgotten influence on New Zealand history.* 2nd ed. Wellington: Whitcombe and Tombs, 1958.

Grady, J., and C. Grocott. *The Continuing Imperialism of Free Trade: developments, trends and the role of supranational agents.* Taylor & Francis, 2018.

Griffith, Penny. *Out of the Shadows: the life of Millicent Baxter.* Wellington: PenPublishing, 2015.

Griffiths, John. *Imperial Culture in Antipodean Cities, 1880–1939.* Basingstoke: Palgrave Macmillan, 2014.

Gustafson, Barry. *From the Cradle to the Grave: a biography of Michael Joseph Savage.* Auckland NZ: Reed Methuen, 1986.

Hanrieder, Wolfram F., and Graeme P. Auton. *The Foreign Policies of West Germany, France, and Britain.* Englewood Cliffs, NJ: Prentice-Hall, 1980.

Harper, Glyn. *Johnny Enzed: the New Zealand Soldier in the First World War 1914–1918.* Exisle, 2015.

———. ed. *Letters from Gallipoli: New Zealand Soldiers write home.* Auckland, NZ: Auckland University Press, 2011.

———. ed. *Letters from the Battlefield: New Zealand Soldiers write home, 1914–18.* Auckland NZ: HarperCollins, 2001.

———. and National Army Museum (NZ). *Images of War: New Zealand and the First World War in photographs.* HarperCollinsPublishers (New Zealand), 2008.

Hawke, G.R. *The Evolution of New Zealand Currency.* VUW Working Papers in Economic History: 84/1. Wellington, NZ: [Victoria University of Wellington, Dept. of Economics], 1984.

Hayward, Dai. *Golden Jubilee: the story of the first fifty years of the New Zealand Meat Producers Board, 1922–1972.* Wellington, Universal Printers, 1972.

Henningham, S. *France and the South Pacific: a contemporary history*. University of Hawaii Press, 1992.

Hett, B.C. *The Death of Democracy*. Random House, 2018.

Higham, Robin. *Two Roads to War: the French and British air arms from Versailles to Dunkirk*. Annapolis, MD: Naval Institute Press, 2012.

Hilliard, Christopher. *The Bookmen's Dominion: cultural life in New Zealand, 1920–1950, AUP studies in cultural and social history, 3.* Auckland: Auckland University Press, 2006.

Hoadley, J. Stephen, and New Zealand Institute of International Affairs. *New Zealand and France: politics, diplomacy and dispute management*. Wellington [NZ]: New Zealand Institute of International Affairs, 2005.

Hodder, E. *Conquests of the Cross: a record of missionary work throughout the world.* Facsimile ed. London: Cassell, 2002, 1890.

Horne, Alistair. *Friend or Foe: an Anglo-Saxon history of France*. London: Weidenfeld & Nicolson, 2004.

Howarth, D.A. *Tahiti: a paradise lost.* Harvill Press, 1983.

Howe, K.R. *Singer in a Songless Land: a life of Edward Tregear, 1846–1931.* Auckland [NZ]: Auckland University Press, 1991.

Hunt, N.C. *Memory, War and Trauma*. Cambridge University Press, 2010.

Hunter, Ian. *Farmers, Your Store for 100 Years*. Auckland, NZ: HarperCollins, 2009.

Hyam, Ronald. *Britain's Declining Empire: the road to decolonisation, 1918–1968*. Cambridge: Cambridge University Press, 2006.

Jenkins, Roy. *Churchill*. London: Macmillan, 2001.

Johnson, Dominic D.P. *Overconfidence and War: the havoc and glory of positive illusions*. Cambridge, MA: Harvard University Press, 2004.

Kahler, Miles. *Decolonization in Britain and France: the domestic consequences of international relations*. Princeton, NJ: Princeton University Press, 1984.

Kent, John. *The Internationalization of Colonialism: Britain, France, and Black Africa, 1939–1956, Oxford studies in African affairs*. Oxford: Oxford University Press, 1992.

Keynes, John Maynard. *The Economic Consequences of Peace*. London England: Macmillan, 1920.

Kier, Elizabeth. *Imagining War: French and British military doctrine between the wars, Princeton studies in international history and politics*. Princeton, NJ: Princeton University Press, 1997.

Kindleberger, Charles Poor. *Economic Growth in France and Britain, 1851–1950*. Cambridge, MA: Harvard University Press, 1964.

King, Michael. *God's Furthest Outpost: a history of Catholics in New Zealand.* Auckland: Penguin Books, 1997.

———. *The Penguin History of New Zealand.* Auckland: Penguin Books, 2012.

Knowles, D. *HMS Hood: pride of the Royal Navy.* Fonthill Media Limited, 2019.

Lambourn, A. *Major Thomas Bunbury: envoy extraordinary, New Zealand's soldier-treatymaker.* Heritage Press, 1995.

Laurenson, H. *Going up, Going Down: the rise and fall of the department store. AUP Studies in Cultural and Social History: 2.* Auckland, NZ: Auckland University Press, 2005.

Lee, John A. *Civilian into Soldier.* London, England: May Fair Books, 1963.

Littératures du Pacifique insulaire: Nouvelle-Calèdonie, Nouvelle-zèlande, Ocèanie, Timor Oriental: approches historiques, culturelles et comparatives. Bibliothëque de littèrature gènèrale et comparèe 114. Paris: Champion, 2013.

Lloyd, David. *Battlefield Tourism: pilgrimage and the commemoration of the Great War in Britain, Australia and Canada, 1919–1939*. London: Bloomsbury, 1998.

Mainwaring, Marion. *Fullerton, William Morton (1865–1952), Journalist and Writer*. Oxford University Press, 2018.

Malthus, Cecil. *Anzac, a Retrospect*. Christchurch NZ: Whitcombe & Tombs, 1965.

———. *Armentières and the Somme*. Auckland NZ: Reed Publishing, 2002.

Marchant, L.R. *France Australe.* Access Press, 1982.

Marks, Sally. *The Illusion of Peace: international relations in Europe, 1918–1933*. 2nd ed., *Making of the 20th century*. New York: Palgrave Macmillan, 2003.

Marshall, T.W.M. *Christian Missions.* Vol. I, II, III, 1863.

Marwick, Arthur. *Class: image and reality in Britain, France and the USA since 1930*. London: Collins, 1980.

Mavor, Carol. *Black and Blue: the bruising passion of Camera Lucida, La Jetée, Sans Soleil, and Hiroshima Mon Amour*. Durham, NC: Duke University Press, 2012.

McAloon, Jim. *Judgements of All Kinds: economic policy-making in New Zealand, 1945–1984*. Wellington: Victoria University Press, 2013.

McGibbon, I.C. *Blue-water Rationale: the naval defence of New Zealand 1914–1942*. Wellington, NZ: Govt. Printer, 1981.

———. *New Zealand Battlefields and Memorials of the Western Front*. Auckland, NZ: Oxford University Press in association with the History Group Ministry for Culture and Heritage, 2001.

———. *The Western Front: a guide to New Zealand battlefields and memorials*. Oxford University Press, 2001.

McKinnon, Malcolm. *The Broken Decade: prosperity, depression and recovery in New Zealand, 1928–39.* Dunedin: Otago University Press, 2016.

McMillan, James F. *Twentieth Century France: politics and society 1898–1991.* New York: Routledge, 1992.

Melman, Billie. *The Culture of History: English uses of the past 1800–1953*. Oxford: Oxford University Press, 2006.

Miles, William F.S. *Scars of Partition: postcolonial legacies in French and British borderlands* [in English]. Lincoln: University of Nebraska Press, 2014.

Mitchell, B.R. *British Historical Statistics.* Cambridge: Cambridge University Press, 1988.

Moon, P. *Fatal Frontiers: a new history of New Zealand in the decade before the Treaty.* Penguin Books, 2006.

———. *Hone Heke: Nga Puhi warrior.* David Ling Pub., 2001.

———. *The Origins of the Treaty of Waitangi.* Birdwood Pub., 1994.

———. *Path to the Treaty of Waitangi.* David Ling Pub., 2002.

Mousley, E.O. *An Empire View of the Empire Tangle*. BiblioBazaar, 2016.

Negrine, Ralph M. *Parliament and the Media: a study of Britain, Germany and the media, Chatham House papers.* Washington, DC: Pinter, 1998.

Neillands, Robin. *The Old Contemptibles: the British Expeditionary Force, 1914.* London: John Murray, 2008.

Nimmo, J.M. 2001. *Somewhere in France*. Christchurch, NZ: Marion M. Young.

O'Farrell, Patrick James. *Harry Holland, Militant Socialist*. Canberra: Australian National University, 1964.

Orange, C. *The Treaty of Waitangi.* 2nd ed.: Bridget Williams Books, 2011.

Overy, R.J. *The Origins of the Second World War*. 3rd ed., *Seminar studies in history*. New York: Longman, 2008.

Palenski, Ron. *Rugby: a New Zealand history.* e-Book ed.: Auckland University Press, 2015.

Pannett, Bryan. *Just a Piece of Wire: the history of the first submarine telegraph cable linking New Zealand with the world*. 2nd ed. Wellington, NZ: B. Pannett, 2013.

Pedersen, Peter. *ANZACs at War: from Gallipoli to the present day.* Crows Nest, NSW: Crows Nest, 2010.

Pedersen, Susan. *Family, Dependence, and the Origins of the Welfare State: Britain and France, 1914–1945*. Cambridge New York: Cambridge University Press, 1993.

Phillips, Jock. *A Man's Country? The Image of the Pakeha Male: a history.* Auckland: Penguin, 1987.

Pickles, Katie. *Transnational Outrage: the death and commemoration of Edith Cavell*. Basingstoke: Palgrave Macmillan, 2007.

Pitts, Jennifer. *A Turn to Empire: the rise of imperial liberalism in Britain and France*. Princeton, NJ; Woodstock: Princeton University Press, 2006.

Posen, Barry. *The Sources of Military Doctrine: France, Britain, and Germany between the world wars, Cornell studies in security affairs.* Ithaca, NY: Cornell University Press, 1986.

Pratt, Larwrence. *East of Malta, West of Suez: Britain's Mediterranean Crisis, 1936–1939*. First ed. Cambridge: Cambridge University Press, 2008.

Priestley, H.I., and American Historical Association. *France Overseas: a study of modern imperialism, 1938*. Octagon Books, 1938.

Pritchard, G., and P. De Decker. *The Aggressions of the French at Tahiti: and other islands in the Pacific*. Oxford University Press, 1983.

Ramsden, E. *Busby of Waitangi, H.M's Resident at New Zealand, 1833–40.* A.H. & A.W. Reed, 1942.

Reddiex, Glenn. *Just to Let You Know I'm Still Alive: postcards from New Zealanders during the First World War*. Grantham House, 2015.

Reeves, W.P. *The Long White Cloud: Ao Tea Roa.* 4th (1898) ed. London: George Allen and Unwin, 1950.

Runciman, S. *A History of the Crusades: the Kingdom of Jerusalem and the Frankish East, 1100–1187.* Cambridge: Cambridge University Press, 1952.

Said, E.W. *Orientalism: Western conceptions of the Orient.* London: Penguin Books, 1991.

Scholefield, G.H. *Captain William Hobson, First Governor of New Zealand.* Oxford University Press, 1934.

Schuker, Stephen A. *The End of French Predominance in Europe: the financial crisis of 1924 and the adoption of the Dawes plan*. Chapel Hill: University of North Carolina Press, 1976.

Siegfried, André. *Post-War Britain: a French analysis.* London, England: Cape, 1924.

Siegfried, André, William Downie Stewart, and D.A. Hamer. *Democracy in New Zealand.* 2nd ed.: Wellington: Victoria University Press, 1982.

Sigley, S. *Transnational Film Culture in New Zealand*. Bristol: Intellect Limited, 2013.

Simmons E. R., *Pompallier: prince of bishops.* Auckland: CPC Publishing, 1984.

Smith, L.V. *Sovereignty at the Paris Peace Conference of 1919.* Oxford University Press, 2018.

South Pacific Action Network. *New Caledonia*. Wellington: Span, 1976.

Steel, Frances. *Oceania under Steam: sea transport and the cultures of colonialism, c.1870–1914*. New York: Manchester University Press, 2011.

Stuer, Anny P.L. *The French in Australia.* Canberra: Miami, Fla: Dept. of Demography, Institute of Advanced Studies, Australian National University; distributed by the Australian National University Press, 1982.

Thomas, James P. *The Military Challenges of Transatlantic Coalitions, Adelphi paper, 333*. Oxford: Oxford University Press for the International Institute for Strategic Studies, 2000.

Thomson, A.S. *The Story of New Zealand: past and present – savage and civilized.* London: Spottiswoode, 1859.

Tombs, Isabelle, and Robert Tombs. *That Sweet Enemy: the French and the British from the Sun King to the present*. London: William Heinemann, 2006.

Toth, S.A. *Beyond Papillon: the French overseas penal colonies, 1854–1952*. University of Nebraska Press, 2006.

Tremewan, Peter. *French Akaroa.* 2nd ed.: Canterbury University Press, 2010.

Trotter, A. *Britain and East Asia, 1933–1937*. London and New York: Cambridge University Press, 1975.

———. & Little Company of Mary. *Mary Potter's Little Company of Mary: the New Zealand experience 1914–2002*. Wellington, NZ: Bridget Williams Books; Little Company of Mary, 2003.

———. & University of Otago. University Extension (eds). *Fifty Years of New Zealand Foreign Policy Making: anniversary volume: papers from the twenty-eighth Foreign Policy School, 1993*. Dunedin, NZ: University of Otago Press in association with University Extension, 1993.

Tworek, H. *News from Germany: the competition to control world communications, 1900–1945*. Harvard University Press, 2019.

Tyrrell, Ian R. *Transnational Nation: United States history in global perspective since 1789*. Basingstoke: Palgrave Macmillan, 2007.

Waite, Fred. *The New Zealanders at Gallipoli.* Official History of New Zealand's Effort in the Great War; V.1. Edited by Ian McGibbon. Auckland NZ: Whitcombe and Tombs, 1919.

Walker, Ranginui. *Ka Whawhai Tonu Matou: struggle without end.* Auckland: Penguin, 2004.

Wards, I. *The Shadow of the Land: a study of British Policy and racial conflict in New Zealand 1832–1852.* Historical Publications Branch, Department of Internal Affairs, 1968.

Weedon, A. *Victorian Publishing: the economics of book production for a mass market 1836–1916*. Aldershot: Ashgate, 2003.

Weisz, G. *The Emergence of Modern Universities in France, 1863–1914.* Princeton: Princeton University Press, 2014.

Wells, P. *The Hungry Heart: journeys with William Colenso.* Penguin Random House New Zealand, 2012.

Williams, H., and C. Fitzgerald. *Te Wiremu – Henry Williams: early years in the north.* Huia, 2011.

Williams, Maslyn, and Barrie Macdonald. *The Phosphateers: a history of the British Phosphate Commissioners and the Christmas Island Phosphate Commission*. Carlton, Vic.: Melbourne University Press, 1985.

Wilson, A.C. *Wire and Wireless: a history of telecommunications in New Zealand, 1860–1987*. Palmerston North, NZ: Dunmore Press, 1994.

Wilson, Keith M. *Empire and Continent: studies in British Foreign Policy before 1914.* London and New York: Mansell, 1987.

Winter, Jay. *Sites of Memory, Sites of Mourning: the Great War in European cultural history.* Studies in the Social and Cultural History of Modern Warfare. Vol. I, Cambridge: Cambridge University Press, 1998.

Wiskemann, E. *The Europe I Saw*. Collins, 1968.

Ziino, B. *A Distant Grief: Australians, war graves and the Great War*. Crawley, WA: University of Western Australia Press, 2007.

Sections of Books

'A Report from the French Consul to the Minister in France.' In *60 Years Ago: Celebrating the Anniversary of Diplomatic Relations between New Zealand and France*, pp.29–36. Wellington, NZ: The French Embassy, 2005.

Akami, T. 2008. 'From the center to the periphery: Hawai'i and the pacific community.' In *Hawai'i at the Crossroads of the U.S. and Japan before the Pacific War*, edited by J. Davidann, P.F. Hooper and E.H. Tamura, pp.13–41. Hawaii: University of Hawaii Press, 2008.

Aldrich, Robert. 'European Expansion in the Island Pacific: A Historiographical Review.' In *The French and the Pacific world, 17th–19th centuries: explorations, migrations and cultural exchanges*, edited by Annick Foucrier, pp.87–102. Aldershot, Hampshire, England Burlington, VT: Ashgate, 2005.

Ballantyne, Tony. 'Putting the Nation in Its Place?: World History and C.A. Bayly's *The Birth of the Modern World*.' In *Connected Worlds: history in transnational perspective*, edited by Marilyn Lake and Ann Curthoys, pp.23–45. Canberra: Australian National University, 2006.

Bargas, I., and T. Shoebridge. 'Mourning, Honourimg, Remembering.' In *New Zealand's First World War Heritage*, pp.369–455: Exisle Publishing, 2015.

Broadbent, John. 'Colin and the European Powers in the Pacific.' In *Catholic Beginnings in Oceania: Marist Missionary Perspectives*, edited by A. Greiler. Hindmarsh: ATF Press, 2009.

Brooking, Tom. 'Economic Transformation.' In *The Oxford History of New Zealand*, edited by Geoffery W. Rice, pp.230–53. Oxford: Oxford University Press, 2000.

Charle, Christophe. 'French Intellectuals and the Impossible English Model (1870–1914).' In *Anglo-French Attitudes: comparisons and transfers between English and French intellectuals since the eighteenth century*, edited by Christophe Charle, Julien Vincent and J.M. Winter, pp.235–55. Manchester, UK; New York: Manchester University Press, 2007.

Clayton, Garry, 'Francophobia in New Zealand' In *60 Years Ago: celebrating the anniversary of diplomatic relations between New Zealand and France*, ed. France. Ambassade (NZ), 2005.

Crouzet, François. 'Trade and empire: the British experience from the establishment of free trade until the First World War.' In *Britain*

Ascendant: comparative studies in Franco-British economic history, pp.385–414. Cambridge: Cambridge University Press, 1990.

———. 'Problems of communication between Britain and France in the nineteenth and twentieth centuries.' In *Britain Ascendant: comparative studies in Franco-British economic history*, pp.464–502. Cambridge: Cambridge University Press, 1990.

———. 'The core and periphery of the core: Franco-British trade in the belle époque.' In *Britain Ascendant: comparative studies in Franco-British economic history*, pp.442–63. Cambridge: Cambridge University Press, 1990.

Curthoys, Ann. 'We've Just Started Making National Histories, and You Want Us to Stop Already?' In *After the Imperial Turn: thinking with and through the nation*, edited by Antoinette Burton. pp.70–90. Durham [NC]: Duke University Press 2003.

Dalley, B. '"Come back with honour': Prostitution and the New Zealand soldier, at home and abroad.' In *New Zealand's Great War: New Zealand, the Allies and the First World War*, edited by J. Crawford & I.C. McGibbon, pp.364–77. Auckland, NZ: Exisle Pub, 2007.

Deacon, Desley. ''Films as Foreign Offices': Transnationalism at Paramount in the Twenties and Early Thirties.' In *Connected Worlds: history in transnational perspective*, edited by Marilyn Lake and Ann Curthoys, pp.139–57: Australian National University, 2006.

Dunmore, John. 'First Relations.' In *60 Years Ago: celebrating the anniversary of diplomatic relations between New Zealand and France*. Wellington: The French Embassy, 2005.

———. *New Zealand and the French: two centuries of contact*. 2nd, updated ed.: Waikanae [NZ]: Heritage Press, 1997.

Farrell, Brian P. 'Coalition of the Usually Willing: The Dominions and Imperial Defence, 1856–1919.' In *Imperial Defence: the old world order 1856–1956*, edited by Greg Kennedy, pp.251–302. London: Routledge, 2008.

Faucher, Charlotte, and Philippe Lane. 'French Cultural Diplomacy in Early Twentieth-Century London.' In *A History of the French in*

London: liberty, equality, opportunity, edited by D. Kelly and M. Cornick, pp.281–98: Institute of Historical Research, 2013.

Foucrier, A. 'Introduction.' In *The French and the Pacific World, 17th–19th Centuries: explorations, migrations, and cultural exchanges*, edited by Annick Foucrier, pp.XV–XIVI: Ashgate, 2005.

Fox, Alistair. 'Exploring the Dynamics of Epochal Change: Shifting Identities in Historical Novels of Heretaunga Pat Baker – *Behind the Tattooed Face* and *The Strongest God*.' In *Littératures du Pacifique insulaire: Nouvelle-Calédonie, Nouvelle-Zélande, Océanie, Timor Oriental: approches historiques, culturelles et comparatives*, édite by Jean Bessière and Sylvie André, pp.81–95. Paris: Champion, 2013.

Gailey, Christine Ward. 'Putting Down Sisters and Wives: Tongan Women and Colonization.' In *The Pacific World: lands, peoples and history of the Pacific, 1500–1900*, edited by Jane Samson. Aldershot: Ashgate, 2003.

Gildea, Robert. *The Past in French history*. Ch.5. New Haven: Yale University Press, 1994.

Gray, Patrick. 'The peculiarities of Irish land tenure, 1800–1914: from agent of impoverishment to agent of pacification.' In *The Political Economy of British Historical Experience: 1688–1914*, edited by Patrick Karl O'Brien and Donald Winch, pp.139–64. Oxford: Oxford Univ. Press, 2002.

Hamer, David. 'Andre Siegfried and New Zealand.' In *New Zealand and the French: two centuries of contact*, edited by John Dunmore, pp.112–15. Waikanae: Heritage Press, 1997.

Harper, G. 'New Zealand and the Catastrophic Year 1917.' In *The Myriad Legacies of 1917: a year of war and revolution*, edited by M. Abbenhuis, N. Atkinson, K. Baird and G. Romano, pp.192–221: Springer International Publishing, 2018.

Hobson, J.A. 'Imperialism: A Study (1902).' In *Politics and Empire in Victorian Britain: a reader*, edited by Antoinette M. Burton, pp.xiii, 343. New York: Palgrave, 2001.

Hoock, Holger. 'Monumental Memories: state commemoration of the Napoleonic wars in early nineteenth-century Britain.' In *War Memories: the Revolutionary and Napoleonic wars in modern*

European culture, edited by Alan I. Forrest, Etienne Francois and Karen Hagemann, pp.193–215. Palgrave Macmillan UK., 2012.

Hynes, Greg. 'Picturing the empire: Enduring imperial perceptions and depictions in British first world war photographic propaganda.' In *Endurance and the First World War: experiences and legacies in New Zealand and Australia*, edited by David Monger, Sarah Murray and Katie Pickles, pp.215–35. Newcastle: Cambridge Scholars, 2014.

Jackson, Stephen. 'Finding Historical Meaning without Britain.' In *Constructing National Identity in Canadian and Australian Classrooms: the crown of education*, pp.207–40. Cham: Springer International Publishing, 2018.

Johnson, Douglas, and Jean-Baptiste Duroselle. 'Entente and Mésentente.' In *Britain and France: ten centuries*, edited by Douglas W.J. Johnson, Francois Crouzet and Francois Bèdarida, pp.265–83. Folkestone, Kent, England: Dawson, 1980.

Kaul, Chandrika. 'Introductory Survey.' In *Media and the British Empire*, pp.1–19. New York: Palgrave Macmillan, 2006.

Keiger, John. 'How the Entente Cordiale Began.' In *Cross Channel Currents: 100 years of the Entente Cordiale*, edited by Richard Mayne, Douglas Johnson and Robert Tombs, pp.3–11. London: Routledge, 2004.

Kempshall, Chris. 'Careless Disasters: Allied Relations in 1918.' In *British, French and American Relations on the Western Front, 1914–1918*, pp.191–246. Cham: Springer International Publishing, 2018.

———. '"My Heart Softened to the French … All at Once I Loved Them": The Entente Cordiale at the Somme.' In *British, French and American Relations on the Western Front, 1914–1918*, pp.107–57. Cham: Springer International Publishing, 2018.

Kray, R. 'Caging the Prussian Dragon: New Zealand and the Paris Peace Conference 1919'. In J. Crawford & I.C. McGibbon (eds), *New Zealand's Great War: New Zealand, the Allies and the First World War*, pp.123–41. Auckland, NZ: Exisle Pub., 2007.

Lambert, Andrew. 'The Royal Navy and the Defence of Empire, 1856–1918.' In *Imperial Defence: the old world order 1856–1956*, edited by Greg Kennedy, pp.111–32. London: Routledge, 2008.

Langton, G. 'A different sort of war: the experience of NZEF transport drivers'. In In *New Zealand's Great War: New Zealand, the Allies and the First World War*, edited by J. Crawford & I.C. McGibbon, pp.344–53. Auckland, NZ: Exisle Pub.

Leask, Rognvald. c.2011. '"Britain's Watchdog' in the Pacific? Seddon's Imperialism as Seen by the French.' In *New Zealand, France and the Pacific: studies in New Zealand culture*, edited by Ian Conrich and Dominic Alessio, pp.23–40. Nottingham: Kakapo, 2007.

———. 'Andre Siegfried and the Discovery of the New Zealand Democracy.' In *60 Years Ago: celebrating the anniversary of diplomatic relations between New Zealand and France*, edited by France. Ambassade (NZ), pp.55–59. Wellington: The French Embassy, 2005.

Lentin, Antony. 'The Treaty That Never Was: Lloyd George and the French Connection, 1919.' In *Lloyd George and the Lost Peace: from Versailles to Hitler, 1919–1940*, pp.47–66. London: Palgrave Macmillan UK, 2001.

Lineham, P. 'First World War religion.' In *New Zealand's Great War: New Zealand, the Allies and the First World War*, edited by J. Crawford & I.C. McGibbon, pp.467–92. Auckland, NZ: Exisle Pub., 2007.

Littlewood, David. 'The Provision of Opportunities: Politics and the State.' In *New Zealand Between the Wars*, edited by Rachael Bell and Massey University Press, pp.32–56. Auckland: Massey University Press, 2017.

Lochhead, Ian. 'Enduring memories: Samuel Hurst Seager and the New Zealand battlefield memorials of the Great War.' In *Endurance and the First World War: experiences and legacies in New Zealand and Australia*, edited by David Monger, Sarah Murray and Katie Pickles, pp.153–76. Newcastle: Cambridge Scholars, 2014.

Lord, Caroline. 'Painting the Road to Le Quesnoy.' In *the Great Adventure Ends: New Zealand and France on the Western Front*, edited by Nathalie Philippe, Christopher Pugsley, John Crawford, Matthias Strohn, pp.357–90. Christchurch: John Douglas, 2013.

Low, Peter. 'Bishop Pompallier and Te Tiriti.' In *The French Place in the Bay of Islands: essays from Pompallier's Printery (Te Urunga Mai O Te Iwi Wiwi)*, edited by Kate Martin and Brad Mercer: Mātou Matauwhi, 2011.

Mallett, D.R. 'Introduction.' In *Monumental Conflicts: twentieth-century wars and the evolution of public memory*. Taylor & Francis, 2017.

McCabe, Jane. '"An Ideal Life": Anglo-Indians in the New Zealand Expeditionary Force.' In *Endurance and the First World War: experiences and legacies in New Zealand and Australia*, edited by David Monger, Sarah Murray, and Katie Pickles, pp.196–214. Newcastle: Cambridge Scholars, 2014.

McGibbon, I. 'The shaping of New Zealand's war effort, August–October 1914.' In *New Zealand's Great War: New Zealand, the Allies and the First World War*, edited by J. Crawford & I.C. McGibbon, pp.49–68. Auckland, NZ: Exisle Pub., 2007.

McGing, Brian C. *Polybius' Histories, Oxford Approaches to Classical Literature*, pp.95–128. Cary, NC: Oxford University Press, USA, 2010.

Metzger, Barbara. 'Towards an International Human Rights Regime during the Interwar Years: The League of Nations' Combat of Traffic in Women and Children.' In *Beyond Sovereignty: Britain, empire and transnationalism, c. 1880–1950*, edited by Kevin Grant, Philippa Levine and Frank Trentmann, pp.54–79. New York: Palgrave Macmillan, 2007.

Mortelier, Christiane. 'Jules Verne and New Zealand.' In *New Zealand and the French: two centuries of contact*, edited by John Dunmore, pp.97–111. Waikanae: Heritage Press, 1997, 2nd updated ed.

Muckle, Adrian. 'Empire in the eyes of the beholder: New Zealand in the Pacific through French eyes.' In *New Zealand's Empire*, edited by Katie Pickles and Catharine Coleborne, pp.163–78. Manchester University Press, 2016.

Muller, Karis. 'The Australian Experience: Teaching French civilisation with an Australian accent.' In *Teaching French civilisation in Britain, the United States and Australia: proceedings of the Anglo-American seminar held at Portsmouth*

Polytechnic, 18th-20th September 1987, edited by Eri Cahm, p.210. London: Association for the Study of Modern and Contemporary France, 1988.

Munro, Jessie. 'Mother Aubert.' In *New Zealand and the French: two centuries of contact*, edited by John Dunmore, p.85. Waikanae: Heritage Press, 1997, 2nd updated ed.

———. 'Colin and Pompallier and the Founding of the Catholic Church in New Zealand.' In *Catholic Beginnings in Oceania: Marist missionary perspectives*, edited by A. Greiler: ATF Press, 2009.

Norrish, Mervyn. 'Political Relations between New Zealand and France.' In *New Zealand and the French: two centuries of contact*, edited by John Dunmore, pp.155–64. Waikanae: Heritage Press, 1997.

O'Meeghan, Michael. 'The French Marist Maori Mission.' In *The French and the Maori*, edited by J. Dunmore. Waikanae: Heritage Press, 1992.

Openshaw, Roger. 'Contradiction and Contestation: Public Education in the Interwar Period.' In *New Zealand Between the Wars*, edited by Rachael Bell and Massey University Press, pp.85–107. Auckland: Massey University Press, 2017.

Otte, T.G. 'The Foreign Office and the Defence of Empire 1856–1914.' In *Imperial Defence: the old world order 1856–1956*, edited by Greg Kennedy, pp.9–29. London: Routledge, 2008.

Parsons, Gwen. 'Challenging Enduring Home Front Myths: Jingoistic Civilians and Neglected Soldiers.' In *Endurance and the First World War: experiences and legacies in New Zealand and Australia*, edited by David Monger, Sarah Murray and Katie Pickles, pp.62–85. Newcastle: Cambridge Scholars, 2014.

Peden, George. 'The Treasury and Defence of Empire.' In *Imperial Defence: the old world order 1856–1956*, edited by Greg Kennedy, pp.71–90. London: Routledge, 2008.

Pérez, Michael. 'New Caledonia and New Zealand: Similar Histories, Parallel Destinies, Converging Diplomacies.' In *New Zealand-New Caledonia: neighbours, friends and partners (La Nouvelle-Zélande et la Nouvelle-Calédonie: voisins, amis et partenaires)*, edited by Fr. Èd Èric Angleviel, Stephen I. Levine and Museum of

Wellington City & Sea, pp.271–79. Wellington, NZ: Victoria University Press, 2008.

Peters, Lars. 'Warrior Sailors and Heroic Boys: Images of masculinity in English nautical novels on the revolutionary and Napoleonic wars.' In *War Memories: The Revolutionary and Napoleonic Wars in modern European culture, war, culture and society,1750–1850*, edited by Alan I. Forrest, Etienne Francois and Karen Hagemann, pp.137–53. Basingstoke: Palgrave, 2013.

Philippe, Nathalie. 'Feeding civilians in occupied France.' In *The Great Adventure Ends: New Zealand and France on the Western Front*, edited by Christopher Pugsley, Nathalie Philippe, John Crawford, Matthias Strohn, pp.75–96. Christchurch: John Douglas, 2013.

Phillips, Jock. 'Passchendaele: Remembering and Forgetting in New Zealand.' In *The Myriad Legacies of 1917: a year of war and revolution*, edited by Maartje Abbenhuis, Neill Atkinson, Kingsley Baird and Gail Romano, pp.245–67. Cham: Springer International Publishing, 2018.

Piekarz, Mark. 'It's Just a Bloody Field! Approaches, Opportunities and Dilemmas of Interpreting English Battlefields.' In *Battlefield Tourism: history, place and interpretation*, edited by Chris Ryan, pp.29–47. Amsterdam Oxford: Elsevier, 2007.

Prochasson, Christophe. 'Fashoda and the Boer War.' In *Anglo-French Attitudes: comparisons and transfers between English and French intellectuals since the eighteenth century*, edited by Christophe Charle, Julien Vincent and J.M. Winter, pp.256–70. Manchester: Manchester University Press, 2007.

Purseigle, P. 'The reception of Belgian refugees in Europe: a litmus test of wartime social mobilisation.' In *New Zealand's Great War: New Zealand, the Allies and the First World War*, edited by J. Crawford & I.C. McGibbon, pp.69–84. Auckland, NZ: Exisle Pub., 2007.

Richardson, Len. 'Parties and Political Change.' In *The Oxford History of New Zealand*, edited by Geoffrey W. Rice, pp.201–29. Oxford: Oxford University Press, 2000.

Roche, Michael. '"A Duty of the Country" Soldier Settlement, 1915–1941.' Chapter Two. In *New Zealand Between the Wars*, edited by

Rachael Bell, pp.32–56. Auckland, New Zealand: Massey University Press, 2017.

Salmond, Anne. 'Marion Du Fresne.' In *The French Place in the Bay of Islands: essays from Pompallier's Printery (Te Urunga Mai O Te Iwi Wiwi)*, edited by Kate Martin and Brad Mercer: Mātou Matauwhi, 2011.

———. 'New Zealand and the New Hebrides.' In *The Feel of Truth: essays in New Zealand and Pacific history*, edited by Peter Munz. Wellington: A.H. and A.W. Reed, 1969.

Scott, Joan Wallach. 'Part II. Debate. Women: A French Singularity?: "Vive La Différence!".' In *Beyond French Feminisms: debates on women, culture and politics in France 1980–2001*, edited by R. Célestin, E. DalMolin and I. Courtivron, pp.225–39. New York: Palgrave Macmillan US, 2016.

Sheffield, G. 'Britain and the Empire at War 1914–18: Reflections on a Forgotten Victory.' In *New Zealand's Great War: New Zealand, the Allies and the First World War*, edited by J. Crawford & I.C. McGibbon, pp.30–48. Auckland, NZ: Exisle Pub., 2007.

Sinclair, Keith. *A History of New Zealand.* rev. ed. Auckland: Penguin Books, 2000.

Smyth, Hanna. '"There Is Absolutely Nothing Like the Carving of Names": Imperial War Graves Commission Sites and World War I Memory.' In *Monumental Conflicts: twentieth-century wars and the evolution of public memory*, edited by D.R. Mallett. eBook: Taylor & Francis, 2017.

St John, Ian. '*Writing to the Defence of Empire:* Winston Churchill's Press Campaign against Constitutional Reform in India, 1929–1935.' In *Media and the British Empire*, edited by Chandrika Kaul, pp.104–24. New York: Palgrave Macmillan, 2006.

Strohn, Matthias. 'Defending Le Quesnoy.' In *The Great Adventure Ends: New Zealand and France on the Western Front*, edited by N. Philippe, Pugsley, C., Crawford, J., & Strohn, M., pp.319–33. Christchurch: John Douglas Publishing, 2013.

Stuart, John. 'Beyond Sovereignty? Protestant Missions, Empire and Transnationalism, 1890–1950.' In *Beyond Sovereignty: Britain, empire and transnationalism, c. 1880–1950*, edited by Kevin

Grant, Philippa Levine and Frank Trentmann, pp.103–25. Basingstoke England; New York: Palgrave Macmillan, 2007.

Taylor, Kerry. 'The Old Bolshevik: Alex Gailbraith, the Communist Party and the New Zealand Revolution.' In *New Zealand Between the Wars*, edited by Rachael Bell and Massey University Press, pp.108–32. Auckland: Massey University Press, 2017.

Thackeray, David, Andrew Thompson, and Richard Toye. 'Imagining Britain's Economic Future, c.1800–1975: Trade, Consumerism, and Global Markets.' In *Imagining Britain's Economic Future, c.1800–1975: trade, consumerism, and global markets*, edited by David Thackeray, Andrew Thompson and Richard Toye, pp.1–18. Cham: Springer International Publishing, 2018.

Tombs, Isabelle, and Robert Tombs. 'Losing the Peace.' In *That Sweet Enemy: the French and the British from the Sun King to the present*, pp.500–25. London: William Heinemann, 2006.

Trentmann, Frank. 'After the Nation-State: Citizenship, Empire and Global Coordination in the New Internationalism, 1914–1930.' In *Beyond Sovereignty: Britain, empire and transnationalism, c. 1880–1950*, edited by Kevin Grant, Philippa Levine and Frank Trentmann, pp.34–53. Basingstoke England; New York: Palgrave Macmillan, 2007.

Unattributed. 'The Queen's Empire: A Pictorial and Descriptive Record (1897).' In *Politics and Empire in Victorian Britain: a reader*, edited by Antoinette M. Burton, pp.278–79. New York: Palgrave, 2001.

Walker-Morrison, Deborah, and Raylene Ramsay. 'Mon Whare, ton Fare: Building a common house through translation in Pacific Literature.' In *Littératures du Pacifique insulaire: Nouvelle-Calédonie, Nouvelle-Zélande, Océanie, Timor Oriental: approches historiques, culturelles et comparatives*, édite by Jean Bessière and Sylvie André, pp.231–48. Paris: Champion: Diffusion hors France Slatkine, 2013.

Ward, Stuart. 'Transcending the Nation: A Global Imperial History?'. In *After the Imperial Turn: thinking with and through the nation*, edited by Antoinette Burton, pp.44–56. Durham [NC]: Duke University Press, 2003.

Watson, James. '"The Greatest Commercial Traveller in the Empire": Massey and Trade.' In *A Great New Zealand Prime Minister?: reappraising William Ferguson Massey*, edited by James Watson and Lachy Paterson, pp.121–28. Dunedin, NZ: Otago University Press, 2011.

———. 'W.F. Massey: New Zealand.' *Makers of the Modern World.* London: Haus, 2010.

Wildenthal, Laura. 'Notes on a History of "Imperial Turns" in Modern Germany.' In *After the Imperial Turn: thinking with and through the Nation*, edited by Antoinette Burton, pp.145–56. Durham [NC]: Duke University Press, 2003.

Winter, Jay. *Sites of Memory, Sites of Mourning: The Great War in European Cultural History. Studies in the Social and Cultural History of Modern Warfare*. Vol. I, Cambridge: Cambridge University Press, 1998.

Woodward, Keith. 'Keith Woodward – Historical Note.' In *Tufala Gavman: reminiscences from the Anglo-French Condominium of the New Hebrides*, edited by Brian J. Bresnihan and Keith Woodward, pp.16–73. Suva, Fiji: Institute of Pacific Studies University of the South Pacific, 2002.

Woollacott, Angela. 'Postcolonial Histories and Catherine Hall's *Civilising Subjects*.' In *Connected Worlds: history in transnational perspective*, edited by Marilyn Lake and Ann Curthoys, pp.63–75: Australian National University, 2006.

Edited Books

60 Years Ago: Celebrating the Anniversary of Diplomatic Relations between New Zealand and France. Wellington: France Ambassade (The French Embassy), 2005.

Ballantyne, Tony, and Antoinette M. Burton. *Bodies in Contact: rethinking colonial encounters in world history*. Durham, NC: Duke University Press, 2005.

Baylyn, Olive, and Katie Pickles. *Hall of Fame: life stories of New Zealand women*. Christchurch, NZ: Clerestory Press, 1998.

Bell, Leonard, and Diana Morrow. *Jewish Lives in New Zealand: a history.* Auckland, NZ: Godwit, 2012.

Bell, Rachael. *New Zealand Between the Wars*. Auckland, New Zealand: Massey University Press, 2017.

Berg, Manfred, and Bernd Schaefer. *Historical Justice in International Perspective: how societies are trying to right the wrongs of the past, Publications of the German Historical Institute*. Cambridge: Cambridge University Press, 2012.

Bleriot, Erika, Brent Coutts, Sylvain Leduc, Lucy Stone, Baradene College of the Sacred Heart (Auckland NZ), *La bataille de la conscience: la desobeissance et la rebellion des soldats et le traitement des objecteurs de conscience dans la Premiere Guerre mondiale en France et en Nouvelle-Zelande – une etude historique comparee (The battle of conscience: disobedience and rebellion of soldiers and the treatment of conscientious objectors in the First World War in France and New Zealand – a comparative historical study)*. Vitry-sur-Seine France: Lycee Professionel Jean Mace, 2015.

Bornholdt, Jenny, and Gregory O'Brien. *The Colour of Distance: New Zealand writers in France, French writers in New Zealand*. Wellington, NZ: Victoria University Press, 2005.

Burton, Antoinette. *After the Imperial Turn: thinking with and through the nation*. Durham [NC]: Duke University Press, 2003.

Clavin, Patricia, and Michel Margairaz. 'Is Economic History No Longer Fashionable?'. In *Writing Contemporary History*, edited by Robert Gildea, pp.xxix, 254. London: Hodder Arnold, 2008.

Eichengreen, Barry. 'International Currencies in the Lens of History.' In *Handbook of the History of Money and Currency*, edited by Stefano Battilossi, Youssef Cassis and Kazuhiko Yago, pp.1–25. Singapore: Springer Singapore, 2018.

Fisher, Denise. 'Power and Politics.' In *France in the South Pacific*. ANU Press, 2013.

———. 'The French Pacific Presence to World War II.' In *France in the South Pacific*. Power and Politics, pp.13–46: ANU Press, 2013.

Gifford, Prosser, William Roger Louis, and Yale University. Concilium on International Studies. *France and Britain in Africa: imperial rivalry and colonial rule*. New Haven: Yale University Press, 1971.

Grant, Kevin, Philippa Levine, and Frank Trentmann. *Beyond Sovereignty: Britain, empire and transnationalism, c. 1880–1950*. Basingstoke England; New York: Palgrave Macmillan, 2007.

Johnson, Elizabeth. *Activities 1914–1919: The Treasury and Versailles* Vol. XVI, *The collected writings of John Maynard Keynes*. London: Macmillan, 1971.

Kaul, Chandrika. *Media and the British Empire*. New York: Palgrave Macmillan, 2006.

Luciano, Bernadette, and David G. Mayes. *New Zealand and Europe: connections and comparisons, European studies, 21*. Amsterdam, New York: Rodopi, 2005.

McClelland, Keith, and Sonya Rose. 'Citizenship and Empire, 1867–1928.' In *At Home with the Empire: metropolitan culture and the imperial world*, edited by Catherine Hall and Sonya O. Rose, Cambridge, UK; New York: Cambridge University Press, 2006.

Monger, David, Sarah Murray, and Katie Pickles. *Endurance and the First World War: experiences and legacies in New Zealand and Australia*. Newcastle: Cambridge Scholars, 2014.

Munz, Peter. *The Feel of Truth: essays in New Zealand and Pacific history*. Wellington: A.H. and A.W. Reed, 1969.

Newbury, C.W. 'Aspects of French Policy in the Pacific, 1853–1906.' In *The French and the Pacific world, 17th–19th centuries: explorations, migrations and cultural exchanges*, edited by Annick Foucrier, pp.31–42. Aldershot, Hampshire, England; Burlington, VT: Ashgate, 2005.

Pérez, Michael. 'New Caledonia and New Zealand: Similar Histories, Parallel Destinies, Converging Diplomacies.' In *New Zealand-New Caledonia: neighbours, friends and partners (La Nouvelle-Zélande et la Nouvelle-Calédonie: voisins, amis et partenaires)*, edited by Fr. Èd Èric Angleviel, Stephen I. Levine and Museum of Wellington City & Sea, pp.271–79. Wellington, NZ: Victoria University Press, 2008.

Philippe, Nathalie, Christopher Pugsley, John Crawford, and Matthias Strohn. *The Great Adventure Ends: New Zealand and France on the Western Front*. Christchurch: John Douglas, 2013.

Pickles, Katie, and Catharine Coleborne. *New Zealand's Empire. Studies in imperialism.* Manchester: Manchester University Press, 2016.

Tolerton, Jane. *An Awfully Big Adventure: New Zealand World War One veterans tell their stories*. Auckland, NZ: Penguin Books 2013.

Journal Articles

Aldrich, Robert. 'Le Lobby Colonial De L'océanie Française.' *Outre-Mers. Revue d'histoire* (1989): 143–56.

———. 'Remembrances of Empires Past.' *Portal: Journal of Multidisciplinary International Studies*, no. 1 (2010): 1.

Anon. 'The Right Hon. Stanley Baldwin.' *The New Zealand Railways Magazine* 1, no. 9 (February 25, 1927).

———. 'The League of Nations Union — Should Individuals Become Members of This Union?' *The New Zealand Railways Magazine*, Volume 3, Issue 5 (September 1, 1928).

Ballantyne, Tony. 'Thinking Local: Knowledge, Sociability and Community in Gore's Intellectual Life, 1875–1914.' *New Zealand Journal of History* 44 (2010): 138–56.

Beckett, John, and Michael Turner. 'End of the Old Order? F. M. L. Thompson, the Land Question, and the Burden of Ownership in England, c.1880–c.1925.' *The Agricultural History Revie*w 55, no. 2 (2007): 269–88.

Belgrave, M. 'Looking Forward: Historians and the Waitangi Tribunal.' *New Zealand Journal of History* 40, no. 2 (2006).

———. Review: 'Webs of Empire: Locating New Zealand's Colonial Past.' *Kōtuitui: New Zealand Journal of Social Sciences Online* 9, no. 1 (2014/01/02 2014): 36–38.

Belich, James. 'Response: A Cultural History of Economics?'. *Victorian Studies* 53, no. 1 (2010): 116–121.

———. 'The Rise and Fall of Greater Britain.' In *Replenishing the Earth* (2009): 456–73.

Berenson, E. 'Fashoda, Dreyfus, and the Myth of Jean-Baptiste Marchand,' Article, *Yale French Studies* 111, (2007): 129–42.

Bingham, Adrian. 'The Daily Mail and the First World War.' Article. *History Today* 63, no. 12 (2013): 1–8.

Birn, Donald S. 'The League of Nations Union and Collective Security.' *Journal of Contemporary History*, no. 3 (1974): 131.

Blair, C., V.W. Balthrop, and N. Michel. 2011. 'The Arguments of the Tombs of the Unknown: Relationality and National Legitimation.' *Argumentation* no. 25 (4): 449–68. doi: 10.1007/s10503-011-9216-9.

Burbank, Jane, and Frederick Cooper. 'Empires after 1919: Old, New, Transformed.' *International Affairs* 95, no. 1 (2019): 81–100.

Chalaby, Jean K. 'Twenty Years of Contrast: The French and British Press During the Inter-War Period.' *European Journal of Sociology / Archives Européennes de Sociologie* 37, no. 01 (1996): 143–59.

Chaudron, Gerald. 'New Zealand's International Initiation: Sir James Allen at the League of Nations 1920–1926.' *Political Science* (Wellington, NZ) (2012).

———. 'Obsession: New Zealand, Money and the League of Nations, 1920–35.' *Journal of Imperial & Commonwealth History* 41, no. 1 (03// 2013): 143–69.

———. 'The League of Nations and Imperial Dissent: New Zealand and the British Labour Governments, 1924–31.' *Journal of Imperial & Commonwealth History* 39, no. 1 (03// 2011): 47–71.

Chenut, Helen. 'Attitudes toward French Women's Suffrage on the Eve of World War I.' *French Historical Studies* 41, no. 4 (2018): 711–40.

Clarke, F.G. 'Fatal Necessity (Book Review).' *American Historical Review* no. 84 (1) (1979):166.

Clough, Shepard B. 'Review of The End of French Predominance in Europe: The Financial Crisis of 1924 and the Adoption of the Dawes Plan, Stephen A. Schuker. *The Business History Review* no. 51 (2) (1977): 271–72. doi: 10.2307/3113498.

Colton, Joel. 'Review of Louis Loucheur and the Shaping of Modern France, 1916–1931, Stephen D. Carls.' *The American Historical Review* no. 100 (2) (1995): 534–35. doi: 10.2307/2169085.

Cook, R. 'J.W. Dafoe at the Imperial Conference, 1923.' *The Canadian Historical Review* 41(1), (1960): 19–40.

Cornick, Martyn. 'The Dreyfus Affair – Another Year, Another Centenary. British Opinion and the Rennes Verdict, September 1899.' *Modern & Contemporary France* 7, no. 4 (1999).

Cotton, James. 'On the Chatham House Project: Interwar Actors, Networks, Knowledge.' *International Politics* Online Ed. (2017).

Derby, Edward George Villiers Stanley, and David Dutton. Paris '1918: The War Diary of the British Ambassador, the 17th Earl of Derby [in English]'. *Liverpool Historical Studies.* Liverpool: Liverpool University Press, 2001.

Desbordes, Rhoda. 'Representing "Informal Empire" In the Nineteenth Century.' *Media History* no. 14 (2) (2008): 121–39.

Dwyer, Jacqueline. 'Ahead of Their Time: The French Economic Mission to Australia 1918.' *The French Australian Review* no. 59 Australian Summer (2015): 30–53.

Einzig, P. 'Prof. Gustav Cassel.' *Nature 155* (02/10/online 1945): 167.

Federico, G. 'The growth of world agricultural production, 1800–1938.' *Research in Economic History* 22 (January 2004): 125–81.

Gale, S.J. 'Lies and Misdemeanours: Nauru, Phosphate and Global Geopolitics.' *The Extractive Industries and Society*, Department of Archaeology, The University of Sydney, Sydney, New South Wales 2006, Australia, 2019.

Ginneken, Jaap van. 'Crowds, Psychology, and Politics, 1871–1899.' *Cambridge Studies in the History of Psychology*. Cambridge [England]; New York, NY, USA: Cambridge University Press, 1992.

Glazebrook, A.J. 'Review: An Empire View of the Empire Tangle. By Edward O. Mousley, with a Preface by the Rt. Hon. W. F. Massey.' *The Canadian Historical Review* 2, no. 4 (December 1921): 396.

Gorman, D. 'Liberal Internationalism, the League of Nations Union, and the Mandates System.' [In English]. *Canadian Journal of History* 40, no. 3 (12/01/2005): 449–77.

Grayson, Richard S. 'The British Government and the Channel Tunnel, 1919–39.' *Journal of Contemporary History* 31, no. 1 (1996): 125–44.

Grayzel, Susan R. 'Belonging to the Imperial Nation: Rethinking the History of the First World War in Britain and Its Empire.' *The Journal of Modern History* 90, no. 2 (2018/06/01 2018): 383–405.

Greenfield, Jerome. 'Gabriel Hanotaux and French Grand Strategy, 1894–8.' *The International History Review* (2015): 1–21.

Gregory, Charles Noble. 'The First Assembly of the League of Nations.' *The American Journal of International Law* 15, no. 2 (1921): 240–52.

Guillebaud, C.W. 'Review of Money., R. C. Mills, E. R. Walker; World Finance since 1914., Paul Einzig; Ten Years of Currency Revolution., Charles Morgan-Webb; The International Money Markets., John T. Madden, Marcus Nadler.' *The Economic Journal* no. 46 (182) (1936): 319–322.

Guymer, Laurence. 'Pressing the French and Defending the Palmerstonian Line: Lord William Hervey and the Times, 1846–8.' Article. *Historical Research* 87, no. 235 (2014): 116–33.

Harland, S. 'Wool Supplies and Consumption: The Requirements of a British Empire Industry Y1 – 1924/06/01.' *Journal of the Textile Institute Proceedings* 15, no. 6 (1924/06/01 1924): 152–69.

Harper, Glyn. 'W. F. Massey: New Zealand.' *New Zealand Journal of History* 45, no. 2 (2011): 271–73.

Hepp, John. '"Principles of Justice, of Equality, of Peace": the Debate over War Crimes and Their Punishment at Paris in 1919.' In *'Peace making after the First World War 1919–1923' conference*. London, 1919.

Hurley, Desmond. 'Edward Opotiki Mousley.' *New Zealand Studies* November (1996): 10–17.

Kayah, Hasan. 'The Ottoman Experience of World War I: Historiographical Problems and Trends.' *The Journal of Modern History* 89, no. 4 (2017): 875–907.

Kennedy, P.M. 'Imperial Cable Communications and Strategy, 1870–1914.' *The English Historical Review* 86, no. 341 (1971): 728–52.

Irwin, Douglas A. 'The French Gold Sink and the Great Deflation of 1929–32.' *Cato Papers on Public Policy* 2 (2012).

Kaul, Chandrika. 'Gallipoli, Media and Commemorations During 2015: Select Perspectives.' *Media History* 24, no. 1 (2018): 115–41.

Khadduri, Majid. 'The Alexandretta Dispute.' *The American Journal of International Law* no. 39 (3) (1945): 406–25. doi: 10.2307/2193522.

Kish, George. 'Obituary: Andre Siegfried.' *Geographical Review* 50, no. 2 (1960): 287–88.

Klein, Charlotte Lea. 'The Dreyfus Affair in the British Press.' *Patterns of Prejudice* 12, no. 2 (1978/01/01 1978): 33–39.

Krogt, Christopher Van Der. 'Imitating the Holy Family? Catholic Ideals and the Cult of Domesticity in Interwar New Zealand.' *History Now* no. 4 (1) (1998):13–20.

Lee, Howard. 'The New Zealand District High School: A case study of the conservative politics of rural education.' *Education Research & Perspectives,* no. 32 (1) (2005): 12–40.

Lentin, Antony. '"Une Aberration Inexplicable?" Clemenceau and the Abortive Anglo-French Guarantee Treaty of 1919.' *Diplomacy & Statecraft 8*, no. 2 (1997): 31–49.

Loucheur, Louis. 'The Essentials of a Reparations Settlement.' *Foreign Affairs* no. 2 (1) (1923): 1–9. doi: 10.2307/20028267.

Maguire, A. 'Looking for Home? New Zealand Soldiers Visiting London During the First World War.' Article. *London Journal* 41, no. 3 (2016): 281–98.

Manovich, Lev. 'Cultural Data: Possibilities and Limitations of the Digital Data Universe.' In *Museum and Archive on the Move: changing cultural institutions in the digital era*, edited by Wendy Coones Oliver Grau, Viola Rühse Boston: De Gruyter, 2017.

Marks, Sally. 'Mistakes and Myths: The Allies, Germany, and the Versailles Treaty, 1918–1921.' *The Journal of Modern History* 85, no. 3 (2013): 632–59.

Marsh, Kate. '"La Nouvelle Activité Des Trafiquants De Femmes": France, Le Havre and the Politics of Trafficking, 1919–1939.' *Contemporary European History* 26, no. 1 (2017): 23–48.

Marshall, Sheila G. 'The Jancy Dress Dance.' *The New Zealand Railways Magazine* 4, no. 9 (1 January 1930).

Martin, Ged. 'Was There a British Empire?'. Article. *Historical Journal* 15, no. 3 (1972): 562–69.

Martin, Germain. 'The Industrial Reconstruction of France since the War.' *Harvard Business Review* 5, no. 3 (04// 1927): 257–68.

McCarthy, H. 'Leading from the Centre: The League of Nations Union, Foreign Policy and 'Political Agreement' in the 1930s.' [In English]. *Contemporary British History* 23, no. 4 (12/01/2009): 527–42.

McIntyre, W. David. 'The Development and Significance of Dominion Status.' Wellington: NZ Government.

______. *The Britannic Vision: Historians and the Making of the British Commonwealth of Nations, 1907–48.* Basingstoke: Palgrave Macmillan, 2009.

———. *Dominion of New Zealand: Statesmen and Status 1907–1945.* Wellington: New Zealand Institute of International Affairs, 2007.

McMillan, James F. 'Review of The Past in French History, Robert Gildea.' *The English Historical Review* no. 110 (438) (1995): 946–48.

McNeill, Dougal. 'Labouring Feeling: Harry Holland's Political Emotions.' *The Journal of New Zealand Studies* 21 (2015): 1–11.

Mort, Frank. 'On Tour with the Prince: Monarchy, Imperial Politics and Publicity in the Prince of Wales's Dominion Tours 1919–20.' *Twentieth Century British History*, no. Electronic Issue (2017).

Mousley, Edward. 'The Empire and Foreign Policy.' *Journal of the British Institute of International Affairs*, no. 3 (1923): 91.

Mouton, Marie-Renée. 'La France Et La Société Des Nations En 1922.' *Guerres mondiales et conflits contemporains*, no. 193 (1999): 101–15.

Munro, D., and A. Fowler. 'Testing the Credibility of Historical Newspaper Reporting of Extreme Climate and Weather Events.' *New Zealand Geographer* 70, no. 3 (2014): 153–64.

Mutch, Carol and Rosemary Bingham, Lynette Kingsbury, Maria Perreau. 'Political Indoctrination through Myth Building: The New Zealand School Journal at the Time of World War 1.' *Curriculum Matters*, no. 14 (2018): 102–128.

O'Hara, Glen. 'New Histories of British Imperial Communication and the "Networked World" of the 19th and Early 20th Centuries.' *History Compass* 8, no. 7 (2010): 609–25.

Openshaw, Roger. 'The Highest Expression of Devotion: New Zealand Primary-Schools and Patriotic Zeal During the Early 1920s.' *History of Education* 9, no. 4 (1980/12/01 1980): 333–44.

Osborne, Ken. 'Canadian Schools, the League of Nations, and The Teaching of History, 1920–1939.' *Historical Studies in Education* 30, no. 2, Fall (2018).

Patterson, Caleb Perry. 'The Admission of Germany To the League of Nations and Its Probable Significance.' *The Southwestern Political and Social Science Quarterly* no. 7 (3) (1926): 215–37.

Pawson, E. 'Monuments, Memorials and Cemeteries: Icons in the Landscape.' *New Zealand Journal of Geography* 92, no. 1 (1991): 26–27.

Peters, Kathryn. 'New Zealand's Attitudes to the Reform of the League of Nations: The Background of the Memorandum to the Secretary-General, 16 July 1936.' *NZ Journal of History* 06, no. No. 1 (1972): 81–98.

Pickles, Katie. 'The Obvious and the Awkward: Postcolonialism and the British World.' *NZ Journal of History* 45, no. 1 (2011): 85–101.

———. 'Transnational Intentions and Cultural Cringe: History Beyond National Boundaries.' In *Contesting Clio's Craft: New Directions and Debates in Canadian History*, edited by Christopher Dummitt and Michael Dawson, pp.141–61. London: UTP, 2009.

Piekarz, Mark. 'Hot War Tourism: The Klive Battlefield and the Ultimate Adventure Holiday?'. In *Battlefield Tourism: history, place and interpretation*, edited by Chris Ryan, pp. 153–69. Amsterdam Oxford: Elsevier, 2007.

Potter, S.J. 'Jingoism, Public Opinion, and the New Imperialism: Newspapers and Imperial Rivalries at the Fin De Siècle.' Article. *Media History* 20, no. 1 (2014): 34–50.

Reeve, L. J. 'The Legal Status of the Petition of Right1.' *The Historical Journal* no. 29 (2009) 02: 257.

Reynolds, David. 'The Long Sacrifice.' *New Statesman* 144 (2015): 36–39.

Rutherford, J. 'The Treaty of Waitangi and the Acquisition of British Sovereignty in New Zealand, 1840.' *Auckland University College, History Series No. 3*, Bulletin 36 (1948).

Siegfried, Andre. 'Franco-American and Franco-British Relations.' *Journal of the Royal Institute of International Affairs* 5, no. 5 (1926): 225.

Seligmann, M. 'Intelligence Information and the 1909 Naval Scare: The Secret Foundations of a Public Panic.' *War in History* 17 (1) (2010): 37–59. doi: 10.1177/0968344509348302.

Stachurska-Kounta, Marta. Review: 'New Zealand in the League of Nations: The Beginnings of an Independent Foreign Policy, 1919–1939. By Gerald Chaudron.' *The Journal of Pacific History* 48, no. 1 (2013/03/01 2013): 105–6.

Sumpter, Caroline. 'The Cheap Press and the "Reading Crowd".' *Media History* 12, no. 3 (2006/12/01): 233–52.

Thompson, J.A. 'Lord Cecil and the Pacifists in the League of Nations Union.' *The Historical Journal*, no. 4 (1977): 949.

Tombs, Robert. '"Lesser Breeds without the Law": The British Establishment and the Dreyfus Affair, 1894–1899.' *The Historical Journal* 41, no. 02 (1998): 495–510.

Troughton, Geoffrey. 'Between the Wars 1918–40.' *Anglican and Episcopal History* 84, no. 3 (2015): 279–297.

Vacante, Jeffery. 'Review of Dummitt, Chris; Dawson, Michael, eds., Contesting Clio's Craft: New Directions and Debates in Canadian History.' *H-Canada, H-Net Reviews* (2010).

Varian, Brian. 'The Economics of Edwardian Imperial Preference: What Can New Zealand Reveal?'. *Economic History Working Papers* 281/2018 (2018).

Vivier, N. 'Agriculture and economic development in Europe 1870–1939.' *XIV International Economic History Congress Proceedings* (Session 60) (21 to 25 August 2006).

Weardale, (Lord). 'The Inter-Parliamentary Union and the League of Nations.' *Advocate of Peace through Justice*, no. 9/10 (1921): 333.

Williams, John Fischer. 'Reparations.' *International Affairs (Royal Institute of International Affairs 1931–1939)* no. 11 (2) (1932): 183–202. doi: 10.2307/3016302.

Winter, Jay. 'The Tomb of the Unknown Soldier, Modern Mourning, and the Reinvention of the Mystical Body by Laura Wittman (Review).' *University of Toronto Quarterly*, no. 3 (2013): 581.

______. 'Commemorating Catastrophe: 100 Years On.' *War & Society* 36, no. 4 (2017): 239–55.

Wood, John Cunningham. 'J. A. Hobson and British Imperialism.' *American Journal of Economics and Sociology* 42, no. 4 (1983): 483–500.

Yearwood, Peter J. Review: 'New Zealand in the League of Nations: The Beginnings of an Independent Foreign Policy, 1919–1939, by Gerald Chaudron.' *The English Historical Review* 129, no. 538 (2014): 760–761.

Miscellaneous

Anon. 'Earl of Liverpool, GCB, GCMG, GBE, MVO, PC.' https://gg.govt.nz/office-governor-general/history/former-governors-general-0.

Ballantyne, Tony, and Australian National University. History Program. 2009. *Talking, Listening, Writing, Reading: communication and colonisation, Allan Martin lecture, 2009.* Canberra: History Program Research School of Social Sciences Australian National University.

Bloch, Marc Léopold Benjamin, Bertrand Müller, and Lucien Febvre. 1994. Correspondence. Paris: Fayard.

Bondarchuk, Sergei. 'Waterloo.' 2h 12 min, 1970. https://www.imdb.com/title/tt0066549/

(The) Covenant of the League of Nations (Including Amendments adopted to December 1924). Yale Law School: Lillian Goldman Law Library.

Campbell, Hugh and Haggerty, Julia. Photo: Astrid van Meeuwen-Dijkgraaf. 'Farming and the Environment – Environmental Impacts in the 2000s.' In *Te Ara – the Encyclopedia of New Zealand.*

Craige, Champion. 2012. Polybius. *Oxford Bibliographies*, http://www.oxfordbibliographies.com/document/obo-9780195389661/obo-9780195389661-0047.xml.

'Gallica.' Bibliothèque nationale de France, http://gallica.bnf.fr/accueil/?mode=desktop.

Gustafson, Barry. 'Massey, William Ferguson.' In *Dictionary of New Zealand Biography*, 1993, updated 2013.

Hall-Jones, John. 'William Hall-Jones.' In *Dictionary of New Zealand Biography*,1993.

Humbert, Jean-Marcel, and Lionel Dumarche. Undated. The Tomb of Napoleon and the Hôtel des Invalides Savoir Decouvrir.

Hunter, George Leland. April–December 1916. '"Scipio" Tapestries now in America.' *The Burlington magazine*, pp.65–66.

Inglis, K.S., and J. Phillips. 'War Memorials in Australia and New Zealand: A Comparative Survey.' Article. *Australian Historical Studies* 24, no. 96 (1991): 179–91.

Koudelka, Jan. 'Age of Empires – Balancing Imperial Commitments between the First and Second World Wars.' *The Forge.*

Lewis, Paul, Seán Clarke, Caelainn Barr. 'How We Combed Leaders' Speeches to Gauge Populist Rise: A Look at the Methodology Team Populism Used to Chart Surge in Populism.' *The Guardian*, 6 Mar 2019. Downloaded 20 March 2019 from: https://www.theguardian.com/world/2019/mar/06/how-we-combed-leaders-speeches-to-gauge-populist-rise

Lochhead, Ian J. 12-Feb-2014. Seager, Samuel Hurst. In *Dictionary of New Zealand Biography. Te Ara – the Encyclopedia of New Zealand.*

Mackay, Ruddock, and H.C.G. Mathew. 'Balfour, Arthur James. First Earl of Balfour (1848–1930).' In *Oxford Dictionary of National Biography*, edited by Lawrence Goldman. Oxford: Oxford University Press, 2011.

McGibbon, Ian. 'Allen, James.' In *Dictionary of New Zealand Biography: Te Ara – the Encyclopedia of New Zealand.* Wellington.

———. 'Jellicoe, John Henry Rushworth'.' In *Dictionary of New Zealand Biography. Te Ara – the Encyclopedia of New Zealand.* 2018.

Marsh, Peter T. 'Chamberlain, Joseph (1836–1914).' In *Oxford Dictionary of National Biography*, edited by Lawrence Goldman. Oxford: Oxford University Press, 2004.

Mathew, H.C.G. 'Edward V11 (1841–1910), King of the United Kingdom of Great Britain and Ireland, and the British Dominions Beyond the Seas, and Emperor of India'. In *Oxford Dictionary of National Biography*. Oxford: Oxford University Press, 2004–2014.

———. 'Gladstone, William Ewart (1809–1898).' In *Oxford Dictionary of National Biography*, edited by Lawrence Goldman. Oxford: Oxford University Press, 2011.

McKinnon, Malcolm. International economic relations – Britain and New Zealand, 1900 to 1940. In *Te Ara – the Encyclopedia of New Zealand.*

Moloney, John Keith. John Keith Moloney Recalls Passchendaele. Ref: 253856 *New Zealand Broadcasting Corporation*, 1964. 00:03:18. Accessed 23 May 2018: https://www.ngataonga.org.nz/collections/catalogue/catalogue-item?record_id=193716

New Zealand and the First World War: a bibliography of non-fiction sources. Edited by Ministry for Culture and Heritage History Group, Wellington, New Zealand.

O'Farrell, Patrick. 'Holland, Henry Edmund.' In *Dictionary of New Zealand Biography*, 1996.

'Ōhaeawai NZ Wars Memorial Cross.' Ministry for Culture and Heritage, https://nzhistory.govt.nz/media/photo/ohaeawai-nz-wars-memorial-cross.Polybius. 2011. The Histories. In *Loeb Classical Library 159*. Cambridge, MA: Harvard University Press.

Oliver, W.H., and Massey University College of Manawatu. *The Inadequacy of a Dependent Utopia: The Anderson Memorial Lecture.* [Hamilton, NZ]: Published by Paul's Book Arcade for the Massey University of Manawatu, 1964.

Olssen, Erik. 'Sidey, Thomas Kay.' In *Dictionary of New Zealand Biography Te Ara – the Encyclopedia of New Zealand.* Wellington, NZ, 1996.

Roberts, Heather. 'Grossmann, Edith Searle.' In *Dictionary of New Zealand Biography: Te Ara – the Encyclopedia of New Zealand*, 1993.

Schuker, Stephen A. 'What Historians Get Wrong about World War I.' *Time Magazine*, 1 August 2014.

Wright, Matthew. 'The Policy Origins of the Reserve Bank of New Zealand.' *Reserve Bank of New Zealand*, September 2006.

Theses

Albers, Thilo Nils Hendrik. 'Trade Frictions, Trade Policies, and the Interwar Business Cycle.' *Doctoral Thesis*. London School of Economics and Political Science, 2018.

Attwood, Bain. 'Apostles of Peace: The New Zealand League of Nations Union: *Research Essay. Presented in Partial Fulfilment of the Requirements for the Degree of Master of Philosophy in History*. University of Auckland, 1979.

Buckley, Mike. 'A Colour Line Affair – Race, Imperialism and Rugby Football Contacts between New Zealand and South Africa to 1950.', *Presented in Partial Fulfilment of the Requirements for the Degree of Master of Arts in History*. University of Canterbury, 1996.

Chaudron, Gerald. 'New Zealand and the League of Nations.' *A thesis submitted in partial fulfilment of the requirements for the degree of Doctor of Philosophy in History*. University of Canterbury, 1989.

Davenport, Carol. 'Trading in Traditions: New Zealand's Exports to the Countries of the European Union, 1960 to 2000'. *A Thesis Presented in Partial Fulfilment of the Requirements for the Degree of Master of Arts in History at Massey University*. MA, Massey University, 2004.

Dingle, Sarah. 'Gospel Power for Civilization: The CMS Missionary Perspective on Maori Culture 1830–1860.' *Doctor of Philosophy in History*. University of Adelaide, 2009.

Gould, Ashley Nevil. 'Proof of Gratitude? Soldier Land Settlement in New Zealand after World War I.' *Presented in Partial Fulfilment of the Requirements for the Degree of Master of Philosophy in History*. Massey University, 1992.

Hickey, Carina. 'Man in His Time Plays Many Parts: Life Stories of William Jordan'. *A Thesis Presented in Partial Fulfilment of the Requirements for the Degree of Master of Arts in History at Massey University*. MA, Massey University, 2003.

Hilliard, Chris. 'Island stories: the writing of New Zealand history, 1920–1940'. *A thesis submitted in partial fulfilment of the requirements for the degree of Master of Arts in History, The University of Auckland*. MA – History, University of Auckland, 1997.

Hopner, Veronica. 'Home from War'. *A Thesis Presented in Partial Fulfilment of the Requirements for the Degree of Doctor of Philosophy in Psychology at Massey University, Auckland.* Massey University, 2014.

Hucker, G. 'The rural home front: A New Zealand region and the Great War 1914–1926'. *A thesis submitted in partial fulfilment of the requirements for the degree of Doctor of Philosophy in History at Massey University.* (PhD), Massey University, 2006.

Kimber, Geraldine Maria. 'Katherine Mansfield: The View from France.' *A thesis submitted in fulfilment of the requirements for the degree of Doctor of Philosophy*, University of Exeter, 2007.

Knuckey, P. 'A global province?: the development of a movie culture in a small provincial city 1919–1945'. *A thesis presented in partial fulfilment of the requirements for the degree of Master of Arts in History at Massey University.* (MA), Massey University, 2012.

Littlewood, David, and Massey University. 'The Tool and Instrument of the Military?: The Operations of the Military Service Tribunals in the East Central Division of the West Riding of Yorkshire and Those of the Military Service Boards in New Zealand, 1916–1918'. *A Thesis Presented in Partial Fulfilment of the Requirements for the Degree of Doctor of Philosophy in History at Massey University*, 2015.

Neill, Carol May. 'Trading Our Way: Developments in New Zealand's Trade Policy 1930s to 1980s.' PhD, Massey University, 2010.

Phipps, Gareth. 'Bringing Our Boy Home: The Tomb of the Unknown Warrior, Its Visitors, and Contemporary War Remembrance in New Zealand.' MA, Victoria University of Wellington, 2009.

Sigley, Simon. 'Film Culture: Its Development in New Zealand, 1929–1972'. *A Thesis Presented in Partial Fulfilment of the Requirements for the Degree of Doctor of Philosophy at Auckland University.* Auckland, 2003.

Turner, Philip. 'The Politics of Neutrality: The Catholic Mission and the Maori 1838–1870.' MA, University of Auckland, 1986.

Um, So Jung. 'Japanese Colonial Policy Studies, 1909–1945: Nitobe Inazō, Yanaihara Tadao, and Tōbata Seiichi'. *A thesis submitted in fulfilment of the requirements for the degree of Doctor of Philosophy.* The University of Michigan, 2017.

Watts, Alistair. 'Why, when the image of the French in the New Zealand Press 1900–1914 was a divided one, did New Zealand enter World War I allied to France?' *A thesis presented in partial fulfilment of the requirements for the degree of Master of Arts in History at Massey University, Albany, New Zealand,* History Department School of Humanities, 2016.

Web Pages

L'Académie française, 'Jacques Bainville.' In *L'Académie française website*. Paris, 11 January 2018. http://www.academie-francaise.fr/les-immortels/jacques-bainville.

———. 'Jacques Chastenet.' In *L'Académie française website*. Paris, 11 January 2018. http://www.academie-francaise.fr/les-immortels/jacques-chastenet.

Atatürk, Mustafa Kemal. *Ari Burnu Memorial Gallipoli.* Ministry for Culture and Heritage, updated 13-Jan-2016, 13-Jan-2016 [cited 24 August 2016]. Available from http://www.nzhistory.net.nz/media/photo/ari-burnu-memorial.

'Feeding Britain.' In *New Zealand History*, Ministry for Culture and Heritage, 4-May-2016 2016. https://nzhistory.govt.nz/war/public-service-at-war/feeding-britain.

French Ministry of Foreign Affairs and International Development. 2016. *A tour of the Quai d'Orsay* 2016 [cited 29 February 2016]. Available from: http://www.diplomatie.gouv.fr/en/the-ministry-of-foreign-affairs/a-tour-of-the-quai-d-orsay/.

Garvitch, Jeremy Veniamin. 'Relief Workers Pulling a Chain Harrow at Petone.' edited by National Library New Zealand, 1932. Accessed 21 July 2018: https://natlib.govt.nz/records/22708013?search%5Bi%5D%5Bcollection%5D=Garvitch%2C+Jeremy+Veniamin%2C+1890-1990+%3APhotographs+and+negatives&search%5Bi%5D%5Bprimary_collection%5D=TAPUHI&search%5Bi%5D%5Bsubject%5D=Petone&search%5Bpath%5D=items

Gustafson, Barry. 'Rushworth, Harold Montague.' In *Dictionary of New Zealand Biography: Te Ara – the Encyclopedia of New*

Zealand, 1998. Accessed 18 February 2018: https://teara.govt.nz/en/biographies/4r30/rushworth-harold-montague

'History of the Labour Party.' https://www.labour.org.nz/history.

Kipling, Rudyard. 'Kipling Society: The Ladies.' Accessed 28 July 2018: http://www.kiplingsociety.co.uk/poems_ladies.htm.

———. 'Puck of Pook's Hill: The Children's Song.' Adelaide: University of Adelaide. Accessed 29 April 2018: https://ebooks.adelaide.edu.au/k/kipling/rudyard/puck/chapter26.html

Lahmeyer, Jan. 'Population Statistics: Historical Demography of All Countries, Their Divisions and Towns.' 17 January 2018, 2006. http://www.populstat.info/.

'League of Nations Union of NZ, 1936.' Ministry for Culture and Heritage. Downloaded from: http://api.digitalnz.org/records/31936274/source.

McGibbon, Ian. *'Something of Them Is Here Recorded': Official History in New Zealand*. Victoria University 2013 [cited 26 June 2016]. Available from http://nzetc.victoria.ac.nz/tm/scholarly/tei-corpus-WH1.html.

'Modern Anzac Day.' Ministry for Culture and Heritage, https://nzhistory.govt.nz/war/modern-anzac-day.

New Zealand in the First World War. Victoria University [cited 26 June 2016]. Available from http://nzetc.victoria.ac.nz/tm/scholarly/tei-corpus-WH1.html and http://nzetc.victoria.ac.nz/tm/scholarly/tei-McGSome.html.

New Zealand Foreign Affairs and Trade. 'Longueval: New Zealand Memorial.' 2018. Accessed 3 June 2018: https://www.mfat.govt.nz/en/countries-and-regions/europe/france/new-zealand-embassy/anzac-day-commemorations/longueval/.

Nutt, Jim S., and Michael K. Warren. 'Diplomatic and Consular Representations.' Historica Canada, https://www.thecanadianencyclopedia.ca/en/article/diplomatic-and-consular-representations.

'Ōhaeawai NZ Wars Memorial Cross.' Ministry for Culture and Heritage, Updated 26-Feb-2015, accessed 21 January 2019, https://nzhistory.govt.nz/media/photo/ohaeawai-nz-wars-memorial-cross.

Pedersen, Susan. *The Guardians, the League of Nations and the Crisis of Empire* [1 online resource]. Available from http://ezproxy.massey.ac.nz/login?url=http://massey.eblib.com.au/patron/FullRecord.aspx?p=2055006.

Photo, akg-images / Alamy Stock. 'French Women Pulling a Plough.' Accessed 21 July 2018: https://www.alamy.com/stock-photo-french-women-pulling-a-plough-wwi-history-world-war-i-war-economies-20731044.html.

Pickles, Katie. *Female Imperialism and National Identity: the Imperial Order Daughters of the Empire* [1 online resource (xi, 209 pages)]. Manchester University Press: Distributed exclusively in the USA by Palgrave 2002. Available from http://ezproxy.massey.ac.nz/login?url=http://search.ebscohost.com/login.aspx?direct=true&scope=site&db=nlebk&AN=133645.

'Recruiting and Conscription.' Accessed 23 July 2018: https://nzhistory.govt.nz/war/recruiting-and-conscription.

Reserve Bank of New Zealand. 'The History of Coins in New Zealand.' https://www.rbnz.govt.nz/notes-and-coins/coins/history-of-new-zealand-coinage.

'Robert Cecil – Facts.' Nobel Media AB, Updated 7 Dec 2017, 2014, http://www.nobelprize.org/nobel_prizes/peace/laureates/1937/chelwood-facts.html.

Rice, Geoffrey W. 'Buddo, David.' In *Dictionary of New Zealand Biography: Te Ara – the Encyclopedia of New Zealand*, 1996. https://teara.govt.nz/en/biographies/3b56/buddo-david.

Smith, Hallam. 'David Mcdougall.' In *Dictionary of New Zealand Biography Te Ara*, 1998. Accessed 18 February 2018: https://teara.govt.nz/en/biographies/4m8/mcdougall-david

Tomb of the Unknown Warrior. Ministry for Culture and Heritage, 2004.

United Nations. 'Population by Sex, Annual Rate of Population Increase, Surface Area and Density.' https://unstats.un.org/unsd/demographic/products/dyb/dyb2012/Table03.pdf.

Winter, J.M. *The Legacy of the Great War. [Electronic Resource]: Ninety Years On.* Columbia: University of Missouri Press; Kansas City, MO: National World War I Museum, c.2009.

Index

A

B

C

D

E

F

G

H

I

J

K

L

M

N

O

P

R

S

T

U

V

W

Notes

Section One

[1] "Untitled," *New Zealand Gazette And Wellington Spectator*, 26 January 1842, p.3.

Chapter One

[1] Ranganui Walker, *Ka Whawhai Tonu Matou: Struggle Without End* (Auckland: Penguin, 2004), p.102.

[2] S. Runciman, *A History of the Crusades: The Kingdom of Jerusalem and the Frankish East, 1100-1187* (Cambridge University Press, 1952), p.460.

[3] J. Dunmore, *Aventures Dans Le Pacifique: From the Accounts of French Voyagers to the Pacific, Australia, and New Zealand* (A. H. & A. W. Reed, 1967) Fitzroy to Stanley, February 24th 1845. Dunmore refers to visits by De Surville (1769, at the same time as Cook), du Fresne (1772), La Perouse (sailed 1788 but did not return to France), d'Entrecasteaux (1791, looking for La Perouse), Baudin (1802, but visited Australia only), Duperrey (1822), D'Urville (1826), La Place (1829), D'Urville again (1838) and La Place (1838, second visit). Dates are difficult to reconcile, some sources giving the year of departure from France, others use the year of arrival in New Zealand and in some cases the secondary sources are in conflict on both.

[4] Anne Salmond, "Marion du Fresne," in *The French place in the Bay of Islands : essays from Pompallier's printery (Te urunga mai o te iwi Wiwi)*, ed. Kate Martin and Brad Mercer (Mātou Matauwhi, 2011), pp.28-30.

[5] L.R. Marchant, *France Australe* (Access Press, 1982), p.250; P. Moon, *The Origins of the Treaty of Waitangi* (Birdwood Pub., 1994), pp.21-22.

[6] Marchant, pp.222-23.

[7] S.A. Toth, *Beyond Papillon: The French Overseas Penal Colonies, 1854-1952* (University of Nebraska Press, 2006).

[8] James Belich, *Replenishing the Earth: The Settler Revolution and the Rise of the Anglo-world, 1783-1939* (Oxford Scholarship Online, 2011); Michael King, *The Penguin History of New Zealand* (Auckland: Penguin Books, 2012), p.116.

[9] P. Adams, *Fatal Necessity: British Intervention in New Zealand, 1830-1847* (Auckland University Press, 1977), p.76.

[10] W.P. Reeves, *The Long White Cloud: Ao Tea Roa*, 4th ed. (London: George Allen and Unwin, 1950, 1898), p.133; Moon, *Fatal Frontiers: A New History of New Zealand in the Decade Before the Treaty*, pp.106-07. Moon, *The Origins of the Treaty of Waitangi*, pp.141,55. Moon states La Place revisited New Zealand in 1838, raising the French flag and further stirring concerns in the Sydney regarding French intentions. Moon's cited source for this reported visit makes no mention of La Place. See: P. Moon, *Path to the Treaty of Waitangi* (David Ling Pub., 2002), pp.8, 94-95

Footnotes 87, 88, 89, referenced to: The Sydney Gazette and New South Wales Advertiser, 16 October 1838. This has no mention of such an event. Retrieved April 11, 2013, from http://nla.gov.au/nla.news-page694018. This account may have been confused with the *Heroine* visit described by Dunmore, p.96; Adams, p.81.

[11] R. Taylor, *The Past and Present of New Zealand: With Its Prospects for the Future* (W. Macintosh, 1868), pp.264-65; A.S. Thomson, *The Story of New Zealand : Past and Present - Savage and Civilized* (London: Spottiswoode, 1859), pp.275-76, 79; Moon, *The Origins of the Treaty of Waitangi*, pp.62-64; Adams, p.68; E. Ramsden, *Busby of Waitangi, H.M's Resident at New Zealand, 1833-40* (A H & A W Reed, 1942), pp.180-81, 94; C. Orange, *The Treaty of Waitangi*, 2nd ed. (Bridget Williams Books, 2011), p.32.

[12] He Whakaputanga - Declaration of Independence, 1835, Updated 17-Oct-2017.

[13] J. Belich, *Making Peoples: A History of the New Zealanders From Polynesian* (Penguin Random House New Zealand, 2007), p.181; T.L. Buick, *The Treaty of Waitangi: How New Zealand Became a British Colony* (Cambridge: Cambridge University Press, 1933), p.32.

[14] Reeves, p.284.

[15] Belich, pp.134-35; John Broadbent, "Colin and the European Powers in the Pacific," in *Catholic Beginnings in Oceania: Marist Missionary Perspectives*, ed. A. Greiler (Hindmarsh: ATF Press, 2009), pp.56-57.

[16] T.W.M. Marshall, *Christian Missions*, vol. I, II, III (1863), 164; E. Hodder, *Conquests of the Cross: A Record of Missionary Work Throughout the World*, facsimile edn ed. (London: Cassell, 2002, 1890), pp.535,41; Malcolm Falloon, *To Plough or to Preach: Mission Strategies in New Zealand During the 1820s* (London: Latimer Trust, 2010), pp.5-6; Adams, p.31. Moon, *The Origins of the Treaty of Waitangi*, pp.37-40.

[17] Simmons E. R., *Pompallier: Prince of Bishops* (Auckland: CPC Publishing, 1984), p.22; Michael O'Meeghan, "The French Marist Maori Mission," in *The French and the Maori*, ed. J. Dunmore (Waikanae: Heritage Press, 1992), p.42.

[18] Peter Tremewan, *French Akaroa*, 2nd ed. (Canterbury University Press, 2010), pp.58,69-70; Philip Turner, "The Politics of Neutrality: The Catholic Mission and the Maori 1838-1870" (M.A. University of Auckland, 1986), pp.15,21,24.

[19] G.H. Scholefield, *Captain William Hobson, First Governor of New Zealand* (Oxford University Press, 1934), p.99. Christine Ward Gailey, "Putting Down Sisters and Wives: Tongan Women and Colonization," in *The Pacific World: Lands, Peoples and History of the Pacific, 1500-1900*, ed. Jane Samson (Aldershot: Ashgate, 2003). Pompallier urged Lavaud to annex the South Island. Gailey links French Catholic mission activity with French annexations in the Pacific from the 1840s on.

[20] Tremewan, pp.58,70; Broadbent, pp.57-58.

[21] Orange, p.19-20.

[22] P. Wells, *The Hungry Heart: Journeys With William Colenso* (Penguin Random House New Zealand, 2012), p.240.
[23] Sarah Dingle, "Gospel Power for Civilization: The CMS Missionary Perspective on Maori Culture 1830-1860" (Doctor of Philosophy in History University of Adelaide, 2009), pp.34,77.
[24] J. Buller, *Forty Years in New Zealand* (Hodder and Stoughton, 1878), p.295.
[25] Buick, pp.197-200. Buick quotes Pompallier as saying that '… I kept myself entirely aloof from politics…'.
[26] Scholefield, p.99; Orange, p.59.
[27] D.K. Fieldhouse, *The Colonial Empires: A Comparative Survey from the 18th Century* (Weidenfeld and Nicolson, 1966); S. Henningham, *France and the South Pacific: A Contemporary History* (University of Hawaii Press, 1992), pp.3-4.
[28] J. Rutherford, "The Treaty of Waitangi and the Acquisition of British Sovereignty in New Zealand, 1840," *Auckland University College, History Series No. 3* Bulletin 36 (1948): pp.34-35; Moon, *The Origins of the Treaty of Waitangi*, p.18.; Orange, p.59.
[29] Tremewan, pp.77-78.
[30] James Cook, *Captain Cook's Journal During His First Voyage Round the World Made in H. M. Bark "Endeavour", 1768-71*, ed. W. J. L. Wharton (London: Elliot Stock, 2005), pp.1102-3; Scholefield, p.121.
[31] Buick, pp.83-84.
[32] Rutherford, p.31.
[33] Scholefield, pp.101,14; A. Lambourn, *Major Thomas Bunbury: Envoy Extraordinary, New Zealand's Soldier-treatymaker* (Heritage Press, 1995), p.71.
[34] Moon, *Fatal Frontiers: A New History of New Zealand in the Decade Before the Treaty*, pp.175-77,91.
[35] Buick, p.202.
[36] Peter Low, "Bishop Pompallier and Te Tiriti," in *The French place in the Bay of Islands : essays from Pompallier's printery (Te urunga mai o te iwi Wiwi)*, ed. Kate Martin and Brad Mercer (Mātou Matauwhi, 2011), p.122,210-13.
[37] Jessie Munro, "Colin and Pompallier and the Founding of the Catholic Church in New Zealand," in *Catholic Beginnings in Oceania: Marist Missionary Perspectives*, ed. A Greiler (ATF Press, 2009), pp.65-85.
[38] King, p.170.
[39] See Introduction.

Chapter Two

[1] Hansard, New Zealand, (UK Parliament, 1840). The Western model of ownership – once introduced to New Zealand – was not forgotten. It still arises in claims to title or possession of the seabed, airwaves and water in a manner that could never have been foreseen when the British first used the concept to secure land for colonisation.

[2] Hansard, pp.524-45 (1840).

[3] T.L. Buick, *New Zealand's First War: Or, the Rebellion of Hone Heke* (Cambridge University Press, 2011), p.3. New Zealand historian Lindsay Buick writing in 1926 largely supported this view when he attributed the impetus for colonisation to the French threat and 'the pressure of social unrest'.

[4] "The French New Zealand," *The New Zealand Journal* (London), Saturday, February 22 (1840), p.18. Sailing dates taken from Tremewan, p.46,80.

[5] Orange, p.18.

[6] Belich, p.338.

[7] "The French New Zealand." Reprinted in New Zealand: "The French In New Zealand," *New Zealand Gazette and Wellington Spectator*, 11 July 1840. p.4. This was a good fit with the Church Missionary Society's ideas on artisans being employed to civilise the natives.

[8] Tremewan, pp.82,89.

[9] "Untitled," *New Zealand Gazette and Britannia Spectator*, 22 August 1840, p.2.

[10] "Untitled," *New Zealand Gazette and Wellington Spectator*, 29 August 1840. p.2

[11] "Untitled," *New Zealand Gazette and Britannia Spectator*, 5 September 1840, p.2.

[12] Orange, p.92.

[13] Scholefield, p.116-17; Lambourn, p.81.

[14] "Proclamation," *New Zealand Advertiser and Bay of Islands Gazette*, 19 June 1840, Advertisements Column 1 ; Rutherford, pp.7, 23-24,39.

[15] Orange, pp.79-80,82,85. There was confusion as both Bunbury and Hobson issued proclamations without either man being aware that they were replicating the actions of the other.

[16] Rutherford, pp.24-27.

[17] William Hobson, Governor Hobson's Letterbook: 25 April - 1 December 1840, Archive Reference No IA4 300, Item Reference 305, Outward Letterbook., New Zealand Archives, pp.28-29. Original documents have been transcribed by the author. Unreadable words shown by a (?) query.

[18] Hobson: pp.34-35.

[19] Proclamations, 1840 Blue Book of Statistics. Dated 21st May 1840 and transmitted to England 12th June 1840.

[20] Scholefield, p.128.

[21] William Hobson, Accession No: 36, Class: G No. 25/1, Ordinary despatches to the colonial office, 16 Feb 1840 – 28 August 1843, 2, pp.16-17, Archives New Zealand.

[22] Waitangi Tribunal, Rekohu: A Report on Moriori and Ngati Mutunga Claims in the Chatham Islands, ; Michael Belgrave, "Looking Forward: Historians and the Waitangi Tribunal," *New Zealand Journal of History* 40, no. 2 (2006): pp.230-50, This Tribunal report has been used because it draws on legal, archival and Māori records as sources and it specifically refers to the South Island claim.

[23] Buick, *The Treaty of Waitangi: How New Zealand Became a British Colony*, p.215.

[24] Buick, *The Treaty of Waitangi: How New Zealand Became a British Colony*, pp.248-49.

[25] William Hobson, No. 16. — Proclamation In The Name Of Her Majesty Victoria, Queen Of The United Kingdom Of Great Britain And Ireland, By William Hobson, Esquire, A Captain In The Royal Navy, Lieutenant-Governor Of New Zealand, 1840, A Compendium Of Official Documents Relative To Native Affairs In The South Island, Volume One. MACKAY, Alexander, 1833-1909, comp. 1873, p.26, The Alexander Turnbull Library Wellington. This copy is in turn cited as: 'Reproduced from the original by permission of the Public Record Office authorities, London'.

[26] "Proclamation: William Hobson," *New Zealand Advertiser and Bay of Islands Gazette*, 19 June 1840, p.1.

[27] Lambourn, pp.82,91; Buick, *The Treaty of Waitangi: How New Zealand Became a British Colony*, pp.233,40; Rutherford, pp.64-65. Orange, p.82. Rutherford states that this proclamation added 'nothing legally' to Hobson's proclamation of 21 May 1840. Sovereignty over both the South Island and Stewart Island was gained by an indeterminate mix of Māori consent, discovery and settlement.

[28] Ordinary Inward Despatches from the Secretary of State: 9 December 1840–16 February 1841, G1/1 Container Code: C484 037, Archives Reference No: G1 1, R 2 606 998, , Enclosure 12/47, pp.203-06, Archives New Zealand, Wellington.

[29] Ordinary Inward Despatches from the Secretary of State: 9 December 1840–16 February 1841: pp.211-14.

[30] Ordinary Inwards Despatches from the Secretary of State: 30 July– 30 December 1844, Container: C 484 016, Archive Ref. No: G1 12, R 2 607 009, pp.927-34, Archives New Zealand, Wellington.

[31] Tremewan, p.49.

[32] Inquirer, "Correspondence: To the Editor of the 'Nelson Examiner.' Nelson May 24," *Nelson Examiner and New Zealand Chronicle*, 5 June 1861, p.4.

[33] Written for the Herald, "To The Nations," *New Zealand Herald*, 6 April 1869, p.5.

[34] Buick, *The Treaty of Waitangi: How New Zealand Became a British Colony*, pp.284,86-88.

[35] Tremewan, pp.109-11.

[36] Tremewan, p.50. Tremewan described Lavaud as 'a very experienced naval officer'.

[37] New Zealand Gazette And Wellington Spectator.

[38] , *New Zealand Gazette And Wellington Spectator*, 16 February 1842, p.2.

[39] "Nelson News," *New Zealand Gazette And Wellington Spectator*, 24 September 1842, p.3.

[40] Hobson: pp.3-5.

[41] Hobson: p.17.

Chapter Three

[1] "English Good Feeling to France," New Zealand Colonist and Port Nicholson Advertiser, 9 December 1842, p.4.

[2] "The Fire at Auckland," New Zealand Gazette And Wellington Spectator, 30 April 1842, p.3.

[3] "Died at Akaroa," New Zealand Colonist and Port Nicholson Advertiser, 23 December 1842, p.3.

[4] "Coporation Dinner," *New Zealand Gazette and Wellington Spectator* 20 May 1843, pp.2-3.

[5] William P Ryan, "Correspondence," *Nelson Examiner And New Zealand Chronicle*, 15 July 1843, p.283.

[6] Belich, p.205. "Narrative Of The Wairau Massacre, And Proceedings Connected Therewith," *Nelson Examiner And New Zealand Chronicle*, 23 December 1843, pp.1,8. The 'Wairau Incident' was provoked by illegal surveying on Māori land. After burning the surveyors' huts, the Māori owners were confronted and fired upon. A prominent chief's wife was killed. Māori avenged the death by killing the settlers/surveyors consistent with Māori custom.

[7] "Narrative Of The Wairau Massacre, And Proceedings Connected Therewith," p.8.

[8] "Narrative Of The Wairau Massacre, And Proceedings Connected Therewith," p.8.

[9] "Address From The Inhabitants Of Kouorarika To Capt. Lavaud," *New Zealand Gazette And Wellington Spectator*, 30 April 1842, p.2.

[10] King, p.184. Walker, pp.102-03. Orange. Claudia Orange provides a detailed discussion on the interpretations of the terms governance and sovereignty as they were translated and used in the Treaty.

[11] Reeves, p.164.

[12] "Important News: Latest Intelligence of Heki," *Nelson Examiner And New Zealand Chronicle*, 26 July 1845, p.83.

[13] R. Burrows, *Extracts from a Diary Kept by the Rev. R. Burrows During Heke's War in the North in 1845* (Upton, 1886), pp.6,8.

[14] P. Moon, *Hone Heke: Nga Puhi Warrior* (David Ling Pub., 2001), p.42.

[15] Wards, p.135.

[16] Burrows, pp.47.

[17] Wards, p.135.

[18] Fitzroy, Duplicate outwards despatches to the Secretary of State 1840-1861, "Duplicate outwards despatches to the Secretary of State 7 September – 31 December 1884(sic, date is clearly an error)," 1844, C 495 253, R3796085, Archives New Zealand, 16585: pp.104-22, G30, Wellington.

[19] Fitzroy: pp.104-22.

[20] "Success and Amicable Settlement of the Native Disturbance at the Bay of Islands," *Daily Southern Cross*, 7 September 1844. This article was reprinted in several New Zealand papers.

[21] Fitzroy: p.155.Despatch No. 34 of 29 September 1844.

[22] George Clarke, "Bay of Islands Disturbance", 30 September 1844 I A 1 R23520311 No. 44/2055, 1849/158. Items redated in pencil.

[23] Fitzroy to Secretary of State, Duplicate outwards despatches to the Secretary of State 1840-1861, "Duplicate outwards despatches to the Secretary of State 1 January – 7 September 1845," February 24th 1845 1845, C 495 254, R3796085, Archives New Zealand, 16585: pp. 253-57, G30 7, Wellington. Fitzroy to Stanley, February 24th 1845.

[24] http://www.archway.archives.govt.nz/ search terms 'Pompallier' filtered '1838–1868, downloaded 10 January 2013. Archway has 173 individual records. Some are letters to or from the Bishop, others simply mention him.

[25] Pompallier to Colonial Secretary, Duplicate outwards despatches to the Secretary of State 1 January – 7 September 1845, 4th April 1845, C 495 254, R3796085, Archives New Zealand, 16585: pp.661-62.

[26] Pompallier to Home, Included in: Duplicate outwards despatches to the Secretary of State 1 January – 7 September 1845, February 24th 1845, C 495 254, Miscellaneous Inwards Letters And Copies Of Outwards Letters [Record Group](16569), R3796085, Archives New Zealand, 16585: pp.656-60.

[27] Buick, *New Zealand's First War: Or, the Rebellion of Hone Heke*, p.180.

[28] Stanley to Grey, Ordinary Inwards Despatches from the Secretary of State – 24 January -23 July 1845, G1 13, R 2 607 010.October, 15th 1845. Pages not numbered.

[29] Grey to Stanley, Ordinary Inwards Despatches from the Secretary of State – 24 January -23 July 1845.

[30]"The French At Tahiti," *Daily Southern Cross*, 13 April 1844, p.2.

[31] "To The Editor Of The New Zealand Spectator: Extract of a Letter from Mr A W Hort dated Tahiti 7th May 1845," *New Zealand Spectator And Cook's Strait Guardian*, 19 July 1845, p.3.

[32]"State Church, Legislative Council," *Daily Southern Cross*, 8 June 1844, p.2.

[33] Buller, pp.295-96.

[34] *New Zealand Spectator And Cook's Strait Guardian*, 13 September 1845, p.2. The former Governor (Fitzroy) had been quoted by the 'New Zealand Journal' in London as referring to the Catholic Bishop and missionaries as agents of the French Government.

[35] *"Nelson Examiner And New Zealand Chronicle," 31 January 1846, p.189.*

Section Two

[1] J.A. Salmond, "New Zealand and the New Hebrides," in *The Feel of Truth: Essays in New Zealand and Pacific History*, ed. Peter Munz (Wellington: A.H. and A.W. Reed, 1969), p.119.

[2] E.W. Said, *Orientalism: Western Conceptions of the Orient* (London: Penguin Books, 1991).

[3] New Zealand Government, "Census Results," (New Zealand Government). Statistics NZ Home > Browse for statistics > Snapshots of New Zealand > Digitised collections. http://www3.stats.govt.nz/historic_publications/1901-

census/1901-report-on-results-census/1901-report-results-census.html#idpreface_1_1042

[4] New Zealand Government, "New Zealand Official Year Books," (Wellington, 1890-1914). See bibliography for online references.

[5] "A report from the French Consul to the Minister in France," in *60 Years Ago : Celebrating The Anniversary Of Diplomatic Relations Between New Zealand And France* (Wellington, N.Z.: The French Embassy, 2005), p.29. Jessie Munro, "Mother Aubert," in *New Zealand and the French : two centuries of contact*, ed. John Dunmore (Waikanae: Heritage Press, 1997, 2nd., Updated ed), p.93. For New Zealanders the occasional glimpses of the Sisters of Mother Aubert's order with their prams collecting goods for the poor are touching in their simplicity and convey a sympathetic French-related image.

[6] "A report from the French Consul to the Minister in France," pp.29-36. New Zealand Government, "New Zealand Official Yearbook," (Wellington, 1915). http://www3.stats.govt.nz/New_Zealand_Official_Yearbooks/1915/NZOYB_1915.html#idsect1_1_115843. Trade statistics from1914 are reflective of the pattern seen in the preceding twenty years. The vast bulk of the £26,261,447 of New Zealand exports went to the United Kingdom (£21,383,891 or 81%). Imports from the United Kingdom, valued at £11,985,946, were 56% of the total. Additional trade via the United Kingdom hub was not recorded.

[7] Michael King, *God's Furthest Outpost: A History of Catholics in New Zealand* (Auckland: Penguin Books, 1997). The frontispiece quotation from Father Theo Wanders MHM refers to his transfer to New Zealand. He uses the term 'farthest' to mean the farthest place from Europe. Such descriptions of distance were common. Tom Brooking, *Richard Seddon : King of God's Own : The Life and Times of New Zealand's Longest-serving Prime Minister* (Auckland: Penguin, 2014), p.28. Seddon referred to migrating via '… the world's longest sea journey to the "farthest promised land"'. James Belich, *Paradise Reforged : A History of the New Zealanders from the 1880s to the Year 2000* (Auckland, N.Z.: Penguin Press, 2001), p.86, p.237. Salmond, p.133. Salmond attributed New Zealand's concerns regarding the French to the realisation that New Zealand and Australia were part of the Pacific world.

[8] Felicity Barnes, *New Zealand's London : A Colony and its Metropolis* (Auckland, N.Z. : Auckland University Press, 2012), p.7. W. H. Oliver and Massey University College of Manawatu., *The inadequacy of a dependent Utopia : the Anderson memorial lecture* ([Hamilton, N.Z.]: Published by Paul's Book Arcade for the Massey University of Manawatu, 1964), p.7. This concept was also mentioned by W.H. Oliver when he said, 'London has been our sole metropolis…'

[9] Glen O'Hara, "New Histories of British Imperial Communication and the 'Networked World' of the 19th and Early 20th Centuries," *History Compass* 8, no. 7 (2010): p.612,; Frances Steel, *Oceania Under Steam : Sea*

Transport and the Cultures of Colonialism, c.1870-1914 (New York: Manchester University Press, 2011), p.9. Steel refers to the possibility of further examining '...the ways in which transport operations were vital to the formation and maintenance of regional colonial history'. I would put it more broadly to include the idea that innovations in communications were what counted. Trade was a by-product or indeed a volumetric gauge of the magnitude of bilateral relationships. P. M. Kennedy, "Imperial Cable Communications and Strategy, 1870-1914," *The English Historical Review* 86, no. 341 (1971): p.121, Kennedy claims that the French considered cable communications more important than the Navy to the UK's power.

[10] This is not to overlook the many extra-Imperial interactions such as the rejected proposal to become part of the Australian Federation and attempts to build a greater New Zealand presence in the Pacific through annexation and Treaty.

[11] Brian P. Farrell, "Coalition of the Usually Willing: The Dominions and Imperial Defence, 1856-1919," in *Imperial Defence: The old world order 1856-1956*, ed. Greg Kennedy (London: Routledge, 2008), p.258.

[12] Ged Martin, "Was There a British Empire?," Article, *Historical Journal* 15, no. 3 (1972): p.562,

[13] Robert A Huttenback Lance E Davis, *Mammon and the pursuit of Empire: The political economy of British imperialism, 1860-1912*, Online ed. (Cambridge: Cambridge University Press, 1 February 2015, 1986), p.7.

[14] Claire Tomalin, *Samuel Pepys: The Unequalled Self* (London: Penguin, 2002), p.144, p.335. Samuel Pepys' diaries provide an insight into a case of the latter in Tangiers. Pepys was part of the expedition sent to destroy and abandon the colony and naval base that he had helped establish there, in favour of a better Mediterranean alternative: Gibraltar.

[15] K. R. Howe, *Singer In A Songless Land : A Life Of Edward Tregear, 1846-1931* (Auckland [N.Z.]: Auckland University Press, 1991), p.61.

[16] Farrell, p.258.

[17] W. David McIntyre, *The Britannic Vision: Historians and the Making of the British Commonwealth of Nations, 1907-48* (Basingstoke: Palgrave Macmillan, 2009), p.21.

[18] George Peden, "The Treasury and Defence of Empire," in *Imperial Defence: The old world order 1856-1956*, ed. Greg Kennedy (London: Routledge, 2008), pp.73-74. This argument was self-fulfilling as during World War I the Empire did prove to be a strategic asset for the supply of raw materials, manufacturing capacity and manpower.

[19] Unattributed, "The Queen's Empire: A Pictorial and Descriptive Record (1897) " in *Politics and Empire in Victorian Britain : A Reader*, ed. Antoinette M. Burton (New York: Palgrave, 2001), pp.278-79. This essay promoted the model of 'Englishmen' (sic) scattered throughout the world. One day they may become a separate race but that would be far in the future owing to the 'ingrained ... qualities inherent in the blood...'. Other races and cultures were simply a pleasant diversion to the mono-Anglo

culture; John Griffiths, *Imperial Culture in Antipodean Cities, 1880-1939* (Basingstoke: Palgrave Macmillan, 2014), pp.1-2.

[20] Brooking, p.335. 'Our' in this context means 'we British', not 'we New Zealanders'.

[21] Keith McClelland and Sonya Rose, "Citizenship and empire, 1867-1928," in *At home with the empire : metropolitan culture and the imperial world*, ed. Catherine Hall and Sonya O. Rose (Cambridge, UK ; New York: Cambridge University Press, 2006), pp.175-76.

[22] Barnes, p.7.; Peden, pp.74-75.

[23] Andrew Lambert, "The Royal Navy and the Defence of Empire, 1856-1918," in *Imperial Defence: The old world order 1856-1956*, ed. Greg Kennedy (London: Routledge, 2008), pp.114-16.

[24] Isabelle Tombs and Robert Tombs, *That Sweet Enemy : the French and the British from the Sun King to the Present* (London: William Heinemann, 2006), p.432, pp.36-37.

[25] T. G. Otte, "The Foreign Office and the Defence of Empire 1856-1914," in *Imperial Defence: The Old World Order: 1856-1956*, ed. Greg Kennedy (London: Routledge, 2008), p.18.

[26] Peden, p.74.

[27] Farrell, p.266-67; New Zealand Government, Correspondence Between The Rt. Hon. The Premier And The Chief Hansard Reporter. Relative To Letters Written By The Latter Commenting On The Despatch Of Contingents To The Transvaal, pp.2-3 (Wellington: Appendix to the Journals of the House of Representatives, 1900 Session I, H-29, 1900, 1900). J. Grattan Grey, Chief Hansard Reporter, had written an article published in the *New York Times* that criticised New Zealand's hasty offer of assistance and the despatch of troops. At issue was whether he did so in a private capacity.

[28] Farrell, p.267. 'Imperial duty forced New Zealand to act'. Seddon in Brooking's view, '…had little alternative but to support the British case…'. The motivation was both an enhanced standing for New Zealand and economic (trade) while currying support for New Zealand's Pacific ambitions. Brooking, pp.304-06; King, *The Penguin History of New Zealand*, p.286. King, in common with other general New Zealand histories, does not address what constituted defending a colony as opposed to suppressing what could be seen as either a colonial rebellion or a fight for independence.

[29] Brooking, pp. 300-01.p.309. Brooking refers to Seddon establishing links with the 'ruling classes' during his UK visit. The latter apparently had doubts about the ability of Seddon and his colonial brethren to govern others. Otte, p.13-15.

[30] Christopher Clark, *The Sleepwalkers: How Europe Went to War in 1914* (New York: Harper Perennial, 2014), pp.300-01. Clark requoting Raymond Poincaré.

[31] Clark, pp.211-13. Otte, p.15. For example the Colonial Office 'worked' on the Australian Government to accept the Anglo-French agreement made by the Foreign Office to settle the New Hebrides dispute.

Chapter Four

[1] Christopher M. Andrew, *Théophile Delcassé and the making of the Entente Cordiale: a reappraisal of French foreign policy 1898-1905* (London: Macmillan, 1968), pp.27,31. Demography, economic growth and technological progress now shows that the world is not a zero-sum system wherein one country's progress must be equalled by another's (territorial) losses.

[2] James F. McMillan, *Twentieth Century France: Politics and Society 1898-1991* (New York: Routledge, 1992; repr., 1992), p.42; John Keiger, "How the Entente Cordiale Began," in *Cross Channel Currents: 100 Years of the Entente Cordiale*, ed. Richard Mayne, Douglas Johnson, and Robert Tombs (London: Routledge, 2004), p.6.; Tombs and Tombs, p.443. Fashoda could have met the needs of both countries, if national pride would allow it.

[3] Jerome Greenfield, "Gabriel Hanotaux and French Grand Strategy, 1894–8," *The International History Review* (2015): p.3,

[4] E. Berenson, "Fashoda, Dreyfus, and the myth of Jean-Baptiste Marchand," in *Yale French Studies* (2007), Article, pp.135-36. Clark.pp.132-5, pp.190-196. Théophile Delcassé on becoming Minister of Foreign Affairs in 1898 attempted to reorder the directionless state of French foreign affairs that had resulted from the domestic political turmoil. Greenfield, p.1.

[5] Clark, pp.132-35.

[6] Greenfield, pp.14-15.

[7] Berenson, "Fashoda, Dreyfus, and the myth of Jean-Baptiste Marchand," p.131, 32, 37-38.

[8] S. J. Potter, "Jingoism, public opinion, and the new imperialism: Newspapers and imperial rivalries at the fin de siècle," Article, *Media History* 20, no. 1 (2014): pp.34-36,

[9] Potter, pp.37-38.

[10] Andrew, p.93.

[11] In that respect the narrative succeeded, as the term 'Fashoda' was used extensively in advertising thus perpetuating memories of the incident beyond the immediate events.

[12] Berenson, "Fashoda, Dreyfus, and the myth of Jean-Baptiste Marchand," p.130.

[13] McMillan, p.42.; Keiger, p.6.; Tombs and Tombs, p.443.

[14] J.A. Hobson pointed out the dangers of imperial territorial acquisitions in 1902 when he referred to the influence of competitive imperialism in Asia and Africa in creating antagonism based on material gain through acquisition of territory, resources and markets. J. A. Hobson, "Imperialism: A Study (1902)," in *Politics and empire in Victorian Britain : a reader*, ed. Antoinette M. Burton (New York: Palgrave, 2001), p.305.; John

Cunningham Wood, "J. A. Hobson and British Imperialism," *American Journal of Economics and Sociology* 42, no. 4 (1983),

[15] William Hobson's announcement at Waitangi in 1840 can probably be interpreted in this context: 'now we are one people' meant (in his century) one people within the British Empire but each in their ordered place socially and geographically, not only in New Zealand, but elsewhere in the world.

[16] The indigenous population were either irrelevant bystanders or victims of French barbarity in the news reports. After the Indian Mutiny (1857) and 'New Zealand Waikato Wars' (1863) (sic) there was a tendency to hold a more combative and less tolerant attitude towards indigenous people amongst settler populations. The consequences were a shared culture/political base between colonial settlers and the metropolitan middle-class British to the exclusion of 'natives' and the 'undeserving poor'. McClelland and Rose, p.272.

[17] For example, M. Delcassé was quoted as refuting suggestions that Marchand was acting for the French Government; he was '... merely an emissary of civilisation'. "An Assurance," *Nelson Evening Mail*, 11 October 1898, p.2; "Editorial Notes and Comments," *Oamaru Mail*, 12 October 1898. p.1.

[18] "British and French Interests," *Marlborough Express* (Marlborough), 12 November 1897, p.2. The use of the term 'native' is a deliberate reflection of the language of the times and is not used to provoke cultural sensitivities.

[19] "The Fashoda Treaty Denied," *Marlborough Express*, 11 October 1898, p.2.

[20] "Current Topics," *Star*, 26 February 1898, p.7.

[21] "Topics of the Day," *Press*, 26 February 1898, p.7.

[22] "British and French Interests," p.2.

[23] Berenson, "Fashoda, Dreyfus, and the myth of Jean-Baptiste Marchand," p.137.

[24] "Britain Warns France," *Otago Witness*, 18 November 1897, p.19.

[25] Typically the public was not invited to consider other points of view, an approach that was to subsequently become useful when it became expedient to change the status of France to that of a friend. See: "The Outside World," *The Daily Telegraph*, 3 January 1898, p.2.; *The Daily Telegraph* was described as a paper with 'a liberal political stance [advocating] equal rights and opportunities for all' See: "Daily Telegraph (Description)," in *Papers Past* (Undated, Wellington: National Library, 3 April 2015).

[26] During this period Balfour was Leader of the House of Commons and First Lord of the Treasury, but not Prime Minister. In Salisbury's absences, through illness and overseas travel, he was also given charge of the Foreign Office. Ruddock Mackay and H. C. G. Mathew, "Balfour, Arthur James. First Earl of Balfour (1848-1930)," in *Oxford Dictionary of National Biography*, ed. Lawrence Goldman (Oxford: Oxford University Press, 2011). "Home and Foreign," *Ashburton Guardian*, 12 January 1898, p.3.

[27] "Race for an Empire," *Auckland Star*, 11 March 1898, p.2.

[28] "Fashoda Incident," *Poverty Bay Herald*, 14 September 1898, p.2.

[29] "British and Foreign," *West Coast Times*, 19 September 1898, p.2.

[30] "At Home and Abroad," *The Daily Telegraph*, 17 September 1898, p.2.

[31] "At Home and Abroad," *The Daily Telegraph*, 6 October 1898, p.2.

[32] "Race for the White Nile," *Wanganui Herald*, 23 February 1898, p.2; "Current Topics," *Star*, 3 March 1898, p.2. "Home and Foreign Cable News," *Oamaru Mail*, 10 March 1898, p.3; "Passing Notes," *Otago Daily Times*, 24 September 1898, p.2.; "France," Editorial, *Northern Advocate*, 24 September 1898, p.2.

[33] "Cable News," *Grey River Argus*, 15 April 1898, p.2.

[34] "The French in the Soudan (sic)," *The Colonist*, 19 September 1898, p.2. During his Egyptian service Kitchener is often referred to as the 'Sirdar', a local native military rank, rather than by name. "Soudan: The Advance on Fashoda," *Press*, 19 September 1898, p.5; "The Soudan Campaign," *Marlborough Express*, 27 September 1898, p.2.

[35] "Summary Notes," *The Colonist*, 27 September 1898, p.2.

[36] "Editorial Notes and Comments," *Oamaru Mail*, 28 September 1898, p.1.

[37] "France's Weakness at Fashoda," *Evening Post*, 28 September 1898, p.5. The Triple Alliance consisted of Germany, the Austro-Hungarian Empire and Italy. The three Powers no doubt observed with interest the bumbling French performance, both diplomatically and on the ground.

[38] "French Claims to Fashoda," *Thames Advertiser*, 30 September 1898, p.2.

[39] "Passing Notes," *Otago Daily Times*, 1 October 1898, p.2. Salisbury was United Kingdom Prime Minister 1895–1902. Paul Smith, "Cecil, Robert Arthur Talbot Gascoyne-, Third Marquess of Salisbury (1830–1903)," in *Oxford Dictionary of National Biography*, ed. Lawrence Goldman (Oxford: Oxford University Press, 2004).

[40] The need for living space for a growing population justified colonisation. Hence with a falling population the legitimacy of French colonial ambitions was in question. "Pater Chats With the Boys," *Otago Witness*, 6 October 1898, p.57.

[41] "Passing Notes," p.2.

[42] "As You Like It," *Taranaki Herald*, 26 September 1898, p.3.

[43] Potter, pp.40-41. One definition of 'the public', prior to the widespread distribution of newspapers, was everyone except manual labourers. Laurence Guymer, "Pressing the French and defending the Palmerstonian line: Lord William Hervey and The Times, 1846-8," Article, *Historical Research* 87, no. 235 (2014): p.116, 18; Caroline Sumpter, "The cheap press and the 'reading crowd'," *Media History* 12, no. 3 (2006/12/01 2006): pp.239-40, The role of the press in debating and developing opinion was much discussed in the late nineteenth century as was the issue of who led opinion and who followed on issues of the day.

[44] Guymer, pp.125,31-33. Although from an earlier period, the Spanish Marriage issue is a fascinating case study of three loci (within the debate) of press, public and politicians.

[45] Robin Neillands, *The Old Contemptibles: The British Expeditionary Force, 1914* (London: John Murray 2008), p.41; Adrian Bingham, "The Daily Mail and the First World War," Article, *History Today* 63, no. 12 (2013): p.1,

[46] Keith M Wilson, *Empire and Continent: Studies in British Foreign Policy before 1914* (London and New York: Mansell, 1987), p.31,36. Despite a Technical Note to the contrary the Foreign Office restricted access to the 1881 Blue Books but granted preferential access to official papers and communications to the (presumably favourable) *Daily Mail* and *Daily Express*.

[47]Advertising was most frequent in Auckland (*Auckland Star*), the West Coast of the South Island (*Grey River Argus*), Hawkes Bay (*Hastings Standard*), and the upper half of the South Island (*Marlborough Express* and *Nelson Evening Mail*).

[48] A search similar to the above using the 'illustration captions' options gave a nil result.

[49]"Advertisements," *New Zealand Herald*, 21 September 1901, p.8.

[50] "Wanted," *Auckland Star*, 31 January 1905, Issue 26, Advertisements, p1, Column 6.

[51] "Advertisements," *Grey River Argus*, 21 December 1898, p.3.

[52] "A Sensational Week," *Hastings Standard*, 2 November 1898, p.3.

[53] "Advertisements," *Marlborough Express*, 17 December 1898, p.3. "Advertisements," *Marlborough Express*, 21 April 1899, p.1.

[54] "Advertisements," *Marlborough Express*, 26 June 1899, p.4.

[55] "Advertisements," *Marlborough Express*, 18 May 1899, p.3.

[56] "Disquieting Cables," *The Wanganui Chronicle and Patea-Rangitikei Advertiser*, 16 November 1898, p.2. Peter T. Marsh, "Chamberlain, Joseph (1836–1914)," in *Oxford Dictionary of National Biography*, ed. Lawrence Goldman (Oxford: Oxford University Press, 2004). Chamberlain was Secretary of State for the Colonies. While both he and Salisbury had ambitions for Britain in Africa, Chamberlain was the more hawkish and confrontational towards French ambitions. Hence he is attributing the French retreat to a united front whereas Salisbury attributes the same result to his more diplomatic methods. In fact both approaches played their part.

[57] "Great Britain and France," *Oamaru Mail*, 17 November 1898, p.1.

[58] "War Preparations," 26 October 1898, *New Zealand Herald*, 26 October 1898, p.5.; "Outstanding Questions Between England and France," *Press*, 26 October 1898, p.4.

Chapter Five

[1] "Untitled Leader," *Otago Daily Times*, 22 September 1899, p.4.

[2] Charlotte Lea Klein, "The Dreyfus affair in the British press," *Patterns of Prejudice* 12, no. 2 (1978/01/01 1978): pp.33-39, "Home and Foreign Cable News," *Oamaru Mail*, 2 November 1894, p.2. "A Traitor to His Country," *Feilding Star*, 2 November 1894, p.2; "Treason," *Daily Telegraph*, 2 November 1894.

[3] McMillan, pp.5-7.; Jaap van Ginneken, *Crowds, psychology, and politics, 1871-1899*, Cambridge studies in the history of psychology., (Cambridge [England] ; New York, NY, USA: Cambridge University Press, 1992), pp.214-15.

[4] Christophe Prochasson, "Fashoda and the Boer War," in *Anglo-French attitudes : comparisons and transfers between English and French intellectuals since the eighteenth century*, ed. Christophe Charle, Julien Vincent, and J. M. Winter (Manchester: Manchester University Press, 2007), pp.264-65. A perception that France was under siege over the matter would not have been helped by allegations of British funding for the Dreyfus defence, an accusation that had some truth. Tombs and Tombs, p.426. It can be nothing more than speculation, but Gladstone's bequest to Madame Dreyfus of £6000 may have been a tacit signal across the channel. Gladstone was a complex and controversial politician who was no shrinking violet when it came to publicity. He was displaying both his liberalism and reformist zeal in his public support for a French woman in such circumstances. See: "A Sympathetic Bequest," *Hawera and Normanby Star*, 6 September 1898, p.2.; H. C. G. Mathew, "Gladstone, William Ewart (1809–1898," in *Oxford Dictionary of National Biography*, ed. Lawrence Goldman (Oxford: Oxford University Press, 2011).

[5] Tombs and Tombs, p.426.

[6] Ginneken, pp.210,14. An important precursor that does not feature in New Zealand press reporting was *Les Deux Frères* (par Louis Létang) published before Dreyfus became a *cause célèbre*. This was a fictional tale that closely followed the real-life story of Dreyfus. It has been suggested that some of those involved were following this script, whether deliberately or through unconscious assimilation, in the controversy that followed.

[7] Robert Tombs, "'Lesser breeds without the law': The British Establishment and the Dreyfus affair, 1894–1899," *The Historical Journal* 41, no. 02 (1998): p.500,

[8] Clark, pp.216-17. McMillan, pp.7-8,13-14,16. Combes had once been rejected by the Church as a candidate for the priesthood. The Left's agenda was a final repudiation of Napoleon Bonaparte's *concordat* with the Church. The Radicals' agenda included hoped-for revenge against Germany for the 1870 loss.

[9] "Editorial: The Charge of the Light Brigade," *The Times* (London), 13 November 1854.

[10] Tombs, pp.497-98; Sumpter, pp.239-40, 42.

[11] "The Dreyfus Case: A Travesty of Justice," *The Daily Telegraph*, 12 February 1898, p.3.; "Astounding Scenes in Court. Evidence Supporting M. Zola.," *Evening Post*, 15 February 1898, p.5.

[12] "The Degradation of Dreyfus," *Tuapeka Times*, 6 March 1895, p.6.

[13] "Topics of the Day," *Press*, 27 December 1894, p.4.; "(Untitled)," *The Southland Times*, 17 January 1898, p.2. A Mr J.G. Cooke, an English lawyer, was credited with investigating and verifying the innocence of Dreyfus in 1898 on behalf of the Dreyfus family.

[14] "French Judicial Methods," *Wanganui Herald*, 4 March 1898, p.2.
[15] "Dreyfus: a Resume," *Oamaru Mail*, 22 February 1898, p.4.
[16] "Passing Notes," *Otago Witness*, 3 March 1898, p.3.
[17] "Captain Dreyfus," *Thames Star*, 13 November 1897, p.1.
[18] "The Personal Premier (Headline but not relevant to this extract).", *Evening Post*, 17 January 1898, p.4.
[19] "Current Topics: The Dreyfus Case," *Star*, 19 July 1898.
[20] "Untitled," *The Grey River Argus*, 3 September 1898, p.2.
[21] "Untitled," p.2.
[22] "Editorial," *The New Zealand Herald and Daily Southern Cross*, 24 February 1898, p.4.
[23] "The Dreyfus Case," *Wairarapa Daily Times*, 6 September 1898, p.2.
[24] "Dunedin Notes," *Tuapeka Times*, 10 September 1898, p.3.
[25] "Turbulent France," *Evening Post*, 17 October 1898, p.4.
[26] "Crisis in France," *New Zealand Herald*, 17 October 1898, p.5.
[27] "Dunedin Notes," p.3.
[28] "At Home and Abroad," *The Daily Telegraph*, 29 September 1898, p.2.
[29] "The Anti-Semitic Movement: Australian Retaliation," *Marlborough Express*, 29 September 1898, p.2.
[30] "The Fate of Dreyfus," *Star*, 13 January 1898, p.1; "Dreyfus," *Auckland Star*, 21 October 1898, p.3.
[31] "Worse than Siberia: The Horrors of a Penal Colony, Fate of Captain Dreyfus," *New Zealand Herald*, 16 March 1895, p.2. Confederation and Annexation. New Hebrides Group and French Convicts, pp.1-8 (Wellington: Appendix to the Journals of the House of Representative, New Zealand Government, Session I, A-03f, 1884). This petition had one of the better summaries of the issues from the Antipodean point of view. The original petition from the Rev. A.J. Campbell, First Convener of the Heathen Mission Committee of the Presbyterian Church of Victoria to Mr Gladstone was reprinted in the New Zealand A to Js.
[32] "Princess Theatre," *Otago Daily Times*, 20 September 1897, p.3.; "George Edwardes 1852-1915," in *The Oxford Companion to Theatre and Performance* (Oxford University Press, 9 January 2016). http://www.oxfordreference.com; "Seymour Hicks (1871-1949)," (Oxford University Press, 9 January 2016). http://www.oxfordreference.com. This production was attributed to George Edwardes and Sir (Edward) Seymour Hicks, United Kingdom-based theatre promoters and show producers.
[33] "Theatre Royal," *Press*, 13 November 1897, p.5.; "Theatre Royal: "One of the Best"," *Hawkes Bay Herald*, 11 February 1898. This report from the *Hawke's Bay Herald* is typical. Although staged in a different theatre, the production had the same promoter and title.
[34] "The Dreyfus Case," *Star*, 20 October 1898, p.2.
[35] "The Dreyfus Case in Wellington," *Wairarapa Daily Times*, 4 March 1898, p.2.
[36] "Table Talk," *Auckland Star*, 24 February 1898, p.1.

[37] Heather Roberts, "Grossman, Edith Searle," in *Dictionary of New Zealand Biography: Te Ara - the Encyclopedia of New Zealand* (1993). Edith Grossmann BA, MA (Hons), née Searle, was one of the earliest New Zealand female scholars. She had strong feminist views, wrote extensively and was, amongst other occupations, a freelance journalist.

[38] Edith H Grossman, "The American in Peace and War," *Star*, 26 September 1898, p.4.

[39] Vigouroux was one of the many social scientists that visited and studied New Zealand as if it were a social laboratory. Described as a representative of the *Musée Social of Paris*, he was part of a mission gathering data on the industrial classes of the world with the objective of developing the emerging social science disciplines into '… an exact science'. His immediate objective was to analyse and exhibit the results of his studies, which included data from South Africa, Australia and New Zealand as well as the USA, at the Paris Exhibition in 1900.
– Comments in a similar vein from Vigouroux: "France and the French: English Ignorance, A Frenchman's Opinion," Interview, *Press*, 3 October 1898, p.3.
– Also: "Special Interviews: Professor Vigouroux and His Mission," *New Zealand Herald*, 26 October 1898, p.3.
–"A Noted Political Economist: Professor Vigouroux on His Way to Paris With Data Concerning Labor Problems," *San Francisco Call* (San Francisco), 18 November 1898, p.2. French diplomats had also been 'surprised' by press reaction in the United Kingdom to Dreyfus.

[40] Martyn Cornick, "The Dreyfus Affair—another year, another centenary. British opinion and the Rennes verdict, September 1899," *Modern & Contemporary France* 7, no. 4 (1999/11/01 1999): p.499, A local reporter would have (understandably) been unaware of the nuances of the French press. Unlike the large, homogenised markets in Britain that supported mass circulation dailies, the French press depended on disaggregated regional and rural markets. Occupational differences led to this disparity. In 1910 most (84%) of British employment was in industry but only 42% of French were similarly occupied.

[41] Jean K. Chalaby, "Twenty years of contrast: the French and British press during the inter-war period," *European Journal of Sociology / Archives Européennes de Sociologie* 37, no. 01 (1996): p.146,; "France and the French: English Ignorance, A Frenchman's Opinion," p.3.

[42] "The Dreyfus Drama: Position of the Anti-Semitic Party, A Frenchman's Ideas," *Press*, 2 September 1899, p.8.

[43] "New Zealand Sympathy for Dreyfus," *Hawke's Bay Herald*, 14 September 1899, p.3.

[44] "Mail Notices. Notice to Correspondents," *Wanganui Herald*, 22 September 1899, p.2.

[45] "Why Dreyfus was Released," *Ohinemuri Gazette*, 23 September 1899, p.2.

[46] "Dreyfus Case: A Policy of Clemency and Oblivion Advocated," *Taranaki Herald*, 23 September 1899, p.2.
[47] Search for 'Dreyfus' filtered for 'Advertising' in selected issues.
[48] "Advertisements," *Press*, 7 September 1898, p.4.
[49] "Mme. Dreyfus *et al*," *Auckland Star*, 5 November 1898, p.7.
[50] "Advertisements," *Ashburton Guardian*, 29 July 1901, p.3.
[51] "Advertisements," *Auckland Star*, 7 October 1901, p.6. "Advertisements," *Auckland Star*, 5 July 1902, p.7. "Advertisements," *Bush Advocate*, 16 November 1899, p.2.
[52] "Advertisements," *Colonist*, 28 September 1899, p.1.
[53] "Advertisements," *Otago Daily Times*, 2 October 1899, p.1.
[54] "Advertisements ", *Star*, 27 February 1899, p.2.
[55] "Advertisements," *Otago Daily Times*, 26 August 1910, p.1.
[56] "Advertisements," *Evening Post*, 28 July 1927, p.2.
[57] "Advertisements," *Auckland Star*, 20 October 1931, p.16.
[58] "Advertisements," *Auckland Star*, 22 October 1931, p.24.
[59] Despite the extensive news coverage, advertising and illustrations related to Dreyfus made up just 5% of the total relevant newspaper content count.
[60] McMillan, pp.42-44.
[61] New Zealand Parliamentary Debates 104: September 13 - October 13, (Hansard, 1898). The index of the cited volume, which covers the period when both events were at their height, was checked.
[62] Lazarus Morris Goldman, *The History of the Jews in New Zealand* (Wellington: Reed, 1958); Leonard Bell and Diana Morrow, *Jewish Lives in New Zealand : A History* (Auckland, N.Z.: Godwit, 2012). A literature search of Jewish history in New Zealand found nothing indicating widespread anti-Semitism in New Zealand society of the period.
"Anti-Chinese," *Daily Telegraph*, 19 May 1888, p.2. Seddon warned the Cook Islands' *ariki* of the dangers of Chinese immigration.
Rognvald Leask, "Britain's Watchdog' in the Pacific? Seddon's Imperialism as Seen by the French," in *New Zealand, France and the Pacific: Studies in New Zealand Culture*, ed. Ian Conrich and Dominic Alessio (Nottingham: Kakapo, c2011), p.31.
[63] "The Crime of the Century," *Wanganui Herald*, 25 February 1898, p.2.

Chapter Six
[1] New Zealand Government, Imperial Naval Conference (Proceedings Of Informal Meeting Of Members Of The House Of Representatives On The Question Of The Representation Of New Zealand At The). p.3-4 (Wellington: Appendix to the Journals of the House of Representatives, 1909 Session I, A-05, 1909). Michael Bassett, *Sir Joseph Ward : A Political Biography* (Auckland, N.Z.: Auckland University Press, 1993), pp.174-5. The New Zealanders' sense of isolation and remoteness led to demands for visible signs that they were defended. Press reports of external threats, together with investment in defence, validated local fears and stimulated the anxiety used to justify defence spending. Michael Bassett

attributed the dreadnought offer to domestic political considerations and Ward's desire to boost his standing within the Empire.

[2] Kennedy, Greg. "Introduction: The Concept of Imperial Defence." In Imperial Defence: The Old World Order 1856-1956, edited by Greg Kennedy, 1-7. London: Routledge, 2008.

[3] O'Hara, pp.612,16. Lambert, Andrew. "The Royal Navy and the Defence of Empire, 1856-1918." In Imperial Defence: The Old World Order 1856-1956, 111-32.

[4] As well as the general histories of Sinclair and King the following were particularly useful: W. David McIntyre, *Dominion of New Zealand: Statesmen and Status 1907-1945* (Wellington: New Zealand Institute of International Affairs, 2007); Farrell, Brian P. "Coalition of the Usually Willing: The Dominions and Imperial Defence, 1856-1919." In Imperial Defence: The Old World Order 1856-1956, pp.251-302.

[5] Tombs and Tombs, p.340.

[6] "Channel Tunnel," *Poverty Bay Herald*, 9 February 1907, p.6.The importance of physical isolation was not as extraordinary as it sounds today. France, it was reported in 1907, was in favour of a channel tunnel with all its benefits of rapid transport, tourism and economic growth. The English, this requoted French newspaper leader claimed, were not in favour because there would be an influx of French people eager to come to London. As a consequence, there would be interbreeding and thus the Anglo-Saxon race would be transformed with a deleterious effect on the British race.

[7] H. C. G. Mathew, "Edward V11 (1841–1910), King of the United Kingdom of Great Britain and Ireland, and the British Dominions Beyond the Seas, and Emperor of India " in *Oxford Dictionary of National Biography* (Oxford: Oxford University Press, 2004-2014).

[8] Andrew, pp.203-07. His position appears to have been heavily influenced by the success of the Egypt–Morocco trade-off in the aftermath of Fashoda, although the '…traumatic experience of the Boer War' was a decisive influence from the English side.

[9] Keiger, p.5.

[10] "France," *New Zealand Illustrated Magazine*, 1 May 1903., p.159; "King Edward in Paris," *Wairarapa Times*, 4 May 1903, p.3; "The King's Tour," *Bay of Plenty Times*, 4 May 1903, p.2.

[11] "The Royal Tour," *Marlborough Express*, 4 May 1903, , p.2; "His Majesty's Visit to France," *Wanganui Herald*, 2 May 1903, p.5.

[12] "King Edward in Paris," p.3.

[13] "The French President's Visit To England," *Wanganui Herald*, 1 July 1903, p.5.

[14] "President Loubet's Visit to London," *Marlborough Express*, 8 July 1903, p.3; "King and President," *Wairarapa Daily Times*, 8 July 1903, p.3.

[15] "Gallicised London," *Press*, 19 August 1903, p.6.

[16] Tombs and Tombs, p.442; "Anglo-French Agreement," *Otago Daily Times*, 31 October 1903, p.9. Owing to differences in publication dates and

news being received from Britain there is ambiguity in the public record as to exactly what was agreed and when; the *Entente* was not signed until 8 April 1904.

[17] Tombs and Tombs, p.441. Interviews published in *Liberte* quoted in: "French Opinion of King Edward's Visit," *Auckland Star*, 5 June 1903, p.8. *Die Zeit, Vienna* quoted in "Local and General," *Wanganui Herald*, 12 June 1903, p.4.

[18] "The Empire's Guest," *Wanganui Herald*, 8 July 1903, p.5.

[19] "France and Great Britain," *Marlborough Express*, 9 July 1903, p.2.

[20] "England and France," *Press*, 10 July 1903, p.4.

[21] "Britain and France," *Ashburton Guardian*, 5 May 1903, p.2. Probably aimed at *Truth*.

[22] "King Edward On Tour," *Feilding Star*, 5 May 1903, p.2..

[23] "Editorial Notes and Comments," *Oamaru Mail*, 6 May 1903, p.1.

[24] "It is Significant: Cable Coddling," Editorial, *Free Lance*, 11 July 1903, p.8. According to the Papers Past Website: 'The *Free Lance* was one of New Zealand's most popular weekly, pictorial newspapers. It was first published in Wellington in 1900 by Geddis and Blomfield as a spin-off from their successful Auckland weekly, the *NZ Observer and Free Lance*. The publishers split the title, with the Auckland paper becoming the *NZ Observer* and the Wellington paper taking the name *Free Lance*'.

[25] "Untitled," *Press*, 1 June 1912, p.10. During a visit to Auckland the British Ambassador to the USA (Rt. Hon. James Bryce) commented that New Zealanders '...know more about what is happening at Home than the Home people do about colonial affairs...'.

[26] Mervyn J. Stewart, "Correspondence: Splendid Isolation," *Bay of Plenty Times*, 1 June 1903, p.2. Stewart was a prominent Bay of Plenty citizen.

[27] "London Letter," Editorial/Opinion Piece, *Poverty Bay Herald*, 27 August 1903, p.1. This editorial quoted the *Spectator* and unnamed Paris journals. In a wide-ranging review of current affairs, the Irish question and British antagonism towards Germany also received considerable comment.

[28] "Anglo-French Controversies," *The Press*, 7 September 1903, p.4.

[29] "British and Foreign," *Wanganui Chronicle*, 16 May 1903, p.5. Lorin was a prominent left-leaning Catholic and professor who had the ear of the French Government of the day. Requoted in the *Chronicle* from the *Depeche Colonial*. "France and Great Britain," *Evening Post*, 22 May 1903, p.4.

[30]"Anglo-French Entente Cordial: The Recent Commercial Treaty," *Evening Post*, 16 November 1903, p.6. The primary source of these opinions is unclear. This piece is by-lined from San Francisco on 19 October, nearly a month before the NZ publication date. It was received both by telegraph and per the SS *Sierra* 'at Auckland'. The most probable links are by telegraph to a San Francisco paper and thence to New Zealand as hard copy. "The Anglo-French Convention," *The Marlborough Express*, 12 April 1904, p.2; Christopher Andrew and Paul Vallet, "The German Threat," in *Cross Channel Currents: 100 Years of the Entente Cordiale*, ed.

Richard Mayne, Douglas Johnson, and Robert Tombs (London: Routledge, 2004), p.23. At its simplest the *entente* meant that France got Morocco and the United Kingdom got undisputed rights to Egypt. Cod fishing by France off the Newfoundland coast (a perennial issue) was unresolved. The French interpretation went beyond these simple compromises and saw the *entente* as the first step to a Triple Alliance with Russia. Tombs and Tombs, p.442.

[31] Keiger, pp.6-7.

[32] Tombs and Tombs, p.443.

[33] "Imperial Fiscal Question," *Southland Times*, 10 October 1903, p.2. This article, in various forms, was printed in at least twenty New Zealand newspapers.

[34] "The Atlantic Fleet at Brest ", *Daily Mirror*, 14 July 1905, p.8. The symbolism is apparent in the British newspaper illustrations. The joint fleet gathering would be better described as a regatta than a display of maritime military manoeuvres. The *Daily Mirror* used captioned photographs to illustrate the point.

[35] "Under Two Flags - French Fleet's Visit to Portsmouth," *The Daily Mirror*, 7 August 1905, pp.8-9. The return event was '...a formal visit to celebrate the *entente cordiale*'.

[36] Peden, p.74. Terminology used as a diplomatic signal in more recent times include *détente* (with China) as well as *glasnost* and *perestroika* co-opted from their Russian roots to describe a new phase of Soviet–US relations.

[37] Other examples include Sir Joseph Ward being asked about the possibility of an *entente cordiale* with the USA, an agreement between Japanese Government and Opposition being so described and Seddon's appointment of King Mahuta to the Legislative Council, described as symbolic of an *entente cordiale* between 'the Maoris' (sic) and the Government. In 1907 there was an *entente cordiale* between employers and employees. There was an *entente* between Holland and Britain post the Boer War and the phrase was used to describe the developing relationship between France and Japan. Spanish warships being built in British naval yards were the result of an *entente cordiale*. There was even reference to an *entente cordiale* between Tauranga and Te Puke. "British and Foreign," *Poverty Bay Herald*, 19 September 1902, p.3; "Sir Joseph Ward in Christchurch," *Star*, 4 December 1901, p.2; "Various Cabled Items: Japanese Political Parties," *Evening Post*, 26 May 1903, p.5. "Maori and Pakeha," *The Southland Times*, 27 May 1903, p.2. "Trade and Labour Notes," *Auckland Star*, 13 February 1907, p.8. "London Chat: Dutch Heores (sic) in London," *New Zealand Herald*, 20 April 1907, p.5. "Home and Foreign Cables," *Oamaru Mail*, 14 May 1907, p.1; "British and Foreign: The Spanish Navy," *Timaru Herald*, 27 April 1907, p.5.

[38] "Personal Notes," *Bay of Plenty Times*, 5 June 1912, p.4. A belief that France was under British influence is shown in Foreign Secretary Grey's offer to Germany to '... keep France neutral...' in British exchanges with Germany just prior to the war beginning.

[39] Ian McGibbon, " Allen, James," in *Dictionary of New Zealand Biography: Te Ara - the Encyclopedia of New Zealand* (Wellington); "Sir James Allen," *New Zealand Herald* (Auckland), 29 July 1942, p.2. Allen was reportedly an able administrator and capable minister as his senior ministerial postings indicate, but he did not have the charisma of Massey (or Ward). Milton was a small town in Allen's South Otago electorate of Bruce.

[40] Electoral Commission, General Election Results 1890-1993, (Wellington 2013). Massey's Parliamentary majorities were only emphatic on one occasion, and he was therefore acutely aware of the need to maintain electoral support.

[41] "Ministers on Tour: Mr. Massey and Mr. Allen at Milton," *Evening Post*, 19 June 1913, p.10.

[42] J Allen, Ministerial Files - English trip 1913, notes of interviews, (1913), pages not numbered. Allen's bid for a coaling station was rebuffed because 'The whole matter rests on acquiring Rapa from the French…'

[43] "Ministers on Tour: Mr. Massey and Mr. Allen at Milton."

[44] James Allen, Minister of Defence - Naval Defence matters - Memoranda from Hon. James Allen to Ministers (R22319686), D3/6, pages are not numbered. (1912).

[45] "Foreign Alliances and Imperial Defence," *Wairarapa Daily Times*, 24 June 1913, p.4..

[46] "New Zealand History," accessed 26 October 2015, http://www.nzhistory.net.nz/. The United Kingdom population in 1914 was about forty-six million; the French some forty million, Germany sixty-seven million and New Zealand's just over one million.

[47] "Our Merchantmen and Trade Routes," *Dominion*, 3 August 1914. A contemporary view on what was likely to happen if war broke out can be deduced from an a priori discussion on trade. New Zealand in 1914 was, as it is now, reliant on exports and therefore dependent on maritime free passage. Those concerned with commerce take a hard-headed, financially conservative view of threats to their businesses rather than assuming an emotional over-optimistic mindset. The consensus from various (unnamed) industry figures was that in the event of a European war, trade would be curtailed since there would be fewer ships available. Much of the speculation centred on the seasonal nature of the trade. 'New Zealand's busy season as far as her export trade is concerned, does not commence till the end of October or November, and it was held that by that time the supremacy of the seas would probably be settled for many years to come.' Winter being a quieter period it was assumed that any war would be contained in the northern hemisphere and it would be naval, decisive and brief. Although dated 3 August 1914, this article was written in the future tense, thus implying it pre-dated the outbreak of hostilities.

Section Three

[1] "French Mission," *Oamaru Mail*, 8 May 1920, p. 6.

Chapter Seven

[1] André Siegfried, *Post-war Britain : a French analysis*, trans. H. H. Hemming (London: Cape, 1924), p.313.

[2] New Zealand Parliamentary debates v.191: 20th Parliament: 3rd session, p.589 (1921). At issue was the British point of view during the Opium Wars. Atmore was quoting Owen Wister to refute an argument from H.E. (Harry) Holland, the Buller MP and Labour Party Leader.

[3] Billie Melman, *The culture of history : English uses of the past 1800-1953* (Oxford: Oxford University Press, 2006), pp.6-7; Barnes, pp.74-75, 76-77.

[4] Holger Hoock, "Monumental Memories: state commemoration of the Napoleonic wars in early nineteenth-century Britain," in *War memories : the Revolutionary and Napoleonic wars in modern European culture*, ed. Alan I. Forrest, Etienne Francois, and Karen Hagemann (Palgrave Macmillan UK.).

[5] Lars Peters, "Warrior Sailors and Heroic Boys: Images of masculinity in English nautical novels on the revolutionary and Napoleonic wars," in *War Memories : The Revolutionary and Napoleonic Wars in Modern European Culture, War, Culture and Society,1750-1850*, ed. Alan I. Forrest, Etienne Francois, and Karen Hagemann (Basingstoke: Palgrave, 2013), pp.139-42. There is no equivalent study or raw data available for New Zealand apart from published lists of public library purchases. The titles hint at the content but without an in-depth study, the subject(s) cannot always be assumed from the title alone. See for example: "Public Library," *Manawatu Times*, 10 October 1925.

[6] Melman, pp.95, 249.

[7] "Books and Writers," *Northern Advocate*, 27 June 1925, p.9.

[8] "The Dickens Entertainment," *Manawatu Standard*, 17 April 1900, p.2. In one example of the intellectual snobbery that could be associated with these events, the anonymous reviewer mentions but excuses the small audience size as being unrelated to the intellect of Palmerston North's citizens while praising the 'expressive rendering' of the lecturer, the Rev. Charles Clark. Clark was a visiting speaker from Britain, who was touring and speaking in several locations. He also lectured on London's St Paul's, described as the 'heart' of the Empire.

[9] "Napoleon," *Bay of Plenty Times*, 9 December 1924, p.3. This story suggested that although he was Corsican born, Napoleon was not Italian but Greek. The hearsay evidence for this assertion came from an 'old lady' who had conveniently died in 1863.

[10] Melman, pp.29-32

[11] "News and Notes," *Ashburton Guardian*, 3 June 1919, p.5.

[12] "German Bells," *Sun*, 16 July 1918; "German Bells," *Poverty Bay Herald*, 24 July 1918; "The German Bells," *Taranaki Herald*, 13 August 1918; "Timely Topics," *Northern Advocate*, 5 September 1925, p.9.

[13] Melman, pp.45-46.

[14] François Crouzet, "Problems of communication between Britain and France in the nineteenth and twentieth centuries," in *Britain Ascendant : Comparative Studies in Franco-British Economic History*, Editions de la Maison des sciences de l'homme (Cambridge: Cambridge University Press, 1990), pp.470-71.

[15] Dougal McNeill, "Labouring Feeling: Harry Holland's Political Emotions," *The Journal of New Zealand Studies* 21 (2015): footnote 50, 'The clippings filed in Holland's papers at the Turnbull – containing Communist papers, Christian articles, independent socialist publications and more from across the world –give some sense of his eclectic range: ATL MS-Papers-1815–11'.

Patrick O'Farrell, "Holland, Henry Edmund," in *Dictionary of New Zealand Biography* (1996). https://teara.govt.nz/en/biographies/3h32/holland-henry-edmund.; Barry Gustafson, "Massey, William Ferguson," in *Dictionary of New Zealand Biography* (1993 updated 2013). https://teara.govt.nz/en/biographies/2m39/massey-william-ferguson.; Michael Bassett, "Ward, Joseph George," in *Dictionary of New Zealand Biography* (1993). https://teara.govt.nz/en/biographies/2w9/ward-joseph-george. All make the same point. Holland showed 'the marks of a self-taught mind: the compilation of a massive amount of knowledge without selective rigour or analytic penetration'. Although Massey attended a 'private secondary school' he possessed 'an impressive library indicative of his wide reading'. Ward was similarly described as 'read widely throughout his life and [in] his retentive memory stored a broad general knowledge'.

[16] G. Weisz, *The Emergence of Modern Universities In France, 1863-1914* (Princeton: Princeton University Press, 2014), pp.96-97. James Watson and Lachy Paterson, eds., *A great New Zealand prime minister? : reappraising William Ferguson Massey* (Dunedin, N.Z.: Otago University Press, 2011). The background of William Massey typified the image of the self-made man in New Zealand political life during the late nineteenth and early to mid-twentieth century. This distinctly New Zealand characteristic was in part due to a broader electoral franchise compared to that used at Home prior to 1919.

[17] Rosemary Bingham Carol Mutch, Lynette Kingsbury, Maria Perreau, "Political indoctrination through myth building: The New Zealand School Journal at the time of World War 1," *Curriculum Matters*, no. 14 (2018), New Zealand's syllabus was strongly biased towards a pro-Empire stance with all that this implied for a reflected – if unmentioned – version of France.

[18] Roger Openshaw, "Contradiction and contestation: Public education in the interwar period," in *New Zealand between the wars*, ed. Rachael Bell and Massey University Press (Auckland: Massey University Press, 2017), pp.91-93; Roger Openshaw, "The Highest Expression of Devotion: New Zealand Primary- Schools and Patriotic Zeal during the Early 1920s," *History of Education* 9, no. 4 (1980/12/01 1980): pp.343-44, 41,

[19] "Second Referendum on the New Zealand Flag: Final Result," updated 30 March 2016, 2016, accessed 15 February 2019, https://www.electionresults.govt.nz/2016_flag_referendum2/.

[20] Alistair Watts, "Why, when the image of the French in the New Zealand Press 1900-1914 was a divided one, did New Zealand enter World War I allied to France?" (MA 2016).

[21] James Allen, Allen to Massey 14 May 1918, R 223 19675, Miscellaneous files and papers - Allen and WF Massey correspondence 1st September - 1st August 1919, C361 202, pp.3-4, Archives New Zealand.; New Zealand Parliamentary debates v.185: 19th Parliament 6th session, p.162 (1919). Allen reported to Massey that Cabinet was considering asking families to send letters, diaries and other records for later use by an 'editor'. Allen clearly favoured the fallen hero genre as he suggested that Fitchett who had written *Deeds that Won the Empire* would be a suitable chronicler. Another suggested author was Canterbury academic Professor Stewart as he 'has seen service in Gallipoli and France'. Mr Seddon (Westland) queried government policy as far as the conservation and exhibition of films and pictures taken in France and elsewhere for patriotic and other purposes was concerned and asked who was to be in charge of their preservation. New Zealand Parliamentary debates v.186: 20th Parliament 1st session, p.854 (1920). There was political pressure to get these official versions into the public domain. Tom Seddon the Westland MP's query to Sir R.H. Rhodes, the Minister of Defence on 13 September 1920 revealed that Col. Hugh Stewart's *The New Zealanders in France* was already 'with the printers'.

[22] Paul Fussell, *The Great War and modern memory* (New York: Oxford University Press, 1975), p.7 Showing fear was an ever-present risk, as Paul Fussell highlighted when exploring the truths that are concealed when war stories are retold. (Fussell quotes Sassoon's poem 'The Hero' with its reference to 'gallant lies' told to cover for a 'cold footed, useless swine' of a son to make his point). The binary contrast between hero and coward allowed no middle ground in the public imagination.

Paul Fussell, *Doing battle : the making of a skeptic*, 1st ed. (Boston: Little Brown and Co., 1996); Fussell, *The Great War and modern memory*. Jock Phillips, *A man's country? The image of the pakeha male: a history* (Auckland: Penguin, 1987). The soldiers' own letters were understated through censorship and the soldiers' wish to reassure those at home. The importance of censorship, both official (in letters) and self-imposed (continued once home) must be acknowledged, as should the convenient protection this self-imposed taciturnity gave from the fear of describing fear. It was better to say nothing than to admit to having shown fear or acted in anything less than a gallant and heroic manner. Phillips' Kiwi-bloke masculinity has come to typify the rugged, taciturn individuality of the inter-war years' male.

[23] Glyn Harper, ed., *Letters from the battlefield : New Zealand soldiers write home, 1914-18* (Auckland N.Z.: HarperCollins, 2001), p.14.; Phillips,

p.203; Stephen Clarke, *After the war : the RSA in New Zealand* (New Zealand Penguin, 2016), pp.13-16.

[24] "New Zealand in the First World War," New Zealand Electronic Text Collection, Victoria University, accessed 26 June 2016, http://nzetc.victoria.ac.nz/tm/scholarly/tei-corpus-WH1.html. These notes are applicable to the inter-war period, but they omit the more recent (post-2015) centennial publications: 'Unlike after the Second World War, no wide-ranging account of New Zealand's participation in the First World War was prepared at the end of that conflict. Only four official volumes were published (1919–1923), and they were written by senior officers who had fought in the campaigns (Gallipoli, Sinai/Palestine, Western Front) but who generally had no training as historians. Although providing detailed accounts of the fighting on the battlefields itself, they did not describe New Zealand during the war, its economy, politics or society, and the home-defence and patriotic efforts, New Zealanders in the naval or air war, and those serving with other British or Australian forces are not included. Despite this, the four official histories became accepted sources for New Zealand's military effort in the Great War, and have never been updated or superseded.'

The last comment should be read in the context of the qualification implied by 'official' and in the knowledge that there are more recent publications (see Bibliography).

[25] "Regimental Histories," *New Zealand Herald*, 12 October 1922, p.9.

[26] New Zealand Parliamentary Debates 169: 18th Parliament 4th session July 22 - September 15, p.553 (Hansard, 1914). Their destination was presumed to be Europe, but they were sent to the Middle East.

[27] Crouzet, pp.464-502.

[28] Watts.Alistair Watts, "Why, when the image of the French in the New Zealand Press 1900-1914 was a divided one, did New Zealand enter World War I allied to France?" (MA 2016)

[29] This is not to understate the importance of the Gallipoli narrative in New Zealand's war histories but most New Zealanders served in France.

[30] Glyn Harper, *Johnny Enzed : the New Zealand soldier in the First World War 1914-1918*, Online ed., First World War centenary history., (2015), pp.1056-7, 65; A. Maguire, "Looking for home? New Zealand soldiers visiting London during the first world war," Article, *London Journal* 41, no. 3 (2016),

[31] Barnes, pp.54-55.; André Siegfried, William Downie Stewart, and D. A. Hamer, *Democracy in New Zealand*, 2nd ed. (London: Bell, 1914), pp.358-59.

[32] Glenn Reddiex, *Just to let you know I'm still alive : postcards from New Zealanders during the First World War* (Grantham House), p.8. Enthusiasm for collecting and using postcards coincided with the war years. Being unsealed, they were easy for the censors to read. A limited writing space may have been an advantage for the sender who in many cases (one suspects) wanted to say as little as possible about their immediate situation.

[33] James Cowan and New Zealand Maori Regimental Committee, *The Maoris in the great war : a history of the New Zealand Native Contingent and Pioneer Battalion, Gallipoli, 1915 France and Flanders, 1916-1918* (Uckfield: Naval & Military Press, 2006).

[34] Penny Griffith, *Out of the Shadows: The life of Millicent Baxter* (Wellington: PenPublishing, 2015), p.96. Requoted from: *We Will Not Cease*, Archibald Baxter, p.185.

[35] Horopapera Karauti, French post cards, "Unused post cards acquired while on active service in France during World War One. Includes booklets of post cards containing views of the Somme and Boulogne," 1917-1918, 8456-31. Note: I have been unable to obtain permission for reproduction of this series. They are available in the National Library collection.

[36] Greg Hynes, "Picturing the empire: Enduring imperial perceptions and depictions in British first world war photographic propaganda," in *Endurance and the First World War : Experiences and Legacies in New Zealand and Australia*, ed. David Monger, Sarah Murray, and Katie Pickles (Newcastle: Cambridge Scholars, 2014), pp.231-2. Powerful propaganda came from images of German 'barbarity' through association with the destruction of cathedrals and churches. These contrasted with the 'moral, just masculinity' of the Empire troops who were shown alongside women and children.

[37] Patrick Douglas Wood, Letters from Douglas Wood to his sister, Evelyn, "MSPapers8911.

Wood family : Letters from and relating to Patrick Douglas Wood. 19161918, 2007. [Collection]," Jan-June 1917, 8911-2, Wellington, New Zealand, Alexander Turnbull Library.

[38] William Pember Reeves, Account of a visit to France during World War One, "MSPapers0129.

Reeves, William Pember, 18571932: Papers. 1852 [ca 1929].[Collection]," [ca 1919], 0129-33, Alexander Turnbull Library, Wellington, New Zealand.

[39] "Travelling French Scholarship," *Oamaru Mail*, 28 July 1920, p.4.

[40] Harper, *Johnny Enzed : the New Zealand soldier in the First World War 1914-1918*, pp.739, 880, 940-2.

[41] Jane Tolerton, ed., *An awfully big adventure : New Zealand World War One veterans tell their stories* (Auckland, N.Z.: Penguin Books, 2013).

[42] Tolerton, p.176. The tone suggests that this soldier recognised that he and his fellows were the intruders.

[43] Roy Jenkins, *Churchill* (London: Macmillan, 2001), p.297; New Zealand Parliamentary debates v.185: 19th Parliament 6th session, p.1393 (1919). Although this view has been challenged, the case is unconvincing. Undoubtedly there were some close military related exchanges at the individual soldier level. See: Chris Kempshall, "'My Heart Softened to the French ... All at Once I Loved Them': The Entente Cordiale at the Somme," in *British, French and American Relations on the Western Front, 1914–1918* (Cham: Springer International Publishing, 2018).

---

[44] Cecil Malthus, *Armentières and the Somme* (Auckland N.Z.: Reed Publishing (NZ), 2002), p.51, 57. New Zealand Parliamentary debates v.236: 24th Parliament 3rd session, p.188 (1933). Much later the war-wounded veteran Labour MP John A. Lee used embellished, anecdotal accounts such as his tale of throwing a bomb simply to stir things up, to add a hint of frivolity to the record.

[45] Clarke, p.15. The gap between the 'home and away' experience for the home-coming soldiers led to 'awkward silences'.

[46] Harper, *Johnny Enzed : the New Zealand soldier in the First World War 1914-1918*, p.1661.

[47] Anton Oliver, "Anton Oliver," interview by Chris Laidlaw, *Sunday Morning*, 27 July 2008, 2008, http://www.radionz.co.nz/national/programmes/sunday/20080727.

[48] Malthus, p.7 Pugsley notes in his introduction that the private soldier, such as Malthus, wrote from the perspective of one soldier within a platoon of forty to fifty men. This limited perspective gives additional weight to, and understanding of, the private soldier's experience.

[49] Harper, *Johnny Enzed : the New Zealand soldier in the First World War 1914-1918*, pp.1660-80.

[50] Maguire, p.291; Harper, *Johnny Enzed : the New Zealand soldier in the First World War 1914-1918*, p.1518-22; Malthus, p.130.

[51] Malthus, p.33.

[52] Harper, *Johnny Enzed : the New Zealand soldier in the First World War 1914-1918*, p.988; John A Lee, *Civilian into soldier* (London England: May Fair Books, 1963) Lee establishes a hierarchy of womanhood from the lowly occupants of the brothels in Egypt, via the 'French slattern' (less than ideal) to the purity of the English girl. The over-used 'frousy old wowser' cliché was probably meant to describe a plain but disciplined, morally upright mumsy-like matriarchal figure. In the literal meaning the juxtaposition of 'frousy' – meaning a dirty or unclean female – with 'wowser', implying abstention from alcohol use, appears odd.

[53] Tolerton, pp.13-14; Clarke, pp.13-16. The real stories were probably shared in the pubs and the RSA bars but these were usually inaccessible to the historians and politicians.

[54] Alexandre Ryder André Dugès (as André Dugès-Delzescauts), "The Soul of France (La grande épreuve, original title)," (La grande épreuve (original title) 1928), Sound Mix: Silent
Color: Black and White.
http://www.imdb.com/title/tt0018956/?ref_=fn_al_tt_1; Alexandre Ryder and André Dugès, "The Big Test," (April 26, 1928 1927). http://www.cinema-francais.fr/les_films/films_r/films_ryder_alexandre/la_grande_epreuve.htm ; "Figaro-Cinema," *Figaro*, 17 August 1928, p.5; "In Filmland," *New Zealand Herald Supplement*, 10 November 1928, p.9.; "Amusements.," *Bay of Plenty Times*, 13 May 1930, p.3; "Amusements," *Auckland Star*, 7 June 1930, p.13; "Amusements," *Bay Of Plenty Times*, 14 May 1930, p.3.

[55] "Entertainments," *Manawatu Standard*, 15 March 1919, p.6.
[56] "The Picture Houses," *Poverty Bay Herald*, 15 April 1919, p.6.
[57] "Photo-Plays," *Evening Star*, 18 August 1919, p.6.; "The Better 'ole," in *Internet Movie Database* (13 March 2017), Fictional film. http://www.imdb.com/title/tt0009923/.
[58] Maurice Agulhon, *The French Republic, 1879-1992*, English ed., A History of France., (Oxford: B. Blackwell, 1993), pp.168-69; Kempshall, "Careless Disasters: Allied Relations in 1918." Kempshall also discusses the clash between political opinion and democratic rights in wartime conditions. The French, he claims, wanted to hold on until the Americans arrived, rather than attempt to win and risk defeat.
[59] New Zealand Parliamentary debates v.185: 19th Parliament 6th session, p.1370 (1919); J.P.T. Bury, *France, 1814-1940* (Methuen, 1969), pp.247-50. Exactly which of the 1917 battles Bury was referring to is unclear but this was a period within which both the French military and political leadership changed as failure to win the war undermined French morale. The British Empire troops carried the load while the French regrouped.
[60] Jean-Jacques Becker, *The Great War and the French people*, trans. Arnold Pomerans (Oxford: Berg Publishers, 1985), p.325. France held, according to Becker, because 'the national fabric was too firm'. Even people who may have wanted revolution realised this was not the time and the population would not allow it. A deep sense of nationhood – France had been a nation too long to blow apart – meant that despite the weaknesses of low population growth, war damage and a 'vague sense of resignation' in the last year of the war, France held.
[61] Hoock."Monumental Memories: State Commemoration of the Napoleonic Wars in Early Nineteenth-Century Britain." In War Memories : The Revolutionary and Napoleonic Wars in Modern European Culture
[62] "A Heart's New Home," *Evening Post*, 9 November 1929, p.22. Although he regular refused promotion, this Napoleon-favoured hero was an officer rather than a common soldier. His ancestry was probably subject to post hoc adjustment to make him appear to have joined the army as a private soldier and then receive a commission on merit.
[63] These images are reminiscent of the medieval cadaver tombs or transi tombs but without the representation of the decaying cadaver.
[64] Hoock, pp.202-04.
[65] "Obituary," *Evening Post*, 8 April 1935..

Chapter Eight

[1] Watson and Paterson; James Watson, "'The greatest commercial traveller in the Empire': Massey and Trade," in *A great New Zealand prime minister? : reappraising William Ferguson Massey*, ed. James Watson and Lachy Paterson (Dunedin, N.Z.: Otago University Press, 2011). Richard Kray, "Caging the Prussian Dragon: New Zealand and the Paris Peace Conference 1919," in *New Zealand's great war : New Zealand, the Allies and the First World War*, ed. John Crawford and I. C. McGibbon (Auckland, N.Z.:

Exisle Pub., 2007); Keith Sinclair, *A History of New Zealand*, rev. ed. (Auckland: Penguin Books, 2000); King, *The Penguin History of New Zealand*; Rachael Bell, ed., *New Zealand between the wars* (Auckland, New Zealand: Massey University Press, 2017). Neither Sinclair nor King make any substantive comment on the Versailles Treaty. James Watson's biography of William Massey and the various specialist studies covering significant concurrent events such as soldier resettlement, the influenza epidemic and the prohibition debate have only passing references to Versailles. Richard Kray's work stands as an exception to this generalisation.

[2] United Kingdom Government, Versailles Peace Treaty - 1919, "Treaty of Peace between the Allied and Associated Powers and Germany and the Treaty between France and Great Britain signed in Versailles - 28 June 1919," 1919, ACGO 8352 IA20/3/5, R18874438, Archives New Zealand. New Zealand's copy, fittingly unmarked and in pristine condition, is filed without supplementary notes or explanation in the National Archive, suggesting that it was never viewed as a working document.

[3] United Kingdom Government, Anglo-French Treaty (Defence of France) Act, 1919, "Copy of the Treaty setting out UK support for France in the event of hostilities with Germany.," 1919, ACHK 8604 G1/249, R24547991, 1919/2802: Archives New Zealand. Antony Lentin, "The Treaty that Never Was: Lloyd George and the French Connection, 1919," in *Lloyd George and the Lost Peace: From Versailles to Hitler, 1919–1940* (London: Palgrave Macmillan UK, 2001); Antony Lentin, """Une Aberration Inexplicable?" Clemenceau and the Abortive Anglo-French Guarantee Treaty of 1919," Article, *Diplomacy & Statecraft* 8, no. 2 (1997), New Zealand's copy of this Treaty is archived without comment or explanation.

[4] A search of the JSTOR article database found 6586 published articles but only a fraction are recent, i.e. published within the last five years.

[5] New Zealand Parliamentary debates v.182: 19th Parliament 4th session, p.26 (1918).; New Zealand Parliamentary debates v.182: 19th Parliament 4th session, p.168 (1918).

[6] New Zealand Parliamentary debates v.185: 19th Parliament 6th session, pp.1281, 388 (1919).

[7] New Zealand Parliamentary debates v.189: 20th Parliament 1st session, p.430 (1920).

[8] New Zealand Parliamentary debates v.190: 20th Parliament 2nd session, pp.192-95 (1921).

[9] New Zealand Parliamentary debates v.190: 20th Parliament 2nd session, p.198 (1921). In typical Holland overreach he went on to claim the financiers had won.

[10] New Zealand Parliamentary debates v.195: 20th Parliament 4th session, p.88 (1922).

[11] Isabelle Tombs and Robert Tombs, "Losing the Peace," in *That Sweet Enemy : The French and the British from the Sun King to the Present*

(London: William Heinemann, 2006), pp.502-3.; "The Economic Situation," *Manawatu Standard*, 19 January 1920 p.5. By January 1920 a group of British notables were alarmed at the deteriorating situation. They signed a memorandum to 'leading Governments' (including France) asking for action on world economic instability. They warned of the consequences of the burden on Germany and the risk of destroying her production by over-taxation. Not only would this reduce the chance of payments but it would also incite 'despair and revolt'. Long-term credit was recommended for countries requiring it.

[12] Kray, pp.125-26.

[13] To maintain balance the following discussion only uses articles from the original random sample (on the basis of mentioning 'France' or 'French') to illustrate the French connection. None of the articles included direct quotations from New Zealand politicians. This is not to infer that New Zealand politicians did not make comment on the broader issues – they of course did – but it does indicate that most comment pertinent to France came from the newspapers' secondary sources. The New Zealand politicians were not engaging directly with the French point of view in the New Zealand press (although the newspapers were using virtually the same British-led views as the New Zealand Government).

[14] "Russia," *Taranaki Daily News*, 31 January 1919, p.6.; "Dantzig (sic)," *Nelson Evening Mail*, 1 April 1919, p.5.; France was keen on using exclusion as a coercive tool. France objected to Russian participation as a 'triumph for Lenin'.

[15] Agulhon, pp.171-77. The Clemenceau Government was appointed in November 1917 (the secularism-advocating Socialists refused to join). Clemenceau managed to concentrate the French national effort on winning the war without political or other interruptions.

[16] "General Pau Arrival in Sydney: "The Enemy Is Beaten"," *The Advertiser* (Adelaide S.A.), 11 September 1918, p.11.

[17] B.C. Hett, *The Death of Democracy* (Random House, 2018), pp.123-24, contains one of the more recent opinions that substantiates earlier historians' views on these points.

[18] Jane Tolerton, *The Armistice and Afterwards. New Zealand soldiers on the Western Front gradually heard that the Armistice had been signed, An Awfully Big Adventure* (Radio New Zealand). Quotations from: Laurent Blyth, Bill Elder, Bert Hughes, Bert Stokes. Many soldiers believed French civilian farming activities were a ruse to conceal spying.

[19] "The Demand For Backbone Against The Entente," *Evening Post*, 31 January 1919, p.7.; "Opinions Of German Delegates," *Nelson Evening Mail*, 10 May 1919, p.5.. United Kingdom/ NZ Government, Countries - France - External Relations - Saar, "All the relevant files sent to NZ from the UK on the French occupation of the Saar," 1921-1924, AAEG 950/12/A, R17708909, 360/2/23: Archives New Zealand. This file is centimetres thick and includes detailed British Government memos covering first-hand discussions that the British had held with the French at

Secretary of State level on these issues. The newspaper reports are consistent with these records that the New Zealand Government was receiving via the Governor-General at the time.

[20] "Peace Conference," *New Zealand Herald*, 29 November 1918.. Massey was clearly in a hurry to return to Europe and attend the Paris Conference – even to the exclusion of other matters. He wanted to both resolve the relevant issues and avoid any backsliding over New Zealand's Pacific territorial claims.

Acquiring the vast quantities of phosphate needed to adapt New Zealand soils for intensive pastoral farming was a significant problem. While the apparent sustainably of a pasture-based production model utilising atmospheric nitrogen fixed by clover plants is commonly identified as the mainstay of New Zealand's farming competitiveness, it was imported phosphate that was the missing element. As New Zealand lacked a readily accessible local source, Massey's plan depended upon securing a suitable phosphate supply that was both adjacent and in a form that could be readily processed into superphosphate. Without it, his plan would fail.

[21] "Wool Supplies And Consumption: The Requirements Of A British Empire Industry Y1 - 1924/06/01," *Journal of the Textile Institute Proceedings* 15, no. 6 (1924/06/01 1924): pp.152-53, This contradicted the concern expressed in a 1916 report prepared for the President of the Board of Trade suggesting that a 'serious decrease' in global wool supplies was in part due a decline in sheep numbers as the freezing trade expanded. New Zealand sheep numbers fell in the five post-war years 1919–23.

[22] "La Conference de la Paix: Les colonies Allemandes," *Le Figaro*, 25 January, 1919, p.1. France was well aware of New Zealand's interest in the former German colonies.

[23] Malthus, pp.14-20. This contradicted the Labour view. Under Holland's leadership Labour viewed capitalism and class struggle as the underlying cause.

[24] "A la Conférence : La Discussion sur les Colonies allemandes - On A Parlé De La Société Des Nations," *L'Humanité*, 29 January 1919.

[25] Kray, p.136.; Tombs and Tombs, p.518.

[26] "German Indemnities," *Dominion*, 14 February 1919, p.8.

[27] "Lull In The Storm," *Manawatu Standard*, 11 February 1919, p.5.

[28] "Peace Treaty," *Waikato Times*, 22 May 1919, p.5.

[29] "A la Conférence : La Discussion sur les Colonies allemandes - On A Parlé De La Société Des Nations."

[30] "Les colonies allemandes," *L'Humanité*, 26 June 1919.

[31] "Continued Prosperity," *Waikato Times*, 3 September 1920, p.4.

[32] James Watson, *W.F. Massey : New Zealand*, Makers of the modern world., (London: Haus, 2010), p.83. WF Massey, Massey to Allen 2 January 1917, R 223 19675, Miscellaneous files and papers - Allen and WF Massey correspondence 1st September - 1st August 1919, C361 202, Archives New Zealand. In early 1917 Massey had told Allen that he did not know what to

make of Lloyd George. He clearly preferred Asquith but believed Asquith would never regain the prime ministership.

[33] Government, Versailles Peace Treaty - 1919. New Zealand's copy in the National Archives seems to be (appropriately) untouched and is in mint condition without annotation or appended comments.

[34] E. Wiskemann, *The Europe I Saw* (Collins, 1968), p.53. On p.656 of *Mistakes and Myths*, Sally Marks claims that Keynes came to regret writing *The Economic Consequences* by implying he came to believe his interpretation of Versailles was incorrect. Her comment is misleading. Marks' source (Wiskemann) makes it clear that in conversation Keynes expressed regret because the book became a source that 'the [Nazi] German's never ceased to quote' not because (as Marks implies) Keynes believed the content was later proven to be incorrect.

[35] "Dans Les Ambassades," *Le Figaro*, 25 August 1921. Massey was rewarded for his pro-French stance with the award of *les insignes de grand officier de la Légion d'honneur* conferred by the French Ambassador in London in 1921.

[36] New Zealand Parliamentary debates v.184: 19th Parliament 6th session, pp.35-40 (1919); New Zealand Parliamentary debates v.200: 21st Parliament: 2nd session, pp.730-32 (1923). In order to support the ideal of a unified Empire speaking with one voice during the subsequent Washington Conference, Massey claimed that despite the Dominions signing at Versailles as separate entities they did not thereby become independent, thus contradicting this earlier statement.

[37] "French Territorial Claims," *The Colonist*, 1 February 1919, p.5.; "Peace Conference," *Feilding Star*, 8 February 1919, p.2. *The Colonist* quoted an article from *The Times* mentioning the Dominions' status as self-governing partners under the Treaty. This gave them two voices – their own and one as partners within the Empire (and presumably thereby in other world bodies). Canadian Premier Borden was already describing the British Empire as a 'commonwealth of free nations'.

[38] New Zealand Parliamentary debates v.190: 20th Parliament 2nd session, p.195 (1921); Government, 13 September 1919 Subject: Anglo-French Treaty (Defence of France) Act, 1919.

[39] New Zealand Parliamentary Debates v.183 19th Parliament 5th session, p.1034 (1918).

Chapter Nine

[1] "Peace Conference.". There are numerous similar reports from this period of plans for Massey and Ward, having just returned in August 1918 from a War Conference/Cabinet meeting, to again leave for Europe to attend the Peace Conference. Both were therefore in close communication with the British.

[2] United Kingdom/ NZ Government, British War Graves in France, "All the relevant files sent to NZ from the UK on matters related to France, especially official matters such as treaties and the like.," November 26,

1918 1922-1930, AAEG 950/36/B, Countries - United Kingdom - External Relations - France, R17708971, 201/4/73 includes:

W4715/ 4715/ 17 Conversations between Briand and Austen Chamberlain on disarmament and the threat of Russian involvement in Germany.

Treaty Series 1919 No.1 'British War Graves in France' (see notes): pp.2-3, Archives New Zealand. This agreement was signed and dated by Pichon (Foreign Minister of France) and Lord Derby, the United Kingdom Ambassador to France, on 26 November 1918. New Zealand's archived copy is dated as received on 7 June 1919. Both the United Kingdom and the Dominions' governments obviously anticipated the war's end and the inevitable requests for repatriation of the soldiers' remains.

[3] I. Bargas and T. Shoebridge, "Mourning, honouring, remembering," in *New Zealand's First World War Heritage* (Exisle Publishing, 2015), p.378.; *Tomb of the Unknown Warrior*, (Ministry for Culture and Heritage, 2004), http://www.mch.govt.nz/files/booklet_0.pdf; "What do we know about Australia's Unknown Soldier?," updated 11 Nov 2013, 3:44pm, 2013, accessed 04 July 2017, http://www.abc.net.au/news/2013-11-11/what-do-we-know-about-australias-unknown-soldier/5081574. Both Australia and New Zealand later made symbolic repatriations of unidentified remains. To preserve the anonymity of the exhumed the authorities deliberately ignored current technology and relied on a few remnants of uniform and badges to make a country of origin identification – a tenuous link. The Australian authorities noted that: 'To our surprise and satisfaction (emphasis added), we only had to disturb one grave'. This hints at just how complex any large-scale repatriation of what relatives may have assumed to be complete bodies would have been.

[4] New Zealand Parliamentary debates v.185: 19th Parliament 6th session, p.571 (1919); New Zealand Parliamentary debates v.186: 20th Parliament 1st session, p.955 (1920). Given that sittings of the House were discontinuous and that it was impossible for MPs to raise in the House every issue brought to their attention it seems likely that the cases that were raised were representative. Once broached the constituent at least knew that the issue had been brought to the Government's attention and the answers could be used to respond to other similar queries; Hanna Smyth, ""There is absoutely nothing like the carving of names": Imperial War Graves Commission sites and World War I memory," in *Monumental Conflicts: Twentieth-Century Wars and the Evolution of Public Memory*, ed. D.R. Mallett (eBook: Taylor & Francis, 2017), pp.3-4.Online edition, pages unnumbered, confirms the denial of repatriation as consistent with the Imperial War Grave Commission's policy of burial at or near the place of death.

[5] Jay Winter, *Sites of Memory, Sites of Mourning: The Great War in European Cultural History*, vol. I, Studies in the social and cultural history of modern warfare, (Cambridge: Cambridge University Press, 1998), pp.23-26.

[6] New Zealand Parliamentary debates v.189: 20th Parliament 1st session, p.734 (1920).; "The Unknown Warrior: Body on the way from France, Impressive Ceremony," *Feilding Star*, 11 November 1920, p.2. The repatriation was accompanied by an impressive ceremony and symbolism; '...the coffin ... was draped in a torn and stained Union Jack, beneath which could be just seen the outline of a sword...'

[7] New Zealand Parliamentary debates v.192: 20th Parliament: 3rd session, p.213 (1921).; Gareth Phipps, "Bringing our boy home: The Tomb of the Unknown Warrior, its visitors, and contemporary war remembrance in New Zealand" (M.A. Victoria University of Wellington, 2009), p.20.; D. Knowles, *HMS Hood: Pride of the Royal Navy* (Fonthill Media Limited, 2019), electronic ed. pages not numbered. Jennings MP (Waitomo) did ask Massey if an unknown warrior from Gallipoli could be brought home as the number of unidentified from Gallipoli was considerably higher than was the case for the dead in France. Knowles refers to the unidentified soldier buried in Westminster Abbey as representative of '...the many thousands of dead from the British Empire'.

[8] "Grave Units Recalled," *New Zealand Herald*, 11 November 1921, p.5; Winter, I, pp.23-26.

[9] "Ōhaeawai NZ Wars memorial cross," Ministry for Culture and Heritage, updated 26-Feb-2015, accessed 21 January 2019, https://nzhistory.govt.nz/media/photo/ohaeawai-nz-wars-memorial-cross. A common practice. After the Battle at Ōhaeawai during the Northern War the bodies of the officers were interred in the graveyard of St John the Baptist Church at Waimate North while the other ranks were buried in massed graves at the battle site. David Lloyd, *Battlefield Tourism: pilgrimage and the commemoration of the Great War in Britain, Australia and Canada, 1919–1939* (London: Bloomsbury, 1998). p.21.

[10] "Les pèlerins d'Amérique," *Le Figaro*, 02 August 1922, p.2; "Les Canadiennes à Paris," *Le Figaro*, 04 August 1922, p.2; David Lloyd, *Battlefield tourism : pilgrimage and the commemoration of the Great War in Britain, Australia and Canada, 1919-1939* (London: Bloomsbury, 1998, 1998), p.21.

[11] Lloyd, pp.26-27; Our own correspondent, "War Graves In France And Belgium: Pilgrimages for the poor," *Otago Daily Times*, 19 March 1924, p.10.

[12] New Zealand Parliamentary debates v.185: 19th Parliament 6th session, pp.1395, 96 (1919).

[13] "War Graves," *Grey River Argus*, 6 May 1920, p.3. There were subtle prompts to 'get on with it'. An anonymous comment pointed out that graves in France with pencil on wood identification would soon be permanently lost without action. A poem attributed to E. Lamont made the point: "Out there in France they did their part, And there in France they lie;" See: "Vagrant Verse," *Southland Times*, 9 June 1920, p.4. James Allen, Allen to Massey 11 June 1919, R 223 19675, Miscellaneous files and papers - Allen and WF Massey correspondence 1st September - 1st August 1919, C361

202, p.3, Archives New Zealand. Allen had written to Massey in the previous year agreeing that battlefield sites in France and Palestine should be 'secured' for memorial construction; Bargas and Shoebridge, p.386.

[14] Lloyd, p.121. Churchill was referring to former battlefields located in France, apparently without consideration for French views.

[15] New Zealand Parliamentary debates v.185: 19th Parliament 6th session, p.243 (1919). James Allen, Allen to Massey 7 July 1919, R 223 19675, Miscellaneous files and papers - Allen and WF Massey correspondence 1st September - 1st August 1919, C361 202, pp.6-7, Archives New Zealand. The cost of surveying and transferring the sites from the Belgian Government was a piffling £150, but (as Allen informed Massey in July 1919) the cost of the New Zealand graves was already £28,766 out of 'over a million' to be spent by the War Graves Commission.

[16] New Zealand Parliamentary debates v.187: 20th Parliament 1st session, pp.254, 131 (1920).

[17] "War Memorials," *Evening Post*, 9 December 1927, p.11.; Ian J Lochhead, "Seager, Samuel Hurst," in *Dictionary of New Zealand Biography. Te Ara - the Encyclopedia of New Zealand* (12-Feb-2014). http://www.TeAra.govt.nz/en/biographies/3s8/seager-samuel-hurst. Seager was the '...official architect of New Zealand battlefield memorials'. His lantern-slide show included the Gallipoli monuments and does not seem to have discriminated between the two locations.

[18] "Local & General News," *Marlborough Express*, 3 April 1919, p.4.. 'Stunts' was synonymous with 'attacks' rather than the more frivolous current usage of the term.

[19] "Tales From France: Philip Gibbs as war lecturer," *Mataura Ensign*, 4 April 1919, p.4.

[20] Ian Lochhead, "Enduring memories: Samuel Hurst Seager and the New Zealand battlefield memorials of the great war," in *Endurance and the First World War : Experiences and Legacies in New Zealand and Australia*, ed. David Monger, Sarah Murray, and Katie Pickles (Newcastle: Cambridge Scholars, 2014), pp.159,63. Unfortunately, Lochhead polishes his narrative by using the weather as a metaphor: he contrasts the 'sodden and undulating' battlefields of France with steeply contoured, hot and dry Gallipoli. On the days this writer visited the French sites the weather was warm and sunny as it had been for Triggs. There were obviously seasonal variations in the weather patterns in both localities.

[21] New Zealand Parliamentary debates v.195: 20th Parliament 4th session, p.229 (1922).

[22] "A la memoire des soldats neo-zelandais," *Le Figaro*, 09 October 1922, p.4. "In memory of the New Zealand soldiers: Under the presidency of Sir James Allen, High Commissioner of New Zealand, a monument was inaugurated yesterday in Longueval, in memory of the 7,000 deaths of the New Zealand division, fallen gloriously in September 1916, on the front of the Somme."

"Petitis Faits," *Le Figaro*, 29 March 1923, p.2. 'Sir James Allen (as High Commissioner to the UK) in France to sign a protocol annexed to the International Air Convention, [and] yesterday morning laid a crown [wreath] on the tomb of the Unknown Soldier.'

"Visit Of Aldebaran," *Akaroa Mail and Banks Peninsula Advertiser*, 15 November 1921.. Commemoration was not restricted to the war cemeteries in France as was the case when the shared sacrifice theme was reprised during the visit of the French Navy vessel *Aldebaran* in 1921. This article quoted from what was described as a 'literal translation' of the French commander's speech supplied by the French Consul: E.Dupriez, "La Vie Coloniale: Souvenirs français - dans le Pacifique: Une visite à Akaroa. Enseigne de vaisseau a bord de l'Aldébaran," *Le Figaro: Économique*, Lundi 9 Juin 1924 1924.. 'Enfin, sur le monument aux morts de fia grande guerre, les noms de Lelièvre, de Mallemanche sont ceux des descendants de colonie; français, dont les corps reposent aujourd'hui dans leur seconde patrie.'

[23] Katie Pickles, *Transnational outrage : the death and commemoration of Edith Cavell* (Basingstoke: Palgrave Macmillan, 2007), pp.202, 05, 09.

[24] A C Watts, *Nurse Cavell Street Sign Paparoa*. Photographed by the author.

[25] War Memorial Lest we forget, Post-1918, Newmarket Borough Council, Auckland City Central Library.

[26] Fred Waite, *The New Zealanders at Gallipoli*, ed. Ian McGibbon, Official history of New Zealand's effort in the Great War ; v.1., (Auckland N.Z.: Whitcombe and Tombs, 1919) "NZDF Support to 2018 Anzac Day Commemorations," (7 February 2019, Wellington: New Zealand Defence Force, 23 March 2019 2019). http://www.nzdf.mil.nz/templates/custom/mediarelease.aspx@nrmode=published&nrnodeguid=_257b00e2c11c-d25b-40b4-872c-063d57729dad_257d&nroriginalurl=_252fmedia-centr081d878e28.htm. An earlier version of this article (since removed) referred to Anzac Day as a commemoration primarily associated with Gallipoli but this later edition has restored the association with the Western theatre.

[27] New Zealand Parliamentary debates v.200: 21st Parliament: 2nd session, p.731 (1923).

[28] "Smyrne, la Thrace et les Detroits," *Le Figaro*, 20 September 1922, p.1.

"Le gouvernement de l'Australie, celui de la Nouvelle-Zélande, ont déjà accepté d'envoyer des "contingents. L'Angleterre a très habilement et dès longtemps exploité le légitime amour-propre que les patries des Anzac tirent des combats de Gallipoli, péninsule sacrée".

[29] New Zealand Parliamentary debates v.200: 21st Parliament: 2nd session, pp.163, 377, 598 (1923).

[30] Lloyd, p.117. At the time of writing (2017) seeking 'closure' (whatever that may mean) is a common reason to visit a place of death or interment. In the post-war years there seems to have been an unrealistic expectation that visiting the scene meant sharing the experience of the deceased. In objective terms that was nonsensical. Not only would the terrain have been

altered, the graves were now marked and memorials erected. Moreover the weather (if not the season) would likely have been different during individual visits thus creating a confusing dissonance between myth and reality.

[31] New Zealand Parliamentary debates v.185: 19th Parliament 6th session, pp.571, 393 (1919).

[32] New Zealand Parliamentary debates v.186: 20th Parliament 1st session, p.415 (1920). The Dunedin Consular record from December 1926 to August 1930 includes a note that lists New Zealand as one of the countries whose citizens do not require a passport or visa for visits to France so this may be simply a wartime legacy requirement, perhaps to control anticipated mass pilgrimages.

[33] New Zealand Parliamentary debates v.186: 20th Parliament 1st session, p.653 (1920). Shipping to the United Kingdom was at a premium as evidenced by the problems with freight.

[34] New Zealand Parliamentary debates v.189: 20th Parliament 1st session, p.600 (1920).

[35] Rhoda Howden, Correspondence re illness and death of her husband, "Howden, Peter, 1884-1917 : Papers. 1915-1921 [Collection]. Includes letters of condolence sent to her on her husband's death and letters to her about headstone on her husband's grave in France.," 1917, 1504.

[36] New Zealand Foreign Affairs and Trade, "Longueval: New Zealand Memorial," (2018), Photograph. https://www.mfat.govt.nz/en/countries-and-regions/europe/france/new-zealand-embassy/anzac-day-commemorations/longueval/. Paeroa War Memorial, Primrose Hill photographed by the author 27 May 2018; Bargas and Shoebridge, p.370.

[37] New Zealand Parliamentary debates v.185: 19th Parliament 6th session, pp.1349-51 (1919). At about the same time as the issue was debated H.G. Ell (Liberal, Christchurch) asked about the dilapidated state of the Dominion Museum and the risk to the collections therein. The issue was eventually resolved when the National War Memorial Museum was constructed in Wellington. Ell was an early conservationist and lobbied for scenic reserves in the Christchurch and Port Hills environs.

[38] James Allen, Allen to Massey 19 February 1919, R 223 19675, Miscellaneous files and papers - Allen and WF Massey correspondence 1st September - 1st August 1919, C361 202, p.21, Archives New Zealand.

[39] New Zealand Parliamentary debates v.187: 20th Parliament 1st session, p.316 (1920). One MP wanted a national memorial in each of the four main centres.

[40] Wellington Cenotaph, *Inscription*, cnr. Bowen Street and Lambton Quay, Wellington. As viewed and noted by the author.

[41] Clarke, p.54. K. S. Inglis and J. Phillips, "War Memorials In Australia And New Zealand:A Comparative Survey," Article, *Australian Historical Studies* 24, no. 96 (1991): p.189,

[42] Melman, p.7. Melman refers to the British self-deception that idealised a past that was inextricably linked to and part of a rural, non-urban country

despite the realities of industrialisation. Michael Roche, "'A Duty of the Country' Soldier Settlement, 1915-1941," in *New Zealand between the wars*, ed. Rachael Bell (Auckland, New Zealand: Massey University Press, 2017), pp.61-62. The lack of consultation contrasts with the liquor prohibition debate when the 'boys' – to use the repeated vernacular – risked being told by those at home what was good for them.

[43] New Zealand Parliamentary Debates v.183 19th Parliament 5th session, p.1020 (1918). Some alternative separation Allowances and Scholarships covering various disciplines were suggested. These included studying overseas techniques such as sugar-beet growing in France.

[44] New Zealand Parliamentary debates v.201: 21st Parliament: 2nd session, p.696 (1923); New Zealand Parliamentary debates v.228: 23rd Parliament: 5th session, p.346 (1931).; New Zealand Parliamentary debates v.224: 23rd Parliament: 3rd session, p.928 (1930). The 1931 comment repeated Ward's warning from 1919.

[45] Roche, p.65. For example, the family home, domestic meat supply and vegetable garden were integral parts of the farm. A residence and sustenance were needed regardless of the equity in the property or its commercial viability.

[46] New Zealand Parliamentary debates v.185: 19th Parliament 6th session, p.877 (1919).. The Avon MP (G.W. Russell) suggested that rural development could involve assisted passages for immigrant ex-soldiers with rural backgrounds from Belgium and France as well as Great Britain. Roche, p.76.

[47] New Zealand Parliamentary debates v.184: 19th Parliament 6th session, p.508 (1919).

[48] New Zealand Parliamentary debates v.182: 19th Parliament 4th session, p.172 (1918); New Zealand Parliamentary debates v.185: 19th Parliament 6th session, p.1074 (1919); New Zealand Parliamentary debates v.182: 19th Parliament 4th session, p.30 (1918); New Zealand Parliamentary debates v.186: 20th Parliament 1st session, p.675 (1920).

[49] N.C. Hunt, *Memory, War and Trauma* (Cambridge University Press, 2010), pp.197-98, requoted in D.R. Mallett, "Introduction," in *Monumental Conflicts: Twentieth-Century Wars and the Evolution of Public Memory* (Taylor & Francis, 2017), p.4.

[50] The Great War, 1914-1918. New Zealand Expeditionary Force. Roll of Honour, xviii (Wellington: Government Printer, 1924). The French battlefields had in fact the greatest number of New Zealand war casualties (some 75 per cent according to the official record).

[51] "In Memoriam," *New Zealand Herald*, 6 October 1933, p.1.

[52] Colonial Office and Predecessor: New Zealand Original Correspondence - Records of the Colonial Office, Commonwealth and Foreign and Commonwealth Offices, Empire Marketing Board, and related bodies, "Bound volumes arranged chronologically within the following subject headings: Despatches (letters of the governors), Offices (letters of government departments and other organisations) and Individuals (arranged

alphabetically). Each volume with a contents list, or précis of each letter giving name of correspondent, date of letter and subject matter.," 1830-1922, CO 61622, CO 61622, 194,197,199, 300, 301, 302, The National archives, pp.95, 96, British Archives, London.

[53] Gwen Parsons, "Challenging Enduring Home Front Myths: Jingoistic Civilians and Neglected Soldiers," in *Endurance and the First World War : experiences and legacies in New Zealand and Australia*, ed. David Monger, Sarah Murray, and Katie Pickles (Newcastle: Cambridge Scholars, 2014), p.67.

[54] Ashley Nevil Gould, "Proof of Gratitude? Soldier Land Settlement in New Zealand After World War I" (Doctor of Philosophy Massey University, 1992), p.12. Gould uses J.B. Condliffe's *New Zealand in the Making* to estimate that some 12,000 soldiers were assisted into urban homes and by deduction a similar number were assisted with rural real estate.

[55] Parsons, p.81. Parsons also claims that these initiatives changed 'attitudes to home ownership in the Dominion'. If that was so, the images from France had an important secondary influence beyond the immediate scope of the rural settlement programme.

Chapter Ten

[1] "French Ideals: The Nation's Place in the World," *Hawera & Normanby Star*, February 3 1919, p.6.

[2] New Zealand Parliamentary debates v.216: 22nd Parliament: 2nd session, p.792 (1927).

[3] "Feeding Britain," in *New Zealand History* (Ministry for Culture and Heritage, 4-May-2016 2016), pp.33, 36. https://nzhistory.govt.nz/war/public-service-at-war/feeding-britain.

[4] "Feeding Britain," p.37.

[5] "Journaux officiels (Paris): Sont nommés vice-consuls de 1re classe," *Archives Diplomatiques: Journal officiel de la République française. Lois et décrets* (Paris), 1911/08 (A51, N7, SER3) -1911/12 (A51, N12, SER3). p.146.. Hippeau first appears in the *New Zealand Yearbook* of 1917 as the French Vice Consular representative in Auckland but he is not listed in the 1921–22 edition. "Consular Changes," *New Zealand Herald*, 22 December 1916, p.9.; "Local And General News," *New Zealand Herald*, 16 March 1917, p.4.. Hippeau was an experienced career civil servant who had held appointments in Havana and at the French Foreign Office in Geneva. He was clearly a new broom.

[6] "A Third Party," *Auckland Star*, 15 March 1917, p.4. To replicate the search results: https://paperspast.natlib.govt.nz/newspapers?phrase=2&query=French+goods+in+lieu

[7] James Allen, Allen to Massey 29 September 1916, R 223 19675, Miscellaneous files and papers - Allen and WF Massey correspondence 1st September - 1st August 1919, C361 202, Archives New Zealand.; New Zealand Parliamentary Debates v.183 19th Parliament 5th session, p.972

(1918). The significance of that note taken in context is twofold: the suggestion came from the British Chamber of Commerce and the Colonial Office passed it on to New Zealand. When a similarly innocuous suggestion was later made in the House of Representatives (9 December 1918) by the Hon. D.S. McDonald, Minister of Agriculture, Industries and Commerce, it did not attract any dissension: 'This country (McDonald said in 1918) may eventually require to establish agents in England, Canada, the Argentine and Australia to look after the interests of our producers'.

[8] Colonial Office and Predecessor: New Zealand Original Correspondence - Records of the Colonial Office, Commonwealth and Foreign and Commonwealth Offices, Empire Marketing Board, and related bodies: p.116.

[9] Colonial Office and Predecessor: New Zealand Original Correspondence - Records of the Colonial Office, Commonwealth and Foreign and Commonwealth Offices, Empire Marketing Board, and related bodies: p.121. Sun, "German Bells."; Poverty Bay Herald, "German Bells."; "The German Bells." A number of articles published in mid-1918 referred to the destruction of the bells originally hung in the Lutheran Church in Christchurch. These were allegedly cast from French cannon captured by the Germans 'some years ago' (during the 1870–71 war in one account). Deemed by Sir James Allen and other politicians as 'offensive' to the French they were removed, smashed and melted down, apparently with the agreement of the French Consul.

[10] Colonial Office and Predecessor: New Zealand Original Correspondence - Records of the Colonial Office, Commonwealth and Foreign and Commonwealth Offices, Empire Marketing Board, and related bodies: pp.123-24. Presumably this is why the recruitment issue went unremarked.

[11] Hippeau to Russell, 10 April 1918 C583 303, Overseas Representation in New Zealand - France- Powers of French Consuls 1918-1942, EA1 309, 61/360/11: Archives New Zealand.

[12] Heenan to the Under Secretary, 18 April 1918 C583 303, Overseas Representation in New Zealand - France- Powers of French Consuls 1918-1942, EA1 309, 61/360/11: p.1, Archives New Zealand.; Liverpool to Long, 1 June 1918 C583 303, Overseas Representation in New Zealand - France- Powers of French Consuls 1918-1942, EA1 309, 61/360/11: Archives New Zealand. Walter Long had already replied when answering Lord Liverpool's earlier request. He had pointed out that such requests should be politely declined without giving offence. Liverpool had indicated he would do so, with some minor adjustments to allow for local sensitivities.

[13] Mervyn Norrish, "Political Relations between New Zealand and France," in *New Zealand and the French : Two Centuries of Contact*, ed. John Dunmore (Waikanae: Heritage Press, 1997). "The French Mission," *Otago Daily Times*, 10 December 1918, p.4.; "French Mission," *Feilding Star*, 20 December 1918, p.3.; "The French Mission," *Evening Post*, 21 December 1918, p.6.; Adrian Muckle, "Empire in the eyes of the beholder: New

Zealand in the Pacific through French eyes," in *New Zealand's empire*, ed. Katie Pickles and Catherine Coleborne (Manchester University Press, 2016).; Jacqueline Dwyer, "Ahead of their Time: the French Economic Mission to Australia 1918," *The French Australian Review*, no. 59 Australian Summer (2015), The Mission's report is vague and simply states that establishing 'closer relations' and giving thanks for the war effort motivated the visit. The New Zealand newspapers successively reported cancellation and then reinstatement of the visit with the arrival port changed from Wellington to Auckland. There are no direct refences in either the Colonial Office files or the Foreign Office records in the British Archives at Kew relating to this initiative. The Archives New Zealand records only include a passing reference to the Mission amongst James Allen's many exchanges with Massey from 1917 to 1918, but little significance seems to have been attached to the visit. Given the extensive publicity at the time and the sensitivity which Hippeau's actions had aroused, the lack of reaction seems odd; the explanation is therefore more likely to be misfiling or removal of the British records to another collection.

[14] "M. Albert Metin," *Wairarapa Age*, 19 August 1918, p. 5.; "The French Mission," *Dominion*, 27 December 1918, p.4.;"Albert Metin dies from war strain," *New York Times* (New York), 17 August 1918 ; Robert Aldrich, *The French Presence in the South Pacific, 1842-1940* (Basingstoke: Macmillan, 1990), p.279. Albert Métin wrote *Le Socialisme sans doctrines* (1901) following his earlier New Zealand visit. Robert Aldrich appears to have incorrectly concluded that Métin died after the Mission returned to Europe as he says both Métin and Andre Siegfried wrote 'lengthy reports' on their return to Paris.

[15] Dwyer, pp.47-49. Two mission members representing labour interests toured Australia but did not travel to New Zealand.

[16] "French Mission in Australia", Oceania, 2nd new series, New Zealand: 31CPCOM / 10: item: report . Archives of the Ministry of Foreign Affairs (MAE), Center of Diplomatic Archives of La Courneuve, p.6, Political and commercial correspondence called "New series" 1896-1918.

[17] "French Mission in Australia": p.7.

[18] Dwyer, p.44. The Australia leg of the tour was meticulously planned but there is no evidence that this was the case in New Zealand.

[19] "The French Mission," *Auckland Star*, 28 December 1918, p.6.;, *Evening Star*, 31 December 1918., p.4. The influenza epidemic and the alleged vector – infection through a failure to quarantine the *Niagara* owing to political pressure from passengers Ward and Massey – was still a live issue, although it was eventually debunked. It was an allegation that the Mission would have wished to avoid. This is the most likely explanation for the delay in travelling to New Zealand and the party making much of being inoculated against the disease prior to embarkation.

[20] Gen. Pau, Telegram Auckland January 31st, 1919: Auckland, le 31 Janvier 1919 – 1 heure recu le 2 Fevrier a 4 h.4: De la part du General Pau, "As soon as the mission was completed, General Pau sent a brief report to Paris

on the commercial orientations to be developed. ," 1919, 31CPCOM / 10 pieces 45 to 49, Center of Diplomatic Archives of La Courneuve. Archives of the Ministry of Foreign Affairs (MAE), p.45.

[21] "Welcome To General Pau," *Auckland Star*, 29 January 1919, p.8.; "French Mission," *Hastings Standard, Volume IX, Issue 14, 30 December 1918*, 30 December 1918, p.6.; "The French Mission," *New Zealand Herald*, 30 December 1918, p.6.; "Tribute To Catholic Clergy," *Evening Post*, 1 January 1919, p.5.

[22] The economic relations between France and New Zealand : report of the French Mission to New Zealand, December 1918-January 1919, 1919, pp.20–21, Mission en Nouvelle Zelande, Paris. It may be that France realised there was some benefit in the bodies remaining where they were, perhaps as a symbolic rallying point should the sacred soil ever again require defending.

[23] "General Pau And The League Of Nations," *Wanganui Chronicle*, 25 January 1919, p.4. Pau advocated excluding countries he considered not qualified to belong. "General Pau," *Ohinemuri Gazette*, 31 January 1919, p.1.

[24] "Why We Must "Get Together"," *Evening Star*, 25 January 1919, p.2.

[25] "The French Mission," *Otago Daily Times*, 19 April 1919, p.8.

[26] Hippeau to Pichon Le Vice Consul de France à Auckland à son Excellence Monsieur Stephen Pichon, Ministre des Affaires Etrangeres, Oceania, 2nd new series, New Zealand: 31CPCOM / 11: item: report "French Mission in Australia"

Archives of the Ministry of Foreign Affairs (MAE), Center of Diplomatic Archives of La Courneuve, pp.52-54, Political and commercial correspondence called "New series" 1896-1918. The 'indigenes' may have referred to rural dwellers or, more probably, Māori.

[27] Kray, pp.125-26.

[28] Documents related to the French Mission Luncheon with the Otago Harbour Board, AG-200-11/04/1953, French Mission, Hocken Collection, Dunedin The visit was frequently treated as a celebration, not a trade mission. Hippeau did refer in his summary report to Siegfried's study of New Zealand democracy, his knowledge of New Zealand generally and his information gathering.

[29] "After-War Problems," *Evening Post*, 24 April 1925, p.17. "André Siegfried," *Le Figaro*, 8 February 1932.. Siegfried did write after his visit but this work drew New Zealand's attention to the problems Britain faced in trade and population rather than issues specific to this New Zealand visit. *Le Figaro* when reporting his election in 1932 to the Academy of Moral and Political Sciences (de l'Académie des sciences morales et politiques) noted he had been mission secretary during the 1918–19 Australasian visit and drew attention to *La Démocratie en Nouvelle Zélande* amongst his many publications.

[30] The economic relations between France and New Zealand : report of the French Mission to New Zealand, December 1918-January 1919: p.12. The

report highlights the perennial French concern with the perceived low birth rate amongst the white population, thereby limiting the potential of the country.

[31] "Yearbook collection: 1893–2012," (Statistics New Zealand), 1919. http://www.stats.govt.nz/browse_for_stats/snapshots-of-nz/digital-yearbook-collection.aspx.; "Commerce With France," *New Zealand Herald*, 25 January 1919, p.10. Imports from Germany in 1914 were four times the value of those from France, although both were tiny compared to imports from Britain.

[32] James Allen, Allen to Massey 17 January 1919 - 18 January 1919, R 223 19675, Miscellaneous files and papers - Allen and WF Massey correspondence 1st September - 1st August 1919, C361 202, pp.8-10, Archives New Zealand.

[33] "The New Zealand Official Year-Book, 1915: Destination Of New Zealand Exports," (Statistics New Zealand, 2 February 2018). The 1923 edition noted that: 'Included in the exports to the United Kingdom, however, are considerable quantities of produce which are shipped to London merely as a convenient depot, and which are retransferred to the Continent or to America. The total re-exports in normal pre-war years amounted to about £4,000,000 annually, but the amount fell, under war conditions, to £2,408,737 in 1915, £985,891 in 1917, and £565,529 in 1918, rising again to £1,691,168 in 1919, and still further to £3,578,617 in 1920.

The largest item in the re-exports is wool, which, to the value of nearly £2,000,000 annually, was redistributed in pre-war years from London to the manufacturing centres of Belgium, northern France, and Germany. This amounted to a big proportion of the Dominion's wool exports, averaging about 25 per cent.'

[34] "The New Zealand Official Year-Book, 1915: Destination Of New Zealand Exports."

[35] New Zealand Parliamentary debates v.189: 20th Parliament 1st session, p.922 (1920).

[36] New Zealand Parliamentary debates v.189: 20th Parliament 1st session, p.922 (1920). Selling wool to France either directly or via the United Kingdom denied supplies to Germany.

[37] "Yearbook collection: 1893–2012," 1920. The economic relations between France and New Zealand : report of the French Mission to New Zealand, December 1918-January 1919: p.26, pp.61-63.

[38] It was this (understandable) desire for interdependence through Continental self-sufficiency that was to lead to the European Economic Community after World War II with its much-ridiculed Common Agricultural Policy. To European interests the policy made perfect sense, given the Continent's long history of conflict and the remoteness of antipodean supplies.

[39] Pau: pp.47-48.

[40] "Yearbook collection: 1893–2012." There are several distortions in the data over the 1919–20 years, probably due to reassignment of volumes between years. Moreover, as the *Yearbook* notes record: 'The high totals for

1918 and 1919 shown for "other countries" are mainly due to temporary heavy exports to France in the former year and Egypt in the latter.' An earlier reference from the *Yearbooks* suggests that 25% of the UK destined clip was re-exported in 1913. Either way, it was a substantial portion of the total.

41 "Fin des restrictions en Angleterre," *Le Figaro*, 28 April 1919. Restrictions on the sale and distribution of goods covered by the General Security Act had been lifted with exceptions, one being New Zealand and Australian wool. This would have favoured British textile producers over their rapidly recovering French competitors.

42 "Our Yorkshire Letter," *Marlborough Express*, 25 June 1919, p.6. Thilo Nils Hendrik Albers, "Trade Frictions, Trade Policies, and the Interwar Business Cycle" (PhD London School of Economics and Political Science, 2018), pp.329-30. Costs associated with visible impediments are often blamed for trade distortions whereas tariffs, regulations and policies are usually more significant disruptors of trade.

43 The referenced reports used for this section are from the random (n=1,000) sample of articles originally drawn and are thus a representative subsample.

44 "London Wool Sale," *Dominion*, 21 February 1920, p.12.

45 "Commercial," *Press*, 4 March 1920, p.7.

46 "Who Creates The Fashion?," *Otago Daily Times*, 12 January 1926, p.14. The creative brains were with the French dyers who cooperated with the manufacturers unlike their English counterparts who had the best quality fabric but lacked the creativity.

47 Dai Hayward, *Golden jubilee; the story of the first fifty years of the New Zealand Meat Producers Board, 1922-1972* (Wellington, Universal Printers, 1972). Instances of 'mislabelling' of imported New Zealand meat claiming an alternative country of production was not unheard of as an example of the country of origin issues primary producers can experience.

48 B R Mitchell, *British historical statistics* (Cambridge: Cambridge University Press, 1988), pp.336, 41.

49 Harland, pp.161-66. The statistics in this source differ slightly but the overall picture is similar. Only about 20% of the wool available in the UK was locally produced, the balance being imported from the Empire and South America. About two thirds of the wool thus available in the UK whether locally produced or imported was retained for local use with the balance (re-)exported. The bulk went to the Continent with France, Germany and Belgium the major importers. Australia and South Africa were concurrently exporting considerable quantities of wool direct to the Continent.

50 "Our Yorkshire Letter," *Marlborough Express*, 25 June 1919, p.6. Although exports of noils (short wool fibres) were soon to be released from the commandeer the buyer still needed a French recommendation to obtain a War Trade Department licence. The issue is obscure but the general point stands – regulations were still in force; "Commercial," *New Zealand*

Herald, 14 December 1921.; " London Wool Sale," *Dominion*, 21 February 1920, p.12.; "Commercial."

[51] "Fin des restrictions en Angleterre," p.1.

[52] New Zealand Parliamentary debates v.191: 20th Parliament: 3rd session, pp.656, 795, 839 (1921).

[53] New Zealand Parliamentary debates v.196: 20th Parliament 4th session, pp.285, 91, 92 (1922).

[54] "The French Mission," *Evening Star*, 13 January 1919, p.4. (Again) a rundown in stock and a significant shortfall in production was the major French concern.

[55] "Yearbook collection: 1893–2012."; Mitchell. The *NZ Yearbook* series shows wool sent direct to France in 1919 was just 1% of the total exported (1,482,037 lbs. out of 274,246,613 lbs.). UK Import Statistics show 254,000,000 lbs. were imported from NZ in 1919 so the export-import alignment is close with only some 20,000,000 lbs. or 7% of the exported total not included in the UK figures. This may be due as much to timing and/or calculation error as any diversion of supplies elsewhere.

[56] The economic relations between France and New Zealand : report of the French Mission to New Zealand, December 1918-January 1919: pp.26, 37-38.

[57] French Consul, Consular Receipts, 1920-24, AG-514-03, AG514-03, Hocken Library, Dunedin.

[58] "Values Of Wool," *New Zealand Herald*, 11 March 1926, p.10.; "Chronique Economique: La situation industrielle," *Le Figaro*, 01 September, 1924, p.5. "Let us point out the growing trend in New Zealand and Australia of making big sales on the spot without wanting to go through London. Thus 90 per cent of the wool production in these two countries is now (sold in) the local market. This is an evolution which it is prudent to take into account."

[59] "La Production et la Consommation de la Laine," *Le Figaro (Illustrated Supplement)*, 20 October 1924, p.2. This report was based on data from the International Institute of Agriculture in Rome. "L'industrie lainiere anglaise," *Le Figaro (Illustrated Supplement)*, 13 October 1924, p.3. *Le Figaro* pointed out that 85% of wool imports came from the Dominions with Australian and New Zealand supplies being counter-cyclical owing to the seasonal offsets between the hemispheres within the annual cycle. The claim that they would even out since New Zealand wool arrived in February–March is specious given the ease with which wool can be stored.

[60] "Un important conférence lainiere a Bradford," *Le Figaro (Illustrated supplement)*, 29 September 1924, p.4.

[61] New Zealand Parliamentary Debates v.183 19th Parliament 5th session, p.972 (1918). The new legislation also happened to suit the interests of the mainly British-owned local processors.

[62] "William Hall-Jones," in *Dictionary of New Zealand Biography, Te Ara - the Encyclopedia of New Zealand* (Encyclopedia of New Zealand, 1993). http://www.TeAra.govt.nz/en/biographies/2h7/hall-jones-william . Hall-

Jones had been a Liberal Cabinet Minister, Acting Prime Minister and High Commissioner in London prior to serving on the Council. He was a remarkably unassuming and deferential politician even to the point of surrendering leadership of the Liberal Government to Ward without contest after Seddon's death.

[63] "Anglo-Colonial Notes: France and Frozen Meat," *Auckland Star*, 16 October 1911, p.7. A report from *Nord Illustre* describes shipment of frozen lamb to France for the 'New Zealand exhibit at Roubaix' but despite apparently acceptable quality no commercial venture followed.

[64] New Zealand Parliamentary debates v.194: 20th Parliament 3rd session, pp.432-33 (1922).

[65] "Frozen Meat Trade," *New Zealand Herald*, 18 March 1921, p.5. Similar prejudices amongst housewives and wholesalers had to be overcome in the early days of the British frozen meat trade.

New Zealand Parliamentary debates v.193: 20th Parliament: 3rd session, p.210 (1921). Massey had assumed that since continental soldiers had been fed frozen meat during the war they would have carried the taste for it back into civilian life but this did not seem to be the case in France or elsewhere in Europe. Massey was accordingly dismissive of this possibility.

[66] The economic relations between France and New Zealand : report of the French Mission to New Zealand, December 1918-January 1919: p.53.

[67] "Our French Visitors," *Auckland Star*, 16 January 1923, p.3. Her consort proceeded direct to New Caledonia. "Through French Eyes," *Evening Post*, 25 January 1923, p.8; "Mission From France," *New Zealand Herald*, 16 January 1923, p.8; "Jules Michelet In Port," *Evening Post*, 25 January 1923, p.8.; "Jules Michelet In Wellington Gift To Dominion," *Hawera & Normanby Star*, 26 January 1923, p.5; "Nos croiseurs en Nouvelle-Zélande," *Le Figaro*, 11 March 1923.. *Le Figaro* described the visit as 'A success which will undoubtedly influence the trade relations between the two countries.'

[68] "The Meat Trust," *Auckland Star*, 26 April 1919, p.12. The fear of Meat Trusts (monopolies) gaining control over the New Zealand meat trade with Britain could have been eased through such diversification. There were indications of French interest in frozen lamb, although New Zealand beef was considered to be of inferior quality. Distance remained a barrier.

[69] "Trade With France," *Manawatu Standard*, 25 January 1923, p.5.; Hayward, pp.5, 7, 13-14. Stubborn loyalty to exporting via the United Kingdom was raised as a cost issue at the time. Hayward notes that rising costs were in part due to the 'clumsy' shipping arrangements and handling in New Zealand – loading delays and calling at numerous ports on the way around New Zealand also highlighted the need to reduce shipping and handling costs.

[70] "Industrial Corporation," *Press*, 21 February 1923, p.12.; This issue was not new. Industrialists had been urging government action to support the development of secondary industries to help solve local economic problems (presumably underemployment) and coincidentally assist their own

business interests. There was always the fear of major offshore manufacturers, of which France was one, penetrating the New Zealand market. See: "A Forecast," *Southland Times*, 25 April 1919, p.2.

[71] "Cost Of Clothing," *Grey River Argus*, 2 June 1920, p.2. Although there were indications by 1920 that both British and American traders had got in early with the German textile trades; moreover, it was alleged, so-called French perfumes and soaps were being manufactured in Germany and re-exported via France which was fraudulently claimed as the country of origin.

[72] "French Commercial Mission," *Bay of Plenty Times*, 7 February 1923, p.2.; "French Industry," *Bay of Plenty Times*, 2 February 1923, p.4.; "Expansion Urged," *Evening Post*, 30 January 1923, p.10. A suggestion of a reciprocal follow-up mission was apparently not pursued, possibly because earlier missions had failed through a lack of specific objectives with their reports eventually ending up in Wellington 'pigeonholes'. See: "New Zealand Trade," *New Zealand Herald*, 31 January 1919, p.4..

"La Production et la Consommation de la Laine." One *Le Figaro* report suggested that France was pleading for additional wool: '…that exporting countries were unable to supply quantities equal to the average quantities delivered during the pre-war period explains the current tension in prices, which can only be overcome if the increase in wool production or the decline in consumption, or these two circumstances together (both caused by the high prices in force), will have helped to restore a better balance between supply and demand.'

[73] The economic relations between France and New Zealand : report of the French Mission to New Zealand, December 1918-January 1919: p.43.

[74] The analysis is based on simple, raw counts of advertisements as measured by Papers Past. This measure is crude but acceptable. While it ignores the size of each advertisement, its prominence (font size, for example), the use of illustrations and the attractiveness of the copy does give a surrogate estimate of the volume. Between 1919 and 1924 Papers Past content had a count of 2,337,754 advertisements (based on the surrogate inclusion of 'the' as explained earlier) but only 104,561 advertisements included the words 'French' or 'France'.

[75] "Papers Past," (Wellington: National Library of New Zealand, 2016). http://paperspast.natlib.govt.nz/. n = 150 Data are from within-year simple random samples. Each year 1919–24 has a sub-sample n = 30. The data are unweighted.

[76] Pau: p.47.

[77] Hippeau to Pichon Le Vice Consul de France à Auckland à son Excellence Monsieur Stephen Pichon, Ministre des Affaires Etrangeres: pp.54-55.

[78] New Zealand Parliamentary debates v.225: 23rd Parliament: 3rd session, pp.91,93 (1930).

[79] New Zealand Parliamentary debates v.228: 23rd Parliament: 5th session, p.447 (1931).

[80] New Zealand Parliamentary debates v.232: 24th Parliament 1st session, pp.487-8 (1932).; New Zealand Parliamentary debates v.233: 24th Parliament 1st session, p.77 (1932). Separately, Alfred Ransom (United Party and Cabinet Minister 1928–35) quoted the value of primary produce imports by country: France imported £52 million while Germany imported £77 million and Canada and Belgium were also importers. New Zealand's direct exports to these nations was just £2,750,000 whereas Australia alone had sent £10 million of her exports direct to France in 1929–30. 'If we are not careful other Dominions will outstrip us in the race for these markets,' Ransom said. He claimed New Zealand producers were too dependent on the Government.

[81] New Zealand Parliamentary debates v.238: 24th Parliament 4th session, p.239 (1934).

Chapter Eleven

[1] Barnes, p.15.

[2] Barnes, pp.68-69, 82-83.

[3] Rachael Bell, "Introduction: A nation on the cusp," in *New Zealand between the wars*, ed. Rachael Bell (Massey University Press, 2017), p.11. This assertion of a new post-war independence is a common feature in the New Zealand historiography. New Zealand's rejection of the 1931 Statute of Westminster provides additional contrary evidence.

[4] David Reynolds, "The long sacrifice," Essay, 144 (2015), The political divisions evident within the Irish Nationalist movement are noted as are the divisions within New Zealand society especially those centred on Māori grievances.

[5] Miles Kahler, *Decolonization in Britain and France : the domestic consequences of international relations* (Princeton, N.J.: Princeton University Press, 1984), pp.7-9, 131, 348. Although support for (and association with) empires is often linked to parties of the political right, parties of the left could also be supportive although not always within the same paradigm. Hence, despite sharing a recognisably socialist philosophy with Britain's Labour party, the Left in France supported the French presence in Algeria whereas Labour favoured decolonisation.

[6] Carol May Neill, "Trading our way : developments in New Zealand's trade policy 1930s to 1980s" (PhD Massey University, 2010), p.3.

[7] "New Zealand Official Year Books" (1939). Post-war French immigrant totals were minor even within what was a very small subset of non-British European settlers.

[8] Stuart Ward, "Transcending the Nation: A Global Imperial History?," in *After the imperial turn : thinking with and through the nation*, ed. Antoinette Burton (Durham [N.C.]: Duke University Press 2003), pp.45-56.

[9] As was common at the time, Balfour's explanation implied an influence from an unstoppable Darwinian progression.

[10] "Mr Massey," *Press*, 25 January 1924. *The Guardian's* term reportedly stung Massey; it was too close to the truth.

[11] Imperial Conference, 1926. Appendix to the Journals of the House of Representatives, 1927 Session, pp.9, 18, 22.

[12] Ronald Hyam, *Britain's declining empire : the road to decolonisation, 1918-1968* (Cambridge: Cambridge University Press, 2006), p.72. The creation of the Dominions' Office in 1925 as a separate entity from the Colonial Office was just a preliminary step.

[13] Aldrich, p.280.

[14] Pau. 'Au sujet des les Nouvelles-Hébrides – opinion à l'exception des missionnaires protestants dont attitude vous est connue, s'intéresse peu question des Nouvelles-Hébrides, qu'elle considère comme appartenant plutôt zone d'influence Australie. Bien que paraissant préférer éventualité rattachement Empire britannique, elle ne soulèverait vraisemblablement nulle difficulté en cas de cession à la République française. M. Allen, Premier Ministre par intérim, déclare que si l'Angleterre et l'Australie sont d'accord, le Gouvernement du Dominion verrait sans objection cession Nouvelles-Hébrides à la France pourvu toutefois que les mesures nécessaires efficaces soient assurées pour la protection race indigène notamment contre l'alcoolisme. Nous avons prié télégraphiquement Thomsen vous tenir directement au courant mission pout Australie.'

[15] Allen, (1913).

[16] Kray, p.140.

[17] Conference Of Prime Ministers And Representatives Of The United Kingdom, The Dominions, And India (Summary Of Proceedings And Documents Of The), Held In June, July, And August, 1921, At London: Appendix to the Journals of the House of Representatives, 1921, pp.34-35.

[18] Marquess of Crewe, France - 1926 Annual Report, 1926, AAEG 950/88/A, R17709125, 360/1/2 1: pp.49-50, Archives New Zealand; France - 1932 Annual Report, 1932, AAEG 950/88/A, R17709125, 360/1/2 1: para.115, Archives New Zealand.; Henri Bernay, "Une Situation Paradoxale: La France aux Nouvelles-Hébrides," *Le Figaro*, 12 March 1928. The Commission's journey was noted in the French press as was the French Government's intention to retain the New Hebrides.

[19] This contrasts with French attempts to impose the *Code Napoléon* in Europe during the early nineteenth century.

[20] Gerald Chaudron, "Obsession: New Zealand, Money and the League of Nations, 1920–35," Article, *Journal of Imperial & Commonwealth History* 41, no. 1 (03// 2013), New Zealand was no less complicit. Massey seemed determined to keep New Zealand's involvement to the minimum by underfunding Sir James Allen's unenthusiastic representation. While this posture achieved its designated purpose of positioning the League as powerless it also removed the opportunity for a greater New Zealand presence in international diplomacy.

[21] Bain Attwood, "Apostles of peace : the New Zealand League of Nations Union : research essay presented in partial fulfilment of the requirements for the degree of Master of Philosophy in History" (Master of Philosophy in History University of Auckland, 1979), p.37. A literal translation of la

Société des Nations as the Society of Nations is a more appropriate description as Attwood has pointed out.

[22] Bury, p.255.; Antony Lentin, "'Une aberration inexplicable'? Clemenceau and the abortive Anglo-French guarantee treaty of 1919," *Diplomacy & Statecraft* 8, no. 2 (1997): p.57, Lentin has an excellent discussion on the broader issues.

[23] "Sir Austen Chamberlain," (October 12, 2019).; Douglas Johnson and Jean-Baptiste Duroselle, "Entente and Mésentente," in *Britain and France : ten centuries*, ed. Douglas W. J. Johnson, Francois Crouzet, and Francois Bèdarida (Folkestone, Kent, England: Dawson, 1980), p.270 ; Watson, p.124. Neither Massey's New Zealand nor the United Kingdom had any intention of occupying Germany in the pursuit of either guarantee. Chamberlain was a highly influential conservative politician but he was out of office in the crucial 1922–24 years.

[24] The League Of Nations. Report Of The Representative Of The Dominion Of New Zealand On The First Assembly Of The League Of Nations, Held At Geneva, In The Year 1920. Appendix to the Journals of the House of Representatives, 1925; The League Of Nations. Reports Of The Representatives Of The Dominion Of New Zealand On The Second, Third, And Fourth Assemblies Of The League Of Nations, Held At Geneva In The Years 1921, 1922, and 1923. Appendix to the Journals of the House of Representatives, 1924 Session, p.13; Gerald Chaudron, "New Zealand And The League Of Nations" (Doctor of Philosophy in History University of Canterbury, 1989), pp.47-75. Allen in his report from the Second Assembly notes the 'practice' of the Empire Delegations to meet and discuss issues with a view to coordinating action, although he does stress that there was not always unanimity in committee.

[25] James Allen, R 223 19675, Miscellaneous files and papers - Allen and WF Massey correspondence, C361 202, Archives New Zealand. Gerald Chaudron, "New Zealand's international initiation : Sir James Allen at the League of Nations 1920-1926," *Political science (Wellington, N.Z.)* (2012): pp.65-66, Allen was, in that respect, the ideal deputy and a model for a succession of steady and reliable Deputy Prime Ministers such as Marshall for Holyoake, Watt for Kirk, Tallboys for Muldoon, Palmer for Lange, Cullen for Clarke, and English for Key. Massey possibly believed that appointing Allen to the London post left him (Massey) with a free hand domestically and a reliable if unimaginative operative in Europe. Chaudron gives Allen rather more credit but even allowing for Massey's controlling style there is little to suggest that Allen was capable of doing more than adhering to League protocol and avoiding controversy, cash-strapped as he was.

[26] The League Of Nations. Reports Of The Representatives Of The Dominion Of New Zealand On The Second, Third, And Fourth Assemblies Of The League Of Nations, Held At Geneva In The Years 1921, 1922, and 1923. Appendix to the Journals of the House of Representatives, 1924 Session, p.10). This related to the Second Assembly.

---

[27] Kate Marsh, "'La Nouvelle Activité des Trafiquants de Femmes': France, Le Havre and the Politics of Trafficking, 1919–1939," *Contemporary European History* 26, no. 1 (2017): p.25, 'Nowhere was this debate more marked than in France. The persistence of regulated prostitution within France meant that during negotiations within the TWC French delegates felt the need to stress the distinction between the traffic in women across borders (an international issue) and regulated prostitution (which, they argued, was a national issue).'

[28] "Brainless Girls," *Auckland Star*, 20 July 1932.; Joan Wallach Scott, "Part II. Debate. Women: A French SIngularity?: "Vive la différence!"," in *Beyond French Feminisms: Debates on Women, Culture and Politics in France 1980-2001*, ed. R. Célestin, E. DalMolin, and I. Courtivron (New York: Palgrave Macmillan US, 2016), p.230. Scott's analysis suggests that the French (male) politicians had resisted change by arguing that women were assiduous supporters of the Church and therefore collectively constituted a reactionary force against French republicanism. Their other justification relied on the contradictory assertion that women were already treated as equals domestically and sexually so they did not need the vote to achieve autonomy or independence.

D. Gorman, "Liberal internationalism, the League of Nations Union, and the mandates system," Article, *Canadian Journal of History* 40, no. 3 (12 / 01 / 2005): p.465, The treatment of women in colonised territories, assuming the other races were recognised as fellow humans, should have raised concerns for New Zealand as well.

[29] Georges Goyau, "Le droit de vote des femmes," *Le Figaro*, 11 October 1922; Georges Goyau, "Comment votent les mères," *Le Figaro*, 06 November 1922; "Les femmes dans la Cité politique," *Le Figaro*, 8 February 1931; "La Séance: Autres arguments," *L'Humanité*, 08 Novembre 1922. Allen's approach is consistent with his behaviour when he reported to Massey on General Pau's visit. In that case he simply noted the visit but attached no significance to it and displayed no curiosity as to why it may have taken place. Nor did he show any interest in the possible consequences or implications for New Zealand.

[30] Steel-Maitland was a British Conservative MP, enigmatically added to the New Zealand delegation on his own recognisance to assist with his worthy cause of combating slavery.

[31] The League Of Nations. Reports Of The Representatives Of The Dominion Of New Zealand On The Second, Third, And Fourth Assemblies Of The League Of Nations, Held At Geneva In The Years 1921, 1922, and 1923. Appendix to the Journals of the House of Representatives, 1924 Session, pp.17-18).

[32] Desmond Hurley, "Edward Opotiki Mousley," *New Zealand Studies* November (1996): pp.10-17; New Zealand Parliamentary debates v.185: 19th Parliament 6th session, p.820 (1919). Massey lectured the New Zealand Parliament on the potential gains possible given ready access to

phosphatic-rich fertilisers. 'The most nutritious pastures in England and the best dairy pastures in France are those richest in phosphates…'.
A. J. Glazebrook, "Review: An Empire View of the Empire Tangle. By Edward O. Mousley, with a Preface by the Rt. Hon. W. F. Massey," Article, *The Canadian Historical Review* 2, no. 4 (December 1921): p.396, Although a copy of Mousley's book has not been located it seems from this review that Mousley was addressing the dilemma of reconciling nationalism with empire. Mousley's credentials and expertise were not universally recognised. Glazebrook's review of Mousley's book was unflattering: 'The great value of this unpretentious little book is that it is symptomatic. Written by a New Zealander who has been educated in England, it is evidence that the problem of Empire is gaining ever widening consideration.' And 'This publication is a collection of press-cuttings. The first chapter consists of a series of cuttings from Dominion newspapers in which the consciousness of nationhood seems to be the main theme, and this is considered against the fact of empire.'

[33] The League Of Nations. Reports Of The Representatives Of The Dominion Of New Zealand On The Second, Third, And Fourth Assemblies Of The League Of Nations, Held At Geneva In The Years 1921, 1922, and 1923. Appendix to the Journals of the House of Representatives, 1924 Session, pp.28, 34). S. J. Gale, "Lies and misdemeanours: Nauru, phosphate and global geopolitics," *The Extractive Industries and Society, Department of Archaeology, The University of Sydney, Sydney, New South Wales 2006, Australia* (2019/04/05/ 2019),

[34] "Robert Cecil - Facts," Nobel Media AB, updated 7 Dec 2017, 2014, http://www.nobelprize.org/nobel_prizes/peace/laureates/1937/chelwood-facts.html.

[35] Alistair Horne, *Friend or foe : an Anglo-Saxon history of France* (London: Weidenfeld & Nicolson, 2004), p.534 Imperial Conference, 1923. Appendix to the Journals of the House of Representatives, 1924 Session, pp.17-22, 25-31, 34-35. Baldwin praised the role of the Washington Disarmament Conference, probably as much for the potential relief to the defence budget as for the prospect for a disarmed peace. It is remarkable that this disarmament conference had to be held in the capital city of one of the leading non-members of the League despite the core purpose of the League being peaceful dispute resolution and disarmament.

[36] "Echos," *Le Figaro*, 10 July 1923, p. 1.. The vague description may have fitted that of the Dunedin-based (honorary) French Consul.

[37] "Une protestation de la Nouvelle-Zélande," *Le Figaro*, 26 March 1924, p.3. 'Vous dites que votre gouvernement est en faveur de la coopération internationale par l'intermédiaire de la Société des nations élargie et renforcée. Je crois devoir répondre à cela. On pourrait en venir à regretter l'existence même de la Société des nations si la défense de l'Empire dépend seulement de cet organisme; l'existence de l'Empire dépend de la marine impériale.'

[38] Protocol For The Pacific Settlement Of International Disputes: Correspondence Relating To The Position Of The Dominions. Appendix to the Journals of the House of Representatives, 1925 Session; Imperial Defence Committee, Report made by Imperial Defence Committee, recommending to the UK government not to ratify the Geneva Protocol, p.6 (UK National Archives, 1925). As Austen Chamberlain said: 'I do see several reasons why the French should be frightened for the future, and while they remain so frightened they go on cultivating, as it were, reproducing that very feeling of bitterness in Germany which is the cause of their fear. It is moving in an unending vicious circle.'

[39] "La Cinquième Assemblée De La S. D. N.: La proposition française touchant l'Institut international est votée à l'unanimité. 1 Genève, 23 septembre. La séance plénière de l'Assemblée est ouverte à 10 h. 10.," *Le Figaro*, 24 September 1924 p.3. In the event the Australian delegation did not vote against the resolution because it required unanimity and so the resolution was passed and the French offer of a Paris headquarters for the Institute was accepted.

[40] The League Of Nations. Report Of The Representative Of The Dominion Of New Zealand On The Sixth Assembly Of The League Of Nations, Held At Geneva In The Year 1925. Appendix to the Journals of the House of Representatives, 1926 Session, pp.2, 8, 9, 19.

[41] "Le Conseil s'est occupé de la question des mandats," *Le Figaro*, 4 September 1926, p.3.

[42] "Bulletin Militaire: Angleterre," *Le Figaro*, 7 August 1921, p. 4.

[43] "Dans la Marine: La défense navale de l'Empire britannique," *Le Figaro*, 5 June 1922.

[44] "La politique extérieure de l'Angleterre," *Le Figaro*, 21 June 1921, p.3.; "Bulletin Militaire: Angleterre."; "Le roi George V a prononcé le discours du Trône, dont voici les principaux passages," *Le Figaro*, 8 February 1922, p.3.; "Dans la Marine: La défense navale de l'Empire britannique."

[45] Henry Bidou, "La Question de Singapour," *Le Figaro*, 28 March 1924, p. 1. The Washington Treaty prohibited the construction of new naval bases in the Pacific so Singapore was interpreted as an enhancement rather than a new facility. More significantly, Baldwin's Conservatives had been replaced by Macdonald's Liberal-reliant minority Labour Party Government.

[46] "Une protestation de la Nouvelle-Zélande."

[47] "Dans La Marine," *Le Figaro*, 30 September 1924, p. 4.

[48] Cabinet Office, Draft Telegram to 5 Dominions, March 1924 1924, Cabinet Meetings and Papers, CAB 23/47 Original Reference CC 7 (24)-25 (24), 1924 23 Jan-7 Apr, p.305, The National Archives, Kew.

[49] Office: pp.308-09. Although Australia, Newfoundland and New Zealand wished to proceed with construction and both Australia and New Zealand were prepared to contribute towards the cost, Australia only wanted the new policy to be used as a bargaining chip in exchange for further arms reduction.

[50] Thomazi, "En Grande-Bretagne: L'Exposition Impériale. Les productions des Dominions et des colonies," *Le Figaro: Economic Supplement Illustrated* 7 April 1924, p.1. 'Le but officiel de l'Exposition est de mettre en présence les producteurs de matières prémières qui sont dans les colonies et les industriels qui utilisent ces matières dans la métropole.'

[51] "New Zealand At Wembley," *Otago Daily Times*, 12 July 1924, p.7; New Zealand Parliamentary debates v.205: 21st Parliament: 3rd session, pp.160, 517, 22 (1924).; New Zealand Parliamentary debates v.203: 21st Parliament: 3rd session 1924, pp.161-2, 71, 268-69, 478-79, 1152 (1924).; T. Clarkson, "N.Z. at Wembley: Truth about the exhibition," *Auckland Star*, 1 August 1924, p.8.. 'A little flock of plump, well-woolled lambs grazing' were included as a backdrop to an exhibition of meat cuts and carcasses as was '... the sheep of the taxidermist, awaiting with plaintive expression, its turn to be led to slaughter'.

[52] Despatches To The Secretary Of State For The Colonies From The Governor-General. Appendix to the Journals of the House of Representatives, 1925 Session, pp.6, 9. New Zealand had declined an invitation to attend the 1927 Paris Exhibition thus bypassing another opportunity to advance the relationship and possibly trade.

[53] Par A. Thomazi (de notre envoyé spécial), "A l'Exposition Impériale britannique," *Le Figaro*, 1 August 1924, pp. 1-2.. 'C'est vraiment un beau spectacle qui complète dignement l'Exposition impériale de Wembley, monument de la puissance, de la richesse et de l'orgueil britanniques.'

[54] A. Thomazi, "Quelques considérations sur l'Exposition de Wembley," *Le Figaro: Economic Supplement*, 8 September 1924, p.1.. One organisation described as the 'Economic Development Branch of the Unionist Party' released tables of statistics showing the value of the imports of British manufactured goods by the Dominions and other imperial territories while omitting any comparative reference to the value of non-Empire British exports. A similar approach was used to demonstrate the loyalty of the citizens of the Empire. The original table did not include the crucial population totals necessary to draw a meaningful comparison.

[55] "Development Of The Empire," *Press*, 6 October 1924, p. 13; Jan Lahmeyer, "Population Statistics: historical demography of all countries, their divisions and towns," (17 January 2018 2006). http://www.populstat.info/.

[56] "Will Prices Decline?," *Evening Post*, 27 November 1922.

[57] "Empire Education," *Evening Post*, 23 August 1924, p.9. The Wembley exhibition was an ideal opportunity to introduce children to the Empire model and many visited as the Duke of Devonshire (the former Conservative Secretary of State for the Colonies) noted. The Triennial Imperial Educational Conference that was held during the exhibition 'under the auspices of the League of Empire at the University College, London' highlighted the important role of education. Mr J. Clark the Director of Education in Glasgow said teachers needed to prevent 'tragedy' for 14-

year-olds by giving them 'better moral and social equipment' and getting them to think imperially.

[58] L'Académie française, "Jacques Chastenet," in *L'Académie française website* (Paris, 11 January 2018). http://www.academie-francaise.fr/les-immortels/jacques-chastenet.; Pierre Villette, "La crise anglais," *Le Figaro*, 3 October 1926, p. 3.

[59] "Le Royaume qui n'est plus « uni »," *Le Figaro*, 24 November 1926.

[60] L'Académie française, "Jacques Bainville," in *L'Académie française website* (Paris, 11 January 2018). http://www.academie-francaise.fr/les-immortels/jacques-bainville.; Pierre Villette, "L'opinion des Autres: Le Royaume qui n'est plus 'uni'," *Le Figaro*, 24 November 1926, p. 3. Bainville, not without apparent glee, described the United Kingdom's disintegration as, 'C'est là consécration d'un fait accompli'.

[61] "La Conférence impériale a terminé hier ses travaux," *Le Figaro*, 24 November 1926, p. 3.

[62] Marion Mainwaring, "Fullerton, William Morton (1865-1952), journalist and writer," (Oxford University Press, 2018). William Morton Fullerton, *William Morton Fullerton papers*. Fullerton had been the Paris based correspondent for *The Times* and after 1910 was an independent journalist. He was therefore well acquainted with the British–French political relationship.

[63] W. Morton Fullerton, "Le Figaro aux Etats-Unis. La fin d'un empire. Que va devenir l'europe? : L'Empire britannique se confesse devant le monde.," *Le Figaro*, 28 November 1926, p. 5.

'It would be useful if the wonderful document which Earl Balfour has just signed on behalf of the Inter-Imperial Relations Committee, which summarizes the work of the British Imperial Conference of 1926, were translated word for word into any language, for consideration by all the statesmen of all the countries. This document is simply one of the more important state papers in the history of England. It records a factual situation that interests the entire universe. It proclaims *urbi et orbi* things known, no doubt, by well-informed people, but sceptically disputed by the mass of observers. It is a confession of ecumenical significance, and its practical significance, which is no less universal, will be endless.'

[64] Fullerton, p. 5.

'Fixons pour le moment notre attention sur une seule des vérités que nous venons d'enregistrer. Elle est la plus pratique de toutes. Il s'agit tout simplement dé l'émancipation de l'Angleterre, mais émancipation par isolement. Remarquez que si les Dominions se lavent les mains de toute responsabilité pour ce qui concerne les initiatives de Londres, Londres se trouve libéré de responsabilité pour pas mal de problèmes, par exemple ceux que l'avenir du Pacifique pourra susciter à l'horizon de l'Australie et de la Nouvelle-Zélande, ou qui pourront rapprocher dans un jiu-jitsu formidable les populations de l'Afrique du Sud et celles de l'Inde. Cela est vrai, malgré les accords jusqu'ici soigneusement cachés sur Sinqapour et sur tout le problème de la défense de l'Empire!'

[65] Hugues Delorme La Société des Rations, "Au Jour Le Jour: La recette du Pudding Royal. Le roi d'Angletérré a voulu que fût rendue publique la recette du pudding que jusqu'ici on ne dégustait qu'à la Cour.," *Le Figaro*, 4 December 1927, p. 1.

"… Et le mouton
Jouant son rôle, il en commande
La graisse en Nouvelle-Zélande
(Toute autre sent le suint, dit-on.)"

"Mr Massey." The *Press* published an article in 1924 that also used the pudding allegory:

'At the reception on the steamer today, his Excellency the Governor-General was represented by Commander Dove, Aide-de-Camp. "Did you bring the plum pudding safely home?" The Prime Minister took the query quite seriously [suggesting Massey had missed an 'in' joke. AW]. He (Massey) thought the presentation of "the plum pudding was very nice. He had been at the Hotel Cecil on five occasions, and had been nice to the staff, and they felt that they ought to give him a plum pudding. That was the sentiment that prompted the gift. "Yes, I have got it somewhere in my baggage," added Mr Massey.'

[66] "Kipling Society: The Ladies," http://www.kiplingsociety.co.uk/poems_ladies.htm.

"For the Colonel's Lady an' Judy O'Grady, Are sisters under their skins!"

Chapter Twelve

[1] Bury, p.271.

[2] Paul Einzig, *World finance since 1914*, Routledge library editions. Banking & finance ; v. 12, (London: Routledge, 2012), p.95 During the nineteenth century New Zealand had experienced the Land Wars, the Boer War and repeated economic booms and busts typical of primary production economies. The associated fiscal problems had led *in extremis* to government moratoriums on both external and internal debt.

[3] David Littlewood, "The provision of opportunities: politics and the state," in *New Zealand between the wars*, ed. Rachael Bell and Massey University Press (Auckland: Massey University Press, 2017), pp.32-56.; Jim McAloon, *Judgements of all kinds : economic policy-making in New Zealand, 1945-1984* (Wellington: Victoria University Press, 2013), pp.23-24. Littlewood argues that austerity narrowed the Right's electoral base leading to skilled workers and tradespeople switching to Labour. According to McAloon, Labour believed New Zealand was implementing stringent budget controls in a land of plenty. The main problem was wealth redistribution and once this was recognised and Labour elected, appropriate policies were implemented and recovery followed.

[4] Malcolm McKinnon, *The broken decade: prosperity, depression and recovery in New Zealand, 1928-39* (Dunedin: Otago University Press, 2016), p.10.

[5] Patriotic Funds. Tables Showing Details Of The Various Patriotic Funds In New Zealand From The Outbreak Of War To The 31st March, 1918: Appendix to the Journals of the House of Representatives, (1918). Poor, suffering France (and Belgium) was a theme used to engender support for the war effort and build national unity.

[6] Christophe Charle, "French Intellectuals and the Impossible English Model (1870-1914)," in *Anglo-French attitudes : comparisons and transfers between English and French intellectuals since the eighteenth century*, ed. Christophe Charle, Julien Vincent, and J. M. Winter (Manchester, UK ; New York: Manchester University Press, 2007), p.235. Charles Poor Kindleberger, *Economic growth in France and Britain, 1851-1950* (Cambridge, Mass.: Harvard University Press, 1964), pp.8-9 The pre-war Anglo-Saxon world presumed that some malaise caused by an unidentified factor (a miasma-like affliction) was infecting the Gallic race and culture. France had to recover to maintain her place as a world power. Confusingly, an apparently afflicted and war-damaged France appeared to rapidly recover and prosper between 1919 and 1929. Although this view of post-war French success has since been modified (Kindleberger gave this view in 1964) a rapid recovery and subsequent prosperity was a commonly accepted state of France in New Zealand in the immediate post-war decade and a half.

[7] Tombs and Tombs, p.511.; Robin Higham, *Two roads to war : the French and British air arms from Versailles to Dunkirk* (Annapolis, Md.: Naval Institute Press, 2012), pp.6-7.

[8] New Zealand Parliamentary debates v.190: 20th Parliament 2nd session, p.66 (1921).

[9] New Zealand Parliamentary debates v.233: 24th Parliament 1st session, p.695 (1932); New Zealand Parliamentary debates v.231: 24th Parliament 1st session, p.250 (1932). "A Challenge To Mr. Nash," *Evening Post*, 30 November 1931, p.10.; King, *The Penguin History of New Zealand*, p.346. Jeremy Veniamin Garvitch, Relief workers pulling a chain harrow at Petone, 1932, PAColl-5584-03, National Library New Zealand, Relief workers pulling a chain harrow at Petone. Ref: PAColl-5584-03. Alexander Turnbull Library, Wellington, New Zealand. /records/22708013; akg-images / Alamy Stock Photo, "French women pulling a plough," (21 July 2018). https://www.alamy.com/stock-photo-french-women-pulling-a-plough-wwi-history-world-war-i-war-economies-20731044.html. Holland, Nash and Coates had clashed over Nash's association with this image. Nash did not disclaim an association but made it clear that an attribution referenced by Coates was related to another article in the same publication. A letter in the *Evening Post* (signed with a nom de plume) claimed the original image was of local workers in Petone and implied there was nothing untoward in the men dragging the harrows within a local park. It was therefore, the writer said, not typical of Depression era farm cultivation. King simply noted the 'famous 1931 Labour Party poster'. I am

grateful to Dr James Watson for drawing my attention to the *Evening Post* article.

New Zealand Parliamentary debates v.236: 24th Parliament 3rd session, p.188 (1933).

On another occasion Lee referred to throwing a bomb in France simply to stir things up. As he prepared to launch the missile he noticed, he claimed, that there were two woodlice on the bomb apparently oblivious to their situation, rather like the Government.

[10] New Zealand Parliamentary debates v.237: 24th Parliament 3rd session, p.77 (1933). Lee was deliberately confusing two issues: whether a local currency was appropriate or not had no bearing on where locally used notes and coins were manufactured.

[11] "Recruiting and conscription," updated 17-Nov-2016, https://nzhistory.govt.nz/war/recruiting-and-conscription. Eligibility was lowered to 19 years old in late 1917.

[12] New Zealand Parliamentary debates v.232: 24th Parliament 1st session, p.iv (1932). Birthdates for MPs in this parliament have been drawn from *Te Ara*, NZTEC and other records including newspaper obituaries. Statistics New Zealand, "New Zealand Long Term Data Series (LTDS) Title: Consolidated Population by Age and Sex," (18 March 2018 2018). https://www.data.govt.nz/. This Parliament was probably no less representative than many others but in this case the difference in life-stage experiences was particularly marked.

[13] Ralph M Negrine, *Parliament and the media : a study of Britain, Germany and the media*, Chatham House papers., (Washington, DC: Pinter, 1998), p.9.

[14] Higham, pp.6-7.

[15] Imperial Economic Conference Of Representatives Of Great Britain, The Dominions, India, And The Colonies And Protectorates, Held In October And November, 1923. Appendix to the Journals of the House of Representatives, 1924 Session, pp.19-21. Massey's general themes were the value of New Zealand's trade with the United Kingdom and the Empire, his vision of New Zealand as the Empire's dairy farm, the case for Imperial Preference and his misplaced belief in the indivisibility of New Zealand and United Kingdom economic interests. "British Farming," *Evening Star*, 3 April 1919. In 1919 a new United Kingdom agricultural policy was proposed. This required intensification of production, as was assumed to be the case in France, while specifically precluding small holdings. Population redistribution within the Empire '...would solve many problems'.

[16] Imperial Economic Conference Of Representatives Of Great Britain, The Dominions, India, And The Colonies And Protectorates, Held In October And November, 1923. Appendix to the Journals of the House of Representatives, 1924 Session, p.18). By late 1922 reports were indicating that butter in increasing quantities was coming onto the world market from Australia, Argentina and Denmark. With France, Belgium and Holland achieving self-sufficiency it was Argentine competition in the British

market that worried New Zealand. Typically, the suggested solution was to cut the price to stimulate demand. See: "Will Prices Decline?," *Evening Post*, 27 November 1922, p.7.

[17] Tom Brooking, "Economic Transformation," in *The Oxford History of New Zealand*, ed. Geoffery W Rice (Oxford: Oxford University Press, 2000), p.232; King, *The Penguin History of New Zealand*, p.342; Sinclair, p.256. The earlier cited works from Littlewood, McAloon, and McKinnon are similarly inclined.

[18] Einzig, p.vii. This analysis has been used because it was accepted as an authoritative, analytically robust and scholarly assessment. At the time it seemed the global economic crisis had abated while the consequences of fascism in Germany, Italy and Japan were not yet obvious.

[19] "The Economic Situation," p.5; "Notes And Comments," *New Zealand Herald*, 5 November 1923, p.6.; New Zealand Parliamentary debates v.190: 20th Parliament 2nd session, pp.199-200 (1921). Holland was already drawing attention to Keynes' view on 17 March 1921.

[20] United Kingdom Government, France - Foreign Policy - General, 1925-1940, AAEG 950/123/E, R17709262, 360/3/1 1A: Archives New Zealand; United Kingdom Government, France - Economic Affairs - Currency, "Various memos and papers relatd to French currency and ability to pay war debts:

- Memo 16/2/1925 Marquess of Crewe to Austen Chamberlain: stronger French economy can pay debts. Increased capacity of textile industry (p.4) exports of wool to the UK (p.8)

1935 Report on Economic Conditions in France (p.1)," 1925-1940, AAEG 950/123/C, R17709260, 123 / C 360/5/4: Archives New Zealand. United Kingdom/ NZ Government, Countries - United Kingdom - External Relations - France, "All the relevant files sent to NZ from the UK on matters related to France, especially official matters such as treaties and the like.," 1922-1930, AAEG 950/36/B, R17708971, 201/4/73 includes:

W4715/ 4715/ 17 Conversations between Briand and Austen Chamberlain on disarmament and the threat of Russian involvement in Germany.

Treaty Series 1919 No.1 'British War Graves in France' (see notes): Archives New Zealand. The latter includes a memo of the conversations between Briand and Austen Chamberlain on disarmament and the threat of Russian involvement in Germany. Churchill (as Secretary of State for the Colonies) copied these to the New Zealand Governor General along with minutes from a meeting on 16 January 1922 between Lloyd George and Poincaré during which (p.2) Lloyd George referred to '...economic revival. Conditions of the latter laid down for discussion include recognition by all countries of their public debts, compensation for property confiscated or withheld, and re-establishment of finance and currency conditions offering reasonable security for international commerce and industry.'

[21] New Zealand Parliamentary debates v.224: 23rd Parliament: 3rd session, p.145 (1930). W.H. Triggs mentioned the rebuilt German fleet to the Legislative Council after his world trip.

[22] New Zealand Parliamentary debates v.227: 23rd Parliament: 4th session, p.112 (1930).

[23] Kindleberger, p.12. Within the considerable literature on the causes of the Great Depression of 1929 there is agreement that the effect was uneven as some newer industries such as 'automobiles, chemicals and electricity' outperformed the traditional sectors.

[24] "Aftermath Of War," *New Zealand Herald*, 22 September 1923, p.10; Crouzet, "Trade and empire: the British experience from the establishment of free trade until the First World War," pp.385, 406.; Pau. At the time of the 1918–19 trade visit New Zealand had, as General Pau noted, just purchased new hydro-electrical machinery from Switzerland, not from the United Kingdom. The best supplier usually won the sale.

[25] New Zealand Parliamentary debates v.233: 24th Parliament 1st session, p.132 (1932).

[26] Siegfried, p.119.

[27] François Crouzet, "The core and periphery of the core: Franco-British trade in the belle époque," in *Britain ascendant : comparative studies in Franco-British economic history*, Editions de la Maison des sciences de l'homme (Cambridge: Cambridge University Press, 1990), p.410; New Zealand Parliamentary debates v.191: 20th Parliament: 3rd session, p.707 (1921).

[28] "Falling Prices," *Press*, 20 November 1930, p.15.

[29] New Zealand Parliamentary debates v.193: 20th Parliament: 3rd session, p.5 (1921). Hall-Jones New Zealand Parliamentary debates v.212: 22nd Parliament: 2nd session, p.396 (1927). Stewart; New Zealand Parliamentary debates v.221: 23rd Parliament: 2nd session, pp.56-57, 209, 520 (1929). Harris, Jenkins, Unidentified interjection; New Zealand Parliamentary debates v.224: 23rd Parliament: 3rd session, pp.95, 322, 508, 674, 934, 45 (1930). Buddo, Unidentified interjection, Armstrong, Semple, Macmillan, Stallworthy New Zealand Parliamentary debates v.226: 23rd Parliament: 3rd session, pp.19, 119-20 (1930). Earnshaw, Buddo; New Zealand Parliamentary debates v.227: 23rd Parliament: 4th session, p.74 (1930). Sinclair; New Zealand Parliamentary debates v.229: 23rd Parliament: 5th session, pp.84, 90-91 (1931).Holland, Veitch; New Zealand Parliamentary debates v.231: 24th Parliament 1st session, p.920 (1932). Coates. These citations all refer to unemployment rates in France.

[30] New Zealand Parliamentary debates v.229: 23rd Parliament: 5th session, pp.84, 90-91 (1931). "Une intéressante statistique : Lê chômage dans le monde," *Le Figaro*, 11 October 1931, p.4. Statistics published by *Le Figaro* showed French unemployment increasing roughly five-fold from 11,214 in 1930 to 53, 673 in 1931. New Zealand's equivalent was a ten-fold increase from 5,371 to 48, 670. The same dataset showed German unemployment was 4,104,000 in 1931 while Britain's total was 2,142,821. King, *The Penguin History of New Zealand*, p.346. King records that 23,000 registered as unemployed when the New Zealand scheme began in February 1931.

[31] New Zealand Parliamentary debates v.231: 24th Parliament 1st session, p.920 (1932). New Zealand Parliamentary debates v.232: 24th Parliament 1st session, pp.62, 69 (1932). "Une intéressante statistique : Lê chômage dans le monde." Coates returned as the second ranked minister and held the Works portfolio. *Le Figaro* published what appears to be a list of selected unemployment statistics on 11 October 1931 showing unemployment in France rising from 11,214 (1930) to 53,673 (1931) with the totals for Nouvelle-Zélande rising from 5371 (1930) to 48,670 (1931). The apparent five-fold increase for France compares favourably with the ten-fold increase for Nouvelle-Zélande but without any total population data or other context no definitive conclusion can be drawn.

[32] New Zealand Parliamentary debates v.233: 24th Parliament 1st session, p.739 (1932). Schramm; New Zealand Parliamentary debates v.234: 24th Parliament 2nd session, p.810 (1932). Nash; New Zealand Parliamentary debates v.241: 24th Parliament 4th session, p.865 (1935). Smith gave his source as the *Evening Post*.

[33] "The history of coins in New Zealand," 2018, accessed 22 March 2018, https://www.rbnz.govt.nz/notes-and-coins/coins/history-of-new-zealand-coinage. New Zealand Parliamentary debates v.186: 20th Parliament 1st session, p.276 (1920). If a currency is composed of the same substance as that in which it is valued it follows that a set amount will purchase the same quantity of goods and services regardless of whether it is in the form of coin or metal. It was nonsense to claim that in the long run gold in coinage form, i.e. literally backed by gold, could maintain a face value greater than its constituent metal. Massey possibly had in mind the problem with medieval currencies that were sometimes minted with a face value that was less than their constituent metal. These were sometimes illegally 'snipped' to harvest the surplus value for smelting, while the face value of the coin was retained. France was quoted alongside the United States and Britain as a reference point but nevertheless it was one that Massey obviously felt added validity to his argument.

Gold coins were gradually withdrawn from circulation in New Zealand from 1914 onwards. Silver coin was debased by approximately 50% from 1920. Moreover, it seems likely that downgrading gold in this way implied (as far as everyday transactions went) that apart from its use for personal adornment, gold and specie were no more important than any other means of exchange.

[34] "Une déclaration de M. Snowden sur la situation financière," *Le Figaro*, 31 July 1931. As *Le Figaro* noted, the then British Chancellor had observed '… it must not be forgotten that Britain's budgetary position is even more satisfactory than that of any other nation in the world. Do not the United States, Canada and New Zealand have large deficits in their budgets?' In the Anglo-Saxon world a lower deficit was a favourable indicator, even during a depression.

[35] Siegfried, p.36.

[36] Einzig, p.46. New Zealand Parliamentary debates v.195: 20th Parliament 4th session, p.144 (1922). Sir J.P. Luke (Legislative Council) did point out that Britain had made a generous offer after the war to cancel the vast war debts that France owed the United Kingdom if the United States would do likewise.

[37] Einzig, pp.121-24, 311.

[38] New Zealand Parliamentary debates v.227: 23rd Parliament: 4th session, p.100 (1930).

[39] New Zealand Parliamentary debates v.227: 23rd Parliament: 4th session, pp.184, 234-35 (1930). Geoffrey W. Rice, "Buddo, David," in *Dictionary of New Zealand Biography* (Te Ara - the Encyclopedia of New Zealand, 4 February 2019 1996). https://teara.govt.nz/en/biographies/3b56/buddo-david

[40] New Zealand Parliamentary debates v.236: 24th Parliament 3rd session, pp.34-35, 389 (1933). There was continual confusion about the importance of gold and the interaction with exchange rates. C.J. Carrington's (Legislative Council) description of the World Monetary and Economic Conference of 1933 alluded to an air of 'scepticism [sic] and self-interest'. Carrington nevertheless still saw all the answers as coming from within the Empire.

[41] New Zealand Parliamentary debates v.227: 23rd Parliament: 4th session, pp.119-20 (1930).

[42] New Zealand Parliamentary debates v.192: 20th Parliament: 3rd session, pp.664, 74 (1921).

[43] "A Disastrous Blunder," *Evening Post*, 20 January 1933; McKinnon, pp.220-21. McAloon, pp.41-42.

[44] New Zealand Parliamentary debates v.238: 24th Parliament 4th session, p.478 (1934).

[45] Barry Gustafson, *From the cradle to the grave : a biography of Michael Joseph Savage* (Auckland N.Z.: Reed Methuen, 1986), p.199 Requote from a letter, George Forbes to Downie Stewart.

[46] McKinnon, p.221.

[47] New Zealand Parliamentary debates v.231: 24th Parliament 1st session, p.811, 89 (1932); Einzig, p.68.

[48] New Zealand Parliamentary debates v.236: 24th Parliament 3rd session, p.27 (1933). Although he was a fellow Labour MP, Carr's point undercut the Lee faction's assertions that New Zealand could act with impunity on exchange control matters.

[49] Agulhon, pp.204-5.

[50] Tombs and Tombs, p.525 ; Agulhon, pp.207-09. The Dawes Plan adjustments in 1929 were superseded by the Young Plan but all to no avail.

[51] "A Dunedin, les chômeurs suscitent une uné émeute ", *Le Figaro*, 11 January 1932, p.3.

[52] "Les troubles de la Nouvelle Zélande," *Le Figaro*, 17 April 1932, p.4.; "EN NOUVELLE-ZÉLANDE: les sans-travail se battent avec les forces

répressives," *L'Humanité*, 16 April 1932. *L'Humanité* also reported the unrest which seemed to be a topic of interest for the French press.

[53] New Zealand Parliamentary debates v.231: 24th Parliament 1st session, p.301 (1932). Chapman's quote came from *Harper's Weekly* published 10 October 1857.

[54] Matthew Wright, The policy origins of the Reserve Bank of New Zealand, (Reserve Bank of New Zealand); " No 11 Reserve Bank of New Zealand Act," ed. Government of New Zealand (1933). http://www.nzlii.org/nz/legis/hist_act/rbonza193324gv1933n11316.pdf.

[55] New Zealand Parliamentary debates v.236: 24th Parliament 3rd session, p.569 (1933). When France had taken similar steps, the state had valued the gold at the new par rate and booked the profits to the Government's account with the Bank of France.

[56] New Zealand Parliamentary debates v.236: 24th Parliament 3rd session, pp.653, 69, 80 (1933).

[57] New Zealand Parliamentary debates v.236: 24th Parliament 3rd session, pp.875, 84 (1933).

[58] New Zealand Parliamentary debates v.237: 24th Parliament 3rd session, pp.230-31, 332, 34 (1933). Despite this an unreasonable fear of inflation persisted. Clinkard claimed that the 'first inflation that we know much about' was the French inflation of the seventeenth century. Despite massive rises in wages and salaries, Clinkard claimed a Paris judge had died of starvation. He therefore simultaneously illustrated that he was aware of the evils of inflation, but that price and wage raises would not solve all problems.

[59] New Zealand Parliamentary debates v.237: 24th Parliament 3rd session, pp.355, 422 (1933).

[60] The League Of Nations. Report Of The Representative Of The Dominion Of New Zealand On The Seventeenth Assembly Of The League Of Nations, Held At Geneva In The Year 1936. Appendix to the Journals of the House of Representatives, 1937 Session, p.13.

[61] New Zealand Parliamentary debates v.231: 24th Parliament 1st session, pp.301-2, 22 (1932).

[62] New Zealand Parliamentary debates v.233: 24th Parliament 1st session, p.731 (1932); New Zealand Parliamentary debates v.232: 24th Parliament 1st session, p.740 (1932).

[63] New Zealand Parliamentary debates v.194: 20th Parliament: 3rd session, p.443 (1921). In reply to a question in the House in 1921, Massey explained that while France and Belgium had priority he still believed New Zealand would get something, although he clearly had doubts as to how much and when. It seems that he was wisely not relying on this source for budgetary relief.

[64] "A Dark Future," *Evening Post*, 8 April 1920, p.9.

[65] Einzig, p.80.

[66] New Zealand Parliamentary debates v.193: 20th Parliament: 3rd session, p.503 (1921).

Chapter Thirteen

[1] Chandrika Kaul, "Introductory Survey," in *Media and the British Empire* (New York: Palgrave Macmillan, 2006), p.15.

[2] Kaul, pp.6-8, 10-11, 14.

[3] Tony Ballantyne, *Webs of empire : locating New Zealand's colonial past* (Wellington: Bridget Williams Books, 2012); Tony Ballantyne and Australian National University. History Program., *Talking, listening, writing, reading : communication and colonisation*, Allan Martin lecture, 2009., (Canberra: History Program Research School of Social Sciences Australian National University, 2009); Tony Ballantyne and Antoinette M. Burton, eds., *Bodies in contact : rethinking colonial encounters in world history* (Durham, N.C.: Duke University Press, 2005). Although the use of diplomatic channels for information exchange has received academic attention, particularly through the work of Tony Ballantyne, much that was in the public environment appears not to have been investigated.

[4] Munro.

[5] "New Zealand Official Year Books."; "Personal Items," *Press*, 10 February 1933; "Shipping News," *Auckland Star*, 7 August 1935. Hotel registrations by significant visitors were still regularly reported. There is one report of a hotel registration by a French visitor (A.G. Boevas). The French warship *Admiral Charner*'s 1933 visit to Auckland was simply recorded as a routine ship movement.

[6] "Billets de Passages," *Le Figaro*, 7 May 1925. This was possibly to counter increased use and therefore competition from the Panama Canal route that negated the advantage of an overland rail link from America's east coast through to the Pacific seaports on the west coast. These advertisements appeared more or less weekly.

[7] Gilbert Charles, "Courrier des lettres: Une âme transparente," *Le Figaro*, 9 July 1931.

[8] Aldrich, pp.240, 68. "In The Far East," *Evening Post*, 4 October 1937.. The (British) Labour opposition was critical of China policy which was to cooperate with France and USA to 'try to keep the peace'. (The UK had previously 'rebuffed' US overtures to 'help'.) Robert Aldrich refers to a 1932 article (written by Pelleray in *Oceanie Francaise*) in which Rear Admiral Castex was quoted as saying that France did not have a strong interest in the South Pacific and could not defend Indo-China against the Japanese.

[9] "The European Crisis," *Press*, 26 September 1938.

[10] """Le Monument De Costume": The French Woman At The Zenith Of Her Power And Charm. A Sketch Of The Grande Dame Of The The Eighteenth Fury In France," *Ladies' Mirror*, 1 December 1925.

[11] "Cléo de Mérode," Wikipedia, https://en.wikipedia.org/wiki/Cl%C3%A9o_de_M%C3%A9rode.; "A Beauty School," *Sun*, 14 February 1920..

[12] "Ramarama Hunt Club Ball," *Pukekohe & Waiuku Times*, 3 October 1919.; "Women's Corner," *Press*, 24 July 1920.; "Fashion Notes," *Auckland Star*, 26 June 1920.; "An Invitation," *Otautau Standard and Wallace County Chronicle*, 18 September 1923.; "Social News," *New Zealand Herald*, 13 November 1925.; "Women's Corner," *Press*, 2 June 1926.

[13] Cecilie Geary, *Celebrating 125 years, 1880-2005 : Smith + Caughey's* ([Auckland, N.Z.] : Smith & Caughey Limited, 2005), pp.63-64.

[14] Ian Hunter, *Farmers, your store for 100 years* (Auckland, N.Z. : HarperCollins, 2009), pp.71-72, 237. Both of the brothers of 'Farmers' founder Robert Laidlaw were employed in the business and both were killed in the war. Robert was therefore not conscripted.

[15] H. Laurenson, *Going up, going down : the rise and fall of the department store*, AUP studies in cultural and social history: 2, (Auckland, N.Z. : Auckland University Press, 2005), pp.55-58.

[16] "Delay Was Dangerous," *Lake County Press*, 11 November 1920.; "Women In Print," *Evening Post*, 10 June 1920.; "Borrowed Plumes," *Auckland Star*, 8 May 1920.; "A Seer's Confessions," *New Zealand Herald Supplement*, 22 December 1923.

[17] "Night Life In Berlin," *Evening Star*, 23 August 1919; "Entre House," *Free Lance*, 4 February 1920; "Cooking Hints: French Recipes," *Auckland Star*, 29 January 1927; "French Recipes," *Otago Daily Times*, 1 May 1928; "Passing Notes," *Otago Daily Times*, 8 April 1922; A Paris Expert, "Fashion Notes: Social Women's Vanity (Mannequins with titles)," *Auckland Star*, 10 December 1932; "Titles Don't Count (in the mannequin business)," *Waikato Times*, 13 April 1928; "Germaine", "Paris In the Mirror," *Evening Post*, 21 April 1928. These columns were attributed to either 'an expert' or 'a Paris expert'. The *Evening Post*'s equivalent – 'Paris in the Looking Glass' (retitled after 1927 as 'Paris in the Mirror') – was credited to 'Germaine'.

[18] "Notes Of The Day," *Dominion*, 29 June 1920, p.4.; "Lawn-Tennis," *Le Figaro*, 15 January 1924, p.6. New Zealand was previously included as a member of the Australasian Team.

[19] "Personal Items," *Mataura Ensign*, 31 July 1919, p.4.; B.J. Clark, "All Blacks taking respect to field with our own poppy," *New Zealand Herald*, 11 November 2017, Online.

[20] "First Impressions," *Evening Post,*, 15 October 1924, p.8.

[21] "Maori Rugby Tourists," *Bay of Plenty Times*, 14 September 1926, p.2; "Table Talk," *Auckland Star*, 17 December 1926, p.1.; "The All Blacks," *Otago Daily Times*, 26 October 1927, p.11..

[22] "Rugby: Les Maoris en France," *Le Figaro*, 6 December 1926; "RUGBY: Courtoisie sportive," *Le Figaro*, 23 December 1926.

[23] Ron Palenski, *Rugby : a New Zealand history*, e-Book ed. (Auckland University Press, 2015), pp.456, 61, 64.

[24] Mike Buckley, " "A Colour Line Affair" - Race, Imperialism and Rugby Football contacts between New Zealand and South Africa to 1950." (Master of Arts in History University of Canterbury, 1996), pp.35-57.

[25] "Le Rugby International," *Le Figaro*, 27 September 1920; Paul Champ, "La France n'est pas admise dans L'International Board," *Le Figaro*, 23 March, 1921.; "Rugby: La Nouvelle-Zélande manifeste," *Le Figaro*, 14 November 1926.

[26] "Sporting," *Press*, 24 April 1922, p.10.; "Racing World," *Auckland Star*, 31 May 1922, p.7.

[27] "Boxe: Tom Henney retourne chez lui," *Le Figaro*, 26 August 1928, p.4.

[28] Arthur Espie (Sir) Porritt, 1900-1994, Letters to his father, "Series 2 Correspondence - Family. 1920-1924. Porritt, Arthur Espie (Sir), 1900-1994: Papers (MS-Group-1812). [Series]. Letters to his father from Magdalen College Oxford, and from Europe, describing his studies and involvement in athletics in Britain, and with the Paris Olympic Games," 1924, 9608-48, Alexander Turnbull Library, Wellington, New Zealand. Porritt barely mentions the Olympic Games in his letters home and has little to say about France. His souvenirs include a copy of the 'Tho. Cook & Sons' map of the battlefields with Porritt's handwritten note: 'Our route thro' the battlefields'.

[29] "L'art et Ia curiosité: La collection André Breton et Paul Eluard," *Le Figaro*, 4 July 1931.

'Un montant de boiserie, deux personages accouplés sur-montés d'un homme debout (Nouvelle-Zélande), 5.200 francs; un pendentif « Hei-Tiki » en néphrite (Nouvelle-Zélande), 3.600 francs; un Hei-Tiki en néphrite d'une translucidité rare (Nouvelle-Zélande), 3.250 francs; un Tiki féminin debout, en pierre grise (îles Marquises), 5,300 francs.'

"Collections de MM. E. V. et L…," *Le Figaro*, 17 March 1932.

'une patou-patou en jadéite verte, Nouvelle-Zélande, 4.000 francs; une herminette (adze) de césenionie, pierre en jadéite verte, Nouvelle-Zélande, 7.000 francs; un grand tiki en jadéite verte, Nouvelle-Zélande, 3.200 francs.'

[30] Simon Sigley, "Film culture : its development in New Zealand, 1929-1972 " (PhD Auckland, 2003), pp.47-48. Sigley notes that films from Europe (i.e. neither British nor American origin) were marketed and (therefore) perceived as 'exotic' while American films promoted a non-British culture that was seen as morally inferior. Nonetheless, American films had more resonance with New Zealand audiences.

[31] "Screen Stars and Films," *Auckland Star*, 18 July 1925, p.28.

[32] "Entertainments," *New Zealand Herald*, 13 March 1918.; Arthur Rosson, "One Hundred Percent American," (5 October 1918 1918). http://www.imdb.com/title/tt0180886/?ref_=fn_al_tt_1. This review is more akin to a promotion of the film than a critical appraisal. Although the movie does not appear to have screened locally, news releases emphasised the patriotism of the American film stars: Pickford was given 'the honorary title of Colonel' and was 'adopted by the entire 143rd Regiment Field Artillery of the 40th or Sunshine Division'.

[33] "Footlight Flashes," *Evening Star*, 4 May 1918, p.2.

[34] "Dramatic And Musical," *Free Lance*, 11 June 1919, p.10.

[35] Tombs and Tombs, pp.520-21. Sigley, p.55. Films from the Continent were promoted on their assumed quality, culture and educational value. The element missing was entertainment.

[36] "Great News For Picturelovers," *NZ Truth*, 4 December 1920, p.2.

[37] René Plaissetty, "The Four Feathers," (May 1921 (UK) 1921), Sound Mix: Silent
Color: Black and White.
http://www.imdb.com/title/tt0012189/?ref_=nv_sr_6. This film has been remade at least seven times, the latest version being released in 2002. None appear to have been an outstanding commercial success.

[38] "Advertisements," *NZ Truth*, 14 January 1922, p.2.

[39] Imperial Conference, 1926. Appendix to the Journals of the House of Representatives, 1927 Session, pp.63-64); "Notes And Comments: British Fim Industry," *New Zealand Herald*, 6 January 1927, p.8.

[40] Desley Deacon, "'Films as foreign offices': Transnationalism at Paramount in the twenties and early thirties," in *Connected Worlds : History in Transnational Perspective*, ed. Marilyn Lake and Ann Curthoys (Australian National University.), pp.139-40. An early equivalent of reality TV shows that are no more representative of real life than these early predecessors.

[41] Deacon, p.151. Despite this setback for the real-life genre, filmmakers such as John Grierson were influenced by experimental natural drama. Grierson was subsequently an advisor when New Zealand's National Film Unit (specialising in local documentaries) was established.

[42] Pauline Knuckey, "A global province? : the development of a movie culture in a small provincial city 1919-1945" (M.A., Massey University, 2012); Sigley.

[43] Simon Sigley, *Transnational film culture in New Zealand* (Bristol: Intellect Limited, 2013), p.122. *The Listener* held monopoly rights to programme schedules and as such had a captive clientele albeit one that was in many cases mainly interested in planning their media consumption. There is no indication from the *Gallica* newspapers that French interests attempted to obtain widespread distribution of French films in New Zealand either before or after the introduction of 'talkies'.

[44] Sigley, pp.54, 223, 363. Walter Harris (interviewer), *Early Cinema In New Zealand – [Interview With] Rudall Hayward* (Archives New Zealand: National Film Unit), R24349834. Hayward had a flair for segmenting the market, in modern marketing parlance. His establishment of a theatre exclusively for screening British films assumed that when the 'talkies' were introduced the correctness of the British accents would be an audience attractant. This plan further exposed the main problem – small New Zealand audiences. No amount of well-intentioned effort could overcome this limitation whatever the genre of film. It was consequently difficult for niche productions to succeed.

[45] (interviewer).; A. H. McLintock, "Feature Films," in *Te Ara - the Encyclopedia of New Zealand* (1966).
http://www.TeAra.govt.nz/en/1966/cinema/page-3. Hayward recalled that

movie shows were regularly screened in Waihi, then a town of 10,000 miners and their families. Waihi's geographic isolation gave exclusive access to a captive audience within the second biggest town (not city) in New Zealand and so it was of sufficient size and thus scale to support a cinema.

[46] "Advertisements," *Northern Advocate*, 4 February 1915, p.1.

[47] Peter Jackson, "They Shall Not Grow Old," (9 November 2018 2018), Sound Mix: Dolby Digital
Color: Color. https://www.imdb.com/title/tt7905466/. This depiction of France 1914–18 persists, as was shown when Jackson released his digitally restored 'documentary about World War I' in 2018.

[48] Frank Mort, "On Tour with the Prince: Monarchy, Imperial Politics and Publicity in the Prince of Wales's Dominion Tours 1919–20," *Twentieth Century British History, Oxford University Press* (2017): pp.19-20, The fate of the Russian imperial family in the Bolshevist's hands would have also heightened concerns.

[49] Mort, pp.16-19, 22-24.

[50] "Notes And Comments: British Fim Industry."; "Notes And Comments: British Films," *New Zealand Herald*, 24 September 1928, p.8.

[51] "Automobile: Le retour du major Campbell," 17 February 1931.. "Une tentative pour le record du monde de vitesse," *Le Figaro*, 21 August 1931; "Nouvelles Du Volant," *Le Figaro*, 16 October 1931; "Nouvelles Du Volant," *Le Figaro*, 10 December 1931. The exploits of Malcolm Campbell were noted because a 'Kaye Dou' was planning to exceed his speed record either in New Zealand or at Daytona. New Zealand was proposed as the venue for a similar endeavour by the Australian Norman Smith Wizard (sic) because 'Kaitaia Beach (New Zealand) (had) a superb natural trail of 145 kilometres in length, including 48 kilometres of packed sand'. 'Kaye Dou' may have referred to 'Kaye Don', the British racing driver.

[52] "Aviation: Nouvelles Aeriennes," *Le Figaro*, 2 April 1931; "Aviation," *Le Figaro*, 2 September 1928; "Derniere Heure Sportive: Les grands raids aériens," *Le Figaro*, 11 September 1928; "Le beau raid de la "Croix-du-Sud'," *Le Figaro*, 12 September 1928. "Les Raids Aeriens: Australie-Nouvelle-Zélande," *L'Humanité*, 21 septembre 1927; "Le raid San Francisco Honolulu," *L'Humanité*, 23 novembre 1927. The geography was not always clear as shown in a report that claimed 'L'aviateur anglais Giles a decolleaisement, hier matin à 7 h. 24, de San-Francisco, pour Honolulu (Nouvelle-Zélande).'

[53] "Aeronautique: A propos des lignes de dirigeables. ," *Le Figaro*, 31 January 1922; "L'immatriculation des avions," *Le Figaro*, 5 September 1932 ; "Nouvelles Aeriennes," *Le Figaro*, 7 November 1930; "Aviation," *Le Figaro*, 9 February 1934; "Un Grand Projet de communications intercontinentales par aéronefs," *Le Figaro*, 09 July 1922; "Vers Le Pole Sud," *Le Figaro*, 18 August 1928..

[54] "Un poste mondial," *L'Humanité*, 24 December 1924; "Le main noire," *L'Humanité*, 07 Octobre 1928.

[55] "Billet du matin," *Le Figaro*, 28 November 1927.

[56] "Création de Télégrammes de fin de semaine," *Le Figaro*, 15 November 1928.

[57] "Les modifications des taxes téléphoniques dans certaines relations avec les pays d'outre-mer," *Le Figaro*, 7 November 1932.

[58] "Le roi d'Angleterre souhaitera Noël par la radiodiffusion à tout son peuple," *Le Figaro*, 22 December 1932; "Christmas Aux Antipodes," *Le Figaro*, 27 December 1932 . The author of the King's message was Rudyard Kipling whose identification with the Empire was as unassailable as any individual's could be.

[59] Siegfried, Stewart, and Hamer.

[60] "L'oeuvre Grancher," *Le Figaro*, 17 December 1922. It may have been only because of this earlier interest in the progressive nature of New Zealand's social reforms that the impact in New Zealand of Pasteur's discoveries was reported by *Le Figaro*. QUOTE Le ministre de l'hygiène et de la. prévoyance sociale, assisté du docteur Ei Rousi, directeur de l'Insfituli Pasteurv présidait hier, dans les salons de Mrà'e Grancher, sa vingtièmie assemblée'- générale, qui fut particulièrement émouvante.' And 'Aussi bien tous les pays d'Europe et l'Amérique, et la Nouvelle-Zélande aussi, se sont emparés de l'idée et multiplient sur leurs territoires des exemplaires de ce mode incomparable de prophylaxie, qui donnera partout et infailliblement les mêmies statistiques admirables! pouryu que les enfants soient choisisavant toute contamination et placés. à la campagne, chez des gens bien choisis, sous la direction d'un médecin chef de foyer, intelligent, et vraiment dévoué. UNQUOTE

[61] "Science sans conscience …Ce qu'on entend par encouragement des recherchas," *L'Humanité*, 31 October 1922.. The article included a passing reference to Arthur Meyer ('Mr. Arthur Meyer drooled'), a press baron whose organisation won control of *Le Figaro* in 1929. The article does not specify what the expedition to New Zealand was.

[62]"Petites Nouvelles," *Le Figaro*, 06 June 1922. 'On ressent chaque jour, depuis le 9 mai, des secousses de tremblements de terre dans la région de Taupo.'

"La terre tremble en Nouvelle Zélande," *Le Figaro*, 4 February 1931.

[63] "Echos: Fantaisie," *Le Figaro*, 20 June 1922. Although scientists agreed that the orbits of the planets made New Zealand the best site to observe Mars, the newspapers apparently could not resist the titillating possibility of 'indisputable signs of vibrant life' as seen from New Zealand but these have as yet to be confirmed. Colonisation and/or civilisation was not just an earthbound possibility.

[64] "Amérique Latine: Pour l'agriculture brésilienne," *Le Figaro*, 27 March 1921. 'Le rapport montre encore le succès de ce système technico-scientifique dans quelques pays, tels que la France, l'Italie, la Grèce, la Suède, la Norvège, le Danemark, l'Australie, l'Indo-Chine, la Nouvelle-Zélande, la Chine, etc.'

"Les colonies ét la vie ...chère ", *Le Figaro*, 27 June 1921.. 'L'industrie frigorifique a fait la fortune de l'Australie, de la Nouvelle- Zélande, du Canada. Demain, elle doit faire celle de notre domaine colonial, qui y trouvera l'un des éléments vitaux de sa prospérité.'

"Les inventeurs devant la Nation," *Le Figaro*, 10 July 1921.. 'C'en était donc fait de l'état de choses contre lequel tout le monde s'était si longtemps insurgé, et il semblait que l'innovation allait être accueillie par une approbation unanime. Il y avait d'autant plus lieu de le croire que des institutions analogues, richement dotées, surgissaient de toutes parts dans les pays alliés, en Angleterre, en Australie, au Canada, en Nouvelle-Zélande, dans l'Afrique Australe, aux Indes, en Italie, en Belgique, au Japon, et que la direction en avait été confiée ici à un homme exceptionnellement qualifié, M. Breton *the right man in the right place* (quoted in English) dont la largeur d'esprit, le désintéressement et le modernisme étaient de nature à désarmer les zoïles les plus irréductibles.'

"Questions Economiques: La bonne guerre," *Le Figaro*, 12 September 1927.

[65] "Agriculture et commerce," *Le Figaro*, 27 May 1923.. Cites 'Gilivrey (New Zealand)' as a representative. M. Meline praised the 'magnificent colonial empire of France' and called for intensification of agriculture production.

[66] Author's photograph. King, *The Penguin History of New Zealand*, pp.433-38. King has an excellent review of these issues and the growing awareness of the environmental damage inflicted as European agricultural practices were imposed on New Zealand.

[67] Harland, p.158. 'Already efforts are being made by the French Government to introduce sheep breeding on a commercial scale in certain of the French colonies, and the Japanese Government are also keenly alive to the necessity of making the Japanese wool textile industry less dependent upon foreign supplies…'

Chapter Fourteen

[1] John Keith Moloney, War diary, "Moloney served on the troopship `Tahiti' and served in Egypt and France. Moloney mainly describes his period of training and leave in England and Ireland; following return to France became ill and was shipped back to England, Nov 1917," 1915-1917, 1194, p.40, Alexander Turnbull Library, Wellington, New Zealand.

[2] There are other examples of an imported bias substituting for first-hand experience in New Zealand's historical narrative but the case of France was unique, owing to the early direct interactions, the wartime alliance and subsequent attempts by France to develop a direct trade and diplomacy-based relationship.

[3] Hagiographic depictions of New Zealand's heroes who have journeyed to the outside world include: Meads at Twickenham, Hillary on Everest, Rutherford at the Cavendish, Mansfield at Menton and the New Zealand soldiers in France. To paraphrase Janet Frame's title, they were 'envoy(s)'

sent to show the others what we (i.e. New Zealanders) could do. Janet Frame, *The envoy from mirror city* (Auckland: Random House, 2000).

[4] The fact that volumetric increases in primary produce do not necessarily equate with proportionate increases in economic gain, although often the two are commonly assumed to be linked.

[5] Tony Ballantyne, "Putting the nation in its place?: world history and C.A. Bayly's *The Birth of the Modern World*," in *Connected Worlds : History in Transnational Perspective*, ed. Marilyn Lake and Ann Curthoys (Australian National University.), pp.29-32.

www.ingramcontent.com/pod-product-compliance
Ingram Content Group UK Ltd.
Pitfield, Milton Keynes, MK11 3LW, UK
UKHW020145250726
13967UKWH00002B/879

9 780473 560362